THE MACHINE HAS A SOUL

AMERICA IN THE WORLD

Sven Beckert and Jeremi Suri, Series Editors

Katy Hull, *The Machine Has a Soul: American Sympathy with Italian Fascism*

Stefan J. Link, *Forging Global Fordism: Nazi Germany, Soviet Russia, and the Contest over the Industrial Order*

Sara Lorenzini, *Global Development: A Cold War History*

Michael Cotey Morgan, *The Final Act: The Helsinki Accords and the Transformation of the Cold War*

A. G. Hopkins, *American Empire: A Global History*

Tore C. Olsson, *Agrarian Crossings: Reformers and the Remaking of the US and Mexican Countryside*

Kiran Klaus Patel, *The New Deal: A Global History*

Adam Ewing, *The Age of Garvey: How a Jamaican Activist Created a Mass Movement and Changed Global Black Politics*

Jürgen Osterhammel and Patrick Camiller, *The Transformation of the World: A Global History of the Nineteenth Century*

Jeffrey A. Engel, Mark Atwood Lawrence, and Andrew Preston, editors, *America in the World: A History in Documents from the War with Spain to the War on Terror*

Donna R. Gabaccia, *Foreign Relations: American Immigration in Global Perspective*

Thomas Borstelmann, *The 1970s: A New Global History from Civil Rights to Economic Inequality*

Rachel St. John, *Line in the Sand: A History of the Western U.S.-Mexico Border*

Ian Tyrrell, *Reforming the World: The Creation of America's Moral Empire*

For a full list of titles in the series, go to https://press.princeton.edu/catalogs/series/title/america-in-the-world.html

The Machine Has a Soul

AMERICAN SYMPATHY WITH
ITALIAN FASCISM

KATY HULL

PRINCETON UNIVERSITY PRESS
PRINCETON & OXFORD

Copyright © 2021 by Princeton University Press

Princeton University Press is committed to the protection of copyright and the intellectual property our authors entrust to us. Copyright promotes the progress and integrity of knowledge created by humans. Thank you for supporting free speech and the global exchange of ideas by purchasing an authorized edition of this book. If you wish to reproduce or distribute any part of it in any form, please obtain permission.

Requests for permission to reproduce material from this work should be sent to permissions@press.princeton.edu

Published by Princeton University Press
41 William Street, Princeton, New Jersey 08540
99 Banbury Road, Oxford OX2 6JX

press.princeton.edu

All Rights Reserved

Library of Congress Control Number: 2020947160
First paperback printing, 2025
Paperback ISBN 9780691208138
Cloth ISBN 9780691208107
ISBN (e-book) 9780691208121

British Library Cataloging-in-Publication Data is available

Editorial: Eric Crahan, Priya Nelson, and Thalia Leaf
Production Editorial: Nathan Carr
Jacket/Cover Design: Layla Mac Rory
Production: Danielle Amatucci
Publicity: Alyssa Sanford and Amy Stewart
Copyeditor: Jennifer Harris

Jacket/Cover image: Workers salute Mussolini during his visit to the Pontine Marshes, Latium, April 5, 1932 © Cinecittà Luce / Scala / Art Resource, NY

This book has been composed in Arno Pro

To Anne Marie and Anthony Hull,
for the past they gave me and the spaces they left behind.

CONTENTS

List of Illustrations ix
Acknowledgments xi
Abbreviations xiii

	Introduction: The Machine with a Soul	1
1	The Good Adventure: Fascist Squads in a War-Weary World	22
2	Mystic in a Morning Coat: Americans' Mussolini in the 1920s	42
3	The Dream Machine: The Fascist State in an Era of Democratic Disillusionment	65
4	Man as the Measure of All Things: Sympathizing with Fascism in the Early Depression Years	84
5	The Garden of Fascism: Beauty, Transcendence, and Peace in an Era of Uncertainty	116
	Conclusion: Searching for Soul under the Sign of the Machine	150

Notes 175
References 229
Index 237

ILLUSTRATIONS

0.1.	Mussolini Walking along the Seashore	2
0.2.	Richard Washburn Child	7
0.3.	Anne O'Hare McCormick	10
0.4.	Generoso Pope	13
0.5.	Herbert Wallace Schneider	16
2.1.	A Sober Mussolini	49
2.2.	Benito Mussolini Poses with Generoso Pope	59
3.1.	Congress as a Tank	71
3.2.	Politics in the Machine Age	73
4.1.	Uncle Sam Faces the Machine	87
4.2.	Mussolini Returns to the Farm	93
4.3.	Franklin D. Roosevelt Surveys New Deal America	114
5.1.	Generoso Pope Rides with Italo Balbo	118
5.2.	Mussolini Conquers Nature	148
6.1.	Generoso Pope in Rome	171

ACKNOWLEDGMENTS

THE MACHINE HAS A SOUL began as my dissertation at Georgetown University. Michael Kazin, my advisor, is a perfect combination of sharpness and cool. His sharpness led to second and third drafts. His cool reassured me it was all doable. I hope some of his sharpness rubbed off on me. I am sure as hell his cool never will.

I wrote much of this book in Europe. At the Free University of Brussels, Pieter Lagrou and Kenneth Bertrams gave me institutional support and a network of peers. The Roosevelt Institute for American Studies (RIAS) in Middelburg welcomed me to their PhD scholars' seminar in the spring of 2016. At the RIAS, Dario Fazzi is a true friend. In Amsterdam, George Blaustein challenged me to present the unexpected—he always will. In Rome, Stefania Cianflone Mottola and Cristiano Carocci gave me a place, and people, to call home. From afar, Katie Benton-Cohen inspired me with her wit and warmth. Rick Bell has done his job, and then some, through the Institute for Humane Studies' mentorship program.

I am grateful to all the organizations that gave me support (and timely boosts to morale): the Graduate School of Arts and Sciences at Georgetown University; the Cosmos Club Foundation of Washington, DC; the Roosevelt Institute; the Academia Belgica; and the Belgian Historical Institute of Rome. Archivists at the Franklin D. Roosevelt Presidential Library in Hyde Park, New York, and the Central State Archives in Rome made my research visits much more productive. Signor Mancini—a retired gentleman who catalogued many of the Ministry of Popular Culture files—pointed me to a trove of materials at the Archives of the Ministry of Foreign Affairs in Rome.

The Institute for Humane Studies at George Mason University enabled the reproduction of many of the illustrations that appear in this book. Edward Cesare helped me to trace the wonderful illustrations by his grandfather, Oscar Edward Cesare, for the *New York Times*. Thank you, Edward and your family, for your openness to this project.

At Princeton University Press, Jeremi Suri and Sven Beckert expressed enthusiasm for this book from the get-go. The anonymous readers who took on my manuscript gave me immensely helpful advice. Eric Crahan and Thalia Leaf are responsive, professional, and wise. Nathan Carr and Jennifer Harris helped me to turn a manuscript into a book. I cannot thank you all enough for your belief and your support.

Leo Ribuffo died in November 2018. He had a formal role in the production of this book, since he served on my dissertation committee. He was also my best teacher. Leo was so very human—prickly, generous, and hilarious. I am one, of many, who feels the loss.

For many years, Sophie thought, "Mummy does yoga." That is because her presence encouraged me to shut down the computer at 6 pm. When Hugh came along, my motivation doubled. Thank you, Sophie and Hugh, for keeping me motivated. And thank you, Jason, for holding us all together.

ABBREVIATIONS

ACS   Archivio Centrale dello Stato
ASD   Archivio Storico Diplomatico
CPI   Committee on Public Information
CWA   Civil Works Administration
DNC   Democratic National Committee
FBI   Federal Bureau of Investigation
FDRL   Franklin D. Roosevelt Library
GUF   Gruppi Universitari Fascisti
HUAC   House Committee on Un-American Activities
NARA   National Archives and Records Administration
NIRA   National Industrial Recovery Act
NLRA   National Labor Relations Act
NRA   National Recovery Administration
OWI   Office of War Information
PWA   Public Works Administration
RFC   Reconstruction Finance Corporation
RG   Record Group (NARA)
RWCP   Richard Washburn Child Papers
SPHWS   Selected Papers of Herbert Wallace Schneider
WIB   War Industries Board

THE MACHINE HAS A SOUL

INTRODUCTION

The Machine with a Soul

AN IMPOSING PHOTOGRAPH of Benito Mussolini spanned the first page of the May 1928 issue of the *Saturday Evening Post*, the United States' most-read magazine. It introduced *Post* readers to "Youth"—the first installment of Mussolini's English-language autobiography. The photograph was, in part, a representation of Mussolini as an efficient administrator. Pictured in a black suit and derby hat, he could have been plucked from Fleet Street or Wall Street. Striding forward with purpose, his arms swinging to hasten his pace, Mussolini seemed in lockstep with the tempo of modern life. But this image represented more than a man qualified to manage the demands of a complex, contemporary state. Although dressed in a business suit, Mussolini was not marching down a city street. He was on a beach. The Tyrrhenian sea stretched out to the horizon. Its waves seemed stiller, somehow, than the man on the shore. It was as if the ocean was holding its breath. And from dark clouds descended broad rays of light, like divine fingers, illuminating *Il Duce* (figure 0.1).

By presenting Mussolini as both an administrative whiz and a spiritual icon, the *Saturday Evening Post* suggested that he was the ideal man for the modern age. Richard Washburn Child, a former ambassador to Italy, helped to fashion this portrait of Mussolini as a combination of speed and stillness, materiality and spirituality. Child had been the United States' chief representative in Rome in 1922 when the fascists seized power. By 1928, he was both a writer for the *Post* and the editor of Mussolini's autobiography. Child argued that, as a "miracle administrator," Mussolini had turned the fascist state into a machine that ran. But, as a spiritual leader, Mussolini would create something more: "the machine which will run and has a soul."[1]

The representation of fascism as a machine with a soul lies at the heart of this book because it explains why Italian fascism appealed to some Americans in the interwar years. Child and other American fascist sympathizers were

FIGURE 0.1. Mussolini Walking along the Seashore, 1928.
Courtesy of Cinecittà Luce / Scala, Florence.

ambivalent about modernity. In this, they were far from alone. In the interwar years, American artists and public intellectuals commonly expressed concerns about aspects of modern life, whether the anonymity of cities, pointlessness of consumption, or dulling effects of standardization. Machines featured frequently in these critiques, both as agents of change and metaphors for the modern condition. Child, for instance, described how mechanical production had "stunted" the "soul" of American workers by making them perform repetitive tasks all day long. He also used images of machines to convey impersonal forces. Reflecting on the feelings of disassociation many Americans had toward their democracy in the mid-1920s, Child described the average citizen as a "slave of a tyrant giant machine," caught in a system beyond his capacity to control.[2]

Although Richard Washburn Child and other fascist sympathizers echoed their contemporaries in their critiques of American modernity, they parted ways with most other Americans in their interpretation of Mussolini and his government. In their telling, fascism was an effective system for managing contemporary challenges because it delivered the material benefits of the machine age while protecting Italians from its emotionally draining effects. If the average American worker was little more than a robot on an assembly line, the average Italian was a farmer who cultivated his crops, noted Herbert Schneider, a Columbia University professor. While the mindlessness of his task deadened the spirit of the American worker, a sense of personal responsibility for his yield ensured that the Italian farmer was satisfied with his job, reported Anne O'Hare McCormick, a *New York Times* journalist. And whereas Americans felt disconnected from their democracy, Italians appreciated their government's presence in their everyday lives, according to Generoso Pope, an Italian-American publisher.

These observers believed that such contrasts between Italy and the United States were not due mainly to variations in geography, history, or culture. Rather, they professed that these differences were due to a fascist regime, which had intervened judiciously to manage change. For instance, they argued that the Italian farmer was able to experience the satisfactions of growing a crop because the government had drained the marshlands of Italy and implemented policies that incentivized urban Italians to move to rural areas. And they claimed that the fascists had intentionally reformed democratic institutions to create a government that was more receptive to the needs of ordinary people. In each case, these observers asserted that fascism produced a different kind of modernity from that which prevailed in the United States—one that upheld traditions, restored connections between government and the governed, and rebalanced the relationship between men and machines.

Two (Very Different) Forerunners to This Study

This project did not begin with the notion that Americans sympathized with fascism because they believed that Mussolini was coping better with the problems of modernity. It began with a more basic curiosity. Prior to this study, the most complete work on the question of American fascist sympathizers was John Diggins's *Mussolini and Fascism: The View from America*, published in 1972. In his book, Diggins demonstrated that fascist sympathizers could be found within many areas of American life in the interwar years, including government, universities, the Catholic Church, and the Italian-American community.[3] Diggins argued that various groups supported Mussolini for different reasons: government officials believed he would create stability in Italy; academics were impressed by his apparent pragmatism; Catholic churchmen appreciated his resolution of the state's conflict with the Vatican; and Italian Americans felt immense pride in Italy under *Il Duce*.[4] This variety of responses, Diggins suggested, was a reflection of the protean nature of fascism and of Mussolini himself, who was all things to all men—a part-time statesman, athlete, and warrior, and a full-time fraud.[5]

Diggins succeeded in demonstrating that fascist sympathies were widespread in American society in the interwar years. But beyond their love of Mussolini, he found little in common across the various groups of fascist sympathizers. Reading *Mussolini and Fascism: The View from America* is like looking through a kaleidoscope at hundreds of brightly colored shards: the details are transfixing, and the big picture is hard to process. The absence of a clear picture—or thesis—was partly due to Diggins's methodology. He incorporated the views of scores of Americans who expressed both sympathies with and criticisms of fascism. This broad approach did not allow Diggins to investigate deeply the mental landscape of individuals. Most notably, Diggins analyzed what American fascist sympathizers thought of Italy, but he could devote very little attention to what they thought about the United States.

No historian since Diggins has revisited the question of sympathies with Italian fascism across American society in the interwar years, although some— notably Philip Cannistraro and Peter D'Agostino—have investigated Italian Americans' and the Catholic Church's support for Mussolini's regime.[6] The absence of scholarly contributions to the study of broader American sympathies for fascism has left the field open to polemics. In 2008, the conservative pundit Jonah Goldberg argued that American liberalism was a "totalitarian political religion." For evidence, Goldberg pointed to the American progressives who simultaneously supported Mussolini and FDR. Goldberg ignored a lot in his version of history, including the American conservatives who admired Mussolini in the interwar years. But then, his objective was not really to write history. Rather, Goldberg used his interpretation of the past to argue that contemporary progressives were self-satisfied elites, intent on harnessing Americans to a gigantic state, and intolerant of anyone who disagreed with them.[7]

Together, Diggins's and Goldberg's contributions to the question of American fascist sympathizers encouraged me to make a contribution of my own. Diggins's research indicated that more work could be done to understand why some Americans sympathized with fascism—to search for commonalities (as well as differences) in the views of Mussolini's American supporters, and to uncover more fully what they thought not just about Italy but also about the United States. Goldberg's *Liberal Fascism* convinced me that there was some urgency in this task, to ensure that warped accounts, which used the evidence selectively to support present-day political agendas, were not the only voices in the debate.[8]

Methodology and Scope

When designing the method and scope of this study, I consciously chose an approach that was different from Diggins's. While Diggins considered the views of many Americans who expressed sympathetic views toward Mussolini, I decided to analyze in depth the intellectual biographies and activities of four American fascist sympathizers. This approach would enable me to consider fascist sympathizers' opinions about both Italy and the United States in equal measure, to contextualize their views within American culture in the interwar years, and to consider how they used Italy to influence policy and public discourse in the United States.

When selecting individuals to research, I had three basic criteria. First, they had to have expressed positive sentiments about fascism for a relatively long period—around a decade or more. This would allow for a sustained investigation that assessed how the same individual's views changed over time. Second, they needed to represent various walks of American life. This would avoid giving the impression (perpetuated by Goldberg, among others) that fascist sympathies were the unique preserve of any one group of Americans. Third, these individuals needed to be men and women of significant influence, whether that influence was on policymakers in Italy and the United States or on a broader swath of American public opinion.

Based on these criteria, I selected four individuals for an in-depth study of fascist sympathies: Richard Washburn Child, the diplomat and writer; Anne O'Hare McCormick, the *New York Times* journalist; Generoso Pope, the Italian-American community leader; and Herbert Wallace Schneider, the professor of moral philosophy.

A large body of source material is associated with these four Americans. Their correspondence and related papers are housed in public archives, including the National Archives and Records Administration and the Franklin Roosevelt Library in the United States, and the Central State Archives and the Archives of the Ministry of Foreign Affairs in Italy. I analyzed papers in these archives in part to determine the extent to which Child, McCormick, Pope, and Schneider influenced domestic and foreign policies in both countries.

Published materials authored by these individuals are also copious, amounting to hundreds of newspaper and magazine articles and dozens of books. I analyzed these published sources informed by theories, articulated as early as 1926 by the philosopher and sociologist George H. Mead. Mead argued that most news stories had an "aesthetic function," which helped readers to make sense of their relationship to their communities, nation, and the wider world. Whether the topic was the Florida real estate boom, the difficulties of enforcing Prohibition, or the future of Bolshevism in Russia, it would resonate with readers insofar as it enabled them to see their own connection to the story.[9] I read Child, McCormick, Pope, and Schneider's published works with a particular attentiveness to their imagery and narrative techniques, and an awareness of their historical context, so as to understand the salience to contemporary readers of the stories they told.

Four Fascist Sympathizers

Richard Washburn Child

Born in Massachusetts in 1880, Richard Washburn Child (figure 0.2) grew up on the outer edges of the American establishment. His father was the proprietor of a boot and shoe company, which he had inherited from his own father and ran poorly.[10] Richard attended Milton—a boarding school in his home state—and then Harvard University. The *Saturday Evening Post* published his first short story while he was still an undergraduate.[11] Child went on to law school, but he was always more of a writer than he was a lawyer.[12]

Child's first job was as the Washington correspondent for a new magazine, *Ridgway's*. He approached the position with a mixture of contempt and

FIGURE 0.2. Richard Washburn Child, 1924.
Source: National Photo Company Collection, Prints and Photographs Division, Library of Congress.

calculation. The job itself had little merit, he wrote to his father upon taking up the position in the fall of 1906. But it was useful "as a means to step into a big place, up and out." Within a few months, it was clear that the magazine was faltering. Child wanted to get out. Rather than quit, he hoped to be fired, since the severance could be three hundred dollars or more. In the meantime, he felt like he was "treading water in a rather dirty stream."[13] He often felt that way.

Child made his living over the next few years by writing short stories for more successful magazines, including *McClure's*, *Collier's*, and the *Saturday Evening Post*. He set up his own law office in Boston in 1911. But either his heart was not in it or the money was not enough.[14] He moved on quickly. By 1912, Child was working for the Progressive Party, supporting his uncle's campaign to become governor of Massachusetts.[15] He cultivated a relationship with the leader of the Progressives, Theodore Roosevelt. In one letter, Child advised Roosevelt that someone on his campaign team ought to attack Woodrow Wilson as a narrow autocrat who was temperamentally unfit for office (although he himself refused to do that particular piece of dirty work on the candidate's behalf).[16] Child cherished his passing connection to Roosevelt, and traded on it for decades to come. TR embodied muscular patriotism with a touch of the "he-man"—qualities that Child admired.[17]

Following a brief stint at the Treasury Department during the war, Child assumed editorship of *Collier's* in 1919.[18] He had, by then, published more than one hundred and fifty short stories in various magazines, and almost no nonfiction. By 1920, he was working as a speechwriter and adviser for Republican presidential candidate Warren Harding.[19] According to Child, the two men got on well, drafting speeches the old-fashioned way, hunched together over a table, with soft lead pencils and plenty of rough paper. No stenographer for Harding and Child![20] The new president appointed Child ambassador to Italy in 1921, to thank him for his contributions to the (notoriously unscrupulous) political campaign.[21]

In the 1920s, Child was a staunch proponent of a conservative worldview. He esteemed individuals and nations who minded "their own business" and argued that the best possible government was the "least possible government."[22] Child's political philosophy changed—or at least appeared to—in 1932, when the depth of the Great Depression and the momentum of Franklin Roosevelt's presidential campaign prompted him to back the Democratic candidate and to express a more capacious view of government's role in Americans' lives.[23] Fickle in his party politics, Child was constant in one regard. Throughout, he expressed a love for big characters—leaders of "breadth," who exhibited their own humanity.[24] To put it mildly, he was drawn to charismatic men. Child put it in blunter terms, in a rare moment of self-criticism: he had "a weakness for listening to charlatans."[25]

As Child's transitions across party lines suggest, he worked hard to align himself with whoever had the most power in Washington, DC. His efforts had mixed results. His direct influence on policymaking circles was greatest between 1921 and 1924, when he was ambassador to Italy. His analysis of the fascist movement and the new Italian prime minister contributed to Washington's positive reception of Mussolini.[26] But after the death of Warren Harding, Child struggled to influence decisionmakers in Washington: he was a marginal figure in the administration of Calvin Coolidge; he had no official role in Herbert Hoover's presidency; and Franklin Roosevelt distrusted him and kept him at a distance.[27]

Child's insecure public position paralleled his unstable personal life. He obsessed about money. He drank too much. He divorced three times and married four.[28] His attitude toward his first wife, Elizabeth Westfield, offers some insights into his character. The couple divorced, after a ten-year marriage, in 1916. Child married a fellow writer, Maude Parker, that same year.[29] While he was ambassador in Rome, Child received word that Elizabeth had died. The news inspired him to reflect on her "sweet and fine soul." He could have chosen to stay in that marriage, he wrote to his father, but it would have come at the expense of his own life, "Maude's development," the creation of their daughters, and the contribution of all of them "to the world." In his mind, the "cost of staying with Elizabeth" was too high; he could not "pay it." Perhaps it was no coincidence that he phrased it all in monetary terms. Swiftly, Child moved on to discussion of Elizabeth's estate—the "furniture, books, silver, rugs" that ought to be heading his way. He asked his father to make the necessary inquiries on his behalf, since he "did not even know where Elizabeth was living or in what city."[30] Sometimes, Child tempered his narcissism with self-flagellation. "I may be rated as 'difficult' in temperament," he wrote soon after Elizabeth's death, as his marriage to Maude Parker disintegrated.[31] He had "made a lot of errors from Christ's point of view."[32]

Child was crumbly on the inside. He did not go from one plum job to another, which was his desire, after his tour in Rome. But despite his private failures and public shortcomings, he exerted sustained influence on American culture through his work for the *Saturday Evening Post*. More than two million Americans subscribed to the *Post* in the early 1920s, and readership continued to rise over the course of the decade. The magazine's editor, George Horace Lorimer, dictated the *Post*'s editorial line, championing individual initiative, old-fashioned values, and small government.[33] Child wrote more than seventy articles for the *Post* between 1924 and 1932, in addition to editing Mussolini's serialized autobiography. In this capacity, Child addressed a variety of topics, including the American presidency, domestic policy concerns, and politics in Europe—as well as in Italy, in particular. He described conditions that resonated with his readers, such as the growing complexity of everyday life, the feeling of disconnection between government and the governed, and the decline of traditional values. And he looked abroad for signs that might point Americans home.

Anne O'Hare McCormick

Richard Washburn Child was an exact contemporary of Anne O'Hare McCormick (figure 0.3). But Child and McCormick were perhaps as unalike as two journalists who sympathized with fascism could be. While Child touted his Brahmin credentials, McCormick's family were recent immigrants, of Irish stock.[34] Thomas and Teresa O'Hare moved to America when Anne was a baby, and made Columbus, Ohio, their home. Thomas was regional manager for the

FIGURE 0.3. Anne O'Hare McCormick, 1937. *Source:* New York World-Telegram and the Sun Newspaper Photograph Collection, Prints and Photographs Division, Library of Congress.

Home-Life insurance company. Teresa wrote poetry. Anne and her younger sisters attended convent schools, where Anne, in particular, excelled in rhetoric, Latin, and church history.³⁵

When Anne was poised to graduate from school, Thomas ran into financial problems. He abandoned his wife and three girls. Teresa tried to support the family by selling dry goods, as well as a book of her poetry, door-to-door.³⁶ Teresa's collection of poems blended religious meditations with intensely personal reflections. "That was not Love, that poor weak flame that died; / It was a taper that lit passion's pride," she wrote, presumably with Thomas in mind.³⁷

Teresa moved her daughters to Cleveland. There, Anne saw terrifying versions of the insecurity that her own family had experienced. The city's population was burgeoning, and many newcomers were foreign-born. They had come to Cleveland to work in steel mills, build ships, and make mechanical parts, furnaces, and sewing machines. Mansions lined Euclid Avenue. But the working poor struggled to survive.[38] Due to their education and connections, the O'Hares escaped the worst of this fate.[39] But Anne's proximity to such precariousness, as well as her religious faith, informed her conviction that Americans must help those who suffered under industrialization.

Both Teresa and Anne found work at a diocesan newspaper, the *Catholic Universe*, and a 1907 pilgrimage to Rome gave Anne the opportunity to write her first foreign correspondence. In these reports from Europe, she reflected on tensions that would occupy her for decades to come—between church and state, capital and labor, tradition and modernity. Anne's work at the *Universe* also helped her to develop elements of her journalistic style. She planted vignettes. From Assisi, for instance, she described a car journey as a jarring disruption to the town's contemplative atmosphere.[40] By suggesting that the car, as a symbol of the machine age, upended spiritual life, she aimed to convey an emotional truth that might resonate with her readers. Anne was an instinctive entrepreneur. In 1910, she married Francis McCormick, a Dayton importer. Accompanying Francis on business trips to Europe, Anne wrote poems and travel articles, which were picked up by *Bookman, Catholic World, Atlantic Monthly,* and *Reader Magazine*.[41] A 1918 poem, "Pompeii," conveyed the persistence of life following mass devastation—the "silence like a voice" that flowed through "muted streams."[42]

In 1920, she approached the managing editor of the *New York Times*, and fellow Ohioan, Carr Van Anda, with a proposal: she would write impressionistic pieces on postwar Europe; the paper would pay per article. It was an ambitious leap for McCormick. But it was a zero-risk deal for the paper, which had to pay neither a salary nor travel expenses. Anne O'Hare McCormick entered her career as a foreign correspondent for the *Times* through the back door, which seemed the only way for a woman to enter it at all in 1920.[43] She arrived in Naples that summer; the newspaper published her first article—"New Italy of the Italians"—on the front page of its Sunday magazine section at the end of the year.[44]

McCormick assumed a mounting influence over American culture and policymaking over the course of the interwar years. Her journalism from Italy was instrumental in advancing her career: she was one of the earliest American journalists to report on the rising fascist movement, and in 1926, she interviewed Mussolini for the first time.[45] Interviews such as this sealed her reputation as a talented writer, capable of humanizing powerful men and translating their policies into terms that her readers could readily understand.[46]

McCormick's political progressivism, Democratic affiliations, and capacity to distill the essence of a man and his policies to the public made her a useful ally for Franklin Roosevelt. Rarely one to miss a public relations opportunity,

Roosevelt used McCormick wisely, to both of their advantages. FDR and McCormick met on numerous occasions in the mid- to late 1930s. During their meetings, the president mined the journalist for her insights into the situation in Europe; the journalist, in turn, mined the president for his views on the changing role of government in the lives of ordinary Americans.[47] A colleague described McCormick's interviews with Roosevelt as "intimate" records that provided insights into his "mind at work on the job."[48] She excelled in this kind of journalism—making big men sympathetic and big ideas understandable.

By the mid-1930s, Anne O'Hare McCormick had established herself as an authority on European affairs—someone with a keen sense of the public mood in various countries, and access to leaders, including Mussolini and Hitler.[49] At the same time, she had built her reputation as an acute observer of the United States. She traveled frequently across the country, reporting on the experiences of Americans in the Midwest, the West, and the South. Drawing on personal anecdotes and snippets of conversation, she relayed ordinary people's anxieties and aspirations to readers of the *New York Times*.[50] McCormick was at her most compelling as a chronicler of the human experience, an artful assembler of details that, combined, told Americans so much about the challenges they faced in the modern world.

The *Times* promoted McCormick onto the newspaper's editorial board in 1936 (she was the first woman ever to occupy this role), and gave her a column devoted to European affairs (another first, not just for a female journalist, but for the newspaper). In 1937, McCormick won a Pulitzer Prize for her European correspondence.[51] She was a very good writer. She had a poet's feel for the redolent detail. One of her colleagues estimated that she was able to "enter almost personally into the hearts and minds" of her readers.[52] It was a talent that was as powerful as it was rare.

Generoso Pope

For his first fifteen years, Generoso Papa (figure 0.4) lived in a hamlet, close to the village of Arpaise, in rural Campania. His mother died when he was six. Generoso migrated to the United States in 1906. He arrived in New York with a stiletto knife and "ten dollars' worth of lire in his pocket," according to family history.[53]

Generoso rose. His first job was underground. He delivered water to the men who dug the subways. Within a year, he was just below sea level, working

THE MACHINE WITH A SOUL   13

FIGURE 0.4. Generoso Pope, 1937.
Courtesy of Bettmann via Getty Images.

as a laborer in the sand quarries of Long Island. Opposition to a walkout endeared him to his bosses, who promoted him to foreman. By the age of twenty-one, he was a supervisor on the docks for the Colonial Sand & Stone Company. Generoso became an American citizen and changed his last name to Pope. In 1916, he took on all the debt of Colonial, which was bankrupt, in exchange for full management and a fifty percent share. Only ten years had passed since he had crossed the Atlantic. Pope turned the fortunes of Colonial Sand & Stone around. He had acumen. This extended to his choice of associates. He counted the mobster Frank Costello among his few good friends, and gave Jimmy Walker $10,000 to support his successful bid for mayor. Contracts flooded in. Competitors folded. By 1927, Colonial Sand & Stone belonged to Pope alone.[54]

Pope understood how politics mixed with business in New York. He aimed to "build" constituencies of Italian-American, Democratic voters and "trade" these for municipal sand and cement contracts.[55] In 1925, Pope had helped to garner votes for Walker through Italian-American political clubs. He would continue to use these personal channels to influence the political fortunes of

Democratic candidates. But when the nation's largest-circulating Italian-language newspaper, *Il Progresso Italo-Americano*, came up for sale in 1928, he saw an opportunity to forge votes on a much grander scale. Pope paid more than two million dollars for a newspaper that hovered on the edge of bankruptcy, based on a calculation of *Il Progresso*'s capacity to shape Italian Americans' voting behavior, and an expectation of the contracts that would flow to him as a result.[56]

Pope was not alone in appreciating *Il Progresso*'s value. Its owner until 1928 had been a steadfast supporter of fascism, and, with his passing, the Italian government was concerned about the newspaper's future. William Randolph Hearst was interested in an acquisition. Although Hearst was a fan of Mussolini, the regime worried about the reliability of his support. The Italian consul general in New York pressured the vendors of *Il Progresso* to sell to Pope.[57] And upon purchase, he signaled to the fascist government that their mouthpiece in America was in safe hands: "the policies and personnel of the paper would remain the same," he announced.[58]

In a private meeting with Mussolini in Rome, in the summer of 1929, Pope assured *Il Duce* that he would continue to sustain fascism, if the government supported his bid for another Italian-American newspaper, *Il Corriere d'America*. Pope relished in quid pro quos. Over the next three years, he acquired three newspapers—*Il Corriere*, *Il Bolettino della Sera*, and the Philadelphia daily, *L'Opinione*—expanding his influence over Italian-American opinion.[59] The fascist government recognized Pope as a valuable ally who could shape the sympathies of the Italian diaspora and the policies of the American government. The benefits of this relationship ran both ways. Every single day, Pope's newspapers disseminated stories of Mussolini's popularity and fascism's success. Pope also intervened with American policymakers on the regime's behalf.[60] In turn, Mussolini's government gave Pope public affirmation of his own importance, of the kind he craved. Jimmy Walker bestowed his first title—Order of the Chevalier of the Crown of Italy—on behalf of King Vittorio Emanuele III, in New York in 1926.[61] The regime organized a second honor—Commander of the Crown of Italy—prior to Pope's visit in 1929.[62]

Generoso Pope's newspaper empire also boosted his usefulness to the Democratic Party. He used his platform to strengthen Italian Americans as a political force; in frequent editorials, he encouraged his fellow ethnics to claim citizenship, reminded them of their duty to vote, and steered them toward Democratic candidates.[63] Mayor Jimmy Walker, Senator Robert Wagner, and Governor Franklin Roosevelt cultivated relationships with Pope, recognizing that positive coverage in *Il Progresso* would result in votes in their favor on election day.⁶⁴ The ties between Roosevelt and Pope tightened after Roosevelt moved into the White House, especially in the second half of the 1930s, as diplomatic relations between Italy and the United States strained. More than ever before, the publisher needed the president to prop up his reputation as a loyal American. And, more than ever before, the president needed the publisher to secure votes. In private, Franklin Roosevelt sometimes expressed distaste for Generoso Pope, but politics dictated that the two men appeared in public as allies and friends.⁶⁵

Herbert Wallace Schneider

Herbert Wallace Schneider (figure 0.5) was born in 1892 in the small town of Berea, Ohio. His father was a professor of theology at the local German college. Schneider would remember his childhood as calm and secure. There was a ritualistic quality to his family's day, punctuated by morning and evening prayers and hymns in the German Pietist tradition. Church was a large part of their life, and Herbert loved the services, the religious activities, and especially the music. His family's milieu was entirely German-American, Protestant, and predominantly academic. Polish Catholics, who worked in the quarries and made grindstones, lived on the other side of the town. Herbert had no contact with the children of these families except when they skated out onto the frozen lakes in the winter.⁶⁶

In 1909, the family moved to Brooklyn, in part so that Herbert could receive a good high school education. His father became the pastor at a Methodist church near Bushwick Avenue, where the older people spoke German and the young people spoke English. The family lived in the parsonage next door. In Brooklyn, the Schneiders reproduced many elements of their prior, small-town existence, at least in Herbert's memory. Their social life revolved around church picnics, activities, and clubs. Herbert went to Brooklyn Boys' High School, which trained him in classics, and then on to City College. After three semesters, he earned a scholarship for Columbia University.⁶⁷

The intellectual ambience of Columbia University in the 1910s and early 1920s shaped Herbert Schneider. As an undergraduate, he took graduate-level philosophy classes. He stayed on for a doctorate, under the supervision of the renowned moral philosopher, John Dewey. Schneider was impressed by the pragmatists' view of philosophy as a mode of action, and he developed a version of instrumentalism that was far more strident than Dewey's own.⁶⁸ According to Schneider's conception, norms had no value independent of their effects. He argued that any thought that "'gets you somewhere' (intellectually speaking)" was a

FIGURE 0.5. Herbert Wallace Schneider, 1948.
Courtesy of Leonard McCombe, The Life Images
Collection via Getty Images.

"good" one; it was not the job of a philosopher to judge whether that destination was ethical or not.[69] In his doctoral thesis, Schneider observed that an idea, such as democracy, was all too often held up as "an ultimate standard" rather than as a means to an end. Such normative absolutism, he argued, prevented social progress.[70] Unlike Child, the sometime Republican, or McCormick and Pope, the committed Democrats, Schneider expressed no public affiliation to one American political party or another. But his agnosticism extended beyond political parties, to entire systems of government. Function trumped all in Schneider's worldview: for him, Democrat or Republican, democracy or dictatorship, mattered less than whether or not the government worked.

In 1926, the influential political scientist Charles Merriam nominated Schneider for a prestigious fellowship from the Social Science Research Council to study fascism in Italy.[71] Schneider's research resulted in a book and a handful of articles, which established him as an authority on Mussolini's regime.[72] His peers responded positively to his analysis, arguing that his research demonstrated the significance of fascism for the modern world.[73] Schneider's work fitted within the zeitgeist of contemporary political science, which challenged reflexive American exceptionalism by ranking objectivity over morality.[74] So enamored was his audience by Schneider's seemingly cold dissection of the truth that only one reviewer paused to reflect on his data. William Yandell Elliott of Harvard noted that Schneider had made no use of the voices of antifascist exiles.[75] It was the fascists, not the facts, who did all the talking in Schneider's work.

One well-reviewed book led to another, and in 1929, Merriam asked Schneider to co-author a study of civic education in Italy.[76] The book was part of a two-year research project, headed by Merriam, that compared methods for "making citizens" across eight countries, including Italy and the United States. The collaborative nature of the work meant that Schneider's observations fanned out among his peers, while Merriam's tacit endorsement boosted his credibility. Informed by Schneider's findings, Merriam suggested that fascist Italy had been successful where most states had failed in adjusting to the changing times.[77]

Schneider's scholarship on fascism culminated in a 1934 award from the Carnegie Endowment for International Peace for a visiting professorship in Rome, at a university headed by Giacomo Acerbo, a fascist economist and politician.[78] By then, Schneider had also developed his expertise in the field of religion. In many ways, Schneider assessed fascism as he would a religion. He examined its rituals, ceremonies, and customs. He measured its success based on its apparent capacity to inspire, galvanize, and bind its followers. He analyzed the sometimes overlapping, sometimes competitive relationship between fascism and Catholicism as he would analyze two religions that coexisted within one state. He adopted an air of moral neutrality around fascism, much as he adopted an agnosticism with regard to various religions.[79]

At least with regard to fascism, this approach was problematic. Schneider never considered the toll that fascism had on human beings, perhaps because this might have required him to adopt a moral stance that he was steadfastly unwilling to take. He built his observations on the evidence that he had at his disposal: fascist propaganda, the various charters and laws of the Italian state, and the words of friendly government officials. His methodology was the equivalent of researching Christianity by going to church, reading the Bible, and talking to some priests. The news was almost always good, and the distance between myth and reality often great.

In sum, Richard Washburn Child, Anne O'Hare McCormick, Generoso Pope, and Herbert Schneider came from a cross-section of American society and asserted their influence through quite different channels. Child was the product of an elite upbringing and education, and a long-standing conservative. McCormick came from far more modest origins and was progressive in her politics. Pope was an immigrant, businessman, publisher, and Democratic Party powerbroker. Schneider was a scholar and teacher, who kept himself one step removed from American party politics. Despite their differences, all these individuals expressed sustained sympathies for fascist Italy. This book explains why.

What Explains Fascist Sympathies?

It is intuitive that one woman and three men as different in their intellectual backgrounds, politics, activities, and proclivities as McCormick, Child, Pope, and Schneider would view the fascist state from different angles. For Anne O'Hare McCormick, a liberal Catholic, the new regime promised the resolution of two conflicts that concerned her very much: one between the church and state, which stymied the pope's temporal powers; and one between capital and labor, which labor invariably lost.[80] To Richard Washburn Child, a conservative, Mussolini offered stability, and—initially at least—a *laissez-faire* approach to economics that would allow businesses to thrive.[81] For Generoso Pope, and many Italian Americans, fascism's claims to order and progress offered gratifying ripostes to nativist stereotypes of Italians as anarchic and archaic.[82] And for Herbert Schneider, a political philosopher, the fascist state seemed to be proof positive of the pragmatists' proposition that the best kind of government was a government that worked.[83] In so far as this study demonstrates that these very different Americans were attracted to fascism for different reasons, then, it supports the arguments of John Diggins, as well as the work of those historians who have considered why discrete groups within American society supported Mussolini's regime.[84]

But this study is not only—or even mainly—about the different reasons why Americans from various walks of life supported fascism. Rather, it is about the common ground that these individuals occupied, in spite of their differences. Child, a conservative writer for a popular magazine; McCormick, a progressive Catholic journalist at the nation's most respected broadsheet; Pope, a businessman, publisher, and powerbroker; and Schneider, an academic schooled in the philosophy of instrumentalism—all worried about the impact of economic, social, and cultural change on the United States and argued that Italy was coping better with the challenges that such changes entailed. Each of these Americans saw fascism as a means of harnessing the benefits of modernity, while resisting its anesthetizing effects. They used fascism's apparent successes to highlight what was wrong in the United States, to offer examples for what Americans could do, and to provide their countrymen with something that filled a lacuna in their own lives.

From the early 1920s to the late 1930s, Child, McCormick, Pope, and Schneider retained their overarching concern with how Italy and the United States were coping with the challenges of modernity. But the interplay of events in Italy and the United States, current themes in fascist propaganda, and American cultural, economic, and political preoccupations affected the specific issues they explored at any given time.

In the early 1920s, as fascist squads engaged in street fights against their political enemies in Italy, the United States returned to peacetime routines of work, consumption, and leisure. As shown in chapter 1, Child, McCormick, and Schneider rendered young fascists as embodiments of a martial ideal to argue that the ennui of modern times was more damaging to society than war.

In the mid-decade, the United States experienced unprecedented rates of economic growth, fueled by speculation and consumption, which provoked concerns about the erosion of older ideals of benevolence, sobriety, and self-control. Chapter 2 describes how Child, McCormick, and Pope used images of Mussolini as a man of old-fashioned values and modern capacities both to critique American culture and to send a reassuring message that it was possible to combine the best of old and new in the contemporary age.

At the decade's end, American political scientists and cultural commentators voiced growing concerns over an apparent mismatch between the static institutions of democracy and the dynamic forces of society. Chapter 3 shows how all four of these American fascist sympathizers invoked the fascist corporate state to highlight weaknesses in the democratic system and to suggest possible reforms in the United States.

In the early 1930s, fascist propaganda asserted that Italy had withstood the worst of the global depression by enabling a return to simpler ways of life. Chapter 4 analyzes how Child, McCormick, Schneider, and Pope used Italy's apparent success to call for policy interventions in the United States that would both enable a short-term recovery from the depression and ensure a long-term recalibration of the relationship between humans and machines.

As shown in chapter 5, in the mid-1930s, these observers responded to an increasingly authoritarian Italy by reproducing images of Italy and Ethiopia as gardens, so as to offer Americans experiences of control, beauty, and even peace, which were lacking in their own unstable nation and an increasingly volatile world.

It was not until the late 1930s, as fascist Italy drew closer with Nazi Germany, issued anti-Jewish edicts, and embarked on a path that would lead to global conflagration, that these observers withdrew their support from Mussolini. They did so with various degrees of silence and noise, and only oblique expressions of remorse.

Why American Fascist Sympathizers Matter

By understanding why Americans of such different backgrounds sympathized with Italian fascism in the interwar years, we can learn something about the nature of the fascist regime—at least as it presented itself. We can also gain insights into the prevailing anxieties and policy challenges of the United States in the interwar years. Last, a fuller understanding of the history of American fascist sympathies has implications for our contemporary societies, as they grapple with cultural, social, and economic change.

The research presented in this study shows that to understand the appeal of Italian fascism, we need to confront its relationship with modernity. As such, it supports the work of other historians—most notably, Emilio Gentile, Ruth Ben-Ghiat, and Roger Griffin—who have attempted to parse out fascism's complex attitude toward the modern world.[85] The responses of American fascist sympathizers show that various tendencies within fascism that might appear contradictory from our vantage point—such as the regime's embrace of modern technology alongside its promotion of rural communities—seemed to be consistent to some contemporary observers. Indeed, for Child, McCormick, Pope, and Schneider, fascism's genius lay at the meeting point between modernity and tradition. This does not suggest that Italian fascism in practice was consistent—too many historians have demonstrated that the regime was riven with internal schisms, and survived for as long as it did because Mussolini was an opportunist, rather than a purist.[86] But it does show that we underestimate fascism if we dismiss it as an eclectic mishmash merely because it seems so to us. Fascism appealed to these observers because it claimed to reconcile the clash between new and old, by ensuring that machines edified rather than eroded the souls of women and men.

By focusing on these four Americans' responses to fascism, this book also helps us to understand modernity as many interwar Americans saw and felt it—as a convergence of individual experiences and an acceleration of materialism, which deprived humanity of its texture and drained living of its meaning. Child, McCormick, Pope, and Schneider stayed in the mainstream of American society in the 1920s and 1930s because they addressed issues that concerned many of their contemporaries, including those who opposed fascism:

the erosion of values of service and honor; the impact of a get-rich-quick ethos; the obsolescence of democratic institutions; the devastating economic and cultural effects of mass-production; and the sense that men and women were overwhelmed by forces beyond their capacity to control. By contextualizing fascist sympathizers' views about modernity, and by demonstrating that these individuals spoke to various public and policy audiences who were eager to hear their words, this book provides insights into the temper and tone of the United States in the interwar years. It shows that the anxieties of these fascist sympathizers were American anxieties.

Last, as the United States grapples with a period of extraordinarily divisive politics, in which each side labels the other fascistic and neo-fascists are emboldened in the public sphere, this book offers a timely dissection of why some Americans were attracted to Italian fascism in the interwar years. In contrast to pundits who use distorted versions of history to argue that fascist sympathies are unique to progressives and Democrats in the United States, I demonstrate that, in the interwar years, fascism appealed to four Americans from very different walks of life because they believed that Mussolini's Italy was managing better with the transition to modernity than the United States. These fascist sympathizers wrote for and spoke to those Americans who felt threatened by various changes, including the decline of communities, the erosion of traditional values, and the sense that the machine—as both a literal presence and a metaphor for modernity—dominated mankind. In the 1920s and up until 1933, Child, McCormick, Pope, and Schneider argued that the United States' political leaders had failed to make democracy relevant, to manage the pace of industrialization, and to support those who felt left behind in the modern world. And even after Roosevelt rolled out the New Deal, they argued that more should and could be done to manage the transition to modernity. If this study suggests a lesson in our present circumstances, the lesson is here. When a system of government fails to protect those damaged by transitions, it will provoke feelings of disenchantment, both with that system of government and with the rate and impact of cultural, social, and economic change. Disenchanted people may seethe quietly. Or they may look for alternative forms of government that promise the restoration of past values, the protection of embattled communities, and the assurance that they—and not outside forces—are in control.

1

The Good Adventure

FASCIST SQUADS IN A WAR-WEARY WORLD

FROM A WINDOW of a stranger's home in April 1921, Anne O'Hare McCormick caught her first glimpse of a formation of *fascisti*. It was Rome's birthday—the first day of its 2,676th year—and the city was animated with gatherings and parades. The temper of Rome in the spring of 1921 was entirely different from the atmosphere in the same city the previous fall. Then, there had been no crowds to celebrate the anniversary of Italian unification, and the standard bearers had been hired men, "shabby wretches," proceeding haphazardly, with about as much enthusiasm for the job as they felt for their country. But in April 1921, there was a large crowd, which carried McCormick from the top of the Capitoline to the streets below. It was a rare kind of crowd that "somehow succeeded in crushing gently," and she welcomed an offer of a temporary shelter in a home on the Via Aracoeli—a typically narrow street, its flat-fronted buildings abutting the road. She "hung" from the window and watched.[1]

Soon, troops of young fascists, sharply dressed and marching shoulder to shoulder, came by. McCormick felt a "thrill" shared by her host, a Piedmontese woman so overcome with "excitement" that she almost fell from the window into the street below. The woman was moved by the presence in one parade of young men from all over Italy; of a wounded veteran, who only months before would have been attacked had he dared to march in public; and of women, not just in the crowd of spectators, but even among the marchers themselves. McCormick was moved by all of this, and by something more basic too. The young marchers, "electric with life" and "conscious of power," made her feel alive once more.[2]

McCormick's initial response to the fascists is indicative of why some American observers were attracted to the movement in its early years. The silence she heard upon first arriving in Italy in 1920 was unnerving. Rome's "shabby" standard bearers and the few "listless" residents who watched them were expressions of a more universal disillusionment.[3] As she moved across the continent, taking in France, Belgium, and England, McCormick breathed stale air that differed only slightly according to national characteristics. Wherever she went, her analysis suggested the same conclusion: the Great War, which had once promised to remake nations and men, had delivered nothing of that sort. In place of national unity, there was apathy. Instead of higher values of service and duty, there was disengagement and despair. Europeans were depressed, she suggested, not because of the changes wrought by the war, but because the war had seemed to change so very little.

Returning to Italy the following year, she was happy to find the country in the early stages of an uprising, and not just because it made good copy. The "excitement" felt by McCormick's host on the Via Aracoeli was primarily a "patriotic" one. Well-dressed young men were harbingers of a national self-respect that had been eroded by the war. The veterans among them indicated a perpetuation of higher ideals: duty, honor, service. The mobilization of Italy's notoriously apolitical women—whether the few who marched alongside the fascists, or the many who cheered them—suggested that the movement could galvanize a divided nation.[4]

For McCormick and other sympathetic American onlookers, fascism in its early stages provided an optimistic rejoinder to the prevailing cynicism of the early 1920s—living proof that the hopes for a moral rebirth that had accompanied the Great War had not been laughably naïve. Service, duty, and honor were not defunct, they argued—the values were embodied in fascist youth. Intertwined in their appreciation of fascism for its war-like values was their appreciation of fascism for its war-like effects on the imagination. For months, McCormick had traveled through Europe, reporting on the lifelessness of its inhabitants. Shell-shocked and poorer than they had been in 1914, Europeans seemed nonetheless bound to the same old patterns of repetitive production, meaningless consumption, and self-serving politics that were part and parcel of the modern condition. No wonder the Europeans were depressed; it *was* depressing. But, leaning out of a stranger's window on the Via Aracoeli, McCormick felt the "thrill" of adrenaline that humans feel in proximity to violence.[5] Adrenaline and depression just do not go together; when the two meet, adrenaline wins out. For that, she was grateful.

Other historians have not given much attention to sympathetic American responses to the fascist movement in the early 1920s. John Diggins did not go into detail about attitudes toward the fascist squads prior to the March on

Rome, suggesting that the *squadristi* failed to capture Americans' imagination. He argued that this changed only once Mussolini became prime minister, in October 1922; then, sympathetic observers welcomed fascism as a bulwark against Bolshevism.[6]

The observations of Anne O'Hare McCormick, Richard Washburn Child, and Herbert Schneider do not bear out Diggins's arguments. First, these observers wrote prolifically about the fascist movement before the March on Rome; the squads fascinated them. Second, anti-Bolshevism did not fully account for their appreciation of fascism in its early stages; of these three individuals, only McCormick insisted on a simple causal relationship between the rise of fascism and the decline of the radical left in Italy. Had Child, McCormick, and Schneider viewed fascist squads as merely a force for order, they would have presented attacks on socialists and communists as a necessary, or even unfortunate, precursor to stability. But instead, they savored the violence, implying that it had a moral and aesthetic value that transcended immediate political needs. To them, the *fascisti* embodied a rebellion not just against communism, but against apathy in the wake of the Great War.

The Wrong Side of Paradise

These fascist sympathizers wrote against the grain of American culture in the early 1920s, when references to the Great War were more likely to evoke expressions of bitterness than nostalgia. The war had promised Americans a lot in 1917. Those on the front lines had imagined that it would provide them with stimulation of senses numbed by modern life: "I constantly feel the need of the drunken excitement of a good bombardment," John Dos Passos wrote from France.[7] Government propaganda suggested that Americans on the home front could also experience the elevating effects of war. The Committee on Public Information (CPI) implied that, by supporting the war effort, Americans could realize higher ideals of duty, obligation, and sacrifice.[8] Richard Washburn Child made his own contribution to this propaganda campaign. In the winter of 1917–18, he wrote promotional materials for the Treasury Department, which portrayed the purchase of war savings certificates as the home-front equivalent to fighting in France.[9] "A Country worth *fighting* for is a Country worth *saving* for" was the Treasury's refrain.[10]

Pro-war intellectuals also imagined that the war would be transformative, remaking not just Americans but the entire world.[11] From the "horror" of war, Walter Lippmann wrote in 1917, "we can dare to hope for things which we never dared to hope for in the past." Predicting that a "Federation of the World" would spring from the war, this was Lippmann at his most millenarian.[12] Child was probably influenced by this (and similar) tracts, when he wrote to his father later that year. Child interpreted the war as a chastening experience—heaven's revenge on men who had pursued "tangibles" at the expense of their "spirit." He imagined that a "new world" would "rise from the wallow of gore and starvation and chaos—a better world." Child even anticipated that a "prophet" would "come forth," although he had no idea, in 1917, who that prophet might be.[13]

Big ideas often sound naïve in retrospect. The war had promised too much. To most Americans, it did not feel like a new world once the mud had dried, countries had counted their dead, and the allies had imposed their punishing peace. Any excitement that John Dos Passos felt in 1917 faded as he cogitated the realities of mechanized warfare. Far from representing a break from modernity, the war seemed to epitomize the dehumanizing effects of machine-made civilization.[14] Civilians also reassessed their wartime experience in a harsh light. In 1920, George Creel, the former head of the CPI, boasted that his campaign had been "the world's greatest adventure in advertising."[15] Although Creel insisted that he had merely sold brilliantly packaged truths, Americans were no longer inclined to believe him.[16] Intellectuals who had favored the war, particularly those of a progressive bent, turned away from their previous optimism in disgust. Walter Lippmann would never again sound millenarian.[17]

The American mood after the war was one of pervasive disillusionment: disillusionment with the high-minded ideals that had fueled the intervention in Europe; with the mechanics of modern war that precluded a good death; with politics, turned propaganda, turned lies.[18] "We have no heritages or traditions to which to cling except those that have already withered in our hands and turned to dust," wrote the critic Harold Stearns, just before he packed his bags for Paris.[19] A young generation "had grown up to find all Gods dead, all wars fought, all faiths in men shaken," wrote F. Scott Fitzgerald.[20] For many of Fitzgerald's contemporaries, the pursuit of individual freedom and personal pleasure seemed to be all that was left.[21]

Italia Disprezzata

Anne O'Hare McCormick presented Italy as a potent expression of what was wrong with the postwar world in her first article for the *New York Times*. She arrived from the United States in the summer of 1920 to a country that was crippled by debt, and stifled by death. Worse, in her mind, than the material and physical impact of the war was its emotional and spiritual effects. The Italian people felt cheated by political leaders, who had dragged them into the war without securing for them the spoils of victory. Fiume, the Adriatic city that many Italians felt should have been theirs, was a focal point for popular resentment. But McCormick did not believe that Gabrielle D'Annunzio, the eccentric and effete poet who led the occupation of Fiume from the fall of 1919 to the end of 1920, could galvanize the nation. By her estimation, most Italians had withdrawn into themselves, in disgust. The country was "tired, drained of emotion," she observed.[22] Schneider and Child sustained this characterization. In the aftermath of the war, the mood was of *Italia disprezzata* ("despised Italy"), according to Schneider.[23] It felt like a nation "drifting toward nowhere," wrote Child.[24]

Child interpreted Italy's *biennio rosso* ("two red years") as a manifestation of Italians' inward turn. He arrived at his post of ambassador in summer 1921, in the later stages of the radical labor movement. In Child's telling, in an overwhelmingly apathetic nation, a minority of Italians had attached themselves superficially to anarchism, socialism, communism, or some hybrid of all three. The radicals who staged protests and strikes in Italy were, in his view, a self-centered faction. In his memoir of his diplomatic tour, serialized in the *Saturday Evening Post*, Child argued that a young Italian, who came to the embassy to petition for Sacco and Vanzetti (the anarchists found guilty of armed robbery in Massachusetts in July 1921), embodied the attitude of the radical left. A few days after his first visit to the embassy, the same young radical returned to ask for a job, according to Child. Italian leftists felt no true fervor, no attachment to causes larger than themselves, he maintained.[25] Child seemed genuinely to believe that, wherever they were located in the world, members of the radical left were motivated only by their own interests. For instance, as editor of *Collier's* magazine in 1919, he had railed against a New York printers' strike as the ploy of a "'something for nothing' minority."[26] But Child's tendency to tie together the various strands of the left, and then dismiss the whole bunch as selfish, was also *de rigueur* for any contributor to the *Saturday Evening Post*. Under the leadership of George Horace Lorimer, *Post* writers portrayed socialism as a creeping disease, blurring almost any distinction between Italian anarchists, Russian Bolsheviks, and the British Labour Party.[27]

Although Herbert Schneider and Anne O'Hare McCormick had more sophisticated understandings of the left, their analysis brought them to very similar observations regarding the temper of Italy in the immediate postwar years. In contrast to Child's tendency to lump together disparate movements, Schneider recognized that the left in Italy consisted of parliamentary socialists and communists, syndicalists, nonparliamentary socialists and communists, and anarchists, among others.[28] For her part, McCormick perceived a causal chain running from economic deprivation and ineffectual governance to the occupation of factories and land, and used interviews with ordinary people to communicate this viewpoint: "In Italy we are reaping what we have sown.... The peasants have always lived too close to the starving line," she quoted a "wise old" man.[29] But despite these more nuanced understandings, McCormick and Schneider echoed Child's perception that the strikes and protests of 1919 to 1921 had failed to capture fully the popular imagination.[30] At the height of the two red years, the predominant attitude of Italians toward the strikers was "exasperation ... diluted with forbearance," McCormick argued.[31]

Child, McCormick, and Schneider all underestimated the appeal of the Italian socialist movement in the postwar years. They characterized the *biennio rosso* as an expression of disillusionment, rather than a concrete bid for better working conditions and land rights. They invoked the economic paralysis caused by strikes as a motif for a wider paralysis—a kind of spiritual death. "One wakes up any morning ... to find a whole city as dead as if it had been asphyxiated in the night," wrote McCormick.[32] Perhaps she wanted American readers to feel something of their own lives in those sensations of listlessness and emptiness.

These observers claimed that Italians had departed so far from wartime values that they turned upon their own veterans: civilians hissed at men in uniforms; children and women threw bottles, water, and stones at them.[33] McCormick, Schneider, and Child argued that Italians felt no pride in their recent past, no trust in their government, and no sense of self-worth. The dominant sensation was of a nation laid to waste by a war that had once promised "re-birth."[34]

Child, Schneider, and McCormick argued that passivity had also become official policy. The Italian government seemed to acquiesce to everything: national humiliation at the hands of other victorious powers; violence against soldiers; the chaos of strikes. For his readers in the *Saturday Evening Post*, Child alluded to ideas of sexual dysfunction to suggest a weak and indulgent state. The government was "flabby," he wrote; its "failure spread" out "like watery jelly."[35] Italy was not only *disprezzata*, according to Schneider, it was *decadenta*—its liberal government seemed to shelter all in its midst.[36] McCormick cited one example of this apparent decadence in government: its seating of Francesco Misiano, a communist and "deserter" in the Great War, in the Chamber of Deputies.[37] By allowing Misiano to take his seat in parliament, the government signaled that liberal ideas of tolerance were more important than patriotic values of service and sacrifice.

Liberalism felt permissive to these observers: "nice, easy, benevolent," and weak.[38] Even as they described the details of Italian politics and society, they seemed to allude to a wider cultural shift toward tolerance at the expense of standards. The world was "shrieking after freedom, self-indulgence and anything bizarre," in the aftermath of the war, according to Child. "[C]are, trouble, toil, service, thrift and even morals"—the values that the Great War had instilled—no longer seemed to matter.[39]

The Weary World

Drifting unmoored, decaying from within, and turning its back on its wartime legacy, Italy, as rendered by these observers, embodied much of what was wrong with the postwar world. To them, gray was the dominant color in Europe in the aftermath of the war, and silence the dominant sound. Child reminded readers of the *Post* that he had attended some of the postwar conferences. He described Paris in 1919 as "wet and weary," and Lausanne in 1922 as "chilly, damp, dull."[40] This was blatant pathetic fallacy—gray weather, a stand-in for both internationalism (which Child considered deceptive and boring) and the popular mood of despondency and withdrawal. A "generation" had "seen the inherent desire of mankind for conflict come to a head, burst disastrously for everyone," he wrote. He felt "no fever in Europe, no high blood pressure," in the early 1920s. He felt, "rather, fatigue and chill."[41]

Similarly, McCormick described a desolate atmosphere in Europe in the winter of 1920–21. McCormick arrived after a wave of strikes, inspired by the revolution in Russia, had subsided (although if her responses to Italy's labor movement were any indication, these protests would have, in any case, left her unimpressed). In the winter of 1920–21, she described a continent devoid of energy. She saw no evidence of the "Gay Paree" of Americans' imagination. The lights were out in Paris; its cafés were quiet by ten, she reported. The Europeans could not muster the energy to celebrate Christmas, let alone build a new world "on the ruins of the old."[42]

McCormick suggested that Europe's—and indeed the United States'—troubles ran deeper than the war. They were the troubles of a world that the war had failed to change. As was often the case in her journalism, McCormick let nameless strangers articulate her ideas. The American tourists who trickled back to Europe in the summer of 1921 were, without exception, bored, she thought. They had come in the spirit of adventure, with a hope of seeing transformation. They found nothing of the sort. They visited the battlefields, but could not remember from one day to the next whether they had been in Arras or Reims. It all blurred in a single gray fog—the war was already far away, the reality of the trenches out of reach.[43]

These visitors emitted an aura of "ennui," and as with any good rendition of ennui it was hard to pinpoint the source of the problem. An American tourist in Cherbourg came closest to explaining it: "What is there over here that we haven't got at home except ruins?" she asked. Americans could be sanguine about uncomfortable trains and bad plumbing, but they could not accept gracefully "the presence of so many home discomforts," McCormick wrote. Had they been at ease with boredom, they would have stayed in the United States. The *Times* underscored this point. In an illustration for McCormick's piece, three American women stood listlessly in an unidentifiable European town. One glanced off into the distance, guidebook in hand. Another suppressed a yawn. The third woman stooped over a cane, her eyes downcast. "I am bored stiff with this life," the caption read. It was Americans' life that was boring; Europe had provided none of the hoped-for stimulation.[44]

In McCormick's telling, mass-production and mass-culture were the main culprits for Americans' world-weariness. Her domestic journalism in the early 1920s contained a critique of these homogenizing forces. Though Americans loved to hate New York, she observed, they all moved reflexively to the same "tickers," and the same jazz. New York, in its lurid representation of the "the temporary in decay" was, "only our town grown big," so when they expressed distaste for New York, Americans revealed an inherent, and usually unconscious, disgust with themselves.[45] As a people, they remained "restless" with the instincts of their pioneering forbears. But since the frontier had shrunk to "Dutch Colonials, tiled bathrooms and twelve-cylinder cars," Americans searched in vain for the emotional satisfactions of a good adventure.[46]

McCormick's ideas were not unique. A critique of modernity had taken on renewed piquancy in the early 1920s. From Paris, for example, Harold Stearns issued a similar warning about the invasion of philistine American tourists as personifications of the enveloping advance of insipid American culture.[47] And in listing items that made up this American standard—a single-family detached home, a gleaming bathroom, and, of course, a car—McCormick echoed one of the literary techniques of the novelist and satirist Sinclair Lewis.

She overwhelmed her reader with the pointlessness of it all. She suggested that, like Lewis's anti-hero, George Babbitt, more and more middle-class Americans defined themselves through their possessions. Like the characters in Babbitt, they worked soulless jobs so that they might fill their lives with more material goods. They hoped for fulfillment in a toothbrush holder, an electric cigar lighter, or a new sedan.[48] The fulfillment would never come.

McCormick argued that this problem spread far beyond American shores. Revealing more about the social circles she moved in than about the reality of European life in the early 1920s, she wrote that Europeans increasingly resembled Americans. They used "the same soap, razors, adding machines," and danced to the same music.[49] This, then, was the "new world," as McCormick perceived it. Not a morally cleaner, more Spartan, world. Just a planet of people who aspired to the same American standard. To paraphrase Lewis, McCormick seems to have preferred people who were miserable and knew it to those who felt an undefinable unhappiness but could not admit it.[50] So she welcomed any differences that alerted Americans to their own misery. In the spring of 1922, she mused:

> I wonder whether in this New World, in which all the nations are so closely huddled together, . . . I wonder whether dissatisfaction with ourselves and a little wistfulness for the ways of others is not what we all most need?[51]

Events in Italy would soon provide McCormick with the differences she yearned for and a sense of nostalgia that she believed would spur Americans to retrieve their better selves.

Renewing War

"In 1920 a disgusted and wretched Italy" had "never wanted to hear of war again," wrote Herbert Schneider.[52] Although on the victors' side at the war's end, the nation had suffered many of the humiliations associated with defeat: first, at Caporetto in the fall of 1917, when the Austro-German army broke through the Italian lines, and Italians, in their hundreds of thousands, deserted; and again, at the Paris Peace Conference of 1919, when Italy gained few of the territories promised to her by Britain and France before she joined their side in the war.[53] Schneider argued that, against all odds, the fascists were able to "renew the war in imagination." Their apparent success seemed all the more noteworthy given the depths of despair to which Italians had sunk.[54] It suggested that under the layers of disillusionment, human beings craved a good war and its accompanying sensations of higher ideals, patriotic spirit, and adrenaline. They just needed something to light the spark.

For these observers, the *squadristi* provided that spark. Fascist squads sprung up across northern and central Italy in the early 1920s. The relationship between the *biennio rosso* and fascism is a matter of historiographical debate. Some scholars have argued that the radical movement petered out of its own accord, while other scholars have emphasized the role of fascist violence in quashing the left.[55] Contemporary observers foreshadowed this debate. Herbert Schneider and Richard Washburn Child suggested that the Italian left was its own worst enemy. Schneider noted that the labor movement lost momentum after the failure of factory occupations in the fall of 1921. He argued that chronology did not support the idea that fascism suppressed socialism, since squadrist violence peaked later, in 1922.[56] Just before taking up his post in Rome, Child told the press that many Americans had overestimated "the extent of the extreme radical movement" in Italy.[57] As ambassador, he continued to portray Italian socialists as paper tigers.[58] Only McCormick argued definitively that squadrism "saved Italy from Bolshevism."[59] In contrast to Schneider and Child, who focused on events in the major cities, she recognized the instrumental role of fascist violence in crushing socialism and communism in the towns and countryside of north-central Italy.[60] But McCormick, too, was less compelled by the strategic necessity of fascist violence than she was by the aesthetics of the fights.

McCormick's first report of fights between fascists and communists was typical in this regard. She relied on the testimony of a "young English girl" (whose wide-eyed ardor made her a conveniently romantic raconteur) to describe the violence in Florence in March 1921. This witness told McCormick that a group of students had been doing nothing more than waving the tricolore in the streets, when a group of communists attacked them. Although the students resisted bravely, they were outnumbered and, seemingly, unarmed. The communists "murdered" around a dozen "nice quiet patriotic boys." Following this act of wanton violence, the fascists rushed in to avenge the young men. There followed "three days of real war," with both sides in "terrible earnest, fighting to kill." To the relief of McCormick's raconteur, the fascists eventually prevailed; she imagined that they beat the communists because their outrage was purer.[61]

The observations of this eyewitness introduced McCormick's readers to a number of characteristics of fascist squads, which were hallmarks of other sympathetic accounts. The first of these was their association with students.

While McCormick's witness described the fascists of Florence as rushing to students' defense (suggesting a link between the two groups), elsewhere sympathetic observers homed in on student members within the squads.[62] In reality, the social composition of squads varied by area, with agricultural laborers and farmers making up around one-third of the entire movement, while perhaps one out of every eight squadrists was a student.[63] But American observers stressed the role of students in squadrism because their presence imbued the movement with élan. Since the Boston police strike of 1919, when Harvard students volunteered as strikebreakers, the student as an upper-class hero in the war against radicals was a familiar image for Americans.[64] In the guise of students, fascist sympathizers could argue that the squadrists were "ardent devotees" of "higher" ideals.[65]

At same time, the image of squadrists as students enabled these observers to dismiss excesses of fascist violence as no more than "fraternity" fun. In Herbert Schneider's hands, the "castor oil treatment," and other forms of political violence meted out by the fascists, were "student pranks."[66] Child, McCormick, and Schneider made no mention of waterboarding, of men assassinated in front of their families, or of those left to bleed slowly to death, although these practices, too, formed part of the squadrists' repertoire.[67] Instead, they limited their descriptions to acts that seemed to be worthy of young gentlemen.

Fascist sympathizers consistently argued that the squadrists embodied honorable values. Often, they used gendered ideas and language to insist on this point. McCormick's "young English girl" was just one of a number of women who seemed to be in awe of the squadrists' tough martial code.[68] McCormick, too, was impressed. She described the impeccable manners of a squadrist leader who met with her in Rome in 1922. This "perfectly groomed" young man came early to their appointment, just to explain that he could not stay. He was part of an elite corps, always ready to perform the fascists' "most dangerous and bloody work." Duty called him that night, in the form of a group of communists on the road heading north, she confided to her reader.[69] According to Child, the squadrist movement gained "lyric and epic" qualities, based around traditions of "sacrifice," "discipline," and "orderly restraint." He described one such tradition: a commander would shout the name of a slain fascist during roll call; and upon hearing their dead comrade's name, the rest of the company would respond in unison, "Here!"[70]

In an era when Americans worried about a decline in "manners and morals" of youth, and a blurring of gender lines, there was something reassuringly old-fashioned to patterns of behavior that were both chivalric and decisively masculine.[71] In an illustration that accompanied a 1921 *New York Times* article by McCormick, fascism appeared in the form of a muscular knight in armor, firmly standing his ground against a weak and cowering socialist.[72] In another piece in the *Times*, she described the fascists as Italy's equivalent to the Rough Riders.[73] McCormick portrayed these young men as continuing traditions of martial honor that had receded in the United States.

For American sympathizers, the fascist squads also represented a righteous outrage against moral laxity. Just as McCormick's young eyewitness hailed the "terrible anger" of the squadrists in Florence in March 1921, the journalist herself suggested that the fascists shored up the country against moral decay.[74] She welcomed the entry of thirty-five fascists into the Chamber of Deputies, following snap elections in May 1921. These men did not share the liberal government's tolerant attitude toward the communist war deserter, Francesco Misiano, who sat among them. In June, the fascists launched a "perfectly legitimate demonstration" against the communist deputy.[75] An embassy report proffered further details, describing how the fascists "attacked" Misiano, "spat in his face," and drove him into the lavatories of the parliamentary building.[76] McCormick wrote that it was "easy to sympathize with" the "patriotic exasperation" of the fascists.[77] They appeared to counteract a modern mood that was part liberal acceptance, part spiritual despondency. Unlike their liberal government, the fascists in and out of parliament would not make "concessions to anarchy"; unlike their liberal government, they were not "weakened by any desire to temper the wind."[78] If the wind was cold and angry, so be it, she believed. At the very least, a cold and angry wind reminded Italians that they were still alive.

In their spirit of intolerance, the fascist squads resembled the American Legion, and, in case the parallel was lost on her readers, McCormick made it explicit.[79] Like Italian fascism, the American Legion was a postwar movement that trumpeted wartime values of sacrifice, service, and nationalism. Its members engaged in violent combat against organized labor, under the rubric of defending the nation against a communist threat. And Legionnaire vigilantes claimed to form a moral police force, which stepped in, in the absence of an adequately forceful state, to rescue society from decadence. But in the United States, the values embodied by the Legion seemed to be on the wane. The vigilante activities of the Legion peaked in 1919; by the early 1920s, the organization's leadership had distanced itself from these tendencies.[80] The Legionnaires who raided the Industrial Workers of the World hall in Centralia,

Washington, in November 1919 and participated in the lynching of a local member seemed to be a rearguard in American society.[81]

By contrast, fascist sympathizers portrayed the *squadristi* as the wave of the future. The youthfulness of the *squadristi*—the majority of whom were born at the turn of the century—was symbolic in this regard.[82] Their age evoked all the clichés that accompany renditions of youth in fiction, poetry, and art. They were "hope," according to Child.[83] Herbert Schneider devoted an entire article, published in the mass-circulation magazine *Century*, to this topic alone: "Giovinezza" (Youth). Schneider described the eponymous anthem as a "rollicking" tune, reminiscent of the "old Methodist Sunday-School" hymns that he had loved so much in childhood. Although these young fascists had not been all that useful in finishing off the communists, they had been essential to energizing Italy, he told readers of *Century*.[84]

These observers argued that the squadrists were a vanguard. They led, and their country followed. Child, McCormick, and Schneider described a swift eradication of sentiments of despondency, depression, and withdrawal, as the nation rallied behind the fascists.[85] Sometimes, they used specific examples to indicate a broader trend. For instance, Child claimed that by the summer of 1922 all the servants in his home in Rome had joined the movement.[86] Child and McCormick cited "conversions" of socialists and communists to fascism, not only as evidence of Italians' superficial attachment to leftist creeds but also as an indication that the Italians (like human beings everywhere) were latent patriots.[87] The movement generated by the squads had brought Italy to a higher level of "national self-consciousness" than it had ever experienced before, wrote McCormick in the spring of 1921.[88] Ignoring the basic reality that most people opt for self-preservation over ideological integrity in the face of violence, these observers imagined that Italians were experiencing a moment of national unity. Such a moment would have felt both familiar and remote to Americans in the early 1920s, and intentionally so: they wanted their readers to feel nostalgic for a recent yet strangely distant time, when they had united behind their country.

Fascist sympathizers suggested that in addition to elevated ideals of service, honor, and patriotism, the squads offered excitement of senses dulled in the postwar years. Although more basic, the sense of invigoration provoked by displays of violence seemed to be just as integral to their appreciation of squadrism. McCormick had raced to Florence from France, in March 1921, but she arrived too late to witness the fight. "Oh, it's too bad you missed it," she quoted the young English woman. The woman's eyes sparkled as she described how she had been trapped in a working-class neighborhood as the conflict unfolded.[89] She suffered from none of the ennui that afflicted typical tourists in

Europe; the violence had brought her to life. Naturally, McCormick welcomed the fascist squads when she finally witnessed them for herself on the Via Aracoeli the next month in Rome. They provided the elation she had craved since arriving in Europe the previous summer. Describing how she "hung" from the window of the stranger's home, she conveyed a desire to get as close as possible to the fascists' violent energy, and a sense that her reader, perhaps, wanted to as well.[90]

Child also courted adventure. He claimed that he walked out in Rome, against the advice of his staff.[91] "I've had dozens of serious warnings that I would be assassinated," he wrote to his father. "I am not bothering much." One "red" had threatened him, but the ambassador responded directly, "tell your crowd to go to Hell"; the two men had ended up laughing with one another.[92] In describing relaxed encounters with dangerous men, Child wanted to convey something of his own hardboiled character. His wife, Maude Parker, wrote to her parents-in-law of "several days of excitement" generated by street fights between communists and fascists in the fall of 1921. Forty people, she thought, had died in the clashes. Forty people killed in several days. Nothing in Parker's words suggested any regret at the loss of human life.[93]

These observers suggested that violence had brought the whole nation to life. After years of silence born of apathy, they bore witness to an atavistic spirit in the Italians. The feeling they described is familiar to anyone who has seen civilians living in a conflict zone: people tend to be unflappable, sanguine, and so very alive. There was "nothing in the least abnormal in the air and atmosphere" of Florence when McCormick visited it in the days following the clashes.[94] Rome, too, maintained its composure under gunfire. The Italians took the violence in their stride, drinking coffee and vermouth in outdoor cafes as bullets flew by.[95] And lest her readers consider this ease with violence as a uniquely Latin trait, McCormick was at pains to argue that Italians were only "overdeveloped" examples of "human nature."[96] Their experiences belonged to everyone. Americans, insulated in their postwar comforts of shower bath, sleeping porch, and frame garage, might feel far from the streets of Florence and Rome, but McCormick hoped to bring them as near as possible to the violence, so near that they might feel its pleasures for themselves.

March on Rome

Of the three Americans discussed in this chapter, only Richard Washburn Child was in Italy during the March on Rome of October 1922. But for all three, the march represented a culmination of the tendencies that they observed in squadrism since its inception: enlivenment of the modern experience; revival of wartime values; and an augur of change, which World War I had once promised but never delivered.

Child's descriptions of these days prickled with energy. His telegrams to Washington barely concealed his delight.[97] In private, he was ecstatic. "We are having a fine young revolution here—no danger, plenty of enthusiasm & color," he wrote to his father, a fortnight before the march. "We all enjoy it. Confidential."[98] Maude Parker too was enraptured by the atmosphere: fascism's "great triumph," she wrote, was its appeal to youth; even their young daughters dressed up in makeshift fascist uniforms and sang marching songs.[99]

In the *Saturday Evening Post*, Child switched style to describe these heady days. Instead of writing from the vantage point of 1925, he relayed the events mainly in the form of diary excerpts. He wanted to bring his readers close to the unique feeling of a city on the brink of violence, in which everyday actions were infused with color. On October 28, Child recorded:

> There is a perversity in human beings which asks that violence happen. The best of us have love of conflict. I could find no one in my office and none of my many visitors whose eyes were not bright with expectancy.[100]

Finally, on Sunday, October 29, the fascist squads entered the city; almost one hundred thousand men flooded into Rome over the next few days, Child estimated. Child had his Sunday lunch in a restaurant on the Via Veneto and rushed onto a terrace when he heard the sound of gunfire. There was not quite enough violence to satisfy him—he "motored about" the city that day searching for disorder, finding little.[101] The March on Rome was as near as Child would ever come to experiencing conflict, and its attendant sensations. He was enjoying himself, and he wanted his readers, too, to appreciate fascism for its invigorating effects.

It rained a lot in central Italy over those days. Child watched from a window at the embassy as troops of fascists marched by on October 30. They were a "muddy, tired, healthy lot," he wrote. Some had marched over open fields for two days. They were hungry, soaked, and sleep deprived. But from faces streaked with mud, their eyes were shining brightly.[102] These descriptions might have called to his contemporaries' minds the homegrown heroes of the Great War: mud-splattered men who jumped from trenches and ran across battlefields in posters advertising liberty bonds.[103] Bored American tourists in Europe had failed to sense the realities of trench warfare, even when they had visited Reims and Arras.[104] The March on Rome, mediated by observers like Richard Washburn Child, tried to bring Americans closer, not to the trenches per se, but to a sanitized battlefield, with something of the aesthetic, little of the suffering, and much of the excitement, of war.

These marching men were an embodiment, also, of a Spartan morality, according to Child. They refrained from raids on food shops in spite of their hunger; they avoided alcohol despite their euphoria and their thirst.[105] McCormick too would interpret the absence of disorder in Rome that October as evidence of the fascists' self-restraint, made more remarkable by the fact that many of them were "country boys," seeing the city for the first time. Wholesome and naïve, these young men remained disciplined, despite the lure of the metropole.[106] The portrait functioned as a riposte to the caricature of the youthful Americans of the jazz age, who flocked to cities to partake of myriad sins.

Child claimed that there were very few opponents of fascism in Italy in the fall of 1922. Those there were would have been familiar types to anyone who read the gossip columns in the daily American press: men like the "terrified, titled wastrel, whose private life had been too public"; libertines who feared the punishment of "notorious cases of scandal in society."[107] The *fascisti* would not tolerate the kind of activities satirized so knowingly by Child's *Smart Set* contemporaries—bacchanalia, the exploration of sexual identity, the pursuit of self.

According to Child, the forces of a new nationalism culminated in the victory parade on October 31. The ambassador and his wife joined the spectators in the Piazza Venezia, enjoying a rare moment of anonymity in the cheerful crowd. There was no longer any reason to fear for his own safety, he suggested: there was no serious opposition to speak of; the nation, to all intents and purposes, had become one. The mud-splattered men had cleaned themselves up for the occasion. Now, the collective face of fascism was a dignified and handsome one, "lean" and "brown." Child described how the marching companies sang "Giovinezza"—Youth—the hymn of the fascists; and how the crowd sang back the same song. The fascists marched up to the steps of the Tomb of the Unknown Soldier, signaling continuity between times of war and times of peace. They passed the Quirinale, where from a balcony King Vittorio Emanuele III, dressed in uniform, acknowledge their cheers with a military salute.[108] Four years after the end of the war, Italy finally had a worthy victory parade.

These descriptions would have struck the chords of memory for most American readers. They would have been familiar to anyone who had participated in spontaneous celebrations of victory in November 1918, when church bells rang, schools were closed, and crowds flooded the streets, and familiar to anyone who had welcomed the troops when they had arrived on domestic shores the following spring.[109] Yet they would have felt strangely remote to Americans who had lived through the subsequent years. In 1922, Armistice Day in the United States was a subdued affair, marked by quiet services in churches or at memorial sites.[110] That same month, thousands flooded onto the streets of Elizabeth, New Jersey, to fete the world welterweight champion, Mickey Walker; the "entire" body of Harvard undergraduates cheered the varsity eleven during practice; and the seventy-five-thousand-seat stadium at Ohio State University opened to capacity crowds.[111] Americans of 1922 seemed more likely to rally around a titleholder or a team than they did their national flag. Child seems to have intended his descriptions of Italy that fall to remind Americans of what they were missing.

The reality of the March on Rome was not as Child described it. One hundred thousand men did not march on Rome.[112] When Schneider cut that number in half, and when McCormick reduced it by ten thousand more, they exaggerated still.[113] Historians now estimate that fewer than thirty thousand fascists joined the march.[114] Many of the squadrists at regional outposts failed to congregate on time. Those who did were poorly armed. They were also poorly fed: the "lean" faces that Child described were "lean" for a reason. It did rain a lot in Rome in late October. For four days, young men hung around the city in the pouring rain.[115] Did the squads clean off the mud and adjust their uniforms to present a dignified countenance, worthy of a victory parade, as Child wrote? Or did all that rain just wash the mud away? Herbert Schneider suggested that none of these details mattered. What mattered was that the March on Rome had created "a ferment of emotion and ideation" that was "much more revolutionary than the event itself."[116] What mattered, he suggested, was that Italians had been susceptible to dreams of battles, heroes, glory. What mattered, he suggested, was that people wanted to believe.

The Leader of the Fascists

Mussolini, as described by these observers, was at first a shadowy figure. Their initial impressions of him were hazy, and ill-informed: "Mussolino," McCormick called him when she first introduced him to her readers in July 1921; the man poised to resign as the leader of the fascists, the embassy informed the Department of State in August that year.[117] It was only in the weeks leading up to the March on Rome that Mussolini came into focus at all. Fascist sympathizers soon portrayed him as the right man to lead a war-weary nation out of its malaise—a man committed to the ideals of war, who scourged liberalism, and electrified a nation.

When sympathetic American observers considered Mussolini's past, they believed that more relevant than his socialism per se was his break with the majority of socialists over Italy's entry into World War I. In 1914, Mussolini was editor of the socialist daily, *Avanti*, noted Schneider and Child. But the party forced him to resign because he wrote in favor of intervention on the side of the allied powers. Mussolini quickly organized a new paper, *Il Popolo d'Italia*, which became an influential champion of Italy's entry into the war.[118] Schneider summarized Mussolini's editorials: a policy of neutrality was morally bankrupt; Italians had to fight, and "make sacrifices," if they wanted to gain anything from the war.[119]

According to the embassy, and later Child, when called to fight in the war, Mussolini conducted himself heroically. "He fought courageously and was seriously wounded," stated an embassy report.[120] Child wrote that Mussolini fought in the ranks and was "shredded by shrapnel in a hundred wounds."[121] (Mussolini had been injured in a training exercise and not by enemy fire, as Child implied.)[122] These observers noted that Mussolini maintained his fervent interventionism, even when Italian morale was at its lowest ebb, in the wake of the humiliating defeat at Caporetto.[123] In this guise, he was fascism's most famous "convert" from socialism—a man who went against the party when the party line interfered with his sense of honor, and his belief in what was right for his country.[124]

Following the war, these observers argued that Mussolini embodied righteous indignation that was sorely lacking in Italy, and much of the rest of the world. In their minds, he was the incarnation of a "spirit which could no longer tolerate drifting."[125] According to Schneider, Mussolini avoided sinking into mood of *disprezzo* that characterized society after the war. Instead, he turned his rage upon Italy's "pessimistic, timid, degenerate" leaders, who, he believed, had failed to secure for Italy the territorial rewards of victory.[126]

When Mussolini entered parliament in June 1921, as leader of the small group of elected fascists, his spirit of intolerance was evident again. McCormick heard his first speech in the Chamber of Deputies on June 21st. She described it as "one of the best political speeches" she had ever heard, "caustic, powerful and telling." In this speech, Mussolini declared the communists to be his enemies and castigated the socialists for their fatalism, materialism, and opposition to the war.[127]

Mussolini's rage seemed to be at one with the "terrible anger" of the squadrists, even if it typically took a less physical form.[128] It was harsh, unforgiving, and uncompromising. It felt refreshing to those who were disgusted with the atmosphere of passive acceptance that seemed to prevail in the postwar years.

For instance, Child described a meeting with the leader of the fascists, in the fall of 1922, just before the March on Rome. The two men drank tea with Maude Parker and laughed about European politics.[129] But within this relaxed encounter, there was an apparent authenticity, which Child obviously relished. He wrote: "Mussolini tears the cover off all pretenses; it is his foremost characteristic. Veneer is nothing; he rips it away and looks at the wood. We got on."[130] As was frequently the case in fascist sympathizers' writing, Child's portrait of Mussolini had sexual undercurrents. In this case, Child suggested that Mussolini's passion was pure, his approach was penetrating, and that their encounters provided Child with an immense sense of relief.

During his precipitous rise to power, Mussolini personified the fascists' spirit of *élan vital*, in the American observer's mind. He was young in age, remarked Child; "*giovane* in spirit," according to Schneider.[131] Although he was not the most bloodthirsty of fascists, Mussolini offered aggressive energy, seemingly contained within a chivalric code. In May 1922, the embassy reported that Mussolini had wounded an editor of another journal, Mario Missiroli, in a duel.[132] The fascist leader seemed to be a man of action, as well as thought, and sympathetic American observers appreciated the theater. He turned politics into a "noble show," in McCormick's words.[133] Schneider interpreted the March on Rome as Mussolini's most triumphant spectacle: he channeled the squadrists' energies; he choreographed their revolution; and he ensured that their violence was held within bounds.[134]

Both Schneider and McCormick commented on the speed with which Mussolini got the *squadristi* out of Rome after their victory parade of October 31. Within twenty-four hours, according to Schneider, and even sooner, according to McCormick, the marchers marched back from where they had come. Schneider and McCormick emphasized this point to suggest that Mussolini represented the vitality of youth, without its associated excesses.[135] His apparent capacity for control seemed to bode well for Italian (and global) stability. But his ability to unleash made these observers, quite simply, happy to be alive. It felt like Child's "prophet" had arrived.[136]

The Promise of a New World

American sympathizers with fascism reacted against the prevailing culture of disillusionment in the wake of World War I. By 1922, they could tell Italy's story in a satisfying narrative arc, starting with despair and ending with redemption. According to their perceptions, Italians in 1920 were extreme embodiments of the modern mood. They were apathetic—even their attachments to socialism, communism, and other manifestations of the left were shallow and self-serving. As a people, they had turned against their government, their nation, and their recent participation in the war. They had turned inward, toward only themselves. Italy, like the rest of Europe, was depressing in 1919, not because it was a nation in mourning, but because it seemed to want to forget.

These observers argued that fascist squads excited senses numbed by the apathetic atmosphere left in the wake of the war. Richard Washburn Child and Herbert Schneider both suggested that fascist violence was not necessary for the suppression of communism. Anne O'Hare McCormick, by contrast, insisted that the fascists prevented a Bolshevik-style revolution in Italy. But whatever their position on the relationship between the *biennio rosso* and fascism, all three of these observers admired squadrist violence qua violence. In this sense, they appreciated fascism, not just as a force for order against communism, but as a force for disorder, which created at least "one diversion in a dull world."[137]

Fascism, they believed, could renew the spirit of the Great War in at least three ways. First, fascist youths demonstrated the inherent dignity of martial ideals. The call to service, American sympathizers suggested, could still be pure—unsullied by self-interest—and powerful—capable of inspiring, galvanizing. Second, nothing awakened one's sense of being alive better than being close to death. McCormick and Child aimed to get as near to the violence as possible so as to benefit from its therapeutic effects. And all three of these observers attempted to bring their readers, too, into the vortex, away from the modern appliances and motor cars, to remind them that there was more to living. Last, fascism—both in and out of politics—promised the beginning of the "new world," which the war had failed to deliver. After she had watched the fascists as they trooped down the Via Aracoeli, in April 1921, Anne O'Hare McCormick expressed her own uncertainty about a future that she deemed to be in the hands of these young men:

> I wondered if the world they will create for us, a world already more solid than the shaken planet of the past few years, will be as liberal, as easy for the nonconformists, as indulgent of the mildly mad, as pitiful of the weak, as the muddling old world we used to know or used to think we knew until that August morning when it crashed![138]

The question was barely a question. McCormick's answer, though never explicitly articulated, was surely a hopeful "No."

2

Mystic in a Morning Coat

AMERICANS' MUSSOLINI IN THE 1920S

HOW QUICKLY RICHARD WASHBURN CHILD turned the youthful, irreverent leader of the *squadristi* into an effective yet soulful administrator. Child caught sight of Mussolini in a limousine on a Roman side street by the parliament on November 16, 1922. The two men saw each other, and then Mussolini raised his eyes and threw his head up to the sky. Child interpreted the gesture as a sign that Mussolini had made a decision, and that he was satisfied with it. Minutes later, the ambassador watched from the gallery as the new prime minister made his first address to the Chamber of Deputies. He spoke quietly, yet firmly, with none of the florid conventions of Italian rhetoric. Child distilled the "essence" of Mussolini's words to his readers. First, he said he had chosen to limit the revolution. Second, he observed that the will to act was more important than programs of action. The fascist government, he said, embodied such will. Last, Mussolini accepted personal responsibility for the trials that lay ahead. He had, he said, a "religious sense" of the difficulties that Italy faced.[1] The celebrations were over; work had begun.

While the image of Mussolini as an effective executive indicated that he could navigate the technical challenges of modernity, it also implied that he would act as a bulwark against modernity's worst effects. Silent in his limousine, speaking quietly in the chamber, and using only those words that were necessary, Mussolini was a calm riposte to the modern tendency of self-expression, words and more words, noise and more noise. Fascist sympathizers suggested that this austerity with words was at one with an economy of character. Their Mussolini embodied older ideals of savings and responsibility that were fading in the United States, flushed, as it was, with cash. Child's description conveyed a man who was driven by an internal impetus rather than external stimuli, who stood, Neptune-like, above the waves, and calmed the storm. In the modern era, when men and women seemed driven by forces outside themselves—the pace of the assembly line, the tempo of jazz, and the speed of cars—Mussolini offered a hope that human beings, endowed with sufficient will, could still be in control.

Despite the apparent directness of the prime minister's words, there was something mystical about him, according to sympathetic onlookers: hidden depths. Child alluded to this mysticism in the silent gestures that conveyed meanings, rather like a Renaissance portrait of a saint. He saw mysticism in Mussolini's "religious sense" of his duty to others.[2] As Anne O'Hare McCormick observed, Mussolini's speech before the Chamber of Deputies marked the first time that any Italian prime minister had bound his secular role to the spiritual realm.[3] Even in this early appearance as prime minister, Mussolini seemed to suggest that he would be more than an effective administrator, and more than an exemplar of old-fashioned values of austerity, inner will, selflessness, and responsibility. He would be a spiritual leader, who could nourish the modern soul.

Fascist sympathizers saw Mussolini as a man who could simultaneously navigate the complexities of the modern world and slow down the breakneck speed of modern culture. They also believed that he could provide Americans with an emotional and spiritual fulfillment that seemed lacking in their own milieu. John Diggins pointed to this idea when he wrote that Mussolini was, for some Americans, the "answer to many . . . things that were wrong with the modern world."[4] In a study that was broader than it was deep, Diggins could offer his readers no more than a tantalizing glimpse of this argument.

Yet the work of other cultural historians demonstrates the validity of the hypothesis that Mussolini appealed to Americans as an antidote to the ills of modernity. According to Warren Susman, the "culture heroes" of the 1920s were men who succeeded in modern arenas while they displayed character traits associated with the late-Victorian era. Henry Ford, for instance, built the archetypal assembly line, while insisting on old-fashioned ideals of simplicity, hard work, and austerity. Ford, argued Susman, eased the transition to modernity by suggesting that Americans could succeed in a new world by playing by the old rules. As the nineteenth-century emphasis on character—defined by internal measures of self-control, hard work, and will—gave way to the celebration of personality—defined by external measures of beauty, likability, and charisma—Ford and other "culture heroes" sent a reassuring message that a man's integrity still mattered.[5]

As Diggins's and Susman's research suggests, fascist sympathizers were attracted to Mussolini for his apparent capacity to navigate modernity while moderating its worst effects. Constructed as the austere administrator with a deep soul, sympathizers' Mussolini drew attention to all that Americans had sacrificed in their race to the future and provided recompense for those who felt lost, lonely, or left behind by change.

The Right Kind of Businessman

Richard Washburn Child used the image of a limousine, idling in a Roman side street in November 1922, to suggest that Mussolini resembled a modern business executive. This was just one of the many ways that fascist sympathizers conveyed the new prime minister's ease in a complex modern world. Some historians, most notably Gian Giacomo Migone, have argued that Mussolini was popular with Americans in the 1920s because he appeared to offer a stable destination for dollar investments, and this argument does indeed go some way to explaining why the Americans studied here reproduced images of the prime minister as a business executive *par excellence*.[6] Child, while he was still ambassador, was involved in discussions with Mussolini about economic opportunities for American investors; Anne O'Hare McCormick advocated dollar outlays as a spur to recovery in postwar Europe; Generoso Pope's newspaper portrayed Italy as a safe home for foreign financiers; and Herbert Schneider argued that, under Mussolini, the country's economy was in capable hands.[7] But after Child retired from the ambassadorship in 1924, none of these onlookers was particularly well-placed to influence decisionmaking in the upper echelons of American government and finance, at least while Republican administrations remained in power. These observers aimed to impact the United States' domestic culture by addressing a much broader public. Financial and business concerns give us only a partial explanation for their reproduction of images of Mussolini as an effective administrator.

Fascist sympathizers portrayed Mussolini as a figure who gracefully mastered the complexities of the modern economy, creating clarity where there was confusion. Child presented his *Saturday Evening Post* readers with a list of figures. In Mussolini's first year in power, he reported, the government reduced the budget deficit by nearly one-half, as private savings increased by fifteen percent. Through a crackdown on evasion, the regime added almost one million taxpayers to its rolls. By sacking "useless personnel," it cut railway costs by 352,000,000 lire. At the same time, it reduced overall unemployment by more than two-thirds, to under 180,000 men nationwide. In reciting these figures, and many more, Child probably did not imagine that many of his readers would pause to analyze them (and those who did would have felt justifiably skeptical about a man who could simultaneously initiate drastic reductions of public spending while stimulating output and employment).[8] His goal was rather to suggest that ordinary Americans, like ordinary Italians, need not concern themselves with these complexities. An administrative genius was in command, a man who could add "a column of cold figures which finely balance a budget" with ease.[9]

Child's Mussolini exuded calm. Child claimed that he met with the prime minister often in his early days of "administrative superlabor."[10] Although busy, Mussolini still had time to reflect on the nature of his work. He was laboring hard, he confided; he was absorbing the details. "'Detail!'" this Mussolini exclaimed, as he "spread his short strong arms apart to indicate the world of detail." There, in his sturdy embrace, Mussolini held the details. It was a comforting image of a strong man assuming a burden so that others need not. And it was made more comforting still by Mussolini's pronounced ability to do away with the details entirely. "Detail interferes with wise solution of the larger problems," Child quoted him as saying.[11] Like a magician, he held the details and, in a flash, they disappeared.

McCormick also portrayed Mussolini as adept at simplifying complex realities. She met *Il Duce* for the first time in the summer of 1926. The regime had only just announced its plans for the corporate state, and international onlookers were uncertain about what this really entailed—their own uncertainties a reflection of the confusion within the fascist government itself.[12] Had McCormick seen clearly, she might have described Italian corporatism as a half-baked attempt to mediate the competing demands of capital and labor, almost always to the disadvantage of the latter.[13] But instead, she described it as a complete system of economic management, not unlike an integrated factory, with Mussolini as the chief of the enterprise. McCormick's Mussolini certainly had all the communication skills of the modern businessman. According to her, he responded enthusiastically to her expressions of interest, "jumping up" to show her a "diagram on the wall" of his office. Speaking calmly and patiently, this Mussolini explained to McCormick the "whole economic structure of the nation."[14] Never have smoke and mirrors looked so simple.

The reality of McCormick's interview with Mussolini in 1926 was far less straightforward than she claimed. The two met in mid-July for what was less of an interview and more of an audience. The following day, McCormick sent *Il Duce* a list of written questions. Did His Excellency, she asked, "wish to say a few words to American readers on his concept of the new corporate state?"

In return, she received a diagram from Giacomo Paulucci, the head of the Cabinet of Foreign Affairs. Perhaps this, or another, diagram of the corporate state also hung on Mussolini's office wall, or perhaps McCormick took a great deal of journalistic license and hung it there herself. But in response to her specific questions, McCormick heard nothing at all. She prodded Paulucci in late July and again in early August. Someone in the government compiled the answers. Mussolini's chief contribution was to delay the process further, in an effort to pace his appearances in the US news. "One month after the Associated [Press] one," he scribbled on top of McCormick's questionnaire.[15] The *Times* was not able to publish the piece until October 1926. In it, McCormick portrayed an entirely different man from the one who had eluded her for more than three months: a man who was honest and open, instead of calculating and indirect; a man who distilled complex realities down to their essence, instead of one who created murky clouds in muddy water.

When McCormick fashioned Mussolini into this alter-ego, she wanted Americans to recognize that they too needed men who could bring calm and clarity to their frenetic and confusing culture. The journalist had spent most of 1925 in the United States, where she had witnessed the Florida land-boom at its peak. From Florida, she had relayed dizzying statistics to her readers: fifteen hundred cars, carrying more than four thousand people, entered the state each day; the tourist industry was worth sixty million dollars a year; and the advertisers for prospective lots on Davis Island had sold three million dollars' worth of land, site unseen (and unseeable, since it still lay below water).[16] McCormick suggested that Florida was a product of the United States in the mid-1920s, moving so fast that you could barely make sense of it.

In contrast to her Mussolini, who made sense of complexities, the American businessmen whom McCormick profiled in Florida compounded and profited from the mayhem. Men like Dave Davis—the investor behind Davis Island—had turned Florida into a land of "high pressure salesmen."[17] McCormick's Mussolini of 1926 suggested the kind of men Americans should find among themselves: executives who faced the chaos, so that others need not; administrators who absorbed complexity, removing its burden on society.

More Modern, More Italian

The claim that Mussolini effortlessly managed modernity was particularly useful for Generoso Pope. On November 2, 1928—the day after Pope assumed leadership of *Il Progresso Italo-Americano*—he stated that his goal was to make the newspaper "*più moderno, più italiano*."[18] The notion of "more modern, more Italian" implied a challenge to nativist prejudices, which equated Italians with, at best, beautiful chaos and an irretrievable past, and, at worst, congenital disorder and immunity to modernity.[19] Images of Mussolini as an effective executive furthered Pope's objective by demonstrating the compatibility of modernity and Italianità.[20]

A typical photograph of the *Il Duce*, reprinted in the newspaper in January 1929, showed him speaking at a meeting of Italian business managers. Standing behind a lectern in a suit, with a neat pile of papers before him, and indoor plants in the background, the image was as suggestive of an American Chamber of Commerce convention as it was of a meeting of the Italian corporate state.[21] "An Italian Genius, He Knows His Business," crowed a headline, which touted Mussolini's managerial capacities, that same month.[22] Photographed in a March meeting of the Grand Council—as the fascist elite hand-picked deputies to replace elected representatives in the parliament—*Il Duce* sat behind a desk loaded with papers, poised to make a decision.[23] Images like this foregrounded Mussolini's administrative skills, while obscuring the loss of Italians' freedoms entailed by his executive actions.

Contributors to *Il Progresso* argued that Mussolini's skills as an administrator were not his alone, but were typical of his countrymen, whether in Italy or in the United States. One fascist official, quoted at length in *Il Progresso*, argued that Mussolini's "capacity for problems of a technical character, and for statistics" showed that Italians were not just good artists, as once was thought.[24] The newspaper's English-language section—a feature launched by Pope to reach second-generation immigrants as well as native-born Americans—published a series of articles on local self-made men titled "Italo-Americans of Whom We Are Proud."[25] In contrast to Child's and McCormick's journalism, which suggested that most Americans had lost control of the economic forces that governed their daily existence, this series portrayed Italian Americans as methodically overcoming challenges, to succeed in a modern United States. The series featured lawyers, like Ferdinand Pecora, who had migrated from Italy as a child, studying and working assiduously to reach the peak of his profession, and bankers, like Italo Palermo, who had "exploited the opportunities" of a booming American financial sector to triple the capital of his company.[26]

Examples such as this implied that Italian Americans were importing Mussolini's talents into the United States. Nobody seemed more suggestive of this claim than Generoso Pope himself, at least as he was rendered in *Il Progresso*. Italo Carlo Falbo, *Il Progresso*'s director, reflected on Pope's pathway to success, from a low-wage worker in a sand company to the unassailable cement king of New York. Pope, wrote Falbo, had succeeded due to his "vigor for organization and administration." Buying up company after company, he had "strengthened and secured" the construction industry for the benefit of all Americans.[27] Falbo's account naturally sanitized Pope's life story of the mafia connections that had facilitated his rise, and eschewed any notion that monopoly produced dangerous economic distortions rather than stability.[28] Pope, in this guise, was the kind of man who was in short supply and much demand in the United States—one who managed the "maelstrom" of modernity, without getting swept up in its force.[29]

In these ways, *Il Progresso Italo-Americano* reproduced and reinterpreted images of Mussolini for its own purposes. Like Child and McCormick's portraits of *Il Duce*, the newspaper's representations of Mussolini as an effective administrator suggested that he had a capacity to absorb the details that overwhelmed many modern Americans. But *Il Progresso* went further, to claim that Mussolini's skills, while scarce among Americans, were innate to Italians, as exemplified, above all, by Generoso Pope. These images rebuffed pejorative stereotypes of Italian immigrants as incapable of incorporation into American modernity, suggesting that Americans needed Italians to live among them, as much as, or even more than, Italians needed to live in the United States.

Italy's Answer to Horatio Alger

Even as they praised him for his abilities to manage the technical challenges associated with modernity, Child, McCormick, and Pope suggested that Italy's leader held steadfast to an older model of manhood. The *New York Times* hinted at this in an illustration, which accompanied McCormick's 1926 piece based on her interview with Mussolini. In this drawing, *Il Duce* appeared in a morning suit—a form of dress that by 1926 was decidedly old-fashioned in the United States.[30]

Il Progresso, too, consistently reproduced images of Mussolini that were reminiscent of older masculine ideals. Pictured at work in 1929, Mussolini's eyes were cast away from the camera, in the direction of the business of government that occupied him.[31] *Il Progresso* invited the viewer to make contrasts between representations of Mussolini and those of other famous men who appeared frequently in the newspaper, such as the boxing champion Primo Carnera and the aviator Italo Balbo. Carnera and Balbo were a source of titillating images and a more modern aesthetic, which emphasized the physical

FIGURE 2.1. A Sober Mussolini. Images similar to this appeared frequently in *Il Progresso Italo-Americano* in the late 1920s.
Source: Bain News Service, Prints and Photographs Division, Library of Congress.

self and used youthful good looks to establish a connection with the audience.[32] The newspaper consistently selected opposing images to represent the leader of Italians. By far the most prevalent image of Mussolini in *Il Progresso* was a sober profile of Mussolini in a dark suit. Face turned to the side, eyes downcast, it suggested that the putative viewer could not have been further from *Il Duce*'s mind (figure 2.1).[33] To employ Warren Susman's distinction, images of Carnera and Balbo evoked "personalities"; those of Mussolini, "character."[34] The difference was between men who had been swept into an easy but often superficial modern world, and a man who held on to a harder but truer self.

Child, McCormick, and Pope's Mussolini shared many characteristics with the protagonist of a Horatio Alger tale of a young man, born in poverty, who achieved success through integrity. They emphasized various features of Mussolini's character—including self-denial, inner will, benevolence, and responsibility—which were reminiscent of one of Alger's protagonists.[35] In attaching these characteristics to Mussolini, these observers had a number of objectives. First, and most obviously, they aimed to make him admirable, and even likable. Second, they insisted on Mussolini's adherence to late-Victorian ideals to critique modern American men, and the society that encouraged them to drift so far from their anchors. Last, they used the example of Mussolini to suggest a reassuring, or "therapeutic," message, that Americans too could become hybrid men, who combined technical capabilities with older sensibilities, thereby escaping modernity's thrall.[36]

Mussolini's reputation for austerity was the invention of Italian propagandists, who recognized that in a relatively poor dictatorship, it was wise for *Il Duce* to claim he preferred black bread to red meat, and few words to constant debate.[37] When American sympathizers reproduced propaganda images of Italy's leader as austere, they suggested that he shunned consumption, physical pleasure, and self-expression in favor of a simple life. These observers insisted that Mussolini learned his austerity in childhood. In the mid-1920s, the regime made a shrine of *Il Duce*'s childhood home in Predappio, Romagna, refurbishing it artfully, to conjure poverty.[38] Dutifully, McCormick described the "tumble-down tenement" where Mussolini had grown up; dutifully, too, she suggested that he never lost the ascetic habits that he had learned as a "half-starved" child.[39]

As editor of Mussolini's English-language autobiography, Child also insisted on this theme. The first two chapters of the autobiography were devoted to Benito's early years of simple play in the fields and simple work in his father's blacksmith shop.[40] Introducing the autobiography to readers of the *Saturday Evening Post*, Child argued that *Il Duce* maintained these habits into his adult life: Mussolini was "abstemious, almost ascetic"; he neither had nor wanted money; he shunned alcohol and cigarettes; and he resisted the distractions of friends or the sycophancy of acquaintances.[41]

In Mussolini's self-abnegation, these observers identified a strong inner will. They argued that his will, too, was evident in his work ethic. McCormick wrote that when she met Mussolini in 1926, he had been working in the summer heat for ten hours, and showed no signs of letting up.[42] The *Saturday Evening Post* summarized Mussolini's approach in a single subheading, which could have been lifted from the pages of a Victorian success manual: *Work and Discipline*.[43] *Il Progresso* similarly stressed that Mussolini was the hardest of hard workers—"*un lavoratore formidabile*."[44]

Il Duce's will to work came from within, according to American sympathizers. He drove himself. In more imaginative ways, too, they suggested that Mussolini's impetus was internal. Child described his habit of listening quietly in meetings with his ministers. Suddenly, he would sit up, and "with a jerk of his stocky body" shoot out his decision.[45] It was not the only allusion to ejaculation that Child made in his descriptions of Mussolini and fascism.[46] In this case, the metaphor suggested that Mussolini's decisions obeyed a rhythm all of their own; they were often contrary to the expectations of others; and, like bodily fluids, they came from the inside.[47]

Similarly, Mussolini's much-touted pragmatism was suggestive of a man who acted out of his own instincts rather than according to external expectations.[48] By this interpretation, Mussolini's changing identities, from a Socialist firebrand in his youth, to fervent interventionist in 1914, to anti-Bolshevik militant in the early 1920s, to effective administrator by the mid-decade, were not the various masks of a modern personality, changing on the outside, hollow in the middle. Rather, they showed that he refused to follow doctrine for doctrine's sake, and that he was willing to make enemies out of erstwhile allies when the welfare of the nation was at stake. These observers argued that Mussolini's love for country was the central axis around which all his decisions turned.[49] There was nothing hollow about that.

To underscore the idea that Mussolini was animated by profound patriotism, fascist sympathizers reproduced a familiar image of regime propaganda: that of *Il Duce* as a lonely figure—a "sad, solitary giant" as Herbert Schneider called him—who carried the weight of the world on his shoulders.[50] The recurrent portrait of Mussolini in *Il Progresso* (see figure 2.1) communicated this notion. He seemed burdened by responsibility—managing effectively, but deriving no personal pleasure from his position of power. The image implied that his dictatorship was a selfless act, which he bestowed on the Italian people even at a cost to his own person. Often the burden had physical manifestations. Child claimed that, when he was ambassador, he would frequently find Mussolini at his desk in the morning, "hollow-eyed and pale—up all night no doubt."[51] McCormick, too, noted that *Il Duce*'s eyes were "heavily weary."[52] He suffered for his country.

The notion that Mussolini cared for his country rather than himself was evident, too, in his reputed benevolence, which consisted, in part, of acts of charity for the deserving poor. For instance, in his autobiography, Mussolini claimed that he had recently rebuilt Predappio, not with the aim of creating a suitable destination for mass political pilgrimages, but to protect its inhabitants from the risk of avalanche.[53] And in January 1929, *Il Progresso* reported that *Il Duce* had personally contributed fifty-thousand lire so that Rome's poorest children could receive gifts on Epiphany.[54]

The claim to benevolence ran further than these discrete acts of giving. "[T]here is bitterness in power when one has no narcotic for it," wrote Richard Washburn Child, as if he, too, understood public service to be something a man did for his country, and not for himself.[55] By this construction, every additional office Mussolini assumed, every extra power he accumulated, was an act of giving to others. By presenting dictatorship as Mussolini's gift to his country, Child suggested that one-man rule enabled the revival of a charitable ethic. In this way, he disguised the deprivations that Italians suffered under dictatorship—a loss of representation and a theft of their political voices—as a gift.

These observers also dressed up dictatorship as the exercise of an old-fashioned code of individual accountability. Frequently, they presented Mussolini's ever-expanding powers as proof that he was "not afraid of responsibility."[56] While he was still ambassador, Child made a speech in Rome praising Mussolini. "I want to see leaders who, instead of telling men of their rights, will lead them to take a full share of their responsibilities," said Child.[57] To him, Mussolini was such a man. Five years later, Child insisted on this theme. Italy's leader, he wrote, took "responsibility for everything." Over those five years, Mussolini had banned the political opposition and made himself minister of the interior, minister of foreign affairs, minister of war, minister of the navy, minister for aviation, and minister of corporations. To Child, this dizzying accumulation of cabinet posts was not a sign of megalomania. Rather, it was proof of Mussolini's readiness to stand and fall on his commitments. This was "admirable courage" of a kind rarely seen in modern life, according to Richard Washburn Child.[58]

Of course, had Child really cared to find examples of men and women of "admirable courage," who were willing to stand and fall for their beliefs, he ought to have looked among Mussolini's political opponents, serving terms of *confino* (domestic exile) in the south of Italy, or unable to access jobs or welfare because they resisted fascist strictures.[59] But none of these observers aimed to find real examples of old-fashioned virtues among the remaining representatives of Italian labor, socialism, or liberalism. Rather, they aimed to make Mussolini's repressive and brutal tendencies palatable to American readers by repackaging them as facets of an old-fashioned character. They hoped to make Mussolini likable or even lovable, even as they insisted that *Il Duce* himself had no interest in the superficial allure of being adored.

Manliness Lost in the United States

By the 1920s in the United States, the heroes of Horatio Alger's novels belonged to a different, and seemingly simpler, time. These observers argued that each of the characteristics that Mussolini embodied had been undermined by alternative notions of masculinity that prevailed in the modern age. Here, they joined a larger chorus of contemporaries, who, not for the first or last time in American history, used the apparent decadence of manliness to express anxieties about social and cultural change.[60] Fascist sympathizers constructed each of the facets of Mussolini's character—abstinence, will, benevolence, and responsibility—as a counterpoint to a modern personality defined by consumption, external stimuli, self-centeredness, and frivolity. In doing so, they took aim at both a new generation of Americans who embodied these tendencies and also the modern culture that had created them.

Modern man was a product of a materialistic society. This reality seemed to strike Anne O'Hare McCormick hard when she visited Florida in 1925. She was recently returned from the Balkans, and had seen the refugee camps of Greece, where families survived on almost nothing at all.[61] In Florida, by contrast, all the conversations McCormick heard were about money. The wealthy talked about getting wealthier, the poor talked about getting wealthy too. She argued that the state offered financial prospects to any man, regardless of his savings, regardless of his "personal habits."[62] Character seemed to count for nothing in Florida, McCormick claimed, and was counting for less and less across the United States, as a get-rich-quick culture eroded the values of savings and self-control that had once been the route to success.

Child too argued that economic and cultural change in the United States had a detrimental impact on American manhood. In search of a job after he left the ambassadorship, he saw an opportunity in an apparent domestic crime wave. In 1924 and 1925, Child published a book, *Battling the Criminal*, which was serialized in the *Saturday Evening Post*, and served on a National Crime Commission alongside his former boss at the Department of State, Charles Evans Hughes, and Franklin Delano Roosevelt.[63] Rehashing ideas that were common among his contemporaries, Child argued that the postwar consumption boom had contributed to a spike in juvenile delinquency. Cheap amusements and roadhouses, he argued, lured young men out of the home, the sanctuary of traditional values. The ubiquitous automobile only facilitated access to degenerate forms of entertainment. Above all, consumerism altered the standards for success, as a new generation sought peer approval through smoking, spending, and speeding. These young Americans claimed "the right to enjoy every luxury" of "a complex civilization," wrote Child. He argued that it was only a small step from this "lawless claim" to lawless behavior.[64]

Child implied that even those men who avoided a life of crime entered amoral territory when they succumbed to the "idleness and excitement" of consumption.[65] As consumers, men derived their impetus from the outside, following passing fads and hoping for the approval of their acquaintances and friends.[66] Another part of the problem, as Child diagnosed it, lay in the nature of work in the 1920s. It had become too easy: the contemporary American executive did not need much of a work ethic, he could spend his winters in Palm Beach, his summers in Europe, cut his day in the office short at 3 pm, and still make a fortune.[67] Manual workers, also, were affected by the ease of their regime. Whereas a working-class man's job had once demanded discernment, craftsmanship, and physical strength, Child argued that by the mid-1920s, it required only the stamina to resist boredom.[68] Deriving little satisfaction in their work, Americans searched for it in movement, the movies, or the latest craze.[69] Child diagnosed "a form of dipsomania." Americans were "amusement drunkards," addicted to "endless entertainments outside" themselves.[70]

McCormick, too, suggested that the modern personality was a weak amalgam of external stimuli. Her domestic journalism often imitated the tempo of American life, each sentence breathless, packed to bursting point. McCormick's writing seemed designed to induce anxiety in the reader by mimicking the pace of "the opulent, self-starting, power-plus" era. "We jazz into the jungle with a 12-cylinder engine and dynamite the protoplasm," she wrote in 1925, the year she deemed the "fastest" in history.[71] It was as if Americans, unable to catch up, had just given in. For once, Child put it best: "We have invented and found nearly everything; about the only thing we have not found is ourselves."[72]

While the self remained elusive, Americans continued to search. They searched for themselves down blind alleyways, according to Child, following doctrines for self-improvement that brought them no closer to enlightenment: Charles Wagner's advice for a Simple Life, Rabindranath Tagore's insights into Eastern mysticism, and Sigmund Freud's doctrine of psychoanalysis. This was pointless self-indulgence, in Child's mind. Men, he suggested, would have more luck realizing themselves if they laid off the self-help literature and did something that helped others.[73]

But civic-spiritedness seemed, to these observers, to be on the decline. There were plenty of professional associations, such as the Rotary and Lions Clubs, that had charitable functions. But McCormick struggled to find men who gave without an expectation of professional advancement in return. Building private fortresses in their suburban homes and country clubs, modern middle-class men cared little about their poorer neighbors, she believed. They paid entrance fees for sanitary or beautiful spaces instead of creating them in public spheres in their own towns. In April 1929, McCormick concluded that the average "citizen grows more selfish as he grows richer."[74] And, in April 1929, there seemed to be no end to this average citizen's accumulation of wealth.

Pulled this way and that by forces that he either could not or cared not to control, modern man lacked a moral center, according to these critiques. "Habitually . . . , he goes more and more his own way . . . he is more irresponsible," wrote McCormick.[75] Child deemed masculine responsibility to be a casualty of various postwar phenomena: the slackening of a culture of public service; an emphasis on rights instead of obligations; New Women, who carelessly withdrew their attention from their sons; psychiatry, with its attendant proposition that an individual was not to blame for his own misdemeanors; and even avant-garde artists, who claimed that their hurried splashes of paint were better than the painstaking efforts of the great masters.[76] The "wine of irresponsibility," he wrote, came "in many bottles."[77] But whatever the bottle, the effects were the same: autonomy and integrity were no longer the *sine qua non* of a man's social worth. Child lamented a precipitous decline: by the late 1920s, an American man could be a speculator, a drinker, a delinquent, or a sloth, and still be a man.

McCormick and Child both argued that, in the early twentieth century, American men had fallen: from self-control to spending; from inner direction to external definition; from benevolence to self-centeredness; and from responsibility to a total lack thereof. The fall of man was, in their minds, due to an indulgent society, which made consumption and work too easy and welcomed degeneration as self-expression, even art. Mussolini, for them, functioned as a foil—a model of late-Victorian manliness who drew attention to the seemingly immense changes in values in the United States. They hoped that through Mussolini, their audience would mourn all that had fallen by the wayside in the race to modernity. They hoped that through Mussolini, their readers would see these changes as a race to the bottom, as well as a race to the top.

For one of these observers, at least, the parable of manliness lost had personal dimensions. To his readers, Child insisted that he too shunned "silky comforts" in favor of "hard" work and the "hard" life.[78] This was far from the truth. Child's only hardship seemed to be that he never had quite enough money, at least for his liking. He obsessed about money: how to make it, and how to spend it.[79] During his tenure in Rome, he confessed to his father that he was trapped in a "silly, vapid, degenerate" social circle. Though he claimed to loathe these contacts, and long for "serious personalities and the clean," he was unable to break away from all the fun.[80] Child succumbed to the rhythms of evening dinner parties and morning hangover cures—the "endless entertainments outside" himself.[81]

Although he did not accept Maude Parker's charge that he was "an adulterer and drunk all the time" in Rome, Child privately admitted that the breakup of his second marriage was his fault.[82] He had had, it seemed, more than his fair share of the "wine of irresponsibility."[83] Seeking beauty among the damned, he wrote to his father, "The human and the humane gutter is better than the inhuman and inhumane palace. I ought to know. I've seen 'em both."[84] By the time the gossip-hungry press picked up on rumors of Child's pending divorce to Maude, he was living with Eva Sanderson. Known affectionately, when affection reigned, as Billy, Sanderson would be Child's third, but not final, wife.[85]

Meanwhile, his career in government floundered. The day-to-day work of a diplomat did not excite him, and he suffered from what may today be called a fear of missing out. Less than two years into his tour, he began to angle for a position back in the United States. Warren Harding's heart attack, in August 1923, was a source of personal consternation for Child, because he "had just worked out the biggest play" of his life. Child lamented the president's poorly timed death, since the "months" he had spent positioning himself would come to naught.[86] He took an extended leave of absence to travel back to the United States. A plausible rumor swirled that the State Department had recalled him due to "dissatisfaction with his attitude."[87] The department, naturally, denied this, but, at the beginning of 1924, Child quit Rome for good. He circled around the Coolidges and even spent an afternoon swimming with the first lady. But the president used him only as an informal advisor and occasional spokesperson. This was certainly not the big "play" that Child had had in mind.[88]

Work at the *Post* was Child's one constant. He admired the *Post*'s editor, George Horace Lorimer, as "one of the biggest men" in America—a quick decisionmaker with a "splendidly contained" life and an "active and sympathetic mind."[89] Child was Lorimer's second choice for the job of editor of Mussolini's autobiography. But the role made good use of his talents.[90] Everyone who knew him seemed to agree: Richard Washburn Child could spin a story. In many ways, the Mussolini of his imagination was the kind of man that Child failed, so spectacularly, to be—austere, moral, and authentic.

The Promise of Manhood Regained

American fascist sympathizers crafted this old-fashioned Mussolini to evoke feelings of loss in Americans. But they did not want to provoke a sense of despair. Rather, they used Mussolini's example to suggest that recovery of manly virtues might be possible in the United States. Sometimes, these observers pointed to specific institutions or policies that might help American men. In his 1928 piece in *Century* magazine, Schneider observed that the *balilla* (fascist boy scouts) had produced "beneficent results" in Italian young men.[91] He presented similar observations to an academic audience in his book on civic training the following year.[92] Based on Schneider's findings, Charles Merriam remarked on the innovative "patriotic organizations" in Italy, which trained boys and men to be loyal, disciplined, and service-oriented.[93] Neither Schneider nor Merriam argued that the United States ought to import carbon copies of fascist institutions to cleanse the morals of American youths. Instead, like a number of their contemporaries in political science, they suggested that Italy and the United States were facing similar problems, and that Italy had implemented "striking" responses, worthy of study.[94] Child, too, implied that Americans could learn from the ways in which fascist Italy was shaping a new generation of men. The United States needed tough law enforcement, the restoration of authority and discipline, and organizations to train youth "in virile and yet restrained conduct," he argued.[95] Child suggested that American men would benefit from a social order that resembled the one he admired in Italy, while maintaining that domestic institutions—from the police, to the law courts, to the boy scouts—could preside over the changes.

But beyond the realm of specific policies, Mussolini functioned as an object of hope for sympathetic observers. Crafted as a man of technical capabilities and old-fashioned values, Mussolini suggested that it was possible for American men simultaneously to pursue the former and recover the latter. According to the owner of *Il Progresso*, Italian Americans had a special role to play in enabling the recovery of manliness lost. Pope styled himself, like Mussolini, as a potent example of old-fashioned virtues. The newspaper's director, Italo Carlo Falbo, wrote that Pope had been "a poor boy, alone and without help," when he had left the small town of Arpaise for New York. He had "walked the 'stations of the cross' of all poor Italian immigrants," taking on the hardest jobs, and persisting despite the indignities and prejudices he suffered. Material success had not changed Pope's character, Falbo insisted. Rather, he had used his wealth to help others, providing electricity to Arpaise, endowing New York's Italian Hospital, and contributing to Columbia University's Casa Italiana, so that all Americans could benefit from Italy's cultural patrimony.[96]

In reality, there was little that was altruistic in Pope's acts of benevolence, which were calculated to win him accolades and influence. Pope used his reputation for generosity to demand recognition from the Italian government: Falbo wrote to Mussolini's private secretary in December 1928, asking that Pope be commended for his philanthropy.[97] The government obliged, and, in February 1929 the Italian Consul General in New York bestowed the Commander of the Crown of Italy on Pope.[98] Speaking at the award ceremony, Mayor Walker commended Pope as a self-made man, whose "tenacious hard work," "formidable will," and generosity had ensured his success.[99]

In June 1929, Pope left for Italy, accompanied by Falbo; his wife, Catherine; and their two eldest sons, Anthony and Fortune.[100] Pope and his entourage had an audience with Pius XI and meetings with various fascist officials.[101] The people of Arpaise gave their prodigal son a hero's welcome.[102] The tour culminated in a meeting with Mussolini. Falbo accompanied Pope.[103] Behind closed doors, this short conference occupied the gray zone, where business and politics met, as *Il Duce* consented to Pope's purchase of another newspaper, in return for the publisher's assurances of editorial support.[104] But to its readers, *Il Progresso* presented the meeting in a brighter light, as a union of two mutually admiring, and admirable, gentlemen.[105] The editors put a positive spin on a photograph, which showed a nervous-looking Pope, smiling awkwardly, next to a recalcitrant Mussolini, who looked like he would rather be anywhere else, with anyone else. An "interesting" picture was how the editors described it, "most welcomingly attesting to the benevolent feelings of the Duce for Comm. Pope."[106] If only the camera, too, could lie (figure 2.2).

Hiccups in the narrative, such as this one, aside, *Il Progresso Italo-Americano* insisted that Pope and Mussolini shared similar characteristics of late-Victorian manliness. The newspaper insisted, too, that these values were Italian values.

FIGURE 2.2. Benito Mussolini Poses with Generoso Pope in Rome, July 1929. Courtesy of Cinecittà Luce / Scala, Florence.

When Mayor Walker lauded Pope in February 1929, it was as "a prototype" of the Italian men of New York. Walker's words, according to *Il Progresso*, were a "hymn to our race."[107] Similarly, the newspaper recounted how a fascist deputy had feted Pope in Naples in the summer of 1929 "as a typical example of Italians abroad: a tenacious worker; a man of audacious initiative, adamant honesty, ardent patriotism, whose fortune is the result of years of tireless effort."[108]

The Italian Americans who featured in the newspaper's self-made man series were invariably cut from this cloth. These men were not just technical whizzes. Like the characters of a Horatio Alger novel, they showed unerring strength of character, overcoming "poverty, prejudice," and "an unfavorable social environment" to advance in American life.[109] When they found fortune, these men gave back to their community, even as other Americans turned toward the pursuit of private pleasure.[110] In contrast to native-born Americans, Italian-born Americans divorced rarely, the newspaper noted—they defended the institution of the family at a time when it was under threat in the United

States.[111] Countering the stereotypical view of Italian immigrants as untethered young men, disproportionately responsible for urban crimes, *Il Progresso* argued that the community helped to stabilize the United States in volatile times. If Mussolini's virtues and Pope's virtues were Italian virtues, it followed that the Italians in their midst could help Americans find the manliness they had recently lost. A wider, and warmer, melting pot was required.

Old-Fashioned and Eternal

In the 1920s, the state of Americans' souls became a talking point not just for fascist sympathizers but also for a range of commentators concerned about the changes wrought by modernity. For instance, the critic Waldo Frank wrote that Americans worshipped the gods of the age—the machine, efficiency, the corporation, sport, and sex—in the hope of fulfillment, but to no avail.[112] Walter Lippmann observed that the results of newfound freedoms were "not as good as" people had anticipated. Freed from the constraints of authority and religion, they stumbled into a "trackless space under a blinding sun."[113] Richard Washburn Child echoed the mood set by his contemporaries, describing the typical American as a "stunted soul without peace."[114]

The editor of *Il Progresso*'s English-language section also made frequent forays into the depths of the American soul. Quoting the Italian playwright and erstwhile fascist sympathizer Luigi Pirandello, Edward Corsi suggested that the United States felt like "a temporary camp, an outpost on the road to the ultimate destination, and nothing more." It was little surprise, then, that Americans were "restless," to the point of despair.[115] Corsi even suggested that rising suicides were the "price" that native-born Americans were paying for their modernity.[116]

These observers argued that part of the problem lay in the absence of a strong leader, to shepherd Americans through a period of unsettling change. The "characters" in American politics were most noteworthy for their paucity, according to McCormick.[117] It seemed that she could count them on one hand: William Borah, Al Smith, and William Jennings's less famous brother, Charles Wayland Bryan.[118] Such men were few in number, and, with the exception of Borah, they had the disappointing habit of losing key elections.[119]

In the presidency itself, Calvin Coolidge's notorious silence enabled Child to present him as an embodiment of old-fashioned austerity.[120] But even Child could not stretch the truth so far as to argue that Coolidge was a "driving, inspiring superfigure."[121] McCormick interpreted Herbert Hoover's 1928 election as a sign that Americans craved a "super-technician"—an engineer, no less—to make sense of their "intricate" world.[122] Hoover, more than any figure in American life, embodied the virtues of the efficient administrator. But there, he seemed to stop.[123] The new president, in McCormick's mind, was all efficiency, the human equivalent of an upgraded factory or modernized home: it looked good, perhaps it even worked well, but it did not feel like much.[124]

Mussolini was different, these observers believed, because he had more than old-fashioned simplicity, and more than technical capacity, although he had these things too, in spades. He was, according to Child, one of the only men he had met who combined organizational capacity with heart and soul:

> This is the combination for which every country—even our own—hungers and thirsts. Efficient administrators who fail really to lead us we can find. Passionate and sincere prophets we can dig up. But rare, indeed, and needed, indeed, is the man who can be two men at once.[125]

Sympathetic onlookers located part of Mussolini's ex-socialist soul in the church. Mediated, as always, through propaganda, fascist policies of the mid-1920s lent themselves to a reconfiguration of *Il Duce* as a man of faith. Invoking the spirit of St. Francis of Assisi, the regime presented its austerity program as a spiritual journey. Mussolini made a pilgrimage to Assisi in 1926, and propaganda materials claimed parallels between *Il Duce* and the saint who had shunned the luxurious life.[126] The regime publicized images like that of the sober Mussolini (see figure 2.1), which were intentionally reminiscent of devotional portraits of the saints.[127] Reproduced in *Il Progresso*, this image suggested that Mussolini's austerity was not just an expression of old-fashioned values—it was a form of Catholic piety.

Mussolini's attempt to appropriate the cult of St. Francis was but one aspect of a larger scheme, by which the fascist leader approached the Catholic Church in a spirit of reconciliation that belied his intention to usurp its spiritual claims.[128] Other manifestations of this strategy included his invocation of God in the Chamber of Deputies and his appearance alongside prelates in ceremonies of state.[129] The policy culminated in the February 1929 Lateran Accords, which seemed to resolve a seventy-year-old conflict by granting the pope a miniscule territory, political sovereignty, and the right to teach religion in Italian public schools.

McCormick, like many Roman Catholics, was struck by the enormity of the Accords. Pope Pius XI called Mussolini "the man of destiny," sent by God to reinvigorate the position of the church. McCormick took up the theme in her coverage of the event, which portrayed Pius and Mussolini as two very different men, each converging on the same point in history, guided by a supernatural force.[130] McCormick could not help but succumb to the idea that God had chosen Mussolini.

Commentators in *Il Progresso* agreed, suggesting that God had chosen carefully, indeed.[131] The Lateran Accords were a product of Mussolini's unique combination of "acute" intelligence, unbending will, and pragmatic flexibility, according to these writers.[132] A less determined man, less focused on a single end, more receptive to naysayers, and more vulnerable to external ideologies, could not have achieved the same result. An entirely modern man, in short, would have failed: "The problem was awaiting a man like Him."[133]

In various photos memorializing the event, Mussolini always appeared in the guise of the sober executive, eyes downcast, absorbed in his task.[134] At the same time, *Il Progresso* supported *Il Duce*'s claim to a god-like status, implicit in the capitalized "Him." The Lateran Accords not only facilitated the "spiritual renewal" of Italy, according to these constructions, but elevated Mussolini to the indisputable position of a spiritual leader.[135]

Child, in particular, argued that *Il Duce*'s spirituality stretched well beyond the realm of formal religion. In his introduction to Mussolini's autobiography, Child claimed that Mussolini was changing Italians' "hearts" through a program of "applied spirituality."[136] A convenient thing about spirituality is that you cannot offer anything concrete to demonstrate its existence. Describing spirituality allows for, and maybe even necessitates, artistic license. Child was in his element there. He returned to a favorite metaphor: the male orgasm. Mussolini, he wrote, was like Theodore Roosevelt, RIP. Each man, had "energy," bubbling "up and over like an eternally effervescent, irrepressible fluid." Upon parting, each man left behind the impression that "one could squeeze something of him out of one's clothes."[137] Mussolini, in Child's words, had even become a "mystic to himself":

> I imagine, as he reaches forth to touch reality in himself, he finds that he himself has gone a little forward, isolated, determined, illusive, untouchable, just out of reach—onward![138]

The editors of the *Saturday Evening Post* added their own emphasis to Child's proposition that Mussolini offered a spirituality that Americans struggled to find in themselves. He was more than an administrative genius— according to the magazine's subheadings he was "Genius and Mystic." And he was not just an embodiment of old-fashioned values—he was "Old-Fashioned and Eternal."[139] This was the Mussolini who appeared in his serialized autobiography, dressed in a suit, taking a brisk, lonely walk. His suit was the executive's uniform, and his walk was the activity of someone who chose hard exercise over soft leisure. But the expanse of sea and sky connoted vast spiritual depths—undefinable, and all the better for that (see figure 0.1).

Panacea, Foil, and Model

American sympathizers with fascism suggested that their fellow countrymen needed Mussolini as a panacea, foil, and model. As a panacea, Mussolini promised to absorb the complexities of modernity, to spare others from anxieties provoked by the abstract forces that seemed, more and more, to dictate their lives.

As a foil, Mussolini drew attention to what Americans appeared to have lost in the transition to modernity, as austerity, inner direction, benevolence, and responsibility had given way to consumption, peer-group approval, pleasure, and self-discovery. These observers used the discussion of masculinity to enter into a critique of the contrasting societies, which had apparently produced these different kinds of men. According to this construction, Mussolini was at home in Italy, a country that was partly of his own making. Italians did not experience the easy pleasures associated with the "American standard." In Italy, men and women engaged in labor-intensive work in the fields; fascist policies seemed to have strengthened traditional institutions—such as the family and the church; and youth training programs emphasized authority and discipline. The average American man seemed to belong to a different place. Money was easier to come by and easier to spend; homes and church pews seemed emptier than before; and the values of service, hierarchy, and honor appeared to have fallen into abeyance with the end of the war. Like many contemporary cultural critics, fascist sympathizers argued that modernity gave, and modernity took away.

As a model, Mussolini suggested both what Americans should look for in their leaders and what they themselves could become. As a model, he countered the pessimistic notes that inhered in criticisms of American masculinity in contemporary society, to offer the promise of change. Part of the change seemed to rest on policy actions—for instance, in the area of education and youth training—as suggested by Schneider and Child. And part seemed to require a shift in attitudes toward Italian Americans, as argued by Pope. But Mussolini, as a model, could also float freely, unlinked to any specific reform or recommendation. His very existence offered a reassuring message that men could span multiple worlds—that they could manage the challenges of modernity while recovering their traditional values and replenishing their empty souls.

Fascist sympathizers' critiques of American modernity and their construction of Mussolini as an antidote to these ills were shot through with ironies, of course. They reproduced propaganda, even as they argued that modern groupthinking rotted the mind. They used contrived images and apocryphal tales to argue for the importance of integrity and authenticity. They aimed to make Mussolini popular, although they lamented celebrity culture. And they decried the tendency to seek quick fixes to profound problems, while suggesting that they had found, in Mussolini, a savior who could make modern men whole.

3

The Dream Machine

THE FASCIST STATE IN AN ERA OF DEMOCRATIC DISILLUSIONMENT

IN HIS 1928 BOOK *Making the Fascist State*, Herbert Schneider presented fascist theories on democracy to his American readers. He described how the fascists viewed democracy as a product of the past, unsuited to the demands of the modern age. According to Schneider, the fascists believed that in the ancient *demos*, citizens had sufficient time and education to grasp the main issues that animated public life; their votes were an expression of well-informed opinion, which directed policies toward the common good. The fascists thought that in contemporary democracy, citizens had neither the time nor the wherewithal to understand complex political issues; votes cast in these circumstances were an expression of half-formed ideas, and public policies suffered as a result. "In the so-called democratic state," the people were "not really sovereign" and their representatives did "not really govern," Schneider wrote, because neither was in command of the principal issues of the day. The shortcomings of democratic institutions left the field wide open to special interest groups, according to fascist thinkers. Democracy, in these circumstances, became "the organized struggle of particular groups and not a government at all."[1]

Herbert Schneider wrote in a way that made it difficult to tell where fascist theories ended and his own ideas began. He used the passive voice almost exclusively. In his writing, ideas were thought; it is unclear whether it was only the fascists, or Schneider too, who did the thinking.[2] It is even harder to disentangle the fascists' ideas on democracy from Schneider's own when we consider his intellectual biography. As a graduate student under the supervision of John Dewey, both before and after the Great War, Schneider absorbed Dewey's concept of instrumentalism more fully than he did Dewey's belief in democracy as a morally superior form of government, worth striving for.[3] In the words of one historian, Schneider approached democracy as "a kind of arbitrary social experiment" that should be dismissed as a "failure" if it did not provide "solutions" for contemporary problems.[4]

Schneider's experiences during the war probably contributed to his own belief that democracy did not offer the best form of government for the modern age. Historians have described how intelligence tests, designed to measure the cognitive abilities of American soldiers during the war, impacted contemporary debates on democracy.[5] Schneider's war work consisted of administering these tests in army camps throughout the United States. Decades later, Schneider would remember his year in the army as "quite a critical experience." He made "lifelong friends" in the army medical corps, where he found intellectuals, like him, who wanted to serve, but "didn't know how to fight." The results of the intelligence tests performed on soldiers who *did* know how to fight came as a surprise to Schneider and his colleagues; the "standards were so much lower than they had anticipated." As Schneider observed, wartime IQ tests proved to be less valuable to military planners than they were to academics.[6] At the war's end, psychologists and social scientists invoked soldiers' low test scores to question whether the average man was capable of fulfilling his democratic duties.[7]

It was befitting to an era that embraced disillusionment and mass activities in equal measure that pessimism about American democracy was pandemic in the 1920s.[8] By 1928, each of the fascist theories on democracy, as described by Schneider in *Making the Fascist State*, had also been articulated by American pundits and political scientists. In 1922, Walter Lippmann argued that ordinary people were incapable of participating constructively in a complex modern democracy.[9] Four years on, the political scientist Benjamin Wright claimed that he had read more than a handful of books and innumerable articles that compared the people in a democracy to a "ventriloquist's obliging dummy."[10] In the meantime, other writers, including the popular journalist Frank Kent, identified special interest groups as a powerful political force in American society, subverting the public interest to promote their own ends.[11] Benjamin Wright, Walter Lippmann, and their many contemporaries who expressed doubts about American democracy were not fascist sympathizers.[12] But their skepticism about the aptness of democracy in modern circumstances sounded similar to fascist political theories, as Schneider described them. This overlap was intentional: Schneider wanted the fascists' critique of democracy to sound familiar to Americans.

In the late 1920s, Schneider, Child, McCormick, and Pope presented a three-part argument about democracy and political reform in Italy and the United States. First, they harked back to the time of a multiparty system in Italy to imply a cautionary tale for the United States. Even if American democracy had not sunk to the same nadir as Italian democracy, a lack of congressional expertise, the rise of special interest groups, and popular disillusionment meant that it was experiencing similar symptoms of decay, they suggested. These observers portrayed Italy, prior to Mussolini's dictatorship, as a harbinger of what might happen in the United States if political dissolution was left unchecked.

Second, they insisted that, through the corporate state, the fascist government had adapted political institutions to contemporary exigencies, enabling expert and efficient management of economic problems, and advancing policies in the direction of the general good. Sympathetic American observers claimed that by separating policymaking from politics, and by encouraging all Italians to participate in the latter, the regime had created a form of government that fulfilled Italians' material, emotional, and even spiritual needs.

Last, these observers argued that the United States, too, needed to look beyond its preexisting institutions of government to create a state that was adept at dealing with the problems of modernity. They asserted that Americans, no less than Italians, needed a government that both managed complex policy issues and captured its citizens' hearts and their souls.

These observers used fascist Italy to transport Americans to a different place, where policies were better managed, and the government was more popular, than in the United States. They encouraged Americans to fantasize, to dream. As in most dreams, their version of fascist Italy contained familiar reference points. For instance, Herbert Schneider described fascist theories on democracy in terms that would have resonated with his audience. Like all psychologically useful dreams, those of fascist sympathizers had enough familiarity to feel relevant, and enough difference to pique the imagination, as Americans surveyed their own democracy, took stock of its faults, and imagined its future.

The Broken-Down Machine

In 1928, Herbert Schneider, Anne O'Hare McCormick, and Richard Washburn Child each revisited political conditions in Italy prior to Mussolini's dictatorship. Between 1919 and 1922, Italy's liberal democracy had been in a state of protracted crisis. "The situation was very complicated," Schneider reminded his readers, but the basic problem lay in a combination of universal manhood suffrage and proportional representation that turned Italy into an exaggerated version of democracy. Elections in 1919 and 1921 brought around a dozen political parties into parliament. The liberals struggled to form stable governing coalitions. Prime ministers resigned at an alarming rate, until it seemed that there was nobody left within the old political elite who wanted the top job.[13]

These were not conditions that were conducive to running a country. Italy's postwar democracy produced a "period of national paralysis," in McCormick's words.[14] According to Schneider, political parties' constant quarrels obstructed the legislative process at a time when Italians desperately needed their government's help.[15] The country faced social and economic problems of the first order: strikes, crippling debts, and inflation.[16] Fascist sympathizers argued that Italians felt disgusted not only with specific iterations of democratic government but also with democracy itself.[17] On the eve of the March on Rome, wrote Schneider, the democratic government "hardly had a single friend in the country."[18]

Mussolini provided his own analysis of the end of Italian democracy in his English-language autobiography, edited by Richard Washburn Child. He suggested that Italian democracy's most fundamental failure had been a failure to adapt. The "historical parties" had not adjusted to the "new conditions of modern life," Mussolini wrote. Traditional politicians clung to old-fashioned customs and institutions, even when these customs and institutions no longer worked for the country. Italy's democracy was a broken-down machine, he argued, which could not be salvaged with "pitiful repairs." Italians needed a different form of government, suited to "the living reality of the twentieth century." They needed a new machine entirely.[19]

The Crumbling Citadel

Child, McCormick, Pope, and Schneider aimed to connect Italy's political crisis of the early 1920s with conditions in the United States at the decade's end. An episode of Mussolini's serialized biography, published on the first page of the *Saturday Evening Post* in June 1928, began with a statement: "I have little doubt that all inefficient party and parliamentary governments die from the same causes and with the same typical mannerisms of decay."[20] *Post* readers, well-versed in contemporary ideas of democratic decline, would have understood Mussolini's statement as it was intended to be understood: a prediction that the United States' democracy of 1928—seemingly so different from Italy's in 1922—risked collapse for similar reasons, and along similar lines.

Richard Washburn Child also preyed upon Americans' fears of democratic decadence. In 1929, he published a new book. *The Writing on the Wall* was a loose reworking of Child's journalism for the *Post*. After he left Rome, George Horace Lorimer gave Child an assignment as a roving reporter. Traveling to London, Paris, Berlin, Madrid, and Istanbul in the winter of 1924–25, Child reached sweeping conclusions.[21] In *Writing on the Wall*, Child described himself as a modern-day prophet, who foretold of the end of liberal democracy, not just in the old world, but also in the United States. The book was a highly selective survey, taking in the conditions of various polities. Child deemed recent dictatorships in Spain, Turkey, and, of course, Italy, to be success stories. By contrast, he asserted, democracies on the continent were in poor shape— flagging in France, struggling to stay afloat in Germany.[22]

Child paid particular attention to the precarious conditions of British democracy. Britain's first weakness, he wrote, stemmed from a decline in the quality of its parliamentary representatives. Members of parliament seemed to lack the technical knowledge to address the "challenges" of a modern state. Britain's second problem, according to Child, lay in a pending change from a two- to a three-party system. The Labour Party had risen because neither of the two major parties had effectively managed the transition to an industrial economy. Child predicted that Labour would fare no better in this regard, and that its failure would give rise to a fourth party, and so on. Unresponsive to the needs of the British people and poised to descend into multiparty chaos, as rendered by Child, the British "citadel" of 1929 looked not so different from the Italian ruins of 1922. Child was explicit about why he was so concerned about British political conditions. If Britain was one of the world's supposed bastions of representative government, then the United States was the other; and since British democracy was "obviously slipping," this did not bode well for the United States.[23] Child used Britain as a stepping stone between continental Europe and the United States to suggest that none of the distances were very great.

Child, McCormick, and contributors to *Il Progresso Italo-Americano* argued that a declining quality of elected officials beset the United States. These observers echoed the frequently articulated notion that, in the modern age, ordinary men and women failed to elect representatives who would best serve their interests. Child sounded a lot like Walter Lippmann when he described the "snapshot, transitory judgments" of the average citizen in a democracy. Child suggested that Americans selected their candidates for office as they might select their brand of cigarettes, responding to "fabricated" images in newspapers and magazines, mediated sounds on the radio, and ersatz advertising campaigns.[24]

Similarly, McCormick interpreted the 1928 presidential election as proof of the supposition that the people's choice in a democracy was rarely the best candidate to meet the people's needs. The election coincided with a crisis in American agriculture, and McCormick suggested that rational assessments of the two candidates' platforms demonstrated that the Democrat, Al Smith, was the best man to help the farmers: in contrast to Hoover, Smith supported direct subsidies as part of a larger program of farm relief. But in the run-up to the election, she struggled to find a rural American who agreed with her. The farmers McCormick spoke to associated Smith with all that was alien to them: urbanism, immigrants, alcohol, and the Catholic Church. The election, McCormick believed, would not be decided by citizens' rational assessments of their interests. It would be decided instead by prejudices, and by fears. McCormick's coverage of the election was tinged with her sense of a tragedy in the making: by exercising their vaunted democratic rights, ordinary Americans were injuring themselves.[25]

McCormick and contributors to *Il Progresso* argued that Americans' limited political capacities were reflected, too, in the representatives they elected to Congress. *Il Progresso* echoed contemporary characterizations of Congress as a frivolous "show"—a circus or vaudeville act, tone-deaf to the serious problems facing the nation.[26] McCormick observed the new Congress of 1929 with a mounting sense of disgust. President Hoover made his own version of farm relief (which stopped short of loans to farmers) a priority.[27] But Congress did not meet the emergency with alacrity.[28] In the spring of 1929, McCormick sat in the visitors' gallery of the House as one congressman made a speech about the sugar tariff. Only the delegate from Hawaii listened. The other representatives were "chatting and reading newspapers, chewing gum, picking their teeth or yawning." According to McCormick, these were not the best, or the brightest, men in the nation. She argued that congressmen were reluctant to pass arcane legislation to deal with problems they barely grasped. Congress, she suggested, was in over its head. If it resembled any kind of machine, it was in her mind a lumbering tank: a blind mechanical beast, so destructive in its potential that its unqualified drivers preferred to leave it behind closed gates.[29] An accompanying illustration in the *Times* featured American citizens fleeing from the tank as it trundled down the steps of the Capitol, afraid of being crushed by its weight (figure 3.1).

FIGURE 3.1. Congress as a Tank. Illustration by Oscar Edward Cesare, for Anne O'Hare McCormick, "Congress: Mirror of the Nation," *New York Times*, May 5, 1929.

These observers argued that special interest groups had risen to fill the void in legislative expertise. Child and McCormick gave voice to a widespread concern about the power of political lobbies. Child tallied the special interest groups in Washington, DC, at five hundred in 1929.[30] The American government was becoming, in his words, "a government by blackmail," which implemented the agendas of "organized minorities" ahead of the national interest.[31] McCormick asserted that with each passing year, the technical capacity of lobbies grew. Possessing the specific sectoral expertise that elected representatives lacked, lobbyists could run circles around Congress, she argued.[32] Not incorrectly, McCormick cited the Hawley-Smoot tariff bill as a typical outcome of this asymmetry of expertise: lobbyists had, in effect, written the tariff schedules for congressmen, resulting in legislation that favored big business over the common good.[33]

Just as he did for Great Britain, Child predicted that the ineffectiveness of the United States' contemporary system risked edging the nation toward "democracy's shortest . . . road to ruin": a multiparty system.[34] In this prediction, as in most other critiques of American democracy, he added a note of hysteria to the more measured ideas of contemporary political scientists.[35] Child interpreted every political lobby as an embryonic party. The longer the American government failed to cope with problems associated with modernity—including the agricultural crisis, industrialization, and a growing urban-rural divide—the higher the risk that new parties would form, and gather strength, he argued. Italy's calamitous political situation on the eve of the March on Rome was merely the end point of a process that was already under way in the United States, Child implied; a multiparty system, entailing "intolerable chaos," was a distinct possibility.[36]

These fascist sympathizers suggested that the United States' democracy at the decade's end was reminiscent of Italy's at the decade's beginning in another way: ordinary people no longer supported the principle of self-government. Around half of the Americans qualified to vote had not done so in the elections of 1920 and 1924. Simplifying the findings of Charles Merriam and Harold Gosnell, who had studied patterns of nonvoting in Chicago, Child ascribed low voting rates to popular disillusionment with democracy.[37] Even the fifty percent of Americans who did go to the polls went ironically, indifferently, or skeptically, Child asserted; it was little wonder, then, that the other fifty percent shunned the "farce" of voting altogether.[38]

In 1928, Anne O'Hare McCormick observed an uptick in public interest in politics, which would be borne out by voting rates that fall.[39] McCormick argued that emotions drew many of her compatriots to the presidential race: prohibition and religion were gut issues, and the contrasting personas of Hoover and Smith made for good political theater. Yet even this, the most animated contest of the decade, did not seem to capture fully the public's attention. Traveling in the West in the summer of 1928, McCormick watched groups of men gather around a radio in a hotel lobby. The group that gathered for Smith's acceptance speech was a little larger than the group that gathered for Hoover's. But she observed that a group ten times that size gathered to listen to the coverage of the fight between the world heavyweight champion, Gene Tunney, and his challenger.[40] McCormick suggested that Americans were hungry for an emotionally engaging experience; politics left them wanting.

"The Old Language of Politics Is a Dead Language in the Age of the Machine."

FIGURE 3.2. Politics in the Machine Age. Illustration by Wilfred Jones for Anne O'Hare McCormick, "Bringing Politics Up to Date," *New York Times*, November 25, 1928.

Reciting an idea that was common among scholars and writers in the late 1920s, these observers argued that the United States' principal problem (just like democratic Italy's had been) stemmed from a failure to adapt its political institutions to modern conditions.[41] In his 1927 *The Public and Its Problems*, John Dewey argued that American political institutions, which had been created for a decentralized, predominantly agricultural society, were insufficient for an interconnected, industrialized, and urbanized one.[42] McCormick restated this argument in an article published shortly after Hoover's election. American political institutions, she argued, were lagging behind economic and social developments in the modern age. An accompanying illustration underlined her concern. It featured the statue of a politician as a nineteenth-century man, entirely incongruous with the dynamic scene around him. Though set in the foreground, the statue seemed lost, and the engraving on its pedestal—*Politics*—was half-obscured by shade (figure 3.2). In this same article, McCormick praised Mussolini's efforts to update Italy's government before she paraphrased *Il Duce* himself: "Why, he asks, should you take government from the nineteenth century when in all other departments of life you have progressed beyond it?"[43] Why, she seemed to wonder, indeed?

The Cadaver Sings

These observers argued that the fascists created an effective form of government for modern Italy. They portrayed the new state as crafted by experts in response to contemporary realties, endowed with sufficient know-how to enable effective legislative action, truly representative of the nation, and responsive to the country's most pressing needs. They frequently invoked images of a machine in connection with the fascist state. Whereas American democratic *Politics* were represented by the statue of a nineteenth-century man, the Italian corporate state was, in McCormick's mind, "the motor power of the only European country actually going forward since the war."[44] In the words of Richard Washburn Child, the corporate state was a machine that would "run," "function," "do," and "accomplish."[45] Metaphors of the Italian state as an efficient machine implied that the fascists had eliminated the lag between political institutions and economic and social realities, hauling *Politics* into the mechanical age.

Sympathetic observers argued that Italy's best minds designed new institutions of government. In the summer of 1924, Mussolini appointed a commission of "solons" (wise lawmakers) made up of "outstanding scholars," according to Herbert Schneider.[46] The head of the commission was the idealist philosopher, Giovanni Gentile, whom McCormick described as Italy's answer to Josiah Royce and William James.[47] Subsequent reforms came with a similar intellectual pedigree. According to sympathetic Americans, Italy's best and brightest painstakingly constructed the institutional foundations of the corporate state.

These observers also claimed that the new institutions of the corporate state insulated parliament from the vagaries of public opinion. Following a 1928 electoral law, Italians no longer selected their parliamentary representatives. As explained in some detail by Child, Schneider, and contributors to *Il Progresso Italo-Americano*, the Grand Council instead selected four hundred members of parliament from a list of one thousand candidates proposed by confederations of labor, employers, and professionals.[48] A March 1929 photograph in *Il Progresso* featured the council members, hunched over long tables in a darkened meeting room, as they selected the four hundred representatives.

Other than Mussolini, no man was distinguishable as an individual.[49] Thus rendered, the members of the Grand Council were a disinterested bureaucratic elite, bearing more than a passing resemblance to the neutral experts whom Walter Lippmann hoped would soon preside over policymaking in the United States.[50] Unlike average men and women, these elites would not resort to simplifications or allow prejudices to guide their choices, images like this implied.

By selecting from a pool of potential representatives nominated by the corporations, the Grand Council would ensure that parliamentarians were sectoral experts, fascist sympathizers argued.[51] In early 1929, *Il Progresso* reprinted an article, written under Mussolini's name, that explained the advantages of the corporate parliament to American readers. Mussolini argued that the traditional democratic system of geographical representation precluded the development of legislative expertise: parliamentarians had to represent the varied interests of their constituents. By contrast, the corporate system required each legislator to have technical knowledge of a specific economic area.[52] By implication, such men would have no need for the advice of lobbyists and special interest groups: they would have all the knowledge they needed to perform their jobs effectively.

Sympathetic observers argued that by, first, representing and, second, reconciling the interests of all groups in Italian society, the corporate parliament would advance the common good. In the spring of 1929, *Il Progresso* provided evidence to support this claim. In May, less than a month after the new chamber opened, the parliament approved the Lateran Accords—legislation of momentous significance to all Italians.[53] *Il Progresso* predicted that the parliament's agenda would be packed with laws of great consequence: measures to control inflation; projects for land reclamation and irrigation; improvements in rural homes; and the construction of transportation and communication infrastructure for remote areas.[54] Portraits such as this suggested that nobody would be yawning, reading his newspaper, or chewing gum in the new corporate parliament: it would be endowed with the requisite representative structures and technical capacity to ensure that all Italians felt the benefits of modernity.

In their descriptions of the corporate state, fascist sympathizers misrepresented the regime's propaganda as reality. Few of the claims that American sympathizers advanced on behalf of fascist corporatism can be sustained. First, although the solons and members of the Grand Council were certainly more educated than the average Italian, they were not impartial bureaucrats.

Personal ambitions, patronage networks, and political debts affected every decision that the fascist elite made, purportedly on behalf of the people. Second, the four hundred men whom the Grand Council chose to fill the corporate parliament were hardly representative of Italian society. The final makeup of the corporate parliament of 1929 corresponded to the political importance of various groups to the fascist state, with veterans and capital overrepresented, and laboring classes sidelined.[55] The corporate parliament was a microcosm of fascism, not a microcosm of Italy, and—contrary to the claims of American sympathizers—fascism and Italy were not the same.

Only one claim that these observers staked for the new Italian parliament rang true: its members passed many laws, quickly. But this apparent efficiency was a testimony to the hollowness of the parliament. It is simple to pass legislation when you lack any discretionary authority; it is natural to pass legislation when your job, or perhaps even your life, depends on it. The fascist corporate state was a skeleton of institutions and laws, which deprived Italians of far more than it gave them.[56] Fascist sympathizers gave it substance where it had none. They breathed life into the skeleton of the corporate state. They made the cadaver sing.

The Daily Plebiscite

Sympathetic observers argued that the corporate state had all the efficiency of a modern machine, with none of the metallic chill. An ordinary machine, even a highly functioning one, did not promise to change the texture of modern life. At best, it would temporarily replace an obsolete form of government, before passing into obsolescence itself. But a machine with a soul had the potential to lift men and women beyond the material world. It combined modern efficiency with the spirituality that was sorely lacking in contemporary society.

Fascist sympathizers provided concrete evidence for the nebulous notion of the Italian state as a machine with a soul. First, they argued that by simplifying elections, the fascists enabled modern men to participate more meaningfully in formal politics than they had under a democracy. Second, they claimed that by expanding the political realm into the informal sphere, fascism enabled Italians to celebrate spontaneously the presence of their government in their everyday lives.

Italy's new system offered a straightforward means for participating in elections, according to these observers. Although Italian men no longer voted for individual candidates for parliament, they were not excluded from the selection process entirely. Instead, in March 1929, they participated in a referendum: Did they accept the four hundred representatives that the Grand Council had chosen on their behalf?[57] Child argued that ordinary people preferred this kind of referendum to complex elections: they wanted nothing less, and little more, than the chance to say "Yes or No to a broad policy," he wrote.[58] *Il Progresso* cited the turnout on election day, March 24, as evidence that the fascist state had created a format that drew people to the polls. Eight and a half million men, or more than ninety percent of those eligible, had voted, the newspaper reported.[59] In the previous three national elections, voter turnout had hovered around sixty percent. According to this analysis, the fascist regime was empowering Italians as they had never been empowered in a liberal democracy, which had demanded more time and intellectual energy than modern men could dedicate to formal politics.

Taken at face value, the results of the elections demonstrated that Italians were happy, too, to outsource the selection of representatives to men more qualified for this task: ninety-eight percent of those who participated in the election, some 8.5 million men, answered "Yes" when asked if they approved of the list of four hundred parliamentarians chosen by the Grand Council.[60] It was a short step from the claim that fascism provided Italians with the form of government they wanted to the idea that it was more democratic than liberal democracy. It was a short step and Child took it. Wherever a form of government arose "from the true will of the people," there was "democracy in the modern ... sense," he wrote.[61] Claiming that Italians had had an "absolute freedom" to vote with their conscience, *Il Progresso*'s Rome correspondent, Rastignac, argued that the 8.5 million yeses signified a passionate identification of Italians with the fascist state.[62]

In Mussolini's words, reprinted in *Il Progresso*, the 1929 election results demonstrated that fascism had "captured the souls of Italy."[63] Fascist sympathizers suggested that the 1929 referendum was proof of a transformation in Italians' relationship with their state, which stretched beyond the event itself. The more cerebral of these observers rooted this development in the political philosophy of Giovanni Gentile, whose concept of the *stato etico* ("ethical state") portrayed the ideal government not as a fenced-off appendage, but integral to all aspects of national life.[64] Sympathetic American observers minimized the militaristic and expansionist implications of an integral state, opting instead for a gentler picture of a government that generated Italians' loyalty by caring for them and living among them. This warm portrait of the corporate state filtered into Mussolini's English-language autobiography. Citing maximum working hours, social insurance, pensions, and women and child labor laws as evidence that Italy's social welfare program was the most advanced in Europe, Mussolini wrote that "to-day the state is not an abstract and unknowing entity; the government is present everywhere, every day."[65]

The progressive connotations of an ethical state fueled the imagination of Anne O'Hare McCormick, in particular. As a Catholic, committed to the principles of social justice, she hoped that the corporate state might be "more representative of all the people" than a traditional liberal democracy.[66] McCormick suggested that the government's contribution to the welfare of the most vulnerable had earned it broad support at the base of Italian society.[67]

This presumed support for the corporate state included the fifty percent of Italians ineligible to vote in periodic national referendums—women. Since the start of the decade, McCormick had suggested that fascism appealed to women because it protected their roles as mothers.[68] *Il Progresso* identified various manifestations of the regime's pro-natal policy, including the National Organization for Maternity and Childhood, which provided healthcare to infants and mothers, taxes on bachelors, subsidies for large families, and stringent anti-pornography laws.[69] Naturally, the newspaper avoided any implication that fascist pro-natalism might be more concerned with military planning than women's welfare. Instead, it suggested that the ethical state had entered workplaces, homes, and nurseries, and that, with every encroachment, Italians loved it a little bit more.

These observers argued that fascism's appeal outside the realm of formal politics was most evident among the youth of Italy. They asserted that young women and men flocked into a movement that inspired them as political liberalism, the organized left, or the church could not. Although the Lateran Accords ushered in a broad peace between church and state, the late 1920s were also years of increased tension between the two institutions with respect to Italian youth. Herbert Schneider argued that the fascist state was beating the Catholic Church on its own territory, by offering religious-like rituals in a "more vigorous and more spectacular" format.[70]

News stories published in *Il Progresso* supported the idea that fascism had a magnetic appeal for youth. The newspaper described how the fascists offered a new team sport, *volata*, as a homegrown substitute for soccer.[71] Fifty thousand Italians gathered to watch the first *volata* game in 1929, and left the stadium singing the fascist anthem "Giovinezza" (Youth), the newspaper reported.[72] Sympathetic Americans suggested that fascism attracted young

Italians by offering more emotional stimulation than a standard political party, a more relevant form of spiritual sustenance than the ministrations of the church, and as much excitement as a sports team. It seemed like an unbeatable combination.

Unlike politics in the United States, politics in Italy appeared to capture emotional currents that would otherwise be frittered away on frivolities, these observers implied. Schneider argued that the fascists had succeeded in insulating government policies from public interference, even as they encouraged the people to express their wholehearted support for fascist politics.[73] Photographs in *Il Progresso* bore out this observation. In dark rooms, far from the hubbub of the streets, serious men went to work crafting policies and passing legislation.[74] Meanwhile, on brightly lit piazzas, passionate crowds, stretching out into infinity, expressed their approval of the fascist state.[75] Every day was like an election day in Italy, the newspaper suggested. And every day, from the bottom of their hearts, the people shouted "Yes!"

There was little truth in fascist sympathizers' claim that, in recalibrating political participation, the corporate state met the capacities and needs of modern men and women. Italian men's participation in the 1929 plebiscite was not a spontaneous demonstration of enthusiasm for a new kind of politics. As antifascist émigrés argued at the time, many men were forced to vote and others arrived at the polls to find their ballots already cast.[76] The difference in the appearance of ballots—the "Si" ticket emblazoned with the tricolore, the "No" ticket plain—undercut secrecy at the polls.[77] Brave, indeed, were the tiny fraction of Italian men who registered their disapproval of the regime by casting a "no" vote in 1929. Most Italians felt that they had no freedom to exercise a veto, which Child claimed the election granted them. The 8.5 million "yes" votes in Italy's plebiscite masked a range of opinions about fascism, from approval, to ambivalence, to outright opposition, to downright fear.

Just as a "yes" vote in the referendum was not necessarily an expression of approval of the regime, the Italians who turned out for youth activities, mass meetings, or *volata* games felt a variety of sentiments toward the fascist state, including apathy and opposition, shrewdly camouflaged as consent. Child, McCormick, Pope, and Schneider willfully ignored the complex texture of grassroots responses to fascism.[78] They also misrepresented the implications of fascism for the poorest and most vulnerable Italians. A state bent on militarization and wars of aggression, fascist Italy was never tending toward social justice.[79] There was little that was ethical about the so-called ethical state.

Homegrown Solutions

In the late 1920s, these fascist sympathizers insisted that the corporate state was fascism's most significant innovation. For once, Herbert Schneider expressed no ambiguity of authorial voice. It was a "simple fact," he wrote in 1928, that Italy's entire political and economic system was "being fused into the corporate state."[80] McCormick similarly argued in 1928 that fascism *was* corporatism.[81]

Fascist sympathizers believed that Italy's apparent successes offered hope for the United States. If Italy had created a new form of government, which both ran and had a soul, then the United States could do the same, they suggested. These observers did not argue that the Italian version of a corporate state should be grafted directly onto the United States.[82] In this, as in most things, they were faithful to the position of the regime itself: anxious to remain on good terms with the American government in the 1920s, Mussolini denied that fascism was "for export" to the United States.[83]

For fascist sympathizers, the corporate state functioned as inspiration, rather than blueprint, for possible reforms in the United States. They observed that in the late 1920s Italy was the only country in the world with an "economic parliament" that had replaced the existing chamber of representatives entirely. But other European countries, too, seemed to be providing political representation for economic interests. McCormick and Child noted that Czechoslovakia, Germany, Hungary, and Romania had created institutions to grant economic groups a role in lawmaking, although neither investigated how these institutions worked in practice.[84] Child observed that Britons, too, were interested in a parallel "Parliament of Human Life and Labor," which would address economic and social problems associated with modernity.[85]

By implication, an equivalent arrangement in the United States could be a uniquely American affair—an expression of indigenous customs and institutions. In 1929, McCormick's suggested starting point was that most American of institutions—the political lobby. McCormick argued that ordinary citizens detested lobbyists for good reasons: without formal status, they had a disproportionate and clandestine influence over legislators. Echoing a proposal, which had been presented in the *North American Review* earlier that year, McCormick argued that if lobbyists' position as a de facto "supplementary government" were formalized, then their expertise could be harnessed for the good of society. She suggested that lobbies presented both a threat and an opportunity for American democracy. As an adverse force, they could outwit congressmen, undermine the public interest, and create additional layers of elitism and secrecy in government. But as a constructive influence, they could provide sectoral expertise, promote necessary legislation, and widen the base of democracy by representing various interests.[86] By institutionalizing and organizing the various lobbies already assembled in Washington, DC, Americans could have an "economic parliament" of their very own.[87]

Child argued that Americans required a form of government that offered "less talk" than their present democracy. He claimed that a corporate parliament would help the United States become a leaner, more efficient machine. Invoking a rose-tinted memory of the United States' War Industries Board (WIB) of 1917–18 (which was neither very efficient nor very popular), Child implied that contemporary political conditions constituted a peacetime emergency. In these circumstances, he maintained, Americans would welcome a government that, like the WIB, prioritized administrative efficiency over democratic process. Child suggested that routine elections, too, could be dispensed with in a remodeled American state. He believed that, just like modern Italians, modern Americans wanted only the "occasional opportunity to say Yes or No to a broad policy," and the chance to veto their government if it overstepped its legitimate (and expansive) authority. Americans, he argued, would welcome a relief from the "fol-de-rol" of frequent elections.[88]

Child suggested that these reforms would go some way to restoring Americans' faith in their democracy. But contributors to *Il Progresso* and Anne O'Hare McCormick suggested that even more could be done to endear the government to the people. In contrast to Child, who in 1929 maintained that an effective "new machine" would be rooted in traditions of small government, these other observers articulated a vision of a more expansive state. Even before the onset of the depression, Edward Corsi, the editor of *Il Progresso*'s English section, argued that Herbert Hoover's conception of "American individualism" made little sense in a modern era, in which man was a "mere atom" within a gigantic system. Corsi implied that the president needed to accept a greater role for government in guiding Americans through their increasingly connected, and unstable, world.[89]

McCormick, too, suggested that the right government for Americans in the late 1920s was one that would intervene, with unprecedented vigor, to even out social inequalities and sectoral discrepancies—a "humanizing" government that would moderate the insecurities that beset entire social groups in an era of infamous plenty.[90] Such a government was not unlike the Italian ethical state, as McCormick imagined it: leaning toward the political left, it would care for its citizens, earning their love. Without a government that cared for them, McCormick implied that Americans would continue to express their joy, and their pain, in other realms. They would crowd around the radio to listen, blow-by-blow, as one boxer knocked another to the floor. They would search for satisfaction in superficial distractions, and, since their spirits would be left wanting, they would continue their restless search.

Realities and Dreams

Child, McCormick, Pope, and Schneider believed that Italy's recent experiences with democracy and dictatorship were relevant to their American audiences. By describing the chaos of Italian politics prior to the March on Rome, they imagined that American readers might find a likeness to their own domestic realities. A proliferation of interests, a failure to pass laws that mattered, and an apathetic public were all features of Italian democracy after World War I, and each appeared as an extreme version of the problems that Americans faced. The Italian corporate state, as described by these observers, seemed to offer a hopeful message that, with major institutional reforms, Americans could update their democracy for the modern age. Academics who absorbed Schneider's analysis of the corporate state interpreted fascism as a "challenge of the democratic faith," not because it was violent or repressive, but because it produced a government that was both effective and popular.[91] Readers of *Il Progresso Italo-Americano* could take pride that Italy appeared to be leading the way in creating innovative political solutions. Those who turned to McCormick's journalism in the *New York Times*, or Child's book and articles in the *Post*, could find some solace in the notion that new and improved forms of government were possible.

But fascist sympathizers' accounts of the destruction of democracy and the creation of the corporate state in Italy presented a monstrously warped version of reality. These observers exaggerated a lot: the role of experts in lawmaking; the representativeness of the corporate parliament; and the enthusiasm that the Italian people felt toward their state. They ignored even more: antifascists' courage in protesting; systematic intimidation and state-sponsored violence; regressive economic outcomes, which benefited businessmen and landowners at the expense of workers and farmers; and countless Italians' silent opposition to their own regime. Fascist sympathizers exaggerated and ignored so as to tell a story, which they believed was relevant to Americans in the late 1920s. It was the story of one broken-down machine that could not be fixed. And it was the story of a successful effort to create another kind of machine altogether: a machine that both worked, and moved women and men, old and young, in body, mind, and soul.

Fascist sympathizers proposed changes to American institutions of government, which would, in McCormick's words, translate "democratic formulas into new forms," suitable for the modern era.[92] As in the Italy of their imagination, these reforms called for greater expertise in policymaking, simpler mechanisms for participation in formal politics, and a more integrated relationship between citizens and their state.

The inherent problems in such suggestions were manifold. Even Walter Lippmann acknowledged that an expanded role for experts in government risked adding a self-serving bureaucracy, without gaining much in efficiency at all.[93] McCormick's imagined parliament of lobbyists would have been to the advantage of big businesses, whose existing influence on legislation she so lamented. Child's suggestion that ordinary people were politically equipped to vote in referenda on broad policy issues was questionable, to say the least. Last, the notion that any, or all, of these reforms combined would result in policies that promoted the common good was illusory.[94] These observers differed among themselves about what the common good looked like in the late 1920s. Was the common good best served by state-sponsored farm relief or a hands-off approach, by a big government or a small one? Who would decide when the opinions of various experts, and the preferences of various interest groups, collided? If fascist sympathizers' suggestions for the United States tended anywhere, it was toward repression and autocracy, not "solidarity" and social justice.[95]

American fascist sympathizers were no more attuned to the flaws in their proposed reforms for their own democracy than they were to political repression and social inequalities within the fascist state. The corporate state, which these observers constructed, was a dream machine in more than one sense of the phrase. In their eyes, it was an ideal instrument for guiding Italians through the perils of modernity—as close to perfection as a man-made institution could get. It was also a mechanism to transport their readers into another world, which seemed better managed and more spiritually satisfying than their own. But to the historian, the dream machine connotes something else: a manipulated reality that tells us more about the dreamers than it does about the machine.

4

Man as the Measure of All Things

SYMPATHIZING WITH FASCISM IN THE
EARLY DEPRESSION YEARS

IN THE FALL OF 1933, *Il Progresso Italo-Americano* carried a short story about a drive that Mussolini took through the Piedmontese countryside. As he motored over the hills, he brought his car to a halt. He had seen a group of peasant women on the side of the road near the village of Niella Belbo. He got out of his car, stood with the women, and asked them simple questions. How many children did they have? Did they work? Before *Il Duce* left, his aide gave each woman some money. He did not travel far before he stopped his car once more, this time at the village of Mombarcaro. Above the sound of his motor, he had heard an old man's request for help with an application for a veteran's pension. Mussolini asked the man for details. He promised that he would find out what had happened to the application and that he would write to the veteran to let him know. He kept his promise. Twice more that day, as Mussolini sped through the countryside, he stopped when he saw ordinary people in need, to listen to them, to ask them direct questions, and to offer them practical help.[1]

This story was consistent with many of the images of Italy and Mussolini produced by American sympathizers with fascism during the depression years. It was in part a caricature of Italy as a country of villages, made up of small communities working the land. Places, however small, had names and local identities. Niella Belbo and Mombarcaro were not wealthy, but their inhabitants were knit together. In other words, economic capital was low, while social capital was high. This story was also an allegory of Mussolini's relationship with technology and with his people. Driving through the countryside, he was at ease with modern machinery and with speed. He used his car to make human connections, and to reach remote villages untouched by previous Italian governments. He was in control of the pace of his machine, and could slow down, even to a stop, at will.[2] He heard a single plaintiff voice, asking for a pension, above the engine's roar. In a government of one man, he provided a humane and responsive regime, which ensured that no peasant went hungry, that no pension went unpaid.

During the depression years, American fascist sympathizers fashioned images of Italy and Mussolini to suggest the kind of country they wanted the United States to be, and the kind of leader they wanted the United States to have. These observers echoed widespread interpretations of the depression as a product of machine-made capitalism, exacerbated by a government that had fetishized technology at the expense of human beings. A silver lining of the crisis, they believed, was that it forced a recalibration of the United States, away from bigness, mass-production, and the metropolis, toward simplicity, the home, and the countryside. In Roosevelt, some fascist sympathizers saw a leader who, like Mussolini, understood ordinary people and wanted, above anything, to help them. And by relaying the apparent successes of fascist policies, American sympathizers argued that the New Deal could succeed in making man, rather than machines, once more the measure of all things.

The Machine-Made Crisis

As the United States sank into a depression in 1930, all Americans struggled to understand the paradox of poverty in a land of plenty. Like many of their fellow countrymen, fascist sympathizers understood the causes of the depression as symptomatic of American modernity, which they deemed to be increasingly mechanical, impersonal, and anonymous. Machines, in both their literal and metaphorical manifestations, figured prominently in their explanations of the crisis.

Echoing ideas that were a hallmark (although by no means the unique preserve) of fascist economics, American sympathizers argued that mechanical production was the principal cause of the depression.[3] In 1930, Il Progresso conveyed Mussolini's understanding of the depression. Il Duce argued that the American system had failed because machines made goods while humans bought them; consumers could not keep up with the pace set by mechanical producers.[4] Contributors to Il Progresso observed that machines created problems of unemployment as well as surplus production. *Il Progresso*'s director, Italo Carlo Falbo, argued that mechanical production had displaced "thousands of human hands."[5] As the unemployment crisis worsened, Generoso Pope insisted on this argument:

> Each mechanical invention liberates the worker from difficult tasks. Each new device, by boosting production, assures unarguable benefits to industry. But, by the same token, new machines diminish the contribution of manual labor to a minimum and throw thousands of people by the wayside.[6]

All of these observations juxtaposed men and machines, warm skin and cold metal. All of these observations suggested that machines, although made by men, had outpaced their creators. McCormick encapsulated these arguments in a piece she wrote for the *Times* in the spring of 1930. Americans were being overpowered by the machines they had themselves invented, she wrote.[7] The *Times* provided an illustration to underscore her arguments. In the cartoon, Uncle Sam stood at the base of a gigantic complex of machinery, his palms raised upward in a gesture of bemusement. Mounted on a pedestal of cogs and wheels, a robot, twice Sam's height and four times his heft, sputtered on, its blank face registering none of the damage it had wrought (figure 4.1).

Anne O'Hare McCormick implied that the machine represented not only mechanical production but also a network of distant forces that governed the modern economy: the stock market, corporations, chain stores. To an unprecedented degree, the fate of the average American was dictated by these impersonal forces, she argued: when the machine rattled, every home in the country shook.[8] McCormick suggested that impassive groups of unemployed men, who crouched in the streets and parks of many American cities, were an inevitable outcome of this system.[9] As Americans had lost control of their own economic fates, they had lost their identity as "self-determinate individual[s]."[10] The end point of this process seemed to be precisely the spectacle she witnessed in the fall of 1932: hundreds of unemployed and homeless men huddled together in a desolate park in Detroit, waiting.[11]

McCormick did not blame the victims of the depression for their misfortune; by definition, she saw the problems as too big for ordinary Americans to control. Instead, she blamed the system, identifying issues of distance, dissonance, and passivity both within and far beyond the economic realm. In the winter of 1931 and the spring of 1932, she wrote two series for the *New York Times* on Hollywood and the radio, respectively. McCormick conceived of neither series as an opportunity to provide her readers with light relief from

FIGURE 4.1. Uncle Sam Faces the Machine. Illustration by Oscar Edward Cesare, for Anne O'Hare McCormick, "A Year of the Hoover Method," *New York Times*, March 2, 1930.

their economic travails. Images of diminutive men eclipsed by machines dominated these pieces. She described actors and radio presenters as emotionally and physically removed from their audiences and argued that passive consumption habits undermined individual autonomy. Lest her readers miss the meaning of these observations, McCormick described the radio as a "perfect example of the way we do things" and Hollywood as a metaphor for "the whole modern show."[12]

Il Progresso also portrayed the depression as an outgrowth of the ills of modernity. With the onset of the crisis, the New York–based newspaper published more vociferous critiques of urban America. Much as McCormick portrayed machines as man-made inventions that overwhelmed man, in 1930 Franco Ciarlantini (a fascist propagandist and member of the Italian parliament) described New York's skyscrapers as "monuments to business" that dominated the "human anthills" they had been built to serve. "Vertiginous New York" diminished people to "moving shadows," wrote Ciarlantini.[13] Similarly, Italian-American contributors to *Il Progresso* described the city as "cold" and unresponsive: an "empire of stone" that crushed human beings "with the inexorability of a necropolis."[14] These observers implied that starving wretches on the Bowery—which one writer described as a "boulevard of beaten men"—were the products of a city that had cared more about making money than building community, and had prioritized materiality over humanity.[15]

Fascist sympathizers were not alone in their criticisms of a machine-made economy and urban culture in the early depression years. They joined a chorus of observers who searched for symptoms of society's ills and pointed their fingers either directly or indirectly at machines. For instance, in 1933, a research committee sponsored by the Hoover administration found that mechanical production outpaced consumer demand and displaced labor, contributing to excess production and unemployment.[16] Intellectuals, including Walter Lippmann, John Dewey, and Lewis Mumford, argued that problems associated with mass production permeated American culture: using mass culture as a "mode of escape," humans had become "more passive and mechanical," in Mumford's words.[17] Meanwhile, mass culture itself was often a vehicle to criticize various manifestations of the mechanical age. As noted by one cultural historian, the popular comic strip *The Gumps* "rejected the materialism and get-rich-quick ethos that many saw as a cause of the Depression," while *Superman* and *Amos 'n' Andy* portrayed cities as bleak, corrupt, and degenerate.[18]

American fascist sympathizers shared many of their fellow countrymen's ideas about what was wrong with the United States in the 1930s. They parted ways only in their argument that fascist Italy, under Mussolini, provided signposts on the road to recovery.

Like Old Times

In the precrisis years, the editors of *Il Progresso Italo-Americano* tended to downplay Italy's poverty; the nation's economic weakness was a source of shame, which fed nativist stereotypes of Italian immigrants as an underclass.[19] But following the crash, *Il Progresso* began to boast about the simplicity of life in Italy. The country, it argued, was surviving the depression in part because Italians were uncorrupted by materialism and unaccustomed to a now worthless "American standard."[20] Herbert Schneider echoed this analysis: the depression had of course created "hardships" for Italians, as it had for almost every person in the global economy. But, in Schneider's view, Italians' suffering was not "excessive." A people who lived modestly had much less far to fall in the depression.[21]

Summarily excluding Italy's industrial north as atypical, both Schneider and McCormick suggested that the country could be best understood through Tuscany. Tuscany, wrote Schneider, was "Italia centrale in more senses than one"—its landscape of bustling market towns connected to their rural surrounds typical of much of the peninsula. In Florence, as in other provincial towns, the "simple economic processes," which had defined Italian life for centuries, persisted.[22] McCormick observed that, in the marketplace, country folk and town folk met, traded, and talked. The small-scale nature of these economies supported constant contact between one human being and another, and between human beings and the products of their labor. The absence of chain and department stores meant that in Florence, as elsewhere in Italy, you bought each component of your supper from a different market stall or shop. Human encounters were woven into the fabric of every exchange and with each purchase you touched, and appreciated, the labor of another.[23]

McCormick was at pains to point out that Italy was not frozen in time. For instance, she noted that Florence had plentiful modern amenities, from "dial telephones" to "garbage reduction." But although they made life more convenient, mechanical devices did not dominate the scenery or society. Florence remained a city of craftsmen and traders, symbiotically linked to the small farmers who lived in the hinterlands. Italy, McCormick wrote,

> suggests answers to most of the questions asked since the beginning of the transition to the machine age and emphasized by the present crisis of mass production. Here are people living on a much lower material level than Americans.... But they have more enjoyment in their work, they perform it without the strain imposed on men by the inhuman speeds of the machine, and they seem to get more amusement out of their simpler play.

If the average Italian was "less depressed by depression," it was because he had a greater sense of control over his daily life than the average American.[24]

These observers noted with approval that the depression had forced Americans to adopt some of the habits, and the values, that came so readily to Italians. Cash poor, many had reverted to growing their own food and preserving the surplus. Americans touched once more the product of their labors. A system of barter and exchange put them in contact with their neighbors. And, in the absence of much government assistance, they formed community drives to help those most in need. The atmosphere in these local voluntary efforts, noted McCormick, was invariably "cheerful, even jolly." Americans were enjoying human connections.[25]

An illustration that accompanied one of Richard Washburn Child's contributions to the *Saturday Evening Post* summed up the mood of Middle America: a sense of relief that, after a decade of lurid consumption and ruthless pursuit of the modern, its children had finally returned home. In this illustration, two fashionable young women sat in the parlor—one played the piano, and the other reintroduced herself to Grandpa. A young man enjoyed the simple pleasures of a book. The family dog barked. It was disturbed, perhaps, by the strangers in its midst. But Ma and Pa were unable to suppress their pleasure that all was, once more, "like old times."[26]

Il Progresso suggested that Italian Americans could help guide their fellow Americans back toward a more satisfying life. In the early depression years, the humbleness of immigrants was a source of pride for contributors to the newspaper. In the fall of 1930, Giacomo De Martino, the Italian ambassador to the United States, suggested that Americans could find the simplicity they craved in Italian-American communities. The Italian street vendor, pushing his cart of fruit and vegetables, provided "a note of individualism on the flat even level of standardization," De Martino wrote.[27] An editorial in the same issue emphasized Generoso Pope's pride in the "homely" qualities that the

Italian people had brought with them to the United States.[28] These observations suggested that, when they ostracized or excluded Italians, native-born Americans harmed only themselves. Even more liberally minded Americans, who stressed Italians' ability to assimilate to the "American system," risked depriving themselves of an important resource: a people who instinctively knew the value of simple things, as Americans searched for a way to survive the leanest of times.

The Search for a Leader

If Americans were fumbling toward a new equilibrium in the early depression years, it was in spite of, rather than because of, their political leaders. McCormick diagnosed a disconnect in government between politicians and their constituents, similar to the separation she saw in the movies between actors and their audience. Congressmen continued to perform. They debated an entertainment fund for diplomats, the vote over Philippines independence, the ins and outs of the eighteenth amendment. In their performance, they showed no understanding of the "human experience," the travails of ordinary Americans.[29] Delegates attended their gaudy conventions in Chicago in the summer of 1932 even as the desperate, the jobless, and the hungry stood silently in a nearby park.[30] They were not unlike screen actors, these congressmen, so distant from ordinary Americans that they felt none of the satisfactions of a "kindling human response."[31] McCormick suggested that Americans were longing for political leaders who would look them in the eyes, understand their pain, and do something to alleviate it.

Herbert Hoover certainly struggled in this regard. Like many of their contemporaries, American fascist sympathizers downgraded Hoover's technical approach to government in the light of the depression. According to McCormick, the "Hoover method" was the political equivalent of the assembly line: it elevated technological process and expertise and neglected the "human touch."[32] Already in the mid-1920s, Richard Washburn Child, though still a Republican, had begun to express a desire for a different kind of governing philosophy. Government could not run on "cold efficiency" alone, he had written. "It needs a soul. It needs a tang of human understanding."[33] When Child finally parted ways with Hoover in September 1932, he cited coldness, to the point of cruelty, as his grounds for separation: the administration, he declared, had given no "expression to the silent and patient rank and file of the American majority."[34] Similarly, the editors at *Il Progresso* criticized a president who seemed at ease in a world of abstract statistics but failed to offer even a "slight note of encouragement to the distressed people."[35]

Such characterizations underestimated Hoover's communitarian convictions and his willingness to expand the reach of federal government to help ordinary Americans. But they gave voice to a widespread belief that the president was cold and uncaring.[36] Hoover's problems were in part an issue of public relations. He was an incumbent president in the midst of a deep economic crisis, with a wooden persona, who had none of the privileges of a pliant press and submissive legislature that were part and parcel of dictatorship. This orphan son of a blacksmith had great difficulty in conveying his own humanity.

Fascist propaganda enabled observers to draw a stark contrast between a democratically elected president's distance from his citizens and a dictator's connection to his people. The depression years saw the multiplication of stories that exaggerated Mussolini's humble origins, sanctified his childhood home in the Romagna countryside, and presented him as a family man.[37] Combined, these images etched away at the austere portraits that had proliferated in the mid-1920s, to soften Mussolini and to humanize him. *Il Progresso* faithfully reproduced images of Mussolini as a man of the soil, a father, husband, and son.[38] Open to visitors, Mussolini's childhood home in Predappio exhibited his modest background. There was the iron bed that his own blacksmith father had made, which he had shared with his brother. There, where a mattress might have been, was a haystack, of the kind that the boys had slept on.[39]

In contrast to earlier interpretations, which had invoked Mussolini's simple upbringing to portray him as a self-made man who had risen out of poverty in the Horatio Alger tradition, propaganda in the early 1930s tended to root Mussolini in his rural past, to suggest that he still belonged there. Mussolini returned to Predappio often in these years—to speak to local villagers and to farm a plot of land—in displays of public intimacy.[40] A typical photograph, republished in *Il Progresso*, showed Mussolini on his land, bent over to harvest the grain by hand, with his son Vittorio by his side (figure 4.2). In these moments of (contrived and heavily publicized) familiarity, Mussolini appeared as almost indistinguishable from the people he talked to, worked with, or walked alongside.[41]

Sympathetic observers suggested that these incarnations of Mussolini were more than superficial postures: they were the symbolic counterparts of concrete policies. The regime facilitated this idea by disseminating stories about the fascist government's efforts to improve the quality of life of ordinary

FIGURE 4.2. Mussolini Returns to the Farm. This photograph, taken in June 1927, appeared in *Il Progresso Italo-Americano* on July 17, 1932. Courtesy of Cinecittà Luce / Scala, Florence.

Italians. Land reclamation, maternal and child welfare schemes, social insurance, and tuberculosis prevention featured frequently in material that the Ministry of Press and Propaganda sent to the Italian Consul General in New York, to pass on to receptive editors in the United States.[42] Stories like this implied that Mussolini, the man of the soil, was ensuring that Italy remained a nation of small plots of land, just as Mussolini, the loving husband, father, and son, was protecting the traditional family as the basic unit of Italian society.[43] Through his most human of experiences, Mussolini had forged his most human of policies.

These observers were not naïve when they reproduced fascist propaganda. Anne O'Hare McCormick had plenty of opportunities to observe Italy up close in the early 1930s. Her reputation as a "sincere friend" of fascism gave her access to senior figures, including *Il Duce*.[44] Following one such meeting, in the winter of 1930–31, she acknowledged that aspects of Mussolini's persona were "make believe." But still, she argued, he was one of the few responsive leaders "in a world peopled by the half-dead."[45] Richard Washburn Child agreed. Mussolini was the rare kind of leader who "knew his people," wrote Child in September 1932.[46] He was animated, when Herbert Hoover, and indeed the entire democratic machinery of American government, seemed to have ground to a halt.[47]

If small-town and rural Italy had existed merely due to accidents of history and geography, it would have always functioned as a romantic escape for American sympathizers, dismayed as they were by the toll that machines and metropolises had taken on American life. But fascist propaganda allowed them to claim that Italy was more than a picturesque alternative. Arguing that sage policies had ensured that Italy had withstood the worst of the depression, they could present Italy as a country that offered practical solutions to the problems that the United States faced. They suggested that, in 1932, all that Americans lacked was the right leader.

His Master's Voice

Franklin Roosevelt's capacity to connect with ordinary people, his ability to speak for the "forgotten man," is so well-known that we risk taking for granted what it meant to those to whom he spoke. Ordinary Americans felt forgotten by their government and lost; Roosevelt told them that he remembered them and would find them, the "farmers of Iowa . . . the cotton pickers of Georgia, the fruit growers in the Santa Clara Valley."[48] By naming them, and individualizing them, he made them count.

Roosevelt promised to humanize government. In September 1932, eager, as ever, to attach himself to a rising star, Richard Washburn Child announced the creation of the League of Republicans for Roosevelt. Child was the league's chairman; Generoso Pope, a lifelong Democrat, was on the board's advisory committee. Signaling a break with George Horace Lorimer, the conservative editor of the *Saturday Evening Post*, Child declared that the nation would find the "greater human understanding" it so desperately needed in FDR.[49] At the league's rally, five days before the election, Roosevelt made this human understanding the centerpiece of his speech. Herbert Hoover, he said, had looked for a "great invention, hidden away . . . in the lockers of science" as a solution to the crisis. But the way out would not come from "some new equivalent of the automobile or electric power." A government of men, not machines, would provide human solutions to human problems.[50]

Fascist sympathizers' simultaneous support of Mussolini and Roosevelt is best understood in this context. McCormick, Pope, and Child interpreted the Great Depression as proof that human beings had lost control of the pace and scale of modernity. As a result, they were deeply skeptical of any government that suggested that the answers to these problems lay in the "scientific method."[51] According to one contributor to *Il Progresso*, "modern society," though credited with "mechanical and scientific perfection," had caused human suffering in its most basic forms: humiliation, hunger, cold. A cure could not be found in the disease.[52]

In Mussolini and FDR, these observers found similarly reassuring characteristics. Child reflected on both men's pragmatism. It was, he suggested, an expression of their ability to adapt government to changing human realities.[53] McCormick commented on both men's capacity to listen. It was, she argued, a mark of their responsiveness.[54] She saw in Roosevelt a "nostalgia for the good life, free and simple, of our rural past."[55] Although he had no appropriately modest childhood home to claim as his own, FDR, like Mussolini, embodied a longing to return to a pared down past. And in his White House, he created an atmosphere of informality that resembled an ordinary American home.[56]

Like Mussolini, as conceived by fascist sympathizers, Roosevelt was comfortable with technology. Mussolini reached remote villages in his fast car; Roosevelt used the radio to enter people's living rooms, establishing an intimate connection with his audience, which contemporary observers— McCormick included—felt that mass media so often lacked.[57] Like Mussolini, Roosevelt sent the reassuring message that, in the right hands, machines could be tamed and returned to their proper dimensions, as servants and not masters of men.

The individuals examined here avoided drawing simplistic equations between Roosevelt and Mussolini, aware that, in the hands of FDR's enemies, such statements would only do him damage.[58] Yet, they could not disguise their satisfaction that the United States had, in Pope's words, found "il buon duce."[59] In 1921, when she had heard Mussolini's first speech in parliament, McCormick had prophesized that Italy was hearing its "new master's voice." This was an observation to which she would return, repeatedly, during the depression years.[60] It was probably no coincidence, no mere slip of the tongue, that, two weeks into the New Deal, she voiced her approval in the same terms: the United States, too, was finally hearing its own "master's voice."[61] McCormick's intention was not to argue that Roosevelt was Mussolini, but rather that each man was the right person to lead his country through the most trying of times, that each would help to make his people whole again.

From the onset of the depression to well into Roosevelt's first term, Child, McCormick, Pope, and Schneider argued that Italy provided examples of policies that would enable the United States to recover economically and spiritually, resist future crises, and restore proportionality in the relationship between men and machines. They pointed to the apparent successes of the fascist state's back-to-the-land policies and job creation programs to suggest the scope of the possible in the United States. At each turn, they expressed a belief that Italy had succeeded in forging human, and humane, solutions to the problems of modernity and that the United States could do the same.

Full Stomachs and Simple Satisfactions

Superficially, since its goal was to boost production, fascist agricultural policy ran in a contradictory direction to the needs of agriculture in the United States, benighted by immense surpluses. But Mussolini's program of *bonifica integrale* ("land reclamation") placed its emphasis on an increase in total (labor-intensive) production, rather than an increase in per hectare (capital-intensive) production. At least as presented by fascist propaganda, Italy would win its "Battle for Grain" by encouraging internal migration from urban to rural areas and supporting smallholder settlement on modest plots of land, where traditional farming methods would be enhanced—but not displaced—by judicious application of machinery.[62] Just as Mussolini had driven his car through the Piedmontese countryside, to meet the villagers of Niella Belbo and Mombarcaro and to give them help, the regime used a bus—*l'autotreno del grano* ("the autotrain of grain")—to disseminate instructions for improved farming methods to rural villages, according to *Il Progresso*.[63] When used carefully, technology could revive traditions, the newspaper implied.

According to *Il Progresso*, although feats of modern technology enabled the process of reclamation, the beneficiaries would be families who moved from larger towns to settle in Littoria, Sabaudia, and other Pontine communities, designed around human beings' spiritual, social, and cultural needs, "each with church, school, dispensary, rural police-station, and after-work recreation hall."[64] By 1931, a successful back-to-farm movement was well under way in Italy, argued *Il Progresso*: 19,142 families had settled in the countryside beyond Rome, it noted, with a precision that both complimented the accounting capacities of the fascist regime and echoed its propaganda that every Italian counted.⁶⁵ The program would benefit poorer families the most, this article claimed, by forcing wealthy landowners who did not cultivate their land to surrender it.⁶⁶ In the summer of 1933, the newspaper described the Pontine settlements as an antidote to contemporary materialism. According to *Il Progresso*, Italians did not flock to Littoria or Sabaudia with a materialistic mindset: they came in search of a simple life, consisting of hard work, community, and bread.⁶⁷

McCormick sustained portraits of the land reclamation program as a successful effort to restore Italians' attachment to the earth. In the fall of 1933, the regime welcomed McCormick back to Rome. The Foreign Ministry had a mounting appreciation of the journalist for her "excellent" and "high profile" interviews with Mussolini, as well as her "very tight relations with major men in American politics." Arnaldo Cortesi, the *Times*'s correspondent in Rome, assured officials that McCormick was a woman of influence, who nurtured "favorable sentiments" toward Italy in the United States.⁶⁸ The ministry had no reason to doubt the Roman-born Cortesi, who was a consistent supporter of the regime.⁶⁹ In November, Galeazzo Ciano, Mussolini's son-in-law and the head of his press office, furnished McCormick with information about the Pontine program and organized a guided visit of Littoria for the journalist.⁷⁰

In an article published in *Ladies' Home Journal* the following spring, McCormick declared Littoria to be a "perfect" rendition of the Italian government's back-to-the-land initiative. She homed in on the experiences of a single family—the evocatively named Padovanis (meaning from Padua). According to McCormick, the Padovanis had moved from the "overcrowded" north of the country, encouraged by the promise of a new home, a sixty-acre plot of land, subsidized rent and farming supplies, and state-run facilities for education, entertainment, and healthcare.⁷¹ McCormick acknowledged that the Padovanis were *mezzadri* ("sharecroppers"), who owed half their crops to the state, but she claimed that this status was merely temporary. The Padovanis were "members of a community being collectively prepared for individual ownership," she wrote. As portrayed by McCormick, the Padovanis seemed happy and proud. They did not enjoy a luxurious life in Littoria: their "solid" six-room home (painted blue, like the sky) accommodated thirteen people, and they worked hard. As portrayed by McCormick, the Padovanis seemed happy and proud, not in spite of their modest circumstances and hard work but because of them.⁷²

The archives do not show for certain if the Padovanis existed, or if they were a synthetic amalgam of the informants and information, which the regime funneled McCormick's way. The archives do show, however, that McCormick was not averse to such dubious forms of journalism. In 1933, she solicited the regime for statistics on average incomes, which soon found their way into *Ladies' Home Journal*, not as cold data, but as the perceptions of a living, breathing person.[73] McCormick quoted Signora Rossi, a "clear-headed" widow, who was the principal breadwinner in a family of five. Signora Rossi was not a farmer herself, she was a journalist, who lived in Rome. But she had detailed knowledge of the income of Italian farmers. In 1929, farm incomes had been low relative to American averages, noted Signora Rossi; since then, they had declined only twenty percent, while cost of living adjustments meant that the real income remained more or less unchanged.[74] McCormick made Signora Rossi a vehicle for the information sent to her by the fascist Ministry of Press and Propaganda. This kind of journalism fulfilled her readers' interests in the lives of ordinary people. But, at least in the case of Signora Rossi, a seemingly ordinary person was an incarnation of fascist propaganda—lies made flesh and blood.

Herbert Schneider took a less imaginative approach to the regime's statistics. He merely presented trumped-up data as facts. Following a six-month stint in Rome, courtesy of the Carnegie Endowment for International Peace, in 1935, the professor updated his earlier assessment of the fascist regime. He remained broadly positive. Schneider cited official figures to demonstrate a recent uptick in real wages in agriculture, an increase in calorie consumption relative to prewar years, and the growth of "independent classes" of farmers.[75] By implication, the back-to-the-farm movement had made tangible improvements to the lives of ordinary Italians, enabling them to live with greater dignity and fuller stomachs.

Unsurprisingly, historians have demonstrated that fascist agricultural programs were neither as effective in boosting incomes nor as sensitive to the welfare of small farmers as claimed by sympathizers with the regime. Mussolini's agricultural policy entailed no significant land redistribution, as *Il Progresso* claimed. Far from encouraging "independent classes" of farmers, the "Battle for Grain" had a punishing effect on them. Protectionism of wheat production crowded out the cultivation of fruit, vegetables, and olives—labor-intensive crops that were independent farmers' traditional preserve. According to one economic historian, there were fewer small producer-owners in the early 1930s than there had been only a few years earlier.[76] On the Pontine lands, all farmers were *mezzadri*, and many were far less happy than the Padovanis about this arrangement. Pontine farmers frequently engaged in sabotage and slowdowns to register their discontent, and absconded from the land, in search of supplementary incomes.[77] They needed the money, since farm incomes had not stayed the same, in real terms, as McCormick's Signora Rossi claimed. In the depression years, Italian farmers were poorer than they had been in the 1920s, their poverty made worse by the scarcity of the nutritious crops and meat that they had previously cultivated and raised. Contrary to Schneider's claims, farmers' stomachs were emptier in the depression years than they were before, sometimes to the point of desperation: in at least one case, families from the Veneto, who had recently settled on Pontine land, ate diseased carrion in their bid to survive.[78]

The regime did its best to hide these realities, and it is perhaps unfair to criticize contemporary American observers for their failure to uncover truths that subsequent historians struggled to tease out.[79] But we can certainly criticize them for their failure to try. Each was in Italy for extended periods in the 1920s and again in the 1930s. If they did not see that Italian farmers were hungrier in the depression years than they were before, it was because they refused to look.

Both self-serving and more public-spirited motives accounted for the selective blindness of McCormick and Schneider, as well as Generoso Pope. Selfishly, these individuals had built their careers upon favorable representations of fascist Italy and felt little incentive to end their mutually beneficial relationships with the regime. An occasional quip about Mussolini's ego or a gentle note of caution about the accuracy of data was all they could afford if they wanted to maintain their reputations as "sincere" friends of fascism.[80] The compliments swamped any caveats. Access to Mussolini's Italy required them to engage in this unequal balancing act. And they engaged in it artfully, with a sense of the benefits that would accrue to their own careers as a result.

More altruistically, these observers believed that the United States needed a success story. The fascist agricultural program, as they portrayed it, combined the best of new-fangled conceptions of collectivity, technology, and government support with old-fashioned values of individual ownership, connection to the earth, and community. These observers hoped that Italy would present Americans with a vision of full stomachs and simple satisfactions, which they would find difficult to resist.

Back to American Soil

While fascist sympathizers praised Italy's back-to-the-farm policies in the early 1930s, they found a similar program at home. In Michigan, Henry Ford was engaged in an experiment in subsistence farming. In semirural areas, far from

Detroit, the godfather of mass-production had created model communities, in which workers' hours were split between small-scale industry and garden farms. In the spring of 1932, McCormick argued that Ford was attempting to create a new equilibrium for the United States.[81] Since Ford had always marched one step ahead of other Americans, McCormick read his experiment as an augur, no less realistic a vision of the near future than the assembly line had been in 1910.[82] The editors of *Il Progresso* shared McCormick's interest in Ford's experiment and were equally confident in its chances of success.[83] Photographs that accompanied this coverage suggested that, in Ford's model communities, the relationship between men and machines was restored to manageable proportions. In the *Times*, two men sat astride a mechanical harvester no bigger than a horse and cart. If anything dominated the scene, it was nature: the fields, the vast sky.[84] In *Il Progresso*, ten men worked side-by-side with hand-held tools on a small plot of land.[85] These images conveyed a simple companionship, between men, and with the earth.

For his part, Generoso Pope was so convinced by the feasibility of the back-to-the-farm idea that he attempted to exert his political influence with Franklin Roosevelt to enable the resettlement of unemployed Italian Americans on farmland in upstate New York. In March 1930, Pope met with then-Governor Roosevelt to discuss the idea. Noting that Roosevelt responded favorably, *Il Progresso* kept up its campaign.[86] The newspaper's director, Italo Carlo Falbo, argued that a back-to-the-land program made impeccable economic and moral sense. A "voyage of return" offered more than survival for impoverished city dwellers. It would provide a corrective to the "mania for urbanization" that had taken a spiritual toll on the United States and furnish "tranquility," and "happiness," of the kind so readily found in rural Italy.[87] Technology could play a supportive role in such communities. According to one contributor to the newspaper, a farmer with ten hectares of land or six livestock had no need for a tractor or an electric milking machine, but he would benefit from a radio, to learn of the latest production techniques. Digging with a spade, milking with his hands, this farmer would touch the fruits of his labor. He would meet his neighbors, and talk to them, at weekly markets. Italian Americans could be at the forefront of a movement to "live on the land as we did as children in Italy and as our relatives still do over there."[88]

Roosevelt was indeed interested in the back-to-the-land movement. "Suppose one were to offer these [urban unemployed] men opportunity to go on the land, to provide a house and a few acres in the country and a little money and tools to put in small food crops," he mused in 1931. Subsistence agriculture, he suggested, could be the difference between starvation and survival, humiliation and dignity, for the families of the unemployed.[89] Interviewed by McCormick during the 1932 campaign, Roosevelt convinced her that, like "Henry Ford, the repentant mass producer," he would go "back to the soil for his solutions" to the economic crisis.[90]

Under the early New Deal, a modestly funded Subsistence Homestead program supported the back-to-the-land movement. Similar to Ford's experiments in Michigan, the program envisaged small communities, each with a school, a post office, a church. Speaking to an Italian audience in his capacity as a visiting lecturer in Rome, Schneider described how American farmers would cultivate "garden plots," and supplement their labor on the land with work in a small, local factory.[91] According to proponents of the program, machines would enhance, but not dominate, human conditions. For instance, farmers' homes would have indoor bathrooms and electricity. But the overall aim was to simplify modern life, enabling adults to enjoy the satisfactions of work and the pleasures of community and providing children with a wholesome environment. Program planners presented the project as an antidote to the "evils of over-urbanization" and a refuge for "outcasts of the jazz-industrial age."[92] They imagined that through Subsistence Homesteads, the New Deal would create a balanced landscape, and a balanced existence, once more.

The Subsistence Homestead program was a typical example of the New Deal's eclecticism: it borrowed from similar experiments in other countries, including Australia and Denmark.[93] In July 1933, Roosevelt met with the Italian pilot (and Mussolini's heir apparent), Italo Balbo, on the occasion of his flying visit to the United States. According to a report soon filed by Balbo, Roosevelt expressed his desire to deurbanize the United States and said that Americans should be "induced to return to the country." Balbo reminded Roosevelt of Mussolini's "pioneering work" in this area. With obvious pride, Balbo reported back to Mussolini that the United States—"the most up to date country in the world"—was moving back to the land.[94] Balbo evidently derived satisfaction from the notion that Italy and the United States were moving in the same direction. The editors of *Il Progresso* went further, to suggest that Italy's experience had directly informed the New Deal's approach to deurbanization.[95] Yet there is little evidence to suggest that the fascist program functioned as more than a loose source of inspiration for the United States.[96] Indeed, when New Dealer Rexford Tugwell, who was then undersecretary for agriculture, visited Italy in the fall of 1934, he declared that he found "nothing of any significance or interest from the point of view of social arrangements" in the Pontine reclamation projects.[97] Roosevelt, ever the politician, was comfortable giving Balbo the impression that the United States had followed in Italy's footsteps. Roosevelt, ever the pragmatist, was happy to cherry-pick from various models, wherever he found them.

In any case, the Subsistence Homestead program was certainly not the backbone of the United States' recovery efforts. Around thirty rural or semirural communities, usually of fewer than one hundred households, had been created by 1935, when the administration merged the program with other resettlement projects under Tugwell's stewardship.[98] Lecturing in Rome, Herbert Schneider anticipated that this administrative merger could be the first step toward an effort to encourage small farming communities on a wider scale.[99] Instead, the merger signaled the expiration of government-sponsored subsistence farming, as Tugwell turned his attention to suburban development, in tacit recognition that modern Americans were, in the main, urban creatures.[100]

The back-to-the-land movement fueled the imagination of the Roosevelts, Eleanor especially.[101] But it would never be writ large. Underfunding may have accounted for some of the program's shortcomings, but its limitations were mainly built-in: economic recovery on a national scale depended in large part on adaptation in the industrial and service sectors.[102] Fascist sympathizers supported the back-to-the-land movement because it seemed to offer both an immediate response to problems of hunger and unemployment and a long-term rebalancing of the relations between men and machines. But subsistence farming could not provide a feasible solution for more than a tiny sliver of crisis-hit Americans.

Making Work

Public works occupied a far more central place in the United States' recovery efforts, and here, too, fascist sympathizers suggested that Italy could be a model for an approach that placed men, rather than machines, at the center of the solution. As these American observers recognized, Italy's portfolio of public works preceded the depression and included the program of land reclamation, as well as hydroelectric power projects, road and railway construction, and the building of workers' homes.[103]

Following his teaching trip to Italy, Schneider claimed that public works were financed by deficit spending during the crisis years: since 1929, Italy's budget balance had shifted from black to red, reaching a debt of over six billion lire in 1933. Quoting no less an authority than Alberto De Stefani, the classically trained economist and ex-minister of finance, Schneider explained fascism's new orthodoxy on deficits. The budget, wrote De Stefani, was the "balance of assets and liabilities . . . between citizen and citizen." On one side of the balance sheet, according to this view, was the work of women and men; on the other, the "human and material aspects" of the entire country. According to Schneider, De Stefani—an erstwhile disciple of Adam Smith—had come to see the budget as an organic arrangement, its columns representing not numbers but people: Italians' work; Italians' well-being.[104]

These observers argued that Mussolini's willingness to spend his way out of the depression had a pronounced effect on the lives of ordinary Italians. McCormick claimed that Mussolini's extensive works program had enriched Italians' lives with an array of public goods—not just new farmlands, but roads, railways, schools, parks, and housing.[105] Reproducing the regime's statistics, Schneider argued that public spending had a "telling" effect on employment rates, leading to year-on-year reductions in joblessness.[106] *Il Progresso* tracked the impact of public works over the 1930s: 36,681 workers would be employed on the Bologna to Florence railway project, inaugurated in the summer of 1930, the newspaper claimed; 339 land reclamation projects, costing 528,110,131 lire (around 27 million dollars), had created 11,695,757 days of work by the fall of 1932.[107] At the end of 1932, the newspaper reported that a New Hampshire judge had returned from Italy with praise for Mussolini's road building program. "No Machines Used," *Il Progresso*'s editors emphasized. Rather, Judge Jacobs had watched hundreds of men breaking stones with small hammers. The men, said the judge, were "satisfied": they received a daily wage of twenty-seven and a half cents, bread, and wine, which was enough to feed their families; they preferred this system to the humiliations of a dole.[108] Once again, McCormick let Signora Rossi speak for the regime. In the imaginary signora's words, Italy's "vast public works program" meant that unemployment had "never reached anything like the proportions" of joblessness in wealthy countries.[109]

A reduced, forty-hour working week was another element of Italy's response to the depression, these observers noted. In the fall of 1932, *Il Progresso* predicted that this program would give jobs to one million additional workers. With this policy, Italy was creating an example for the rest of the world, the newspaper editorialized.[110] In the first year of the program, the forty-hour rule for industrial work created jobs for two-hundred thousand unemployed men, according to Schneider. The new rules amounted to state-mandated risk-sharing—in theory, they meant that communities as a whole would experience higher levels of social protection: fewer men without jobs, and fewer hungry families.[111] Put another way by *Il Progresso*, work-sharing was a "substitution" for unemployment.[112] When presented in these terms, it seemed like a beneficial trade-off. *Il Progresso* argued that Americans should seek solace in Italy's example: work-sharing demonstrated that some solutions to the problem of unemployment were simple; all that was required was political will.[113]

Using heavily distorted evidence, fascist sympathizers argued that Italy's government had created jobs for men and security for their families. For instance, *Il Progresso Italo-Americano* claimed that, as a result of the fascist government's combined policies of public works and reduced hours, only three in every hundred Italians were without a job in 1933.[114] Over the course of decades, others would provide more realistic representations of employment rates and living standards for ordinary Italians in the early depression years. Already in 1934, the antifascist exile Gaetano Salvemini argued that the regime "systematically distorted" unemployment statistics. Every so often, a fragment of the truth slipped out, as it did when newspapers published jobless rates based on the 1931 census. In Ferrara, 8,930 men described themselves as unemployed, noted Salvemini—seven times the number of unemployed men counted in official statistics "faked in Rome."[115] The regime acted quickly to suppress damning evidence of this kind. Historians would later piece together the reality as best they could. According to two economic historians, public works gave full-time employment to between 3 and 8.8 percent of jobless Italians between 1931 and 1933.[116] Like every country in the world, Italy faced an unemployment crisis that was not amenable to simple solutions.

In all probability, Italians' own coping strategies during the depression had a greater impact on their well-being than official interventions. Disregarding the regime's ruralization policies, Italians moved regularly between rural and urban areas, picking up informal work in cities and short-term jobs in factories. They worked fewer hours for lower income not because of government-mandated work-sharing programs, but because less work at lower pay was all that was available.[117]

Survival, in these conditions, was far less dignified than fascist sympathizers imagined. In 1934, McCormick wrote that soup, pasta and sauce, fish, meat, eggs, vegetables, fruit, and cheese were among the daily standards of the Borgheses of Florence—an "average" family, whom she described to readers in *Ladies' Home Journal*. Of course, there was nothing "average" about such a diet in Italy in the depression years.[118] Perhaps the working-class women of Trieste, described in a confidential government report, were more representative. They sent their boys onto the principal piazza in February 1933 to kill pigeons "because their families were dying of hunger."[119] At the very least, the women of Trieste, unlike the Borgheses of Florence, pass muster with a historian.

Why Can't We?

From the onset of the depression until the winter of 1932, these observers invoked Italy's apparent success in creating work to chide President Hoover for his inadequate responses. In the early years of the depression, Hoover's program for recovery emphasized private initiatives and voluntarism, both for job creation and shorter working hours.[120] In the absence of a bold federal intervention to create jobs, Generoso Pope took matters into his own hands, in his own community at least. In the spring of 1930, he employed Italian-American men to work on New York City's roads. *Il Progresso* named each man whom Generoso Pope put to work. Men like Antonio Salina, of East 105th Street, a father of seven children, who had been unemployed for nine months, and Giuseppe Lo Tauro, of Cherry Street, a father of eleven children, who had been without work for a year. Each man had a name, a home, and a family to feed. Each man had an identity as a breadwinner, which needed to be revived.[121] For every man whom Pope could employ, the newspaper acknowledged, there were hundreds of thousands of American men who had been abandoned to the indignities of charity and waiting, day-in day-out, in line.[122]

Pope probably had a number of goals in mind when he created this modestly sized and highly publicized program of private employment. As was always the case, he aimed to use his beneficence to strengthen his reputation as a leader of New York's Italian-American community. Perhaps, too, he wanted to demonstrate that the task of job creation was a relatively simple one: it did not need expert commissions, bureaucratic processes, and long debates; it required only an injection of cash, and a willingness to act. But Pope's uncharacteristically modest recognition of his own limitations—of the hundreds of thousands of men whom he would never be able to help—was suggestive of an additional goal. It seems that Generoso Pope wanted to show that private individuals, even those with deep pockets and seemingly big hearts, could never substitute for a government that cared.

In a similar vein, Pope was a vociferous proponent of state-mandated work-sharing. Many American businessmen backed a voluntary "share-the-work" movement in the early depression years.[123] Pope's newspaper, however, went further, to argue that the state should enforce new caps on working hours. "The conflict between men and machines has reached the stage where we can no longer take a laissez faire approach," wrote Pope in September 1932. Just as the fascist government had done in Italy, the US federal government needed to forge a better balance between human beings and technology, he suggested.[124]

Italy was frequently the reference point for these observers. After meeting with Mussolini at the end of 1930, McCormick claimed that she had asked him what he would do if he, not Herbert Hoover, were the American president. As was often his way, Mussolini avoided giving a direct answer to a difficult question. As was often her way, McCormick filled the void. "One saw how the imagination of an autocrat kindled to the opportunity presented by the idle millions, men and dollars, available in the United States," she wrote. If Italy, "a poor country," had created jobs for two hundred thousand men that winter, then the United States could do so much more, McCormick implied.[125]

The following summer, *Il Progresso* featured an editorial, titled "If Italy Can Do This, Why Can't We?" According to this piece, Mussolini had already earmarked forty-five million dollars to provide work for unemployed Italians during the winter of 1931–32. The editorial suggested that the American government should use the "undeniable wealth" at its disposal to do the same.[126] In *Il Progresso*, articles of this kind combined feelings of outrage toward the Hoover administration with a sense pride in Mussolini's achievements. But the genre was common, not only in the Italian-language press, but in English-language media in the early 1930s, as an expression of yearning for a decisive response to the unemployment crisis, which observers felt was well within Herbert Hoover's reach.[127]

Even when President Hoover finally accepted the necessity of federal programs for public works, Generoso Pope argued that the president offered too little, too late. In July 1932, Hoover authorized the Reconstruction Finance Corporation (RFC) to disburse 1.5 billion dollars of loans to the states for public works, but not before he vetoed a more expansive relief bill, proposed by House Speaker John Garner and New York Senator Robert Wagner.[128] Pope registered his disapproval of the government for its failure to implement "more generous" measures. "Give Work to the Unemployed!" his front-page article implored.[129] In September, with the election approaching, Pope argued that the government needed to move more quickly, to implement the public works enabled by the recent law. Bureaucratic barriers, he implied, prevented the legislation from taking effect.[130] In this, Pope was not incorrect. Under the Hoover administration, qualifications for RFC loans were so stringent that only a tiny fraction of funds were actually disbursed. Hoover's program helped very few unemployed men.[131] Pope argued that, if the administration implemented a combined policy of public works and reduced working hours with alacrity, millions of jobless Americans could have work by winter time.[132] But he held out little hope for Hoover.[133] In the fall of 1932, Generoso Pope was thinking less about the onset of winter, and more about the upcoming spring.

"Let's Try It!"

For many Americans, Franklin Roosevelt's election offered hope that the government would create jobs for the unemployed. At the League of Republicans for Roosevelt preelection rally, chaired by Richard Washburn Child, FDR described himself as the answer to the "blighted hopes" of "ten million unemployed men" and reminded his audience that, as governor of New York, he had been responsible for a program of work-based unemployment relief. He promised that, if elected, he would provide "two great human values—work and security."[134] But he offered few details regarding his plans for the country.[135] Immediately after his inauguration, McCormick met with Roosevelt to discuss his ideas for the nation. She argued that FDR's approach would be active and experimental, as encapsulated by the phrase, "Let's try it!" But McCormick was unable to offer any precision about what "it" was.[136]

As Americans waited for the new president's policies on unemployment to emerge, Generoso Pope offered his own opinions. In late January 1933, the *New York World Telegram* published Rexford Tugwell's proposal for at least five billion dollars of spending on public works. Conservatives decried the plan as a revolution in government.[137] Responding to the backlash, Pope wrote that ordinary Americans had experienced the "ruinous effects of disinterested government" for too long; in 1933, they needed the very kind of "paternalistic" state that conservatives feared. He could only hope that the president-elect's program of public works would be as generous as the one Tugwell proposed.[138]

Similarly, Richard Washburn Child argued that the time had passed for a miserly approach to public finances. In the spring of 1933, he acknowledged that large-scale job creation entailed unprecedented expenses for government and, ultimately, taxpayers. But he claimed that this was a necessary price to reverse the spectacle of poverty and humiliation. In 1933, Child, once the champion of a small federal government financed on a shoestring, argued for loose money and increased taxation to create jobs for men.[139]

Public works spending in the early New Deal fell short of the five-billion-dollar mark supported by Generoso Pope, but it was still far more expansive than anything the federal government had initiated before. The National Industrial Recovery Act (NIRA) of June 1933 authorized the president to borrow 3.3 billion dollars for public works.[140] "We're Going Back to Work," read Pope's headline, two days after Roosevelt signed the NIRA into law. Pope believed that Americans already felt the moral effects of the NIRA: "pessimism" had given way to hope; a sense of abandonment had been replaced by "trust" in government. He predicted that soon they would also feel its material effects: "within months," or even "a few weeks," millions of men would be back at work; families, "abased" by years of poverty, would know once more the "simple" comforts of economic security.[141] Pope also roundly approved of the new administration's efforts to reduce working hours. "How many times did I write that the best way to give the unemployed work was not to burn machines, the inexorable rivals of manual labor, but to reduce working hours?" he crowed in September 1933.[142]

In 1933, these observers gave voice to hopes that permeated the United States in the wake of Roosevelt's action. Sometimes, their faith that the government would create millions of jobs substituted for tangible progress. New Dealers theorized that government-sponsored construction projects would stimulate up-stream private sector employment in concrete and steel; the newly employed would then spend a portion of their wages on goods and services, stimulating further job creation. But in practice, this process took time. To mark Labor Day, a frequent contributor to *Il Progresso*, who wrote under the name Glaucus, engaged in the same kind of wishful thinking that the newspaper applied to Italy throughout the depression years. The government had "begun the process of distributing $1,023,966,201" for public works, Glaucus wrote. Men were busy once more, laying roads, constructing dams, and building ships. And for every man whom the government paid to mix concrete, break stone, or lay grout, others would find work in revitalized factories, labor yards, and docks.[143] In its enthusiasm for the New Deal, Pope's newspaper declared, quite prematurely, that the pump was primed.

Flawed Realities

For Richard Washburn Child and Generoso Pope, no subsequent period of FDR's administration would produce the heady mixture of relief and hope that characterized the summer and fall of 1933. Inertia and uncertainty, it seemed, had given way to action and clarity; the New Deal, they anticipated, would rebalance the relationships between towns and countryside and men and machines. But by 1934, their initial enthusiasms had tapered off.

Having recently reinvented himself as a New Deal progressive, Child returned to conservative traditions. Publicly, Child insisted that he still favored "humane relief" for the "deserving jobless."[144] Privately, he told FDR that he still admired his "love of humanity."[145] But, increasingly, Child argued that Roosevelt's programs risked producing an unsustainable budget deficit and long-term dependency on government-sponsored jobs.[146] The once necessary costs of the New Deal struck Child, suddenly, as too high.

Child's abrupt turn against Roosevelt came as no surprise to administration insiders, based on what they knew of him. His criticisms were an expression of disillusionment with the New Deal, not so much because it had failed in its promises to the country, but because it had failed in its promises to Richard Washburn Child. Breaking Republican ranks in the fall of 1932, he had severed his relationship with George Horace Lorimer. Child had probably calculated that a high-profile position in the new administration would more than compensate for his loss of influence through the *Saturday Evening Post*. But such a position had never materialized. Soon after Roosevelt's inauguration, the administration had given Child a bureaucratic role, working on problems related to foreign bonds. The position had not satisfied him.[147] In May 1933, a member of the League of Republicans for Roosevelt had warned the president that Child would start to criticize the New Deal if the administration did not reward him for his loyalty.[148] Richard Washburn Child had always had a fuzzy understanding of loyalty.

Starting in January 1934, Child made good on this threat. Writing in William Randolph Hearst's *New York American*, he implied that the New Deal was the opening gambit of a socialistic revolution.[149] Concurrently, Child approached the president, suggesting that he was just the man to represent the United States in Ireland. Roosevelt forwarded Child's request to the secretary of state, Cordell Hull, with a wry note: "What do you think of this rather happy thought?"[150] The prospect of putting three thousand miles between Child and the White House appealed to Roosevelt, but, in the end, the ambassadorship went to the former head of the American Legion (and Mussolini admirer) Alvin Owsley.[151] The State Department offered Child an improvised position of touring economic representative in Europe, designed to give him a little publicity but no power. The president deemed this appointment "an excellent idea"; he hoped it would keep Child quiet.[152] It did not. In the spring of 1934, the American ambassador to Italy, Breckinridge Long, reported that, while in Rome, Child had met with a conservative publisher, Frank Knox, and agreed to write a series of articles against the National Recovery Administration (NRA). His price was one thousand dollars per article.[153]

Roosevelt never met with Child again. Child continued to write to Roosevelt. His letters bristled. Summarizing a series of career disappointments that he had suffered at the hands of the president, he stated, "I am ready to help you, but not by any loss of self-respect."[154] It was rather too late to be worrying about that. Child made his last journey to the White House in January 1935. It was the third time that he had gone to Washington that winter, hoping to see FDR. He wrote once more. "I would ascribe the fact that nearly a year has passed without seeing you to a loss of confidence, interest and perhaps friendship."[155] In all of this, he was correct.

Child kept his selfish reasons for disillusionment with the New Deal hidden from the public, instead articulating a form of fiscal conservatism that was widespread among his contemporaries in the 1930s. By contrast, any disappointment that Generoso Pope felt with Roosevelt in early 1934 was due to precisely those fiscally conservative tendencies. In February 1934, the publisher expressed disbelief that FDR would bow to political pressures to limit the costs of the Civil Works Administration (CWA).[156] The president, wrote Pope, had promised that Americans would no longer suffer from hunger. How, then, could he deprive the four million CWA beneficiaries of the wages that had fed them, and their families, during the winter months? Pope hoped that FDR's sense of "justice and responsibility" would prevail over the orthodoxy of a balanced budget. He hoped, in short, that the American government would adopt the same humane (or, others might say, creative) approach to accounting that Herbert Schneider attributed to Italian public finances in the depression years.[157]

On the same day that *Il Progresso* criticized FDR's fiscal prudence, it published news from Italy: the fascist state had spent seventeen billion lire (around one and a half billion dollars) on public works.[158] In praising Mussolini's approach to job creation, Pope's suggestion was always the same: the US government, wealthy and powerful, could and should be doing much more to give jobs to men. While Richard Washburn Child and fiscal conservatives wanted FDR to tighten his belt, Pope and social progressives called upon the president to loosen it some more. Unintentionally, their criticisms revealed that it is difficult for a democratically elected leader to be all things to all men.

Generoso Pope and his colleagues also expressed disappointment over the fate of the National Recovery Administration, which the administration had launched with such pizzazz in June 1933. For Pope, the early days of the NRA were days of triumph. Editorials in *Il Progresso* expressed a mixture of relief that the government had taken decisive action and pride that the NRA appeared to echo the corporative policies pursued by Mussolini's regime.[159] But here, too, contributors to *Il Progresso* expected too much from the New Deal. Glaucus (*Il Progresso's* resident champion of optimism in 1933) imagined that the NRA would enable decent wages, boost workers' purchasing power, eliminate "illegitimate" competition, stabilize industrial production, and ensure peaceful cooperation between capital and labor.[160] But such claims were no more realistic for the NRA than they were for the fascist corporate state.

In the summer and fall of 1933, *Il Progresso's* fervent support of the NRA merged with its desire to see Americans cohere seamlessly around the government's goals. Editorials in the newspaper endorsed conformism as a positive good. *Il Progresso's* vision was unabashedly authoritarian: a little reminiscent, perhaps, of the United States' home front in World War I, but much more redolent of the contemporary fascist state. "The politics of self is an insupportable luxury in moments of grave crisis," editorialized Italo Carlo Falbo, using a phrase that might as well have been plucked from Mussolini's mouth.[161] In September 1933, the chairman of the NRA in New York, Grover Whalen, denied any similarities between the NRA and the Italian corporate state. Whalen argued that the NRA welcomed voices of dissent, in contrast to the fascist state. Falbo demurred. The fascist government allowed constructive criticism but not "systematic opposition," he wrote. If the NRA were to succeed, the Roosevelt administration should take the same approach as the Italian government, Falbo insisted: opposition could not be tolerated.[162]

This was not the direction that the New Deal was heading in, and no one in the administration, with the notable exception of Hugh Johnson, the eccentric head of the NRA, seemed to welcome the comparison between the NRA and the Italian corporate state.[163] The NRA could not succeed, in part because the American government could not control voices of dissent and dominate the press with apocryphal success stories. Under pressure from Roosevelt to demonstrate the difference between the NRA and authoritarian regimes, Hugh Johnson launched a "field day of criticism" for the NRA at the end of February 1934. And criticize it Americans did, for problems ranging from rising prices and mounting red tape, to lack of compliance and poor labor conditions.[164] Pope subsequently muted all his praise of the NRA, which had delivered neither the economic miracles nor the "disciplined" unity *Il Progresso* had anticipated.[165]

Only Anne O'Hare McCormick lost no enthusiasm for the New Deal as the winter of 1933–34 gave way to spring, summer, and fall. Traveling around the United States in the latter half of 1934, McCormick described the effects of public works in "the new roads or old roads widened and beautified, new parks or neglected parks replanted, bridges, dams, waterworks, sanitation systems, hospitals, schools, municipal buildings." She described the impact of the New Deal, in other words, as a list of public goods that rivaled the list of private ones, which had defined the lost American souls of the 1920s. And she suggested that more valuable than the practice of "throwing away and building new," was a rediscovered habit of "making over," whether through publicly funded projects of rejuvenation or private endeavors. The government paid men to plant trees and flowers along roadways and in parks; other, and sometimes the same, men supplemented their shorter workdays by painting their porches and mending their fences.[166]

With the help of New Deal public works projects, McCormick reported that the center of gravity had shifted away from big cities and away from New York. Although its skyscrapers still stood, McCormick suggested that the city's financial center was as humbled as Icarus, after his fall. The city had shrunk back to human proportions, and she found its pulse not in the corpse of Wall Street but uptown, in the outdoor cafés, where New Yorkers sought the company of one another. In the place of one big city, dominating the culture and economy of the United States, tens, or even hundreds, of small towns had become lively centers, with modest spheres of influence all of their own. And while Malthusian processes accounted for the subdued atmosphere of Wall Street, there was nothing *laissez faire* in the revival of Atlanta, Des Moines, and Kansas City. Government support for agriculture and job creation had, in McCormick's estimation, revived provincial towns. By stimulating civic life and injecting cash into local economies, federally funded public works had chipped away at the veneer of standardization, to reveal peculiarities of place, culture, and heritage that had lain dormant for so many years.[167]

The United States that McCormick rediscovered in 1934 had much in common with Italy as she described it in the early depression years: life was simple, emotionally gratifying, and local; town and countryside survived in symbiosis with one another, and with the government's support. But while McCormick conceded that there was something of the "Old World" to this new United States, she believed that it was a product of uniquely American traditions and environments and a uniquely American democratic process.[168]

In this patchwork landscape, McCormick found a new harmony. An illustration that accompanied her journalism in the New York Times portrays a nation in equipoise (figure 4.3). From a domestic interior, an avuncular Roosevelt looks out at a richly textured scene. In the background is a lightly sketched city, its skyscrapers merely a suggestion, partially eclipsed by the gentle wisps of smoke that rise from the factories before it. Like the city, these factories do not dominate the scene; their horizontal profile echoes the landscape around them. Closer to the president still is a small town, its silhouettes evoking a church, a bank, local stores, and family homes. There is space in this composition for nature: perhaps half of the image is made up of the sky, mountains, fields, gardens, and parks. In the very foreground, almost as if they are in the president's own front yard, are two men: a farmer in overalls, and a mechanic whose only tools are contained in a box, which he carries by hand. These two men are muscular from physical labor, strong from adequate food. They are standing tall, with pride of work well-done. The illustration, like McCormick's journalism in 1934, suggested to readers of the New York Times that Roosevelt's New Deal had rehumanized Americans.

While she was touched by the changing landscape of the United States, McCormick was more touched still by the people she met across half a dozen states, most of them in the heartland. Were Americans happier, she wondered, than they had been in the "feverish, straining" decade past? They were certainly more fully realized. The people who spoke to her were wounded, scarred, and chastened. Their pain was heartrending, it felt like "the ache of a thousand fears." But so was their hope. Tentatively, so very tentatively, they told her that their government was helping them to find their way out of the depression. The Americans who spoke to McCormick were often critical of elements of the administration's policies. But whether they fully approved of the New Deal or not, Americans understood their system of government in startling detail. Government was no longer a gigantic machine, beyond human capacity to control or comprehend. It was a personal experience, a lived reality. Lived reality was flawed reality, McCormick suggested. And what could be more human than that?[169]

FIGURE 4.3. Franklin D. Roosevelt Surveys New Deal America. Illustration by Oscar Edward Cesare, for Anne O'Hare McCormick, "Roosevelt Surveys His Course," *New York Times*, July 8, 1934.

Solutions in Strange Places

Why did some Americans sympathize with fascism in the early depression years? Uncomfortable with the toll that modernity had taken on the fabric of their society, fascist sympathizers were primed to understand the depression as blowback from a decade of urbanization, agglomeration, machine-made production, and mindless consumption. They searched for solutions that would enable not only economic recovery but also a recalibration of the relationship between machines and men. The predominantly rural and small-town Italy of sympathizers' imagination functioned as more than a therapeutic salve for the "acids of modernity"; interpreted as a product of deliberate government policies, it offered concrete solutions for similar problems in the United States.[170] Heartened by Americans' seemingly instinctive gravitation toward the home and the local community in the depression's wake, they argued that humans were happiest, and most themselves, when they had the greatest contact with one another and the products of their labor. In Roosevelt, they saw a leader who, like Mussolini, could shepherd men back into a seemingly more natural state, in which their lives could be enhanced, but never again overpowered, by modern technology.

These fascist sympathizers were pragmatic patriots. They were pragmatic, because they looked for solutions wherever they could find them, whether in Henry Ford's experimental farms or in the reclaimed marshlands of fascist propaganda. They were patriots, because they sincerely wanted what they thought was best for their fellow Americans. It seemed simple, all too simple: if Italy, a cash-strapped, resource-scarce nation, had implemented appropriate policies to manage the depression, then surely the United States, a country of plentiful resources and vast lands, could too.

It is ironic, perhaps even absurd, that fascist sympathizers saw a model for making man the measure of all things in a regime that demanded ever greater conformity from its subjects and ruthlessly exploited individuals for production and, soon, for violent expansion. But if we are to engage in the (admittedly dangerous) practice of using the present to understand the past, then perhaps an instructive observation is that in times of economic stress, when humans feel overwhelmed by forces seemingly beyond their control, they admire leaders who reflect their anxieties and offer deceptively simple responses to their problems. People will search for solutions in the strangest of places.

5

The Garden of Fascism

BEAUTY, TRANSCENDENCE, AND PEACE IN AN ERA OF UNCERTAINTY

IN THE SUMMER OF 1933, Italo Balbo embarked on a feat that many believed impossible: a formation flight of seaplanes across the North Atlantic, in an east to west direction.[1] One hundred Italian airmen, in twenty-five seaplanes, left Orbetello airfield in Tuscany on July 1, 1933. Their first alightment, in Amsterdam, did not go to plan. One seaplane capsized, and a mechanic, Sergeant Ugo Quintavalle, died. The next stopover, in Londonderry, was smoother, and the airmen pressed on to Reykjavik on July 5th. Then the fog set in, and, for six days, Balbo waited.[2] In the United States, the press and the public prickled with anticipation.[3] Richard Washburn Child, a member of the Chicago welcoming committee, was impatient, also.[4] He telegrammed the White House on July 11th: "Suppose President understands [B]albo delay means me here Hotel Sherman."[5] For once, Child was where Roosevelt wanted him: far from Washington, with nothing to do but wait.

On July 12th, the Icelandic fog cleared, and Balbo's fleet took off from Reykjavik to face the toughest leg of their journey, over the Labrador Sea. The airmen stopped, serviced, and refueled their planes three more times, in Newfoundland, New Brunswick, and Montreal.[6] In the late afternoon of Saturday, July 15, Chicagoans caught their first glimpse of the seaplanes, approaching Lake Michigan's shoreline. The vision moved a *Tribune* reporter to lofty heights: "In formations at once proud and flexible they rode out of the evening clouds"; then the "silvery seaplanes" sunk "like swans to majestic rest on the sunlit bosom of the city's water gate."[7]

On the evening of the airmen's first full day in Chicago, five thousand guests, including Mayor Edward Kelly and Governor Henry Horner, gathered at the Stevens Hotel, for a dinner sponsored by the Italian-American society.[8] Vast silhouettes of Mussolini and King Vittorio Emanuele III adorned the ballroom's wall.[9] Balbo wore a formal dress uniform, with a cropped white mess jacket; his aviators wore uniforms of white linen suits, white shoes, white gloves.[10] When the airmen entered the ballroom, the guests rose for a fifteen-minute standing ovation; hundreds held their arms aloft in the fascist salute.[11] Ceremonies and speeches followed. Maintaining a tradition established in the early squadrist days, Balbo called the roll. To the name Ugo Quintavalle, the mechanic who had died in Amsterdam, the airmen responded in chorus, "Presente!"[12] Next, Balbo addressed the five thousand guests. The objective of the flight, he said, was "to demonstrate Italy's good will for America" and to strengthen "the ties of friendship" between the two countries.[13] Then Richard Washburn Child read a telegram of congratulations from Franklin Roosevelt. The crossing, wrote the president, marked a major step toward "the conquest of the air." Child added that all Americans could learn from the "practical bravery and discipline" of these Italian men.[14]

Italo Balbo's flying visit to the United States also provided Generoso Pope with some high-profile moments. The airmen visited New York after Chicago. As the chairman of the city's welcoming committee, Pope was at Balbo's side at every official engagement, and in his orbit for every photo opportunity. Pope stood on a pier to meet the Italians when they flew in to Jamaica Bay on Wednesday, July 19, and rode with Balbo in a police escort to his hotel.[15] On Thursday, Pope posed for photographers with Balbo, as the general changed into his flying clothes in preparation for a flight to meet with the president in Washington, DC.[16] On Friday, Pope waited for the returning airmen at Pennsylvania Station, at the beginning of a jam-packed, triumphal day. The two men rode together in a ticker-tape parade down Broadway (figure 5.1). Pope introduced Balbo to the mayor at City Hall. He hosted the airmen at lunch at the Pennsylvania Hotel. He was there, by Balbo's side, at an afternoon rally at Madison Square Garden Bowl, and again at dinner at the Commodore Hotel. At an after-dinner dance, in the ballroom of the Waldorf Astoria, the two men sat together in a box.[17] For both of them, Friday, July 21, represented the apogee of everything they had worked toward. For Balbo, it was a spectacular celebration of a feat that he had planned meticulously for years. For Pope, it was evidence of Italian prowess and a testament to his role as the de facto leader of his community.[18] Perhaps Italo Balbo breathed a sigh of relief when he said goodbye to Generoso Pope. Certainly, Pope had been solicitousness, ubiquitous, and ever ready to bask in his guest's reflected light.

FIGURE 5.1. Generoso Pope Rides with Italo Balbo down Broadway, July 1933. Courtesy of New York Daily News Archive via Getty Images.

Italo Balbo's flight provided these fascist sympathizers with more than fleeting moments of celebrity. It gave them an opportunity to present fascism in terms that were appealing to many Americans. The airmen affirmed a human capacity to contrive beauty. Their white suits, white shoes, and white gloves were part of their choreography. Balbo himself was immensely photogenic, his appearance conjuring up a modern romanticism.[19] He was the kind of man who changed in and out of his flying clothes in public but honored his fallen comrade with a roll call, in timeworn fashion.[20] In Balbo, most Americans saw only beauty. They were unaware of the cruelty that lay beneath.[21]

The airmen's beauty on land was outdone only by their beauty in the air. They flew the seaplanes in formation, in flights of three, each flight a triangle, each triangle part of a larger design.[22] Soaring above Chicago's Century of Progress exhibition and Manhattan's skyscrapers, the seaplanes were visually stunning. "Our eyes," wrote Generoso Pope, "have never seen such a spectacular sight."[23] As noted by a reporter for the *Baltimore Sun*, Balbo's presence in the United States provided distractions from the problems of the day. When those problems were the nitty gritty of "competitive business codes, stock markets, wheat prices" as well as the larger issues of poverty and unemployment, there was nothing superficial about light relief.[24] It was good for the spirit, and good for the soul.

Balbo's successful flight demonstrated that man could overcome the most binding of constraints. Today, flight is so quotidian that many of us find it a banal experience. We may skim over a phrase like Franklin Roosevelt's "conquest of the air" without really absorbing its meaning. But in 1933, observers used phrases like this in the truest of senses. They understood that the Italians had prevailed over powerful elements.[25] Balbo and his men had successfully played with space and time in the air, and this seemed to give them ample license to play with space and time on land. In Chicago and New York, the Italians were often late, and they often skipped official engagements. But their recalcitrance provoked nothing but understanding.[26] Those white linen suits were not only beautiful in appearance, they connoted transcendence: the usual constraints no longer applied.[27]

Fascist sympathizers also used Balbo's flight to insist on the peaceful intentions of Mussolini's regime. At the Stevens Hotel in Chicago, Balbo emphasized that the flight was a symbol of Italy's "goodwill" toward the United States.[28] He frequently repeated this claim throughout his visit.[29] Although Mussolini's investments in aviation were inextricably linked to his ambitions to wage wars of conquest, fascist sympathizers insisted that Balbo's flight was an expression of amity. In 1933, President Roosevelt was inclined to agree. In a telegram to King Vittorio Emanuele, the president wrote that Americans had welcomed the expedition as proof of the "true friendship" that existed between their two people.[30] In private, he was equally sanguine about the intentions of the fascist state. Roosevelt, in 1933, believed that Mussolini's "honest purpose" was to "prevent general European trouble."[31] In this context, those white linen suits took on additional meaning. They connoted more than beauty and more than transcendence. They implied an innocence of purpose and they promised peace.

In short, fascist sympathizers represented Balbo's 1933 North Atlantic flight as something beautiful and peaceful, in which man conspired with nature to surpass it and, in doing so, came a little bit closer to heaven. Paradoxically, the metaphor that most readily encompasses all this comes not from the air, but from the earth. The garden is a place of beauty and peace, where humans sensitively manipulate nature and find their god or gods. The garden is also the product of careful editing, and throughout Balbo's visit, sympathetic observers did their fair share of gardening of this kind, ignoring the uglier side of Balbo's personality—his irritability and torpor—and cleansing their reports of antifascist protests.[32]

In 1933, American society at large echoed fascist sympathizers' interpretation of Balbo's flight. There were voices of criticism, both in the form of protests on the streets of Chicago and New York and in editorials in antifascist publications.[33] But the mainstream press characterized the airmen as embodiments of physical beauty, conquerors of nature, and representatives of peace. As a welcome escape from reality, an act of transcendence, and a thing of beauty, Balbo's flight seemed to sit comfortably within contemporary American culture: fantasy was a popular genre in books and films of the 1930s; and various forms of art and design—from swing dancing to streamlining—expressed an urge to break free from constraints.[34] In 1933, it was easy for most Americans to celebrate Balbo's feat.

Fascist sympathizers' interpretations of Italo Balbo's flight also signaled the start of a shift in how they represented Italy. At the end of the 1920s and the beginning of the New Deal, these observers mined fascism for practical examples of human-scale responses to economic and social challenges, which could bear lessons for the United States. In the mid- to late 1930s, their interpretations of Mussolini's Italy were not devoid of relevant implications for American policy. But, more than before, they invoked Italian fascism to take Americans out of their own realities, by portraying the regime as capable of surpassing nature.

Writing in the late twentieth century, the sociologist Zygmunt Bauman described the modern state as a "gardening state." By this, Bauman meant that all modern governments used bureaucratic processes to master forces—such as demographics—that had proceeded for the most part naturally in premodern times. Bauman's ideas are chilling because he argued that the Holocaust was a product of the weeding tendencies inherent in all modern states. The gardening state, in Bauman's conception, was merciless.[35] Writing in the 1930s, McCormick, Pope, and Schneider had a rather different conception of the fascist state as a gardening state. They admired Mussolini's regime for its capacity to resist the forces of nature. But they also expressed an appreciation of the Italian state's capacity to nurture and create. They suggested that the garden of Italian fascism was generative rather than destructive. Weeding occurred in this garden, certainly, but never at the expense of beauty and growth.

In the mid-1930s, Mussolini pursued three policies that interested sympathetic American observers: first, he executed a project of archaeology and urban planning in Rome; second, he augmented youth training programs; and third, at the end of 1935, Italy invaded Ethiopia. These policies were interlinked. Mussolini envisaged Rome as an *imperial* city, and the regime became more intent on training and disciplining youth in preparation for its first major war. McCormick, Pope, and Schneider chose not to present these policies as expressions of an increasingly oppressive and violent regime. Instead, they portrayed them as evidence that the fascist state had created places of productivity, sustenance, and harmony.

While it had been easy for most Americans to agree with fascist sympathizers' characterizations of Italo Balbo in July 1933, the claims that Italy represented beauty, transcendence, and peace felt more farfetched as the decade progressed. Balbo alighted in Chicago only a few months after Adolf Hitler assumed dictatorial powers in Germany. The Italian airmen's flight helped to distance Italy under Mussolini—seemingly so beautiful and benign—from Germany under Hitler—blatantly brutal and threatening. These distinctions between Nazism and fascism became increasingly important for fascist sympathizers over the course of the mid-1930s, under mounting evidence that the two regimes were drawing closer together, both in style and in fact. Metaphors of the garden, which seemed so natural for many Americans on the occasion of Balbo's flight in 1933, felt increasingly false, forced, and strained by 1937, given the realities of life in Italy and the foreign policy of the fascist state.

Wildflowers and the Wilderness

One can understand the appeal of alternative worlds to Americans in the 1930s. The economy did pick up slowly (before another recession in 1937), but joblessness was a stubborn problem, particularly among the ranks of the long-term unemployed. In the mid-decade, one in five Americans remained without a job.[36] Initial feelings of hope that Roosevelt would save the country gave way to the realization that the United States could be in the economic doldrums for years to come. "Pessimism stalks upon us at every turn," wrote a columnist in the African-American newspaper the *Atlanta Daily World* at the end of 1934.[37] Populism—of the kind offered by Upton Sinclair, Francis Townsend, Charles Coughlin, and Huey Long—appealed to those who were convinced of, or at least hopeful for, simple solutions for the economic crisis.[38] But other Americans acknowledged that the issues they faced were of a deep-seated and complex nature: there was no "fell-swoop solution" to the United States' problems, wrote a contributor to the *North American Review* in 1935.[39]

The ongoing conflict between capital and labor was one aspect of these problems. In 1934, there were strikes across the country, and the responses of local vigilantes, police, and the national guard were often violent.[40] The strikes confirmed that the NRA had not fulfilled its (unrealistic) promise of resolving industrial strife. A year before the Supreme Court struck it down, the NRA was unraveling: consumers blamed it for price increases; the left disliked it because it favored big business; and the right believed it encouraged labor militancy.

The Roosevelt administration worked to salvage the NRA's guarantee of collective bargaining through the National Labor Relations (or Wagner) Act of 1935, and historians agree that the NLRA created a much firmer basis for industrial relations than the NRA.[41] But for many Americans at the time, the NLRA seemed to leave unanswered more than it resolved. Lecturing in Rome in early 1936, Herbert Schneider said that the Wagner Act had "obvious limitations": it did not address the "broader problem of class struggle" or "curb strikes."[42] Glaucus, the *Il Progresso* journalist who, in 1933, had predicted that the New Deal would usher in a permanent truce between capital and labor, painted an entirely different picture in 1937. He described the sit-down strikes in Michigan that year as an expression of a "bitter and unceasing" conflict between capital and labor in the United States, which had been "resolved in Italy for quite some time."[43] On these issues, fascist sympathizers seemed to voice the sentiments of many Americans: the majority of those polled argued that sit-down strikes should be illegal and that the Wagner Act should be either repealed or revised.[44]

Fascist sympathizers presented the widespread strikes as just one aspect of an unsettled American landscape. Schneider identified the United States' principal problem as the failure to agree. Americans, he said, had "a multitude of faiths; in other words, nothing but doubts." Policymakers were "still hesitating, wondering, debating, or, at best, experimenting." Schneider told his Italian lecture audience: "American morality is still a wilderness, where occasionally the wild flowers bloom (sweet, but essentially wild) amid vast stretches of desert sand." Democracies are by definition pluralistic, people within them rarely agree. Instead of characterizing such democratic pluralism as a fertile orchard, with many varieties, ripe for the picking, Schneider described it as an arid desert, where the odd plant might self-seed. Schneider portrayed Italy, by contrast, as a well-established garden. The Italians, he said, had agreed upon "the fundamental lines" of their "new order"; all that was required in Italy was "the daily application of intelligence and labor."[45] In an era of uncertainty, clarity (even at the expense of pluralism) had a certain appeal.

Of course, there were also international dimensions to Americans' sense of insecurity in the mid-decade, and the garden that fascist sympathizers designed catered to these anxieties, too. Public awareness of the threats presented by Germany, and Japan (and Italy), was exceeded, and often overwhelmed, by the conviction that the United States should never again fight in Europe. At the end of 1936, ninety-five percent of Americans believed that the United States should not take part in another World War.[46] Fascist sympathizers keyed into their fellow Americans' wishful thinking that Mussolini would help to moderate Hitler, and perpetuate the uneasy peace that had prevailed on the continent since 1918. Their agenda was made easier by the attitude of the Roosevelt administration, which premised much of its foreign policy in the mid-1930s on a belief that Mussolini was intent on avoiding war in Europe.[47]

Herbert Schneider's 1935–36 trip to Italy, sponsored by the Carnegie Endowment for International Peace, was itself an expression of the kind of blinkered optimism, vis-à-vis fascist Italy, that ran through policy circles. Schneider's stay coincided with the Italian invasion of Ethiopia, prompting a letter from Carnegie officials reminding him to "confine" his "public and private talks to non-controversial matters." Schneider was there to promote and maintain "the friendly feeling" that existed between "the people of Italy and of the United States," wrote the assistant of Nicholas Murray Butler (who was the director of the endowment, and well-known for his fascist sympathies).[48] Schneider needed no such reminder: he could be counted on as someone who avoided making moral judgments about fascism, not just as a matter of tact, but as a method of inquiry.

For their part, Italian propagandists familiar with the United States understood that the regime needed to tailor its image according to the specific sensitivities of American audiences. In 1935, Carlo Boidi, the head of the Italian

Fascist Students' Group, informed Mussolini that Americans' "confusion" of fascism and Nazism represented the "greatest danger" to Italy's reputation in the United States.[49] In 1936, Angelo Flavio Guidi, a fascist journalist whose work appeared often in *Il Progresso*, recommended that the regime send to the United States materials evoking "beauty and great works" in Italy, to help overcome "simplistic confusions between Nazism and fascism."[50] Similarly, the Italian ambassador in Washington, Fulvio Suvich, recommended that propaganda bound for the United States should emphasize the constructive, creative, and peaceful nature of Italian fascism.[51]

Sympathetic Americans helped the regime in this regard.[52] Often, these observers provided juxtaposing portraits, which suggested that German Nazism was sick, unnatural, and bellicose, while Italian fascism was healthy, natural, and peaceful. For instance, a 1934 editorial in *Il Progresso* described Hitler's plan for autarchy as the product of a "diseased mind," which aimed to make Germany reliant on chemists for sustenance and "detach" Germans from "the rest of humanity."[53] A contemporaneous image published in *Il Progresso* featured Mussolini participating in the wheat harvest in Littoria—communing with nature, connecting with men.[54] On more than one occasion, Anne O'Hare McCormick invited Mussolini to spell out the differences between Nazism and fascism for American readers.[55] In 1936, she reported that *Il Duce* had told her that there were "profound" differences between the two regimes, and that the Italians were "not a warlike people" and would never become one.[56] As constructed by these observers, the garden of fascism did not just look beautiful, it produced the kind of sounds that most Americans wanted to hear.

Urbs es Hortus—City Planning in Italy and the United States

Ideas of the garden had the most literal of manifestations in Italian and American cityscapes of the 1930s, since in both countries, planners envisaged greener inner cities, and airier and more verdant suburbs. Writing in *Il Progresso*, Angelo Flavio Guidi claimed that earlier Italian governments had done nothing to control urbanization. They had allowed buildings to encroach upon Rome's open spaces, much in the same way that a negligent gardener would turn a blind eye to the spread of weeds. Guidi described the changes made by Mussolini's government. He claimed that the regime had created twenty-five new gardens and more than one hundred and fifty kilometers of tree-lined streets in the capital.[57]

According to sympathetic observers, the regime did not only turn Rome into a greener city, but it also improved urban dwellers' access to nature beyond the city limits. In 1928, the government had built a "speedway"—the Via del Mare—between Rome and the ancient seaside town of Ostia; by 1934, it had lined the route to the sea with 6,321 elms, oaks, and pines, by Guidi's count.[58] That same year, Mussolini discussed his love of skiing with Anne O'Hare McCormick. He promised that, within a year, a new road would make the Apennine Mountains accessible to all.[59]

Fascist sympathizers claimed that by creating gardens in the city and access to nature beyond, the regime mitigated the harshness of the urban environment. Thanks to Mussolini, the Roman breeze was more refreshing, the city streets were cooler, and the air smelled of mimosa flowers.[60] They argued that these changes created respite from the most grating aspects of modernity: the regime moved factories to the outskirts of the city and banned car horns, turning Rome into a peaceful sanctuary.[61] The impact of these policies seemed evident on contemporary Romans themselves, who suffered fewer of the tensions associated with modern life. McCormick wrote that the sporty Mussolini, whom she met in 1934, was more "physically fit" and "cheerful" than ever before. By building a road to the mountains, Il Duce would extend the benefits of fresh air and exercise to all, she suggested.[62] "You see happy and satisfied faces everywhere" in Rome, wrote Generoso Pope, following a visit to the capital in 1937.[63] Removing the sources of urban strain and giving Italians air, space, and light, the fascists seemed to provide a refuge from the ills of the modern era.

The fascist project for Rome entailed more than creating green space in the city and transportation networks to get out. In McCormick's telling, it also included the construction of a "modern city on the periphery of the old."[64] Fascist sympathizers stretched the idea of the garden of Rome from the literal to the metaphorical realm, observing that the government took control of the urban environment. In the fall of 1934, *Il Progresso* described how Mussolini took the lead in slum clearance in one of the "filthiest quarters" of the medieval city. *Il Duce* climbed onto the roof of one of the decrepit homes and ripped up the tiles with his bare hands.[65] McCormick's 1934 *Ladies' Home Journal* article included a photograph of a modern apartment complex, which the regime had built in the suburbs of Rome. The building had almost more windows than stone, and curved around a wide street, basked in daylight.[66] All Italian families wanted to exchange their medieval hovels in dark alleyways for "large buildings exposed to the sun," fascist sympathizers implied.[67]

There were parallels between the ideas of Italian and American urban planners in the 1930s.[68] In both Italy and the United States, landscapers and architects reacted against density, envisaging greener cities and more spacious, horizontal buildings. And in both countries, the governments conceived of suburban development as a healthier alternative to life within cities. At times, fascist sympathizers appreciated these parallels. Thanks to New Deal projects, American cities offered "more public gardens" than they had in the past, wrote McCormick in 1934.[69] Two years later, she noted that the gentle "puttering" of the Works Progress Administration and Civilian Conservation Corps had helped to beautify the suburbs.[70] McCormick suggested that, in a similar fashion to fascist policies, the New Deal had helped to soften some of the sharp edges of urban life.

But these observers also suggested that the United States lagged behind Italy in urban planning, especially with regard to the provision of low-income housing. Both McCormick and Pope remarked on the prevalence of slums in the United States. Pointing to whole areas of "dilapidation and decay" in Cleveland, Chicago, and Detroit, McCormick argued that the "margins" of American cities were "the ugliest in the world."[71] Pope described New York's housing conditions as a source of "deep shame for metropolitan America." Why, he wondered, did a city as wealthy as New York still have slums, while Italian cities like Milan and Rome had done so much to increase their stock of popular housing? In June 1934, Pope welcomed a public housing project in Williamsburg, Brooklyn, as the first step toward the "transformation of unhealthy neighborhoods into oases of health, peace, and happiness."[72]

Pope's hope that all New Yorkers would soon have decent housing was not realized. As documented by historians, with Public Works Administration (PWA) funds, the Williamsburg public housing project went ahead, alongside a smaller project in East Harlem. But at the end of 1937, New York still offered only 2,330 public homes to a city of seven million people. New York's limited progress providing low-income housing was replicated in other American cities, where solutions to housing problems were held back by New Dealers' slow uptake of the issue, the resistance of conservatives in Congress, and the vested interests of private sector groups.[73]

Writing in *Il Progresso* at the start of 1935, Glaucus described some of these obstacles to housing policy in the United States. He argued, quite correctly, that the low priority afforded to public housing at the start of the New Deal was reflected in the small budget and weak leverage of the housing division of the PWA. By 1935, initial complacency in the administration had given way to a consensus that some form of intervention was required to relieve the housing problem. But, as Glaucus observed, New Dealers failed to agree on a policy approach. The journalist pointed to various positions in the government: Harry Hopkins, the Federal Emergency Relief Agency chief, called for billions of dollars of public spending to build rural and semirural homes; Harold Ickes, the secretary of the interior, suggested a program of about half that size, to be administered through the PWA; James Moffett, head of the Federal Housing Administration, advocated for government interventions in the mortgage market to stimulate private purchases. Just as Herbert Schneider would argue that New Dealers' "multitude of faiths" left them "hesitating," Glaucus suggested that a variety of positions within the government resulted in paralysis.[74] To employ Schneider's imagery, it seemed that wildflowers bloomed in government, while on city streets the wilderness prevailed.

But even Glaucus himself acknowledged that there was no easy way forward in housing policy in the United States. In his view, any intervention would entail unintended consequences. For instance, by encouraging near-subsistence lifestyles in rural areas, Hopkins's proposal could depress consumer demand, Glaucus observed. Employing hundreds of thousands of men on "relief wages," both Hopkins's and Ickes's programs could undercut private-sector salaries, he noted. Meanwhile, Moffett's preferred course of action would entrust recovery to the kinds of "speculators" who had provoked the boom-to-bust cycle of the 1920s, Glaucus argued.[75]

This kind of analysis represented a significant change from *Il Progresso*'s earlier position on government responses to the depression. In the New Deal's first eighteen months, the newspaper had supported unequivocally programs of rural resettlement and public works; and Glaucus had anticipated that the PWA would effect an almost instantaneous economic recovery.[76] Two years on, Glaucus still argued that government action was preferable to inaction. But he also highlighted the downside risks of every possible intervention. The chastened tone of his analysis was at one with other articles in *Il Progresso* in the mid- to late 1930s, which stressed the complexity of policy options in the United States, and the negative externalities that might accompany public interventions.[77] For instance, whereas Generoso Pope had once welcomed unconditionally New Deal public works, arguing the more, the better, from 1935 onward, he expressed anxieties about a mounting budget deficit, rising taxes, and the danger that public spending would crowd out private-sector investment.[78] So while Pope continued to lament the housing crisis, and in particular the persistence of "old, lurid, unhygienic hovels" in urban areas of the United States, he no longer argued that a solution to the housing problem, or indeed the depression at large, was a simple question of government spending.[79]

Il Progresso Italo-Americano shed light on some of the real constraints under which the New Deal operated in the mid-decade. Housing policy was in disarray within the administration in late 1934 and early 1935, just as Glaucus described.[80] And conservative instincts, of the same kind that Glaucus and Pope expressed, held the government back from developing a more comprehensive approach to public housing. The administration's most important contribution to public housing came in the form of the Housing Act of 1937. As originally conceived by Senator Wagner, the act would provide low-interest federal loans to local authorities to enable them to build homes for low-income families. With equivocal support from President Roosevelt, Wagner's bill drifted for two years, and when it finally passed into law, Congress had deprived it of its most forceful elements.[81] Real-world economic and political constraints hit housing and urban policies hard in the United States.

In contrast to the all too evident limitations of urban planning policies in the United States, fascist sympathizers offered Rome as a place that defied constraints entirely. For example, they presented Rome as a city where policies went into effect "at once without the slightest delay."[82] The idea that policymaking was faster in fascist Italy was not a new one: since the early 1920s, fascist sympathizers had argued that Mussolini's dictatorship represented the height of administrative efficiency. But, increasingly, such claims assumed a paranormal quality. Words like "miracle," "magic," and "supernatural" appeared frequently in sympathetic observers' descriptions of fascist Rome, to refer to phenomena that defied conventional expectations of space and time.[83] The regime decided to develop gardens, parks, and tree-lined streets in Rome, and "straight away" the city turned green, eliding the time it took to implement policy, or even the time it took for seasons to change, for trees to grow, and for flowers to bloom.[84]

The regime's archaeological program also demonstrated its time-bending capacities.[85] Fascist-sponsored archaeology skipped over problematic eras—postimperial decline, competitive city-states, and liberal democracy—to draw a direct line from ancient to contemporary Rome. Sympathetic Americans saw nothing artificial in this program (although both Schneider and McCormick recognized the political value of reviving imperial Rome as "a symbol of unity").[86] Instead, they argued that the fascists resuscitated Rome's ancient past as "the natural and organic structure out of which the present" would grow.[87] In 1935, McCormick observed that Trajan's market was once more an "emporium," that the Circus Maximus hosted public expositions, including a recent modern housing fair, and that the forum was again a "Civic Centre." McCormick implied that by reviving the past, the regime recovered part of Italians' authentic identity, which had been neglected by previous governments; Rome was made whole again, and, with it, Italians too.[88]

These observers claimed that the regime had bolstered Rome's longstanding status as the Eternal City: Schneider argued that, under Mussolini, Rome "more than ever," was "assuming an 'eternal' aspect and temper."[89] The regime intentionally blurred the lines between imperial, Catholic, and fascist Rome, and foreign sympathizers willingly consumed the resulting hybrid—part pagan, part Christian, part statist.[90] To readers of *Ladies' Home Journal*, McCormick described a sunny Sunday morning that she spent in Piazza dell'Esedra (now Piazza della Repubblica). She stood in the center of the square, sprayed by water from the fountain, taking in the Christian Basilica of Santa Maria and Diocletian's baths on one side, the massive train station, and the "fleet" of "shining" new buses on the other. "It was a lusty scene. Everything was mixed up in it: Christ, Caesar and Mussolini," she wrote.[91] One contributor to *Il Progresso* described how it was easy to "find religion in Rome": thanks to fascist town planning and archaeology, the city was more beautiful than ever before; and thanks to the ban on car horns, it was more peaceful. On a "wonderful spring morning," this writer felt "reborn" as he listened to "the silver music of Rome's thousand bells."[92] To sympathetic observers, the city was "*Roma cristiana, cesarea e fascista*"; its bells rang for God, the gods, and Mussolini.[93]

The regime endorsed for American consumption these portraits of fascist Rome as both a triumph of urban planning and a place of spiritual fulfillment. For instance, in 1935 the Ministry of Popular Culture asked the Luce Institute to send films about Rome to the Italian Embassy in Washington, for distribution in the United States.[94] The precise content of these films is unknown, but recent Luce productions had included "Demolition of Slums . . . and the Building of New Homes"; "Sunny Days in Roman Winter," filmed at the seaside in Ostia; and "Excavation of the Roman Forum."[95] The regime used portraits of fascist Rome to portray Italy as a carefully tended land, which both ensured a good quality of life and elevated human existence above a material world.

The regime was also conscious that such images of Rome could help to distinguish Italian fascism from the German strand. Anne O'Hare McCormick echoed the regime's line, using metaphors of space and place to designate fascism as welcoming and welcome, and Nazism as beyond the pale. After interviewing Hitler in 1933 and visiting again the following year, McCormick described Germany as a barren land. She found physical parallels to the destructive spirit of Nazism in Hitler's "modernistic" office, cleansed of books, history, and art, and in the demolition of Munich's Köningsplatz, including its lawn, to make way for the party headquarters.[96]

The fate of German Catholics and Jews worried McCormick immensely: although Hitler had made overtures toward the Catholic Church in early 1933, he proceeded to attack both Catholic and Jewish institutions. During the Night of the Long Knives, in July 1934, the Nazis murdered Dr. Erich Klausener, the leader of a Catholic Action group.[97] Reaching for architectural metaphors to describe Nazi Germany, McCormick situated the regime in the dark, middle ages. Years before the construction of physical ghettos, she wrote that the Third Reich was "erecting a social and spiritual quarantine as dividing as medieval walls."[98] Writing in the *Times*, McCormick insisted that the different aesthetic forms of the two fascisms were expressions of fundamentally different regimes. Nazism was, in her mind, "humorless-Gothic," whereas Italian fascism was "mellower and more humane," softened by history and brightened by the occasional "flourish of the baroque."[99] She suggested that the difference between Nazism and fascism was the difference between a wasteland and a garden.

Rome, as represented by fascist sympathizers, gave health to modern bodies and peace to modern souls. It was a very different city from the one the fascist government actually created. Not all Romans were happy to be transferred from their existing homes in the central city; not all Romans found modern amenities, spacious architecture, and transportation infrastructure in their new neighborhoods. Often, working-class Romans interpreted rehousing as an attempt to break up left-leaning communities; sometimes, their new homes had no more facilities than their old ones, and cut them off from their city and from one another.[100] Instead of connecting Italians with their history, many Italians felt that the fascist regime had deprived them of it. Known as a "disemboweling" (*sventramenti*), Mussolini's archaeological and construction program tore up vast swathes of medieval Rome. Rome's "great parkways" and newly open spaces, which looked so beautiful to Anne O'Hare McCormick, felt like "scars" to many Italians—emblems of the regime's readiness to raze all that stood in its way.[101]

Sympathetic American observers ignored the darker side of fascist Rome to produce an imaginary place that differed in quality and kind from cities of their own. Both the fascist regime and the US government reckoned with problems related to urbanization in the 1930s. Both looked to solutions in the form of public spaces and parks, accessible cultural events, suburbanization, and public housing. But Mussolini appeared to offer more complete solutions to these problems in Rome: a place that was greener, culturally richer, and with better amenities than any American city. At times, and particularly in the early days of the New Deal, these observers drew comparisons between Rome and American cities to argue that their own government should and could do more. But at other times, they seemed to offer up Rome as a pure escape. There was magic to Rome, just as there was to Italo Balbo, and his team of airmen, dressed in white. Fascist sympathizers understood that when real-world solutions to real-world problems were elusive, people craved magic.

The Valley of Youth

When fascist sympathizers criticized urban conditions in the United States in the 1930s, their voices merged with other Americans who argued that inner cities were breeding grounds for juvenile delinquency. In the 1920s, sociologists had developed an "ecological theory" of crime, which described the environment as the chief factor in criminal behavior.[102] Highly influential in the field of criminology, these ideas led the Wickersham Commission—a 1931 government-sponsored investigative committee—to conclude that juvenile delinquency resulted "not from any racial disposition toward crime but from the influence of the social environment."[103] Although the "ecological theory" of crime had its detractors, by the mid-1930s it was well-entrenched in the American public consciousness. Put simply in the *New York Times* in 1935, most Americans understood that criminals were "made, not born."[104] When McCormick lamented the zones "of dilapidation and decay between the business district and the suburbs" of Detroit, Cleveland, and Chicago in 1934, she was referring to the "back of the yards" zones identified by sociologists as breeding grounds for young criminals.[105] And when Generoso Pope stated (as he did frequently) that Italian Americans were not criminals by nature, he could claim that social science was on his side.[106]

Americans sympathetic to fascism used these environmental explanations of delinquency to argue that Mussolini's regime was nurturing young men and women to develop into socially adjusted, responsible adults. Writing in *Ladies' Home Journal* in 1934, McCormick quoted her "friend," an Italian man called Carlo Bonfigli. Carlo had been eighteen when the fascists seized power in

1922—a little too old to benefit from government youth training programs. But Carlo's younger brother, Vito, was a product of fascist youth. Carlo admired Vito and his friends; he described them as "a better generation ... simpler, healthier, more at home in their world." In Carlo's mind, Vito and his friends were "like the saplings growing in the new forests ... growing straight because they have the air and soil most favorable to their development."[107]

Sympathetic American observers argued that the fascist regime channeled natural adolescent instincts that would otherwise be consumed by a life of crime. Herbert Schneider had already praised fascist Italy's education policy and youth training programs when he contributed to Charles Merriam's comparative study on civic education in the late 1920s.[108] After his Carnegie-endowed visit to Italy from 1935–36, he described the fascist athletics program as "little short of spectacular." The goal of such programs, Schneider wrote, was to direct the energies of young people toward a "healthy outdoor life to diminish the sickly fruits of private passion."[109] Here, too, Schneider suggested that fascism was on the cutting edge of social science: contributors to the Wickersham report had emphasized the importance of social relationships for adolescents, suggesting that organized youth groups could compete with gangs.[110] The fascist state succeeded, these observers argued, first because it pursued its sports program wholeheartedly—providing magnificent free training grounds, and making athletics a central aspect of public life—and second, because it offered activities that genuinely appealed to young people. Through the *balilla* (the fascist boy scouts) the government provided a "substitution for the gang to come," wrote one contributor to *Il Progresso*. Like the gang, the *balilla* offered "companionship." Like the gang, the *balilla* provided a "program and code of ethics." But unlike the gang, the *balilla* shaped young people into "good citizens," this writer maintained.[111]

McCormick, Schneider, and contributors to *Il Progresso* noted that, in addition to the weekly activities of fascist youth groups, the government provided summer camps for young people at the mountains or by the sea.[112] As interpreted by these observers, the principal purpose of these camps was to remove children from potentially damaging urban environments. According to one contributor to *Il Progresso*, the state had taken control of these camps (which had once been run by private organizations) to ensure that all children—and the poorest in particular—could "benefit from the cures of the climate."[113] Angelo Flavio Guidi portrayed the camps as health resorts: children ate an enviable diet of pasta, cheese, tuna, and meat, prepared by a chef from a grand hotel; they returned to their families physically stronger and tanned—*the* contemporary emblem of excellent health.[114] These observers argued that the healthy effects of fascist summer camps extended from the "physical" to the "moral" sphere.[115] Removed from urban environments that were breeding grounds of bad behavior, young Italians were nurtured along a straighter and narrower path.

Weekly youth activities and summer camps furnished fascist sympathizers with very obvious examples of the gardening principle: young Italians grew up healthily in outdoor stadiums, on hillsides, and by the sea, they argued. But these observers also applied an environmental understanding of youth development in less direct ways. For instance, McCormick and contributors to *Il Progresso* suggested that the government had revived religious practices among Italian youth. McCormick noted that there were ten thousand chaplains assigned to the fascist boy scouts and "even a Bishop of the Balilla"; photographs in *Il Progresso* featured Catholic prelates performing masses at youth camps. McCormick again referred to her friend, Carlo Bonfigli, and his brother, Vito, to demonstrate the effects of fascist youth organizations. "Like many of my generation, I don't practice my religion," Carlo confided, but, "with all his comrades [Vito] goes to church as naturally as he eats and breathes." McCormick suggested that fascism had effected a transformation in the values of young men. While Carlo had some of the skepticism associated with the modern condition, Vito was an idealist, through and through. She had Carlo convey this idea in two words, made more powerful by their simplicity. "Vito believes."[116]

These observers also identified maternity and infant care as another way in which the fascist state successfully applied an ecological theory of youth development. As *Il Progresso* correctly recognized, one of the main purposes of the *piccole italiane* and *giovane italiane* (the female fascist youth groups) was to prepare girls to become mothers.[117] But rather than presenting such groups as loci for indoctrination, the newspaper portrayed them as sensitively compensating for the effects of modernity, since maternal know-how, which was readily transferred in traditional societies, could be lost in contemporary environments. Mussolini had identified a lacuna in modern society, wrote the editors of *Il Progresso*, and used the state to fill the void.[118] On her tour of Littoria in late 1933, McCormick saw the House of Motherhood and Infancy, which she described to *Ladies' Home Journal* readers as a "combination of baby clinic, nursery, school and hospital for mothers."[119] Such provisions were available throughout Italy, *Il Progresso* observed, offering advice, health care, and even square meals, to women and their children.[120] Fascist nurseries enabled a woman to work if her family's "economic status" necessitated it, while providing the tender administrations of the ideal mother, even in her absence.[121] As rendered by these observers, the fascist maternal state would ensure that children got the best possible start in life.

According to fascist sympathizers, the effects of the state's efforts to nurture and develop youth were evident in the human results. *Il Progresso* cited Italy's success in international athletics as proof that the fascists had molded a new generation. A 1935 cartoon illustration featured three Italian cycling champions—alert, strong-jawed, highly muscled. In the same cartoon, a diminutive Uncle Sam asked, "Where do they come from?" In the center of the composition, Mussolini provided the answer: the men were the "sons of sunny Italy"—a product of their environment.[122]

Fascist sympathizers insisted that the effects of fascist youth programs extended beyond the physical realm. Contributors to *Il Progresso* argued that low crime rates in Italy were the product of youth training and maternity programs. By offering summer camps and weekly activities, the state provided boys with a moral framework and took youth "off the street."[123] By teaching women maternal arts, the regime ensured that mothers were more protective of their children, especially in "big cities," where temptations abounded.[124] And by providing nursery care to vulnerable infants and children, the state had "rescued" thousands "from vice."[125] In short, the fascist state appeared to have abolished juvenile delinquency by reshaping the environment, as sociologists prescribed. In place of cramped cities and absent parents, the fascists offered spacious landscapes and loving authority, according to these observers. And instead of the juvenile delinquent, they produced young men like McCormick's earnest and virtuous Vito Bonfigli—a surname that, perhaps not coincidentally, meant "good son."[126]

All these observers suggested that the United States could learn from the Italian regime's approach to youth training. Indeed, *Il Progresso Italo-Americano* argued quite directly that "America, rich in material and spiritual resources, could readily follow" the Italian example.[127] In early 1937, Generoso Pope launched a "crusade" against juvenile delinquency in the United States. Week after week, Pope's newspaper described how interlocking problems of slum housing, scarce amenities, low income, and working mothers had shaped American urban youth.[128] *Il Progresso* argued that private organizations in the United States had developed the correct approach to tackling the problem of juvenile delinquency, by providing after-school activities to channel "pent-up emotions," and countryside camps to improve young people's physical and moral conditions.[129] The principal problems were related to supply: the boy scouts and most summer camps required fees, which most poor families could not pay; as a result, low-income youth depended on piecemeal programs offered by charities.[130]

Generoso Pope funded one summer camp, Villa St. Joseph, in the "green, woody mountains" of New Jersey. Every summer, groups of Italian-American children left their "asphyxiating hovels" in New York, *Il Progresso* reported, to spend fifteen days in the "oxygen and sunshine" of the countryside. Under the moral guidance of a kindly priest, Father Congedo, and the care of two matronly women, these children developed in body, spirit, and mind. *Il Progresso* presented Villa St. Joseph as a bucolic escape from the ills of modernity—the run-down tenements of New York City, and the families stretched so thin that they could not supply the education or love required for children's healthy growth.[131] Villa St. Joseph was a "Paradise," according to Generoso Pope, but it was "little Paradise" that could extend only as far as Generoso's generosity allowed.[132] Pope and other fascist sympathizers suggested that as long as the efforts to combat delinquency remained piecemeal, the United States would continue to suffer its consequences. Arguing that the fascist government had eradicated the problem by intervening systematically in the environment that shaped youth, they used Italy to suggest that the state and federal governments ought to do more in the United States.

While the fascist government's approach to youth training, summer camps, and nursery care functioned as a practical reference point in the mid- to late 1930s, it also provided opportunities for escapism. Italy, as rendered by fascist sympathizers, was not only a country that had reduced crime, it was also a country that had eliminated organized and systematic crime entirely.[133] Images published in *Il Progresso* reinforced a sense of a miracle at work, in a land of perpetual sunshine. In the Foro Mussolini, in the summer of 1935, thousands of white-shirted young men stood in preternaturally tidy lines.[134] In the middle of the Borghese gardens, in the summer of 1936, perfectly choreographed athletes, dressed in white, auditioned for a place in the Berlin Olympics.[135] At an exhibition on child welfare, in summer of 1937, a carousel in motion carried toddlers in white clothes on miniature mules, as *Il Duce* padded gently by.[136] There was a beauty to these images, but it was a very particular kind of beauty. Photographs are always still, and they are always silent, but these photographs *felt* still and *felt* silent, almost uncannily so.

By reproducing these images, fascist sympathizers aided the regime in its efforts to minimize the bellicose spirit of fascist youth policies. The regime was concerned that Americans would (correctly) interpret fascist youth activities as militaristic in intent and oppressive in spirit. For instance, in September 1937, Luigi Villari, a fascist propagandist familiar with the United States, wrote to the Ministry of Propaganda. He cautioned that some Americans were under the misapprehension that Italian children were "taken from their families at the most tender of ages and closed in institutions to be trained in arms." The Ministry of Propaganda needed to soften the image of its youth programs for an American audience, Villari maintained.[137] McCormick, Schneider, and Pope's newspapers all helped the Ministry of Propaganda in this regard, arguing that the regime did not infringe on the private relationship between parents and their children.[138] McCormick's formulation was typical: parental consent was required before a child could join the fascist youth; the state did not "detach" children from their families, she reassured the readers of *Ladies' Home Journal*.[139]

More generally, these observers emphasized the natural settings and maternal spirit of fascist youth programs to suggest their innocent purposes. These features were especially prominent in their descriptions of camps designed for Italian boys living abroad. In the summer of 1934, *Il Progresso Italo-Americano* published a photograph of one such camp at the "Alpine summer resort" of Cortina. The image was horizontal and wide—as wide as a full page of the newspaper—conveying a sense of openness and space. The figures—more than a hundred boys and a dozen or so grown men—took up only the bottom third of the photo. The loose formation of the assembled group carried little suggestion of regimentation. The boys convened in clusters, snaking around a valley floor in a pattern that echoed the curves of the hills behind them. They were gentle, rolling hills—hills that welcomed, without imposing a shadow on the sun-filled valley below.[140] Angelo Flavio Guidi argued that for the foreign boys who attended the fascist camps, Italy was "Mamma twice over": Mother Nature of "power and beauty"; and Mother nurture of "plenty and grace."[141] According to these formulations, fascist training programs were as healthy as the Alpine air, and as innocuous as a mother's embrace.

Regime propagandists were at pains to characterize government-run camps in Italy as harmless, natural, and nurturing to distinguish them from their Nazi equivalent.[142] In this respect, too, American sympathizers echoed the regime's goals. In contrast to healthy and fully realized young Italians, McCormick described young Nazis as physically and spiritually "undernourished" by a state that propounded unnatural theories of racial hatred and throttled synagogues and churches. She implied that German youth programs were unfit for human consumption; even the brown shirts of young Nazis suggested something indigestible, like an acerbically "strong mustard" or a rancid, "green beer."[143] McCormick argued that while the National Socialist regime superimposed unnatural organizations onto German youth, the Italian state supplied institutions that met young Italians' physical and spiritual needs.[144] "Youth in movement," was "the most formidable sight in Italy—not the heavy arterial excitement, the racial passion, of Germany, but a flourish of young life," she wrote in the spring of 1934.[145] Like the regime itself, she wanted to send the reassuring message that fascism, unlike Nazism, was not bellicose in nature or intent.[146]

In short, sympathetic American observers fashioned the fascist approach to youth as a kind of gardening project, nurturing children as they grew. Italians' actual experience with these programs differed from sympathetic portraits in many respects. The conditions at fascist summer camps were far from idyllic; even the *balilla*'s own inspectors frequently found them to be "marginal."[147] Although Anne O'Hare McCormick argued that participation in fascist youth groups had made young Italians more Catholic, there is little evidence to suggest that this was the case. It was certainly not the intention of the regime, which aimed to displace the church as young people's principal source of authority.[148] Fascist youth programs did not tread lightly around families' private spheres, as fascist sympathizers argued. Although membership in the *balilla* was officially voluntary until 1939, parents faced economic incentives to enroll their children, and risked censure if they did not.[149] Parents signed their children up for fascist youth activities, just as mothers availed themselves of the services of day nurseries, for a number of pragmatic reasons—of which free healthcare and food were the most obvious. But this does not mean that they loved their state, or approved of its broader childrearing objectives.

When we consider what fascism's broader childrearing objectives were, it is easy to imagine that many Italians resented the state's approach. The state did not design its nurseries around the emotional and practical needs of working women, whose contribution to their families' economic survival it only grudgingly recognized.[150] Rather, nurseries were another expression of fascism's ambition to produce a generation large enough, and strong enough, to fight and win a war. Historians have pointed out that the state was not particularly effective in indoctrinating young Italians, many of whom participated in premilitary training without absorbing premilitary mentalities.[151] But preparation and indoctrination for war was certainly the regime's goal. As noted by the historian Richard Bosworth, at fascist camps, "sports and other leisure activities were meant always to have a militant, pugnacious and xenophobic purpose."[152] Perhaps the fascist state did not achieve similar levels of discipline and obedience in youth as the National Socialist state. But this was due less to lack of intention and more to a failure to execute policies effectively. If the state modeled itself on any woman at all, this woman was neither Mother Nature, nor mother nurture, but Bellona, the Roman goddess of war. And if the valley of youth had any color, it was not green but gunmetal gray.

Escape to Abyssinia

Just as they did for Rome and youth training programs, McCormick and Pope used gardening metaphors to reconfigure the fascist invasion of Ethiopia as a thing of beauty, transcendence, and peace. In October 1935, after months of Italian incursions along Ethiopia's border with Somalia, Italy launched a full-scale invasion of Ethiopia. Within days, the League of Nations voted for the imposition of sanctions against Italy. As a *Times* reporter noted, the Geneva vote demonstrated that "[f]ifty-one governments representing four-fifths of mankind," considered Italy's invasion of Ethiopia illegal (only Austria and Hungary opposed sanctions; Germany abstained).[153]

Far from Geneva, the United States invoked neutrality legislation, which blocked the sale of arms to either side in the war. To the administration's evident discomfort, US neutrality legislation did not prevent the shipment of oil, or other necessary war supplies, to Italy. Roosevelt and Cordell Hull encouraged oil companies to conduct a self-imposed "moral embargo."[154] American manufacturers and oil companies ignored these pleas, and by the winter of 1935, some advisers in the State Department and a few members of Congress were pushing for further formal sanctions against Italy.[155]

In the face of international opprobrium, fascist sympathizers used metaphors of the garden to legitimize Italy's invasion of Ethiopia. Employing arguments that were familiar to all imperial powers, both McCormick and contributors to *Il Progresso Italo-Americano* presented Ethiopia as untamed territory. McCormick, who had never set foot in Africa, described Ethiopia as neglected land in a "dark but almost empty continent."[156] *Il Progresso* consistently presented Ethiopia's sophisticated, adaptable, and diverse agricultural systems as primitive, careless, and fatalistic. Incorrectly, contributors to the newspaper claimed that Ethiopians had not controlled their forests, drained their swamps, irrigated their lands, or bred and fed their herds to produce higher yields of milk, meat, and hide.[157] The Ethiopians, wrote one contributor, were unable to "bend nature"; "chance" was their "only cultivator."[158]

Sympathizers of the regime's invasion suggested that Ethiopia was untamed, too, in a figurative sense: a land where disfiguring diseases—leprosy, syphilis, and elephantiasis—spread unchecked; and a place where the government had made no effort to eradicate "barbaric" customs.[159] According to Generoso Pope, Ethiopia remained shut off from "any civilizing influence, under the most retrograde feudal system, exposed to the horrors of slavery and even cannibalism."[160] Pope's claim of cannibalism merged with feature stories and photographs in his newspaper, which recounted legends of an Abyssinian queen who bathed in human blood, and a light-skinned "beautiful dancing slave" who escaped to Italy.[161] It was all fiction. And it all served to form a portrait of Ethiopia as wild, decadent, going to seed. Some observers even likened Ethiopian society to the most avant-garde expressions of modernism. In their minds, both lacked order.[162] In their minds, both accepted ugliness, disease, and discordance in their midst.[163] According to these interpretations, there was too much freedom in Ethiopia—"secular abandon" as the Italian secretary for press and propaganda, Dino Alfieri, termed it—just as there was too much freedom in modernists' visions of unrestrained art and an open society.[164] Ethiopia, as portrayed by fascist sympathizers, was a country in which lepers lived among the healthy, a country where the diseased, the lame, the blind, and the disabled were allowed to approach kings.[165] It was a country where nothing seemed cleaned, contained, or controlled.

Into the Ethiopian wilderness stepped Italy, as a cultivator, healer, and civilizer, according to fascist sympathizers. The idea of imperialism as the taming of wild land—a literal and figurative gardening project—was, of course, not unique to fascist Italy.[166] And, by using this idea, American observers facilitated Italy's claim to equivalency with (and demands for noninterference by) other great powers.[167] Prior to the invasion, McCormick met with Mussolini. Claiming that roaming Ethiopian bands threatened Italian Somalia and Eritrea, he asserted that Italy had a right to protect its colonies against "savage attack," adding that this was "a point that Americans, remembering their own history, should understand."[168] A January 1936 cartoon in *Il Progresso* featured Christopher Columbus and a Native American standing on a shoreline. "What have I come here for? To discover America," said Columbus. "But did you receive permission from the League of Nations?" asked the Native American. This cartoon implied that it was absurd for Americans to sanction Italy for taming savages in Ethiopia, when Americans celebrated Columbus and the settlers for doing the same thing in the United States.[169]

Fascist sympathizers provided ample examples of the ways in which Italy, following in the footsteps of other imperial powers (beginning with Rome), conquered the wild. Italy's goal was to turn Ethiopia's arid spaces into "productive fields, in perpetual fertility," wrote Generoso Pope as the invasion began.[170] Following the cues of regime propaganda, sympathetic observers stressed the importance of roadbuilding both to the war effort and to Italy's colonization plans.[171] Roads would be followed by dams, irrigation systems, land reclamation, labor-saving farm machines, and scientific breeding, wrote one journalist in *Il Progresso*.[172] In contrast to Ethiopians' primitive and fatalistic approach to their surrounds, the Italians would care for the conquered territory, demonstrating man's capacity to mine nature for all that it was worth.

Fascist sympathizers applied the idea of taming the wilderness in Ethiopia in a metaphorical sense too. They repeatedly claimed that the Italians were improving the health of Ethiopians.[173] Whereas the previous rulers of Ethiopia had fatalistically accepted the illnesses in their midst, the Italians were quarantining, vaccinating, and curing so as to gain control of the environment.[174] A garden, after all, was not a place where things survived or died according to the whims of nature. Rather, it was a place where man tended to life, to ensure that it thrived.

This same kind of intentionality was evident in fascist plans for Ethiopia's cities. In the fall of 1936, *Il Progresso* published plans for the transformation of Addis Ababa from a "Native Hut Village" into a "Roman City" of wide boulevards and neoclassical monuments. At the root of the idea of city planning was a philosophical opposition to the purportedly lax attitude of Ethiopians to fate, *Il Progresso* implied. The newspaper claimed that the atmosphere of the capital transformed upon the Italians' arrival: there was no more loitering or ambling in Addis, because everyone had a place to be and a sense of something to strive for.[175] Dino Alfieri, the secretary for press and propaganda, described this phenomenon as one of "arranged fate"—the fascists took control of processes that Ethiopians had abandoned to nature, to chance, and to time.[176]

These observers consciously employed ideas that were familiar to all imperial powers, insisting that, by gaining control of a neglected environment, the Italians had earned the right to settle in Ethiopia; the United States, they suggested, should not interfere in the war. They further bolstered the case for American noninterference by employing an equally familiar argument that colonies would relieve the metropole of pressing constraints of land and raw materials. McCormick, Pope, and Schneider all insisted on the (perfectly true) notion that Italy was a narrow peninsula, scarce in natural resources, and teeming with people.[177] They insisted, too, on the (far more fanciful) idea that

Ethiopia would release Italy from these biding constraints. Herbert Schneider wrote that Ethiopia would provide Italy with outlets for labor, supplies of cotton, and perhaps even oil and gold.[178] McCormick predicted that the colony would provide permanent settlement for between two and three million Italians.[179] *Il Progresso*'s estimations of the settlement opportunities in Ethiopia were more fantastic still: the country, claimed one contributor, could easily be home to thirty million Italians.[180] In Glaucus's words, the Ethiopian conquest would ensure that the Italians would never again "be strays of the world, in search of bread and work."[181]

The notion that Ethiopia would relieve Italy of the constraints forced upon it by nature had a bearing on the fate of all of Europe and the United States, fascist sympathizers claimed. McCormick first floated the idea that a war in Ethiopia would be conducive to peace in Europe in the spring of 1935. Following a meeting with Mussolini in May, she sent him an "unfinished" draft of an article, assuring him that she welcomed his "corrections" and "amplifications." In this draft, she quoted *Il Duce*: "Our African colonies must form the background of Italy. They must become increasingly important to us if we are to work for the general peace by relieving the intolerable pressure in Europe." In response to this draft, Mussolini (or his press office) seems to have corrected McCormick not at all, and amplified her quite a bit. Her final article differed from the draft in only one respect: she emphasized Mussolini's earnest desire for peace. "That is one thing we want—peace in Europe," she added to the quotation. It was the most memorable sentence in the piece, although it seems unlikely that Mussolini ever uttered it to his interviewer.[182]

The regime, and its sympathetic observers, believed that the notion that war in Ethiopia would preserve peace in Europe could sway American policymakers' responses to Italian aggression. They insisted upon this argument, through 1935 and 1936. A month after her spring interview with Mussolini, McCormick repeated the idea that Italian expansion in Africa was a feasible (and preferable) alternative to an intra-European conflict over living space and raw materials.[183] That winter, as Secretary of State Cordell Hull explored the possibility of expanding the American embargo to encompass oil, McCormick argued that, by blocking Italian action in Ethiopia, such actions would increase the likelihood of a European war.[184] Concurrently, Generoso Pope launched an unremitting editorial campaign against any changes to American neutrality laws, and encouraged Italian Americans to write to their congressmen, reminding them that 1936 was an election year. "Neutrality Means Peace," insisted Pope.[185]

Arguments like this shifted the onus for peace-inducing behavior away from the fascist regime and onto American policymakers to accept the Italian conquest of Ethiopia as a price for peace elsewhere. This, of course, was the logic of appeasement—an idea that appealed to many Americans, and not just those who actively sympathized with fascism, in the mid-1930s. At the end of January 1936, Generoso Pope went to Washington to meet with President Roosevelt and Secretary of State Hull. There, Pope received the message he wanted to hear: the United States would continue to allow Italy to buy the oil and other supplies necessary to prosecute its Ethiopian war.[186] Pope did not singlehandedly sway American policy, although the protests of the Italian-American community against changes to neutrality legislation certainly gave a Democratic administration pause for thought.[187] Rather, Pope and McCormick's vision for American foreign policy coincided with the administration's in 1935 and 1936. As Herbert Schneider recognized, the United States' primary concern in the mid-1930s was to "safeguard its own peace," and the most obvious way to do that was by preventing a war in Europe.[188] This meant granting Mussolini his empire in Ethiopia so that the rest of the world could remain a garden of sorts—albeit a compromised, fragile, and sullied Eden.

While McCormick and Pope aimed to contain the American embargo, they continued to protest the League of Nations' sanctions. Not for the last time in history, sympathetic observers used sanctions to claim that the aggressor was the injured party, by portraying Italy as a country with few natural resources of its own, oppressed by a punishing international regime. "Italy Squeezed," read one of McCormick's headlines.[189] Both she and Pope argued that the Italian people banded together to overcome the constraints imposed by sanctions. McCormick watched women forming queues outside the fascist headquarters in Rome in December 1935 to donate their wedding rings to the war effort. She likened these women to Cornelia, mother of the Gracchi—an archetype of feminine beauty, who saw her sons, not her jewels, as her only treasures.[190] Sacrifice, these observers suggested, brought men and women to a purer state. *Il Progresso* quoted the futurist poet Benedetta Cappa. Upon giving, Italian women realized that true beauty was found not in their worldly possessions, but in nature. Benedetta wrote: "We have the blue of the sea, the roses from our gardens. . . . And on our hair the sunshine."[191] They needed nothing more.

Generoso Pope garnered Italian Americans' financial support for the war by arguing that they could help Italy to overcome the constraints imposed by external forces and participate in something greater than their daily travails. *Il Progresso* responded to the League's sanctions with a highly effective fundraising campaign.[192] On the same day that the sanctions went into effect, November 17, 1935, the newspaper submitted a one-hundred-thousand-dollar check to the Italian Red Cross.[193] There would be seven such checks over the course of the next year.[194]

In addition to calling on Italian Americans to donate their dollars, the newspaper encouraged them to engage in symbolic acts of sacrifice. The newspaper published the names of individuals who had given gold to Italy: men like Edoardo Lettieri, who gave two rings and one tooth; women like Elvira Foglia, who gave her wedding ring and a pendant on a long chain.[195] *Il Progresso*'s fundraising campaign suggested that Italian Americans could experience transcendence twice over: by giving their money, they could help Italy break through the economic barriers imposed upon it by the League of Nations; by giving their treasured possessions, they could feel the spiritually elevating effects of sacrifice. Pope's efforts pleased the regime, which bestowed upon him another knighthood when he visited Rome in June 1937.[196]

Fascist sympathizers suggested that feelings of spiritual edification on the home front were matched by scenes of transcendence on the front lines. Glaucus found beauty in the most war-like of places. As the Italians rained bombs down on civilians in Ethiopia, Glaucus homed in on Mussolini's sons, Bruno and Vittorio, and son-in-law, Galeazzo Ciano, as the beautiful heroes of the Italian campaign. When the engines of Bruno's, Vittorio's, and Galeazzo's airplanes blasted through the sky, they "left an echo in the hearts of the people of Asmara," wrote Glaucus. And as the young men flew overhead, the Asmarans lifted "their vision . . . high, high, high."[197] Easter Sunday, 1936, provided *Il Progresso*'s editors with the opportunity to make a pairing in the newspaper's illustrated section that seemed far from accidental. A reproduction of a painting of Christ, triumphant and resplendent in light, *Surrexit Sicut Dixit* ("Risen Again, as He Said"), appeared alongside a photograph of Italian airplanes after battle, flying in nearly perfect formation, the sky flooded with light.[198] Together, these images suggested that any suffering was eclipsed by a state of grace.

In sum, fascist sympathizers employed various gardening metaphors when they described Italy's invasion of Ethiopia. The Italians were cultivators in Ethiopia, and peacemakers in Europe, according to fascist sympathizers. By claiming that Italy's invasion of Ethiopia was both the legitimate act of a civilizing nation, and a necessary precursor to a broader peace, they hoped that the Roosevelt administration would maintain its policy of *de jure* neutrality (which, in practice, enabled Italy to prosecute its war). The administration's limited response to the war fulfilled fascist sympathizers' hopes, although it is unlikely that they had a tangible effect on the direction of policy: in 1935–36, the American foreign policy establishment did not need to be convinced on the logic of appeasement.

Like any good garden, the one that fascist sympathizers created in Ethiopia also functioned as a place of escape. It suggested that man could overcome external constraints and seemed to lift up all those who participated in its production—supporters on various home fronts, airmen, even their victims—toward heaven. The counterimage of this garden was a place where man was overwhelmed by forces beyond his control and unable to access God. The counterimage of this garden felt a lot like the modern world.

If gardening is partly a work of pruning and artful disguise, then these observers did a great deal of gardening too, to produce this image of an Ethiopian wilderness tamed and nurtured by Italian hands. They maligned Ethiopia as "barbaric" and "savage," sidelining sophisticated indigenous systems and rulers' successful contributions to modernization and reform.[199] They ignored the brutality of the invasion, finding beauty in the choreography of airplanes that rained bombs, some filled with poison gas, on civilians as well as soldiers, long after the hostilities came to an official end.[200] And they vastly overestimated Italy's capacities to cultivate, cure, and create in Ethiopia. The country was under formal Italian control for only five years, but they were five long years for the Ethiopians, who faced sky-rocketing inflation, the collapse of local businesses, and scarcity of basic commodities, such as wheat and other grains.[201]

Italian Abyssinia was certainly not a paradise on earth for the Ethiopians. Nor did it function as any kind of a garden for the Italians. It was never a fertile supplier of raw materials: the Italians found neither oil in Ethiopia nor sufficient gold for export; even coffee was in short supply by the decade's end.[202] It was not a place where large numbers of Italians escaped to, to lay down roots of their own: according to historians' best estimates, the total number of Italian workers across East Africa in the late 1930s never exceeded 200,000, the vast majority of whom were repatriated; only 400 or so Italian farmers settled in Ethiopia, 150 of whom were joined by their families.[203] Even plans to bring tree-lined boulevards to Addis Ababa never left the drawing board.[204]

The wishful thoughts of fascist sympathizers were an extension of the chillingly optimistic visions of the fascist regime itself. They imagined that Italy could create a productive colony, but Ethiopian resistance and Italian mismanagement ensured that the short-lived empire drained, rather than contributed to, the metropolitan economy.[205] Abyssinia was less of a garden, and more of a quagmire, for Italy.

The Overstretched Metaphor

In the mid- to late 1930s, sympathetic Americans used the metaphor of the garden to reconfigure some of the most intrusive and aggressive of fascist policies, so that they might appeal to their fellow countrymen. They presented urban planning in Rome, youth training, and the invasion of Ethiopia as wholesome and life-affirming projects. And they argued that all of these programs were compatible with, or even conducive to, forms of peace. At times, these observers used the seemingly positive examples provided by fascist Italy to urge on New Deal interventions, much as they had done in the early 1930s. But they also portrayed fascist Italy as transcending the constraints that bound Americans, offering a flight from the realities of democratic compromise, economic scarcity, and global instability.

It is worth questioning whether metaphors of the garden had their intended effect on an American audience. When they offered Italy as an escape from the realities of the United States, American fascist sympathizers were exercising other forms of escapism—from the impact of fascist interventionism, militarism, and violence on Italians and East Africans. The more grotesque the regime became, the more fascist sympathizers had to stretch the metaphor of the garden as a place of beauty and peace. When airplanes rained bombs on Ethiopian villages, Glaucus elevated the garden above ground level, into the sky where the airplanes soared. Such representations were surely an overstretch for most Americans. Indeed, while fascist sympathizers' representations of Italo Balbo's 1933 flight coincided with most Americans' interpretation of the event, support for Italy's empire in Ethiopia was strong only within the Italian-American community.[206] Perhaps we should understand the garden as fascist sympathizers' way of doing their best with bad material; there is no question that, by 1936, most of the material they had at their disposal was pretty bad.

As the decade wore on, Americans became more and more skeptical of characterizations of Italian fascism as wholesome, peaceful, and fundamentally different from National Socialism. The observations of various fascist officials that the regime must carefully calibrate its propaganda for an American audience were themselves signals that, by and large, the regime was failing in this regard. For instance, Ambassador Rosso lamented that American newspapers published preponderantly militaristic images of Italy in the mid-decade, while his successor, Fulvio Suvich, observed that most Americans associated fascism with "authoritarianism, the negation of all liberties, dictatorship, militarism, preparation for war."[207]

In the meantime, the activities of militant American fascists undermined any efforts to soften the image of Mussolini's regime. In July 1937, blackshirted Italian Americans marched alongside brown-shirted German Americans at the opening ceremonies of Camp Nordland, a New Jersey summer camp, organized by the German American Bund.[208] And later that summer, at a twelve-thousand-person rally at Camp Nordland, Donald Shea—a man who described himself as "founder of the National Gentile League, Inc." (and whose black cap was decorated with the words "American Fascist")—called for "a boycott against all Jewish merchants," to cheers of "Viva Mussolini!" and "Heil Hilter!"[209] While McCormick, Pope, and Schneider presented Italian summer camps as Alpine health resorts and insisted on the difference between fascism and Nazism, the likes of Donald Shea created a very different impression.

It became harder and harder for Schneider, McCormick, and Pope to configure fascism as a garden. Herbert Schneider's 1936 book would be his final publication about fascism. In keeping with the intentions of the Carnegie Endowment, there was little in this assessment that could have offended Schneider's Italian hosts. Schneider maintained his characterization of fascist Italy as well-established and well-tended: institutions of the corporate state were fully operational, and the government was manned by competent executives, he insisted.[210] Schneider's Italy was a relatively gentle place: he cautioned the "inexperienced reader" against interpreting the notion of a totalitarian state literally; in Italy, just as in the United States, government actions had an "incidental, occasional, possibly crucial, but never all-inclusive" impact on private citizens, he argued.[211] Writing during Italy's invasion of Ethiopia, Schneider could hardly ignore fascist imperialism. But he did ignore fascist militarism: he dispensed of the Blackshirts in a single paragraph, mentioned the army and navy only in passing, and the air force not once.[212]

This book—titled *The Fascist Government of Italy*, and targeted at American college students—received none of the acclaim that had accompanied Schneider's earlier research on fascism. It prompted one bland review, in the *American Political Science Review*, and a stunning rebuke, in *Public Opinion Quarterly*.[213] Herman Finer, a professor at the London School of Economics, took Schneider's work to pieces. Schneider had not revealed the mechanisms that prompted "even the brave to be silent" in Italy, noted Finer. Nor had he encapsulated the essence of authoritarian government, which was not to be found in its various formal institutions, but in what it "does to your soul."[214] Finer's review was the sort that could leave a self-respecting academic cringing for decades. Perhaps it had this effect on Herbert Schneider, since he never wrote about fascist Italy again.

At the end of January 1937, Anne O'Hare McCormick penned her last article that would garner the blessing of Mussolini's regime. The piece had many of the hallmarks of the fascist garden. McCormick had met with Mussolini earlier in the month.[215] "Fresh from skiing in the mountains near Rome," he looked "bronzed and hard," she informed her readers. The accompanying photograph of a bare-chested Mussolini in the Alpine snow probably struck many *Times* readers as absurd. But it must have pleased the regime, since it showed Mussolini battling nature and winning—"Il Duce defies weather," read the accompanying caption (figure 5.2). Mussolini, a man of nature, was also Mussolini, a man of peace, according to McCormick's construction. At the height of Italy's intervention in the Spanish Civil War, she described *Il Duce* as anxious to end the conflict, so as to prolong peace in Europe. McCormick saw nothing in the recently announced Rome-Berlin axis that made this outcome less likely. Mussolini, she observed, thought of the axis as a "bridge" that would enable communication across the continent. According to McCormick, *Il Duce* showed a "lively" interest in President Roosevelt's tentative idea of a conference of great powers to promote peace. Roosevelt and Mussolini, she suggested, had more in common than Hitler and Mussolini.[216] McCormick sent Mussolini a draft of this article on January 27, 1937. "[A]*utorizzazione a pubblicare*" ("authorized for publication") read a hand-written note on McCormick's cover letter.[217] Those words would not appear on her writing again. Although McCormick continued to hope for the best in fascist foreign policy, after the winter of 1937, she no longer defended it in terms that were acceptable to the upper echelons of the regime.

While McCormick gradually separated herself from the fascist regime after January 1937, Generoso Pope helped to maintain the garden of fascism for a while longer. Pope and his editors obfuscated Italy's involvement in the Spanish Civil War. Italy did not furnish any aid to the Spanish rebels, lied the newspaper's editors.[218] Even as the regime sent airplanes, munitions, and men to Franco, Glaucus implied that the fascist government's only contribution to the rebel side was as an exemplar. According to this construction, in Spain, as in Italy prior to fascism, the government had neglected to reform and modernize the country; and in Spain, as in Italy prior to fascism, the Bolsheviks threatened to raze history, tradition, and religion to the ground. Fascist Rome provided Spain with a shining example of a "new system of government" that was both updated for modernity and respectful of religion and history, according to Glaucus.[219] He suggested that Mussolini's only role in Spain was as a distant

FIGURE 5.2. Mussolini Conquers Nature. This photograph, taken in January 1930, appeared in the *New York Times* on February 2, 1937. Courtesy of ullstein bild Dtl. via Getty Images.

teacher, who could show his apprentice how to create a "new civilization."[220] Only brazen lies about Italy's actions in Spain enabled *Il Progresso* to continue to characterize Italy as a force for peace.

Meanwhile, events at a May 1937 rally for Spanish relief, in Madison Square Garden, set alarm bells ringing for Generoso Pope. Almost every one of the fifteen thousand Americans who attended the gathering was sympathetic to the rebels in Spain. But, as Pope noted, several speakers used the platform not only to call for help for Spanish noncombatants but also to condemn religious discrimination in Nazi Germany, and to "bind Nazi and fascist politics together in a single bundle" ("un sol fascio"). That more than one orator could suggest before a crowd of socially conservative Catholics that Germany and Italy were converging did not bode well for Generoso Pope. It clearly worried him a great deal. Pope had spent the best part of a decade arguing that Italian Americans' support for fascist Italy was perfectly compatible with their identity as loyal Americans; the speakers at the May rally challenged this argument more effectively than left-wing antifascists could ever have done. Pope responded head on. It was time to end the "unfair and foolish confusion" between Italy and Germany, he wrote. Italian fascism was "against any kind of racial discrimination." Pope cited the 1929 reconciliation between church and state and the legal equality of Jews in Italy as concrete evidence that Nazism and fascism were not alike in spirit or intent.[221] In May 1937, he must have been hoping that this would always remain that case. But gardens do not survive on hope alone.

CONCLUSION

Searching for Soul under the Sign of the Machine

FOR MOST OF THE INTERWAR years, Richard Washburn Child, Anne O'Hare McCormick, Generoso Pope, and Herbert Schneider sympathized with Italian fascism. These four prominent and influential Americans had little in common in their backgrounds. They had various political affiliations. They moved in different circles. But they were drawn to fascism for many of the same reasons. All of them believed that Italy was coping better with the challenges of modernity than the United States.

Child, McCormick, Pope, and Schneider expressed concerns that preoccupied many of their contemporaries. "Modern man lives under the sign of the Machine," wrote Matthew Josephson, an American intellectual who had sequestered himself in Paris in the 1920s. Capitalized, the Machine had replaced the Bible. It had replaced God. By Josephson's estimation, Americans in particular suffered under its sign. There was no other country in the world where people's daily lives were so sped up, so synchronized, and so automated. The Machine affected not just patterns of work and leisure, community, and family life, but the human spirit, the human soul. Men had "the natural illusion of facing the Machine alone."[1] Perhaps it was the aloneness that stung the most.

For its many critics, modernity had its own momentum. There was no escape. The writer Joseph Krutch described his fellow Americans as victims of their own progress, unable to retreat. Illuminated by science, they could not return to the comforts of religion. Educated by Freud, they could not find solace in romantic love.[2] Americans seemed trapped by progress in other ways, too. There was a feeling of inevitability in the onward march of chain stores, mass production, and canned music, movies, and food. "You can't give a synthetic egg individuality or expect the chick to have a soul," quipped the sculptor, Gutzon Borglum, in 1929. The artificial egg would produce an artificial chicken. And on, and on, it would go.[3]

By understanding the United States as their contemporaries understood it—as a nation living "under the sign of the Machine," unable to turn back—we can appreciate the appeal of fascism as a machine with a soul. The idea of a machine with a soul feels incongruous to us now, since it combines two things that normally lie far apart. A machine is a tangible, noisy, and man-made thing. A soul is ethereal, silent, and beyond human comprehension. The idea of a machine with a soul would have felt equally, if not more, incongruous to Americans in the interwar years, when they were exposed to frequent ruminations on the soulless aspects of their mechanized society. The incongruity of the conceit explains its appeal. Most Americans did not believe it was desirable, or even possible, to reject modernization. The machine with a soul indicated that there was no need. Mussolini's Italy, as configured by these fascist sympathizers, suggested that it was possible to have both: the energy, efficiency, and high-sheen glamour that they associated with machines; and the feelings of fulfillment, connectivity, and peace that felt so elusive in the modern age.

The Machine with a Soul through Time

For more than a dozen years, Child, McCormick, Pope, and Schneider argued that Americans could learn from and seek reassurance in fascist Italy's experience of modernity, even as they reacted to events in Italy (as mediated through regime propaganda) and changing social and cultural contexts in the United States. Child and McCormick arrived in Europe in the aftermath of the Great War to find a continent scarred by conflict. Instead of emphasizing the differences in welfare standards between the United States and Europe, each described a homogenization of the transnational experience. This was evident in the material details of daily life: the American products—from chewing gum to razor blades—that were ubiquitous in McCormick's accounts of postwar Europe.[4] These superficial markers seemed symptomatic of a deeper problem. The dominance of materiality suggested a nearly universal retreat from the values that had animated so many during the war: service, honor, and duty. Europe was gray, as the United States was gray, for McCormick and Child, because Europeans and Americans had turned against wartime ideals.

In contrast to the American writers and artists who left for Paris in the 1920s, distrustful of governments, systems, and organizations, Child and McCormick wanted to believe in something bigger than the individual.[5] Herbert Schneider, who researched Italy's postwar experience a few years after the fact, also yearned for evidence of the kind of values that characterized nations at war. In fascist youth, these observers did not see primarily a bulwark against Bolshevism. Instead, they saw disciplined and courteous members of a patriotic organization, energized with a spirit of adventure that pierced through the postwar malaise. Child, McCormick, and Schneider suggested that the *squadristi* presented traditional values in a modern form. They were young and beautiful—"sleek" and "burnished as a blooded race horse," as McCormick described one.[6] They could have been futurist sculptures, their smooth lines and shiny surfaces speeding through space and time.[7] These observers used fascist squadrism to suggest that the future could have as much meaning as the past.

Following the March on Rome, Child and McCormick interpreted Mussolini as both an efficient administrator and a spiritual force. Mussolini's capacity to manage the demands of government suggested that he could create simplicity where there had once been chaos. The chaos, these observers suggested, was not a uniquely Italian phenomenon: it was part of the modern condition. Marshall Berman's characterization of modernity as a "maelstrom" is pertinent here—contemporaries, indeed, sensed that it was such, and that the men and women who stayed abreast would eventually succumb to its thrall.[8] Mussolini, by contrast, seemed both to keep up with the demands of the modern era and to withstand its pull. Upon assuming ownership of *Il Progresso Italo-Americano* in 1928, Generoso Pope recognized the value of this portrait of Italy's leader, since it suggested that Italian Americans could bring the same qualities of technical capacity and spiritual calm to the United States.

By the decade's end, fascist propaganda presented a fully functioning corporate state, endorsed by a plebiscite in the spring of 1929. Child, McCormick, Pope, and Schneider each argued that the corporate state was a form of representative government for the modern age. The state worked under fascism because its institutions had been carefully crafted in response to contemporary challenges, they claimed. For instance, they suggested that by substituting plebiscites for parliamentary elections, fascism was based on a realistic assessment of ordinary people's capacity to engage in complicated matters of governance. And they maintained that sectoral specialists within the corporate parliament had the expertise necessary to draft legislation for the common good. Fascism, they insisted, captured Italians' imagination. This was no easy feat given the distractions of contemporary life. By their estimation, the fascist state was both adapted to popular desires for mass entertainment and attuned to something that was lacking in most ready-made productions—the spiritual hunger of the audience.

With the onslaught of the depression, these American observers shifted their attention to the fascist government's response to the crisis. They reproduced images of Mussolini as a down-to-earth leader, who could be found harvesting crops alongside the Italian people. Child, McCormick, Pope, and Schneider suggested that Mussolini's policies were an extension of his persona. Families thrived on Italy's reclaimed marshlands, according to this interpretation, where Italians felt reconnected to their land, their neighbors, and themselves. In the eyes of these observers, the fascist response to the depression typified the fascist response to modernity. Machines had a place: Mussolini reached remote villages by car; the government spread agricultural information by bus, and cleared the marshlands with mechanical dredgers. Men kept machines in their place: they used them to make humans feel more human.

Fascism was increasingly interventionist in the mid-1930s, both domestically and abroad. Urban planning in Rome, fascist youth training, and the invasion of Ethiopia were three manifestations of a more aggressive state. McCormick, Pope, and Schneider implied that these policies represented a successful effort to overcome constraints that inhered in nature. The garden had a literal manifestation in the green spaces, rolling hills, and fertile farmlands that, in fascist sympathizers' imaginations, abounded in Rome, youth camps, and occupied Abyssinia. But the garden also had a metaphorical meaning, since it suggested that, at every turn, fascism was harnessing the forces of nature to create environments that were healthy, inspiring, and life-affirming. The fascist state, as a gardening state, cleared without sanitizing, disciplined without indoctrinating, and cultivated without eradicating anything of worth.

From the earliest manifestations of squadrism until Italy's conquest of Ethiopia, Child, McCormick, Pope, and Schneider warped reality, and ignored a great deal, to construct fascism as a machine with a soul. They overlooked the brutality of the squadrists, whose practices of kidnapping, torture, and extortion persisted long after the March on Rome.[9] They neglected the aspects of Mussolini that ran counter to their portrait of him as an inner-directed man—his showmanship, insecurity, and multiple personas. They mischaracterized the corporate state, which neither functioned effectively nor inspired all Italians. It was hard for Italians to feel enthusiastic about their state when the militia accompanied them to the polls and instructed them to sing on their way.[10] And they denied the increasingly intrusive nature of fascism. As a political theory, fascism had always been heavy with machinery rather than light with spirit. But, by the mid-1930s, Italians and Ethiopians were pressed down as never before by the weight of the fascist state. How far fascism changed the customs and mentalities of Italians will always be a matter of debate. But in its efforts to do so, it maimed many bodies, and crushed many souls.

Richard Washburn Child Caught a Bad Cold

In the late 1930s, it became difficult for American fascist sympathizers to present fascism as the antidote to those modern ills that blighted the United States. The metaphor, stretched to breaking point by Italy's invasion of Ethiopia, collapsed as the regime drew closer to Nazi Germany. Americans who had expressed sympathies for fascism for more than a decade had to adapt to new realities. They faced decisions. Should they continue to support Mussolini? Should they condemn his policies and regime? Or could they turn to silence, as if to wish their past affinities away?

Only Richard Washburn Child had no decision to make. He had been nursing a very bad cold in January 1935, when he visited the White House to demand, once more, that Franklin Roosevelt give him a good job.[11] That cold turned into pneumonia. On January 30, Child requested a Catholic priest. It was time for a final conversion. The priest performed a baptism and, less than twenty-four hours later, Child died.[12] Among those who attended the funeral were Antonio Grossardi, the Italian consul general; Dorothy Everson, Child's fourth wife; and Anne and Constance, Child's two daughters from his marriage to Maude Parker, who, as young girls in 1922, had dressed up as *fascisti* and sung marching songs.[13]

Italian fascism outlived Richard Washburn Child. Herbert Schneider, by contrast, outlived the fascist state by four decades. In the late 1920s and mid-1930s, Schneider had investigated fascist Italy with the financial and institutional support of major institutions—the Social Science Research Council and the Carnegie Endowment. The investment of these organizations in his research was indicative of a broader interest among political and social scientists in Mussolini's regime, which appeared to offer credible alternatives to the institutions of liberal democracy, as well as a far more active approach to youth training and "civic education" than the American state.[14] In the late 1930s, that broader academic interest in fascism fell away. Schneider had no institutional support to continue to research fascist Italy, and no apparent desire to do so independently.

The Turning Axis, 1937

Generoso Pope and Anne O'Hare McCormick continued to write about fascist Italy in the late 1930s. Both argued that the axis alliance did not represent a threat to global security in 1937, but their arguments rested on increasingly shaky ground. In January of that year, Herman Goering, the Nazi minister of aviation, met with Benito Mussolini and Galeazzo Ciano in Rome. Reports in a number of American newspapers emphasized the significance of Goering's visit: the Germans and Italians discussed wide-ranging plans to ensure General Franco's victory; and Goering predicted an inevitable confrontation between fascism and communism in Europe.[15] *Il Progresso*, by contrast, understated the importance of the meeting. During Goering's stay in Italy, Generoso Pope wrote two messages to his readers on American domestic policy, and uttered not a word on Italian foreign policy.[16] On the inside pages of the newspaper, Pope's editors did some talking for him, arguing that as Germany drew closer to Italy, the axis tended toward peace, while also emphasizing the differences between Nazi and fascist policies regarding Judaism and Catholicism.[17] *Il Progresso* even tried to trivialize Goering's visit with a story of a fencing match between Goering and Mussolini, which Mussolini, apparently, won.[18] Writing from Rome for the *New York Times*, McCormick, too, down-played the significance of the meeting: the Italians gave Goering an "almost conspicuously official" welcome; behind the veneer of a united front, the two powers had nothing in common, she maintained. She saw little in Goering's visit to suggest that the axis was even a formal alliance, still less "an alliance for war."[19]

Over the rest of 1937, it became increasingly difficult for Anne O'Hare McCormick simultaneously to defend Italy and remain credible to her readers. She managed to do this, after a fashion, but not in terms that pleased the regime. McCormick argued that Mussolini and the Italian people were pulling in opposing directions. She observed, quite correctly, that neither the Italian intervention in Spain nor the alliance with Germany was popular in Italy. But she used these observations to imply that Mussolini would not persist with unpopular policies.[20] Here, she was wrong.

In September 1937, Mussolini met with Hitler in Munich. Hitler announced that the private meeting of two fascist dictators spoke "for itself" as an expression of their ever tighter bonds.[21] McCormick tried to pierce this claim by reverting to old formulations of Mussolini and Hitler as pragmatist and prophet—opposite in "tastes, temperament, appearance, manner, mentality, habits, methods, range of interests." In her eagerness to separate fascism from Nazism, McCormick claimed that, as late as 1936, Mussolini had agreed that "the worst thing that ever happened to fascism was Hitler" (an opinion she had not recorded at the time).[22] McCormick aimed to characterize Italian policy as changeable and, quite possibly, changing. As the "supreme opportunist among the wind-blown weathercocks" of Europe, Mussolini could soon turn his back on Germany, she implied.[23]

There was plenty in this coverage that could, and did, anger senior members of the Italian government, including the claim that Italians *en masse* opposed fascist foreign policies, and the notion that Mussolini was vacillating and two-faced in his attitude toward Germany. McCormick tried to justify her critical coverage, so as to remain in the regime's good favor. Visiting Rome in November 1937, she stopped in first at the Ministry of Press and Propaganda, to request a meeting with Mussolini. There, an official pointed out that she had not expressed her usual "sympathies" for fascist Italy in her recent journalism. McCormick defended herself, arguing that, in the United States, "friends of fascism" had "sometimes to be critical so as to avoid being labelled propagandists."[24] But the regime rebuffed McCormick's requests for interviews with Mussolini or, as a second best, his son-in-law and the foreign minister, Galeazzo Ciano.[25]

Perhaps more revealing than the regime's snub was the discussion that McCormick's requests prompted between various members of the Italian government. From Washington, DC, Ambassador Fulvio Suvich advised the Ministry of Press and Propaganda that McCormick ought to be granted a meeting with Mussolini: her journalism was influential, Suvich noted, and she could help the regime to present its alliance with Germany in a favorable light.[26] In Rome, Guido Rocco, the head of the Directorate General of Foreign Press, wrote to Ciano in support of McCormick: she was "undoubtedly sincere in her friendship and admiration" for the regime, he argued.[27] Suvich's and Rocco's interventions show that some members of government wanted to maintain an open approach toward the United States, and perhaps even hoped that McCormick's perspective on the "debatable points" of Italian policy could convince Mussolini that Italy's future was not intertwined with Nazi Germany.[28]

Whatever hopes Suvich and Rocco had were in vain. Their superiors in government would not give McCormick any more access.[29]

While Anne O'Hare McCormick employed the tried-and-tested characterization of Mussolini and Hitler as the odd couple, destined for divorce, to diffuse the threatening nature of their September meeting, Generoso Pope reverted to another customary formula of Mussolini as a force for peace. Both Pope and *Il Progresso*'s director, Italo Carlo Falbo, presented the Munich meeting as proof of Italy's unprecedented influence in Europe, which Mussolini could then leverage to promote a continent-wide peace.[30] Although such claims seem absurd in hindsight, in the fall of 1937 they were plausible enough to appeal to wishful thinkers everywhere. While Germany and Italy strengthened their alliance, the fascist government pursued a simultaneous rapprochement with Britain, prompting some observers (including William Phillips, the American ambassador in Rome) to hope that Mussolini might be in the process of reviving the lapsed Four Power Pact between Great Britain, Italy, Germany, and France.[31]

But the notion that Mussolini could moderate Hitler, and use the axis alliance to promote peace, was losing credibility. President Roosevelt, for one, had become more skeptical of such optimistic interpretations of Italian policy. FDR's "quarantine speech" in Chicago, on October 5, 1937, signaled a shift in the president's attitude. Without naming Germany, Italy, or Japan, Roosevelt made bedfellows of them all, suggesting that superficial differences between the dictators, and equally superficial lip-service to peace, counted for less than their flouting of international boundaries and international law.[32] In the fall of 1937, McCormick and Pope could continue to excuse Mussolini without running too far afoul of mainstream public opinion: as evidenced by negative responses to Roosevelt's "quarantine" speech, many Americans still resisted the idea that the axis tilted the world toward war.[33] But their defense of Mussolini felt more tenuous by the day.

Responses to Fascist Antisemitism

While Pope and McCormick continued to misread and misrepresent the significance of Mussolini and Hitler's relationship, one manifestation of the regimes' strengthening rapport was deeply troubling to both of these observers. In the spring of 1937, the fascist regime sent the first of many signals of pending policy changes with regard to race and religion. On May 25, Mussolini's Milan newspaper, *Il Popolo d'Italia*, published an editorial stating that Italy's Jews should not criticize Hitler's racial policies. The story made it on to the front page of every major American newspaper the following day: Americans were watching Mussolini's attitude toward Jewish Italians closely, both for what it meant for Italy's Jews, and for what it implied about the axis alliance.[34]

The headlines of May 26 were the kind that Pope dreaded, since they challenged his frequent claim that Italy and Germany were unalike in their approaches to religion and race.[35] The next month, Pope went to Italy for a post-Ethiopian war tour: he expected, and received, a hero's welcome for his fundraising efforts on Italy's behalf.[36] Pope probably wished that his June 10 meeting with Mussolini needed to consist only of *pro forma* expressions of mutual admiration, but Pope had a serious issue to which to attend.[37] He wanted Mussolini to make a declaration that would reassure Americans about the status of Italy's Jews.

In late June, Pope returned to the United States on board the SS *Rex*. As soon as the *Rex* docked in New York, he spoke to the *New York Times*. In a scene that reads now like a minor foreshadowing of Neville Chamberlain, standing on the tarmac, waving a flimsy piece of paper in his hand, Pope informed the *Times* that Mussolini had assured him that Italian Jews would be "treated just like all other Italians."[38] A fuller enunciation followed in both *Il Progresso Italo-Americano* and *Il Corriere d'America*. Mussolini had authorized Pope to tell all Americans that "the Jews in Italy have received, receive, and will continue to receive the same treatment accorded to every other Italian citizen," the publisher reported. The statement allowed Pope to continue to defend fascist Italy in the United States, since he could claim that the head of the government had provided him personally with an assurance of Italian religious freedoms. More than ever before, Pope vested his own credibility into the claim that there would "never be persecution of race or religion" in Italy.[39]

Changes in Italian policy and law belied Pope's statements. In mid-July 1938, a government-sponsored report asserted that Jews and Africans living under Italian rule did not "belong to the Italian race."[40] Rather than disavowing the regime, Pope tried to deny reality. While the headline in the African-American *Chicago Defender* read, "Italy Plans Racial Terror à la Nazi," the headline in *Il Progresso* read, "Italy Will Not Alter Its Policies toward the Jews."[41] There could be "no talk of persecution" of the Jewish people of Italy, Pope wrote in August, reminding his readers of the promise that Mussolini had given him the previous year.[42] Only four days after Pope's message to his readers, on September 1, 1938, the fascist government announced that all Jews who had entered Italy since 1919 had six months to leave the country. The next day, it banned Jewish students and teachers from any legally recognized school or university. While most American papers reported the news objectively, *Il Progresso* did its best to bury it under innocuous titles. "Italy Exiles Jews," headlined the *New York Times*; "New Measures Adopted Yesterday," headlined *Il Progresso*.[43] "Schools of Italy to Keep Out Jews," headlined the *Times*; "New Measures of the Council of Ministers," headlined *Il Progresso*.[44]

In the meantime, the tensions induced by Italian racial laws played out in New York City.[45] While the majority of Italian Americans tried to distance themselves from fascist antisemitism, a minority felt emboldened by the news from Italy to express racial animosity: *Il Grido della Stirpe* (*The Cry of the Bloodline*)—a newspaper that had always been far to the right of *Il Progresso*—expressed open antisemitism, and some Italian Americans joined Father Coughlin's Christian Front.[46] Jewish Americans expressed their concerns by boycotting the services and products of Italian Americans.[47] These local tensions prompted Pope to publish an editorial on September 11, 1938. Instead of condemning the regime's policies toward the Jews, Pope argued that Italian and Jewish Americans must rise above "the turmoil of Europe" and embody the values of the "American melting pot." Pope's motives were transparent. He expressed concern that American Jewish organizations would press for an embargo on Italian imports, which would inevitably impinge further on Italian-American businesses and service providers.[48] As always, Pope wanted to ensure that his identity as a proud Italian did not hinder his progress in the United States.[49]

The Italian Embassy in Washington, DC, considered Pope's September 11 editorial significant, and sent it on to the Ministries of Foreign Affairs and Popular Culture. The embassy's chargé d'affaires, Giuseppe Cosmelli, interpreted Pope's editorial for his colleagues in Rome.[50] Cosmelli observed that Pope had "found himself in a quite delicate personal situation" since the regime's policy changes toward Jews. By Cosmelli's estimation, the sentiments expressed in Pope's article corresponded "to the intimate attitude not only of Pope but of the majority of Italian Americans." Feelings of "perplexity" about the recent iterations of fascist racial policies abounded among Italian Americans in New York and Chicago, Cosmelli observed.[51] Cosmelli could not add that these feelings reached into the embassy itself, although perhaps they did, since Ambassador Suvich was known for his opposition to closer ties between Italy and Nazi Germany and, like Pope, had staked his credibility on the claim that the fascism was not antisemitic.[52] Cosmelli used Pope's article to warn Mussolini's government that its anti-Jewish policies risked alienating Italian Americans.[53] This warning had no effect on the regime.

No sooner had Cosmelli transmitted Pope's September 11 editorial to the Ministry of Foreign Affairs than the chargé d'affaires cabled again. Pope had unexpectedly asked the embassy to pass on an urgent telegram to Mussolini, requesting a meeting in Rome between *Il Duce* and a committee of both Italian and Jewish Americans "to ensure continued good relations in business."[54] The regime did not entertain Pope's request.[55] Less than a month later, and one day after the Grand Council issued the first of Italy's formal racial edicts, Pope's friend, the New York Supreme Court Justice Salvatore Cotillo, tried to reach out to Mussolini once more.[56] Cotillo warned the regime that relations between Italy and the United States were at a tipping point, and asked for a meeting in Rome.[57] Cotillo's message made it as far as the foreign minister, Galeazzo Ciano, who dismissed it as similar to the proposal made by Pope. Using a phrase familiar to human rights abusers, wherever they are located in space and time, Ciano noted that any "international initiative to interfere with Italian internal politics will be decisively rebuffed."[58] By the fall of 1938, Ciano was far less interested in courting the favor of Italian Americans, or any Americans, than he was in cultivating a robust relationship with Nazi Germany.

Writing in 1972, John Diggins described Generoso Pope's response to fascist Italy's racist and antisemitic policies as "courageous."[59] This seems to be a misreading of history. There was nothing brave or moral in Pope's stance, or in the position of millions of Americans and Europeans who acquiesced in antisemitism in the 1930s. In the face of declarations from the fascist government that Italian Jews would be divested of their political, economic, and civil rights, Pope's newspaper obfuscated, relativized, and diminished the significance of the regime's policies. For instance, in the week following the Grand Council's racial edict of October 1938, *Il Progresso* claimed that the regime would provide homes for Italian Jews in sunny Ethiopia, that the council had exempted tens of thousands of Jewish people from restrictions, and that "only" ninety-eight university professors had "left" their jobs.[60] Privately, Pope lamented fascism's anti-Jewish turn, but for selfish reasons: he had vested his reputation in claims that German and Italian fascism were opposite in their approaches to race and religion, and he feared the repercussions of fascist policies on the social, economic, and political status of Italian Americans.

Pope never made a definitive statement against fascist antisemitism. Instead, he tried to distance himself from the fascist persecution of Jews for motives of self-protection. Diggins cited Generoso Pope's message to his readers of December 25, 1938, as evidence of his brave stand against Mussolini's repression of the Jewish people. In this message, Pope wrote that while the "anti-Semitic campaign in Europe" persisted, Americans must retain their commitment to nondiscrimination.[61] It was Christmas Day, 1938—the end of a year in which the fascist government had passed legislation to exile eight thousand Jews from Italy, bar Jewish children from schools, exclude Jews from public life, ban intermarriage between gentiles and Jews, and divest Jews of their businesses and property.[62] In his Christmas message to his readers, Pope did not even name the fascist regime as responsible for antisemitism in Europe, still less denounce its policies.[63]

Anne O'Hare McCormick's interventions about fascist anti-Jewish laws, although far less frequent than Generoso Pope's, were much more robust. McCormick encouraged her readers in the *Times* to see the significance of the government-sponsored report on race as soon as it was published in July 1938. She suggested that her readers should not seek solace in Mussolini's past utterances about the "childishness" of Nazi-style racial theories; instead, they should focus on his *volte-face*, and what that meant for Europe.[64] Writing from Rome in January 1939, after the Grand Council's racial edict had gone into law, McCormick urged Americans not to underestimate the new policies, even if they were unpopular among ordinary Italians and executed only half-heartedly on the ground. The regime had excluded Jews from public offices and deprived them of their businesses. Americans should be aware that the discriminatory legislation caused Italy's Jewish people immense pain and distress, she wrote.[65]

This January 1939 article earned McCormick the animosity of the regime, in large part because she described its antisemitic regulations and laws as "universally unpopular" with ordinary Italians. An official in the Ministry of Press and Propaganda underlined her statement that if a "fair plebiscite" were held on the policy, eighty-nine percent of the country would vote against it.[66] The regime knew of the article before it was published, since it intercepted a *Times* correspondent, Camille Cianfarra, telephoning the text to New York.[67] Speaking to fascist officials, Cianfarra scrambled to distance himself from McCormick's article. He claimed that he had implored her not to write the piece, which was "full of inaccuracies and malevolence" toward the regime.[68] Cianfarra's deference to the fascist government was demonstrative of the constrained position of in-country correspondents in dictatorships: they could not write or speak the truth and keep their jobs. McCormick, two years into her position on the *Times* editorial board, was not so bound. By the time the regime had organized itself to expel her, she was in Hungary.[69] She would be back.

The fascist regime's initiation of anti-Jewish policies and laws horrified Anne O'Hare McCormick and Generoso Pope, for different reasons. As the effects of fascist antisemitism reverberated in the United States, they threatened to undermine Pope's position as a business leader and powerbroker. Since 1937, Pope had feared this outcome, and vested his credibility in the assertion that fascism was not antisemitic. More than any previous policy of the Italian government, the turn toward official antisemitism undermined Pope's dual identity as a loyal American and a fascist sympathizer. Rather than accepting that these two identities were irreconcilable, Pope attempted to patch them together by claiming that little had changed for Italy's Jews, while working behind the scenes, with no effect whatsoever, to moderate the regime's policies.

McCormick's position was much simpler. She could criticize fascist antisemitism, without putting her identity, credibility, or professional reputation on the line. In the early stages of her career at the *Times*, McCormick's friendly disposition toward fascism had helped to advance her career. Glowing reports about Italy under Mussolini in the early 1920s had cleared a pathway to interviews with *Il Duce* himself. The resulting profiles helped to seal her reputation as a journalist who could humanize even the most synthetic of men. Fascist reports about Italy had been instrumental in McCormick's rise to a powerful position at the *Times* and in the United States. That position was secure in 1938. She could speak some truths about fascism, aware that she would alienate the pro-Germany hardliners in the regime. And yet, she had not given up on Mussolini entirely.

Anne O'Hare McCormick and the Road to War

Despite her unvarnished assessment of the meaning of fascist racial laws for Jewish Italians and European geopolitics, McCormick continued to put a hopeful gloss on fascist foreign policy at the decade's end. She persisted with two well-worn, and related, themes: first, of the Rome-Berlin axis as a weak partnership, which could disintegrate at any time; and second, of Mussolini as the key to European peace. Since Hitler had come to power in 1933, McCormick had argued that temperamental differences between Hitler and Mussolini reflected an ideological divide between Nazism and fascism. For her readers in the *Times*, she interpreted many of the major events in Europe in 1938 through this lens. For instance, she assessed the Anschluss of March as a blow to Italy, which cracked "wide open the Rome-Berlin axis."[70] And in September 1938, she characterized Mussolini as working in concert with Chamberlain and Daladier (and Roosevelt, from afar) to make Hitler see sense in Munich, enabling the prolongation of peace in Europe.[71]

As Czechoslovakia, and then Poland, buckled under the weight of invading Nazi troops, the basic tenets of McCormick's analysis changed very little: while Nazism was irredeemable, the fascist regime could still be detached from the axis, she argued throughout 1939.[72] Rather than interpreting Italy's invasion of Albania in April as evidence of fascism's similarities with Nazism, McCormick argued that by taking over Albania, Mussolini's goal was to protect the Adriatic against German expansion.[73] Citing the Nazi-Soviet pact as both an expression and a source of the widening gulf between the two right-wing dictatorships, McCormick wrote that no European leader was expending more effort "to prevent a war" than Benito Mussolini.[74] And when (in spite of Mussolini's presumed efforts) the war came, she characterized Italy as a "pendulum," which might swing either way. McCormick even allowed her readers to imagine that Mussolini might use the axis "to pivot" Italy, so that it would exert more sway when it entered the war on the allies' side. McCormick used images of a pivot and a pendulum to convey the sense that fascist policy was both determinative and fluid.[75]

As 1939 gave way to 1940, McCormick persisted in her argument that fascist Italy could be separated from Nazi Germany. In Rome, that January, she emphasized the shared interests of the "greatest" of "noncombatants" and "neutrals"—Italy and the United States—and suggested that the two nations were "destined to work together" in shaping the postwar peace.[76] It was not until April, when the Italian press adopted an intensely pro-German stance, and Nazi officials arrived for military talks in Rome, that McCormick's predictions assumed a far more pessimistic tone.[77] But still, on May 10, the same day that Germany invaded Belgium, she wrote that Italian officials were considering "the possibility of closer relations with the United States."[78]

If McCormick's analysis of the events of 1938 to 1940 seems naïve as we look back at these years from our present perch, it is worth remembering that a number of American policymakers shared her views. For instance, the American ambassador to Italy, William Phillips, argued that the Anschluss drove a wedge between Mussolini and Hitler. President Roosevelt and some of his advisers believed that Mussolini was instrumental in Hitler's acceptance of a "peaceful" solution to the Czechoslovakia crisis at Munich in September 1938. And while Italy's annexation of Albania in the spring of 1939 gave some policymakers, including the president, pause for thought (as proof of the very obvious contention that Mussolini, like Hitler, was bent on aggressive expansion), the Nazi-Soviet Pact that summer weakened any supposition that like attracted like.[79]

164 CONCLUSION

Above all, there was nothing naïve in McCormick's assertion that Italy might remain neutral in World War II. In February 1940, the undersecretary of state, Sumner Welles, traveled to Europe, with the aim of convincing Mussolini to stay out of the war. Meeting with McCormick in January, just before she left for Italy, Roosevelt asked her to convey to Mussolini that good relations between Italy and the United States were naturally contingent on Italian neutrality.[80] Roosevelt probably conceived of McCormick as an informal counterpart to Welles, hoping that she might lay some groundwork for his upcoming mission. Upon reaching Rome, McCormick stopped in at the Ministry of Popular Culture, to request meetings with Mussolini and Ciano, as was her custom. And, as had become its custom, the Ministry of Popular Culture refused her request. But an official at the foreign press section passed on McCormick's reflections to Alessandro Pavolini, the minister of popular culture, emphasizing that they were based on her recent meeting with Roosevelt. McCormick had "insisted" that both American public opinion and the president were firmly opposed to intervening in the war, this official wrote.[81]

Just as she had been instructed to do, McCormick communicated to the fascist regime Roosevelt's hope that both countries could stay out of the war.[82] And although she was denied direct access to the uppermost echelons of the fascist hierarchy, she used her journalism from Rome in January 1940 to convey American policy, confident that officials in the regime read her words. When she painted idealistic images of two great "neutral" powers, united in their nonbelligerency, and working side by side to shape a postwar world, she wrote not only for her broad American audience, but also for her very narrow Italian one.[83]

Back in Rome, once more, in the spring of 1940, and refused, once more, a meeting with Mussolini, McCormick wrote *Il Duce* a long letter. It was April 30, the last day of a month that had seen Nazi technical experts and military representatives in Rome, and a sharp uptick in Italian anti-ally propaganda. After apologizing for any offense that her recent journalism had caused, McCormick lamented that she had not been allowed to meet with Mussolini:

> I am deeply concerned about the relations between our two countries. Your Excellency knows better than I do that public sentiment in the United States is violently and almost unanimously anti-German, and that the better feeling towards Italy since the war grows out of two facts: first, that Italy is not in the conflict on the German side, and second, that for the first time in several years[, W]ashington and Rome have a strong bond of common

interest in their desire to limit the conflict and to uphold certain non-belligerent rights.

McCormick understood why the regime felt affronted by her characterization of Italian mass opinion as anti-German and anti-war. But she argued that "the best thing that can be said to increase sympathy for Italy in the United States is that Italians do not support German policy and action." As both the Nazi and fascist regimes signaled the imminent start of a more active phase in their partnership, she realized that the world was at yet another crossroads:

> My own country, I am always repeating in print, is not prepared to enter the war, militarily or psychologically, but if Italy goes in with Germany . . . I am firmly convinced that such action will powerfully affect our policy and eventually lead to our participation. This is the reason—because Italy is the brake against illimitable war; because . . . the Powers that succeed in keeping out of this exhausting and revolutionary struggle will be the strong powers at the end, the only powers capable of shaping the future—this is the reason that I pile up evidence to prove that your country, and consequently mine, may not be dragged in.

McCormick may have written her final words to Mussolini to appeal to his own sense of greatness, but there is no doubt that she also truly believed that upon his decision rested "what chance there [was] of saving the civilization of Europe." "Believe me, Your Excellency," she signed off, with words that felt less like a formality, and more like a prayer.[84]

By the late 1930s, McCormick was an establishment insider in the United States. And like a number of other establishment insiders, she argued that Mussolini could be split from Hitler not because she believed that this outcome was highly probable, but because it was a possibility in a world of shrinking possibilities. In so far as McCormick could contribute to this outcome, she did so, communicating FDR's hopes for Italian and American neutrality, and arguing (correctly, and insistently) that neither the Italian nor the American people were eager for war. McCormick projected a vision of Italy and the United States as two great neutral powers shaping the postwar world not because this was a likely scenario, but because she hoped against hope that it would strike Mussolini as the most appealing one. Hope is not naïve when it is the only option available.

Suffice to say, you did not need to be a fascist sympathizer to make sympathetic-sounding noises about fascist Italy in 1938, 1939, and 1940, you just needed to be a sensible strategist, who recognized that it would be self-defeating to preemptively foreclose an option, however remote its possibility. McCormick, by the late 1930s, had become this kind of a strategist. Certainly, neither Mussolini nor Ciano considered her a friend of Italy any longer: she was far too critical of dictatorship, the suppression of freedoms, and the growing distance between official policies and public opinion to count as a "friend" in their minds. Too disorganized to expel McCormick for her criticism of its anti-Jewish policies in January 1939, the regime (in its often haphazard fashion), kept an eye on McCormick's comings and goings over the next eighteen months, suggesting politely, pointedly, and probably quite intimidatingly, that she would be better off going than coming, and, better off still if she stayed away for good.[85]

McCormick's love affair with fascist Italy was well and truly over, and yet, one can sense her own feelings of sadness as she mulled over what had happened. Upon her return to New York, in the spring of 1940, she reflected upon the scenes in Rome as she departed. It was the 25th of May, less than three weeks before Mussolini declared war on Britain and France. Consciously or not, McCormick's description of the city she left behind echoed a scene that she had described so vividly for *Times* readers almost twenty years earlier. In the spring of 1940, she watched masses of young men—"boys," really—streaming down the Via Veneto. On the face of it, these young men were not unlike the young *fascisti*, whom McCormick had watched descending from the Capitoline and into the narrow Via Aracoeli in the spring of 1921. But for McCormick, the tragedy lay in the differences between these two parades. In the spring of 1921, the young fascists had, in her mind, embodied all that was good about wartime—vigor, patriotism, and higher ideals—without the threat of full-blown war. In the spring of 1940, the young men's battle cries were real—all "too real," the "shrill tuning up for a summons" to an imminent war. In the spring of 1921, she had believed that the fascists had spoken for Italy; they were cheered along by adoring crowds. In the spring of 1940, the young marching men elicited only feelings of disgust and dismay from passersby on the streets. Twenty years earlier, McCormick had used the words of a "starry-eyed" woman from Piedmont to sum up Italians' view of fascism as a triumphant rebirth. In 1940, she cast a taxi driver in the spokesperson's role, as he "cursed under his breath," and muttered, "Young fools!"[86]

McCormick seemed to think that there had been a corruption of fascism's initial promise and ideals. If Italy entered the war on Germany's side, she wrote, it would be due to the influence of "reckless elements" within the party—a minority of "extreme Fascists under the sway of the Nazis."[87] McCormick conceived of the fascism of 1940 as the inverse, rather than an extension, of the fascism of 1922. She did not perceive Italian fascism's extremism, chauvinism, and violence as inherent to Italian fascism.[88]

Generoso Pope and the Finest of Lines

At the end of May 1938—a month that had begun with a meeting between Hitler and Mussolini in Rome—Generoso Pope received a letter from Frank E. Mason, the vice president of the National Broadcasting Company. Mason and Pope were friends, and Mason wanted to offer Pope some friendly advice. In a polite, but direct, way, Mason told Pope to shut up. Italian Americans were in a delicate situation, Mason noted, due to Italy's tightening relationship with Germany. Mason warned:

> There is no question that there is a rapidly growing sense of nationalism in the United States. You as a good fascist nationalist cannot object to that. And with the growing nationalism, unfortunately comes a certain xenophobia.... Gene, you can't identify Rome with Berlin in the minds of America ... without creating in the minds of our people [the idea] that you are endorsing and are taking responsibility ... for your allies' activities, philosophies and ideologies.

Gallup opinion polls showed remarkably high anti-German attitudes among Americans, wrote Mason.[89] While Americans were less anxious about Italian fascism, either at home or abroad, these feelings would shift if influential men, like Generoso Pope, continued to affirm the axis alliance in Americans' minds. Mason noted that Pope was one of the few Italian Americans who had gained entry into "the salons and drawing rooms of the leaders of industry, the press, of thought and of government." He cautioned Pope that his consistent defense of fascist Italy risked undermining all that he had worked for, and built up, in the United States.[90]

Mason's letter is a fascinating source for a number of reasons. First, it is a restatement of the observation (made as early as 1934 by Italian officials) that ties between the fascist and Nazi regimes were detrimental to the reputation of fascism in the United States. Second, it offers an unusually frank description of Pope as a "fascist nationalist" by an American who was "very fond" of Pope. Such labels were usually the preserve of Pope's antifascist opponents, who used it to question his credentials as a loyal American. The assumption that this letter was a private correspondence, between friends, allowed Frank Mason to describe Pope frankly. It thus offers us a rare insight into how Generoso Pope's friends saw him, and probably how he saw himself.

Last, Mason's letter is a remarkable source because it did not remain private. Pope forwarded it to Fulvio Suvich, the Italian ambassador in Washington, who passed it onward to Dino Alfieri, the minister of popular culture in Rome. Alongside the letter, Pope asked the Italian government for instructions: should he follow Mason's advice and back down, or should he continue to make interventions on behalf of Mussolini's regime in the United States?[91] This correspondence indicates that by May 1938, if not before, Generoso Pope was acting on the specific orders of the fascist government. By coincidence, May 1938 was the same month that Congress passed the Foreign Agents Registration Act, which defined a foreign agent as someone who worked "at the order, request, or under the direction or control" of a foreign government.[92] Pope certainly fit this description; the regime even had a code name for him: *Camerata Casagrande*—Comrade in a Big House.[93]

Generoso Pope's journalistic interventions in late 1938 show how far he was willing to go on behalf of the fascist regime. In a similar fashion to McCormick, Pope claimed that Mussolini was the principal peacemaker at Munich: *Il Duce* had saved Europe from the "seemingly inevitable catastrophe" of war, wrote Pope. But unlike McCormick, Pope also used the precedent set by Germany's acquisition of the Sudetenland to demand further revisions of the Treaty of Versailles in Italy's favor. In a December 1938 editorial in *Il Progresso*, Pope revisited the theme of Italy's "mutilated victory" after the Great War. Europe would not know a "secure and lasting peace until the injustices of the past" were "rectified," he wrote. Pope's editorial was destabilizing, and intentionally so: he aimed to whip up irredentist sentiments among Italian Americans, with a view to pressurizing the US government to accept the regime's demands for territories along the Adriatic.[94] Unwittingly, Pope suggested that the critics of appeasement were right: peace of the kind secured at Munich came at a mounting price.

The German invasion of the rump state of Czechoslovakia and then Poland elicited no condemnation from Generoso Pope. While McCormick would soon exert any influence she had to keep Italy out of the war, Pope's principal concern was to ensure that the United States would not intervene, should a war come to pass. And, in contrast to McCormick, who backed an American policy of "so-called" neutrality (which made it abundantly clear which side the United States was on), Pope insisted that neutrality should be conceived strictly, for the United States' own good.[95] The wounds inflicted by the Great War had not yet healed: "disabled veterans" burdened American institutions; soldiers' pensions drained national resources, Pope wrote. He suggested that to enable a full recovery from the Great Depression, the American government had to keep the country out of war.[96]

Pope's position on neutrality differed from McCormick's in another regard. McCormick was motivated by strategic concerns: she projected an image of Italy and United States as the world's great powers in a last-ditch effort to convince the fascist regime that its interest lay outside the axis. But for Pope, the idea of the United States and Italy as fellow neutrals had intensely personal dimensions. The only way that he could reconcile his own identity as both a fascist sympathizer and a loyal American was by claiming, against the mounting evidence, that the United States and Italy were on the same side as two truly neutral powers in the war.[97] It was, then, with heartfelt regret that Pope acknowledged Mussolini's declaration of war on Britain and France, on June 10, 1940. His hope that Italy and the United States would continue their "cooperative" relationship had not been realized, he wrote. Pope still did not disavow the axis powers.[98]

Pope's editorials fueled the indignation of antifascist intellectuals in the United States. There was nothing new in the Italian *fuoriusciti*'s ("exiles'") condemnation of Pope for using his influence to promote Mussolini's interests in the United States.[99] New, however, was the willingness of native-born Americans to take antifascists' complaints about Generoso Pope seriously. *Il Mondo*, a monthly journal published between 1938 and 1941 by Giuseppe Lupis (a politically moderate antifascist), was particularly influential, since the mainstream press used it as a source for their own investigations into fascist sympathizers.[100] For instance, in November 1940, *Fortune* published articles that criticized Pope's muted Americanism following Italy's entry into the war, and praised *Il Mondo* as the "finest" antifascist paper in the United States.[101]

Running from 1938 until 1944, the House Committee on Un-American Activities (HUAC) whipped up further suspicions of foreign agents of the fascist regime. Italian Americans had been effectively immune in an earlier congressional investigation, chaired by Samuel Dickstein of New York—a representative who depended on the Italian-American vote. But under the leadership of Martin Dies, a representative from Texas, the HUAC heard testimony about the long reach of Italian propaganda. In 1938, the chairman of a New York antifascist group testified that all the major Italian-American dailies were "under dictation from fascist agents."[102] Other stories of fascist radio and information networks surfaced over the committee's long lifespan.[103] In this charged atmosphere, in June 1941, J. Edgar Hoover launched an investigation into the activities of Generoso Pope.[104]

Although it would take more than three years for the FBI to complete its investigation, law enforcement's scrutiny had an almost instantaneous impact on Pope. Upon realizing that he was under investigation in July 1941, Pope met with Max Ascoli, a prominent antifascist intellectual and exile, who together with Lupis had founded the liberal antifascist organization the Mazzini Society in 1939.[105] As the FBI reported, at this meeting, Pope agreed to end *Il Progresso*'s "pro-Fascist editorial policy." The same month, Ascanio Colonna, the Italian ambassador to the United States, reported back to Rome that Pope's newspaper's English-language editorials had become critical of Mussolini. Colonna described Pope as a political opportunist who could not be trusted.[106] It was a fair assessment.[107]

In September 1941, Pope strengthened his antifascist rhetoric, to make his allegiances evident to his American watchers. As a "loyal American," he wrote in *Il Progresso*, he stood against any foreign power that opposed the United States and against the "diffusion of any foreign or anti-American ism," on American soil.[108] Beyond the pages of his own newspaper, Pope was clearer still. He appeared on the front page of the *New York Post*. "The quicker Hitler and the Axis powers are destroyed the better off the world will be. And when I say Axis powers that includes Mussolini," Pope told *Post* readers. *Time* magazine celebrated this statement, snarkily, as evidence of the tardy "Americanization of Mr. Pope" at the hands of antifascist Italians.[109]

Generoso Pope worked hard to get back into the good graces of the American government, and Franklin Roosevelt in particular. He telegrammed FDR following Japan's attack on Pearl Harbor, claiming that he prayed that the world would be liberated "from the shackles of the barbarian dictators."[110] A week later, he wrote to the White House again: "Will you please tell the President for me that if I can be of service to him personally or through my newspapers, I am at his command."[111] Unbeknownst to the White House, Pope had used the identical formulation in a letter to the Italian minister of popular culture, eighteen months before.[112] Although Pope did not acknowledge the ongoing FBI investigation in his correspondence with the White House, he attempted to forestall its findings. At the end of December, he sent the president a statement of loyalty, signed by all his newspapers' staff. Roosevelt passed it on to his press secretary, but not before he scribbled on a note: "I don't believe it."[113]

FIGURE 6.1. Generoso Pope in Rome, June 1937. Generoso Pope is in the center, in a dark business suit. He is surrounded by fascist officials. Courtesy of Bettmann via Getty Images.

Franklin Roosevelt did not trust Generoso Pope. While the FBI investigation proceeded slowly, the White House ordered the Office of War Information (OWI) to come up with a faster report. The OWI report used articles from *Il Mondo* and a letter from Max Ascoli of the Mazzini Society to assemble proof of Pope's prior sympathies for fascism. The most striking evidence that these Mazzini society intellectuals provided was a photograph, taken during Pope's 1937 trip to Rome. Standing at the tomb of the unknown soldier, between the founder of the Fascist League of North America and the director of the fascists abroad (*Fasci all'Estero*), Generoso Pope raised his right arm in a fascist salute (figure 6.1). Luckily for Pope, by the time this image reached the White House, the story was six years old.[114]

Franklin Roosevelt did not trust Generoso Pope, but nor could the president afford to live without the publisher. Reluctantly, Roosevelt acknowledged that in every even-numbered year, on a Tuesday in early November, the Democratic Party depended on Generoso Pope. And 1940 was one of those years. Roosevelt's speech upon Italy's invasion of France on June 10, 1940, had alienated Italian Americans, who did not appreciate the image of Italy as "the hand that held the dagger" that struck into its neighbor's back. It was probably with the November elections in mind that Roosevelt called Pope to the White House in late July.[115] By September, the Democratic National Committee (DNC) had created a new organization, the Democratic Council for Americans of Italian Origin, to campaign for Roosevelt and his running mate, Henry Wallace. The leader of the council was Generoso Pope.[116]

The year 1944 was another presidential election year, and the dynamics were again illustrative of the mutual dependency between FDR and Pope. In late September, Oscar Ewing, a DNC official, contacted the president. It was of the utmost importance that FDR meet with Pope, who could do more than any other Italian-American leader to garner his community's vote, Ewing wrote.[117] Roosevelt saw the value of the meeting, but still it did not occur.[118] Two weeks later, the former DNC chairman, Ed Flynn, telephoned, twice, to "urge that the President let Generoso Pope come in just for a handshake and to be seen coming out of the White House."[119] On October 17, against his will, but in the light of his better judgment, Franklin Roosevelt met with Generoso Pope.[120]

The Federal Bureau of Investigation finished its report on Generoso Pope in October 1944. The report did not reveal anything that the White House did not already know about Pope. The FBI found no clear-cut evidence, such as a money trail, to prove that Pope was a foreign agent; it found less, in fact, than the future historian could find in the Italian government archives.[121] In any case, by October 1944, the atmosphere in the United States was more secure. Italy had surrendered to allied forces the previous year. Mussolini was hemmed in as the nominal head of a fiefdom in the north of Italy, protected by German arms. Nothing in the FBI report would change Roosevelt's overly generous assessment of Generoso Pope, made earlier that year:

> It is perfectly true that he was friendly to Mussolini and his gang while the latter were in control of Italy. So were the great majority of Americans of Italian birth who had to maintain relations with Italy and its de facto government. I do not think it is true that Pope had Fascist tendencies. He merely "hunted with the hounds" chiefly as a business proposition.... The point is that at no time has Pope been accused of working against the United States.[122]

Generoso Pope had walked the finest of fine lines. He survived the war years because a Democratic administration depended on him, as he depended on it, and because US government officials were never aware of the extent of his links with the fascist state.

For Their Sins

McCormick and Pope's attitude to Mussolini's Italy on the eve of American entry into the war reveals something about the nature of their support for fascism. McCormick extricated herself from her fascist-sympathizing past with alacrity. For Pope, the process was more gradual, due to the deep investment of his own identity and credibility in the fascist regime. But each of them cut their ties to Italy when those attachments became incompatible with their claims to be loyal Americans. The same was true for Herbert Schneider, whose silence about fascism after 1936 spoke volumes about his desire for distance from the regime. In his silence, Schneider implied that Americans had nothing good to learn from Mussolini's Italy. Conversely, fascist sympathizers had praised fascism for as long as they had believed that Americans *did* have something good to learn from Italy. They conceived of their own fascist sympathies as a form of patriotism—a desire to make the United States a better version of itself.

In the 1920s and early 1930s, Child, McCormick, Pope, and Schneider had been in the mainstream of American society not in spite of their fascist sympathies but because of them, since Italy's apparent successes enabled them to reflect upon, and suggest solutions to the problems that beset the United States. They addressed concerns that animated many of their fellow countrymen in the interwar years, including the effects of consumption on moral values, the impact of technology on human intelligence and the democratic process, and the repercussions of mechanization on jobs and communities.

Their interpretations of fascist Italy had the potential to help Americans make sense of, and perhaps even feel better about, the vast changes that they experienced. For people concerned about a decline in moral values in their own country, it might have been reassuring to read that, in Italy, the future belonged to aggressively patriotic young men. For those intimidated by the intricacies of modern governance, it could have been a relief to learn of a leader who was capable of simplifying complex realities. For Americans who believed that their democracy was obsolete, there may have been inspiration in a form of government that seemed to be both effective and worthy of popular support. And for those who both suffered in the Great Depression and worried about the long-term effects of technology on their jobs, it might have been tempting to believe in a country that promised economic resilience without significant sectoral transition.

Child, McCormick, Pope, and Schneider did not know what fascism was to become when they voiced their support for Mussolini and his regime in the

1920s and 1930s. But they also did their best to ignore the regime's cruelties and oppressions, so that Italian fascism after 1938 seemed more like an aberration and less like an outgrowth of its inherent chauvinism and authoritarianism. If any of these individuals believed that they had made mistakes when they sympathized with fascism, they never recognized their errors, at least publicly. Herbert Schneider asserted that there was "nothing" he would "change" in the books he wrote about fascism.[123] Generoso Pope lied, allowing his newspaper to claim that it had "consistently and vigorously denounced Mussolini and his fascist cohorts."[124] Only Anne O'Hare McCormick ever came close to expressing regret, and this in private, in a 1941 letter to Franklin Roosevelt, half a year before the United States entered World War II. McCormick addressed the president:

> I can only pray for you when I realize that your judgment and your decision are the fulcrum on which our future turns. The future, indeed, because I am more and more certain that about the only thing worth saving is the idea and the pattern we stand for—not just democracy but this democracy, which has no counterpart anywhere. I hope God will forgive us our sins against it—and give us another chance.[125]

By distorting the realities of Mussolini's Italy, fascist sympathizers had undermined the value of democracy for many Americans. It took fascism, in its full expression, to make Americans appreciate their democracy once more.

NOTES

Introduction. The Machine with a Soul

1. Richard Washburn Child, "The President," *Saturday Evening Post*, April 17, 1926; Richard Washburn Child, "Foreword," in Benito Mussolini, *My Autobiography*, ed. Richard Washburn Child (New York: Scribner's, 1928), xvi.

2. Richard Washburn Child, *A Diplomat Looks at Europe* (New York: Duffield, 1925), 273–77.

3. John P. Diggins, *Mussolini and Fascism: The View from America* (Princeton, NJ: Princeton University Press, 1972). Diggins also analyzed groups that were opposed to Mussolini, including Italian-American antifascists and American communists and socialists.

4. Diggins, *Mussolini and Fascism*, 77–110 (on Italian Americans), 182–97 (on Catholics), 221–32 (on academics), 262–86 (on government).

5. Ibid., 58–73.

6. Philip V. Cannistraro, *Blackshirts in Little Italy: Italian Americans and Fascism, 1921–1929* (West Lafayette, IN: Bordighera, 1999); Peter R. D'Agostino, *Rome in America: Transnational Catholic Ideology from the Risorgimento to Fascism* (Chapel Hill: University of North Carolina Press, 2004), 158–257.

7. Jonah Goldberg, *Liberal Fascism: The Secret History of the American Left from Mussolini to the Politics of Meaning* (New York: Doubleday, 2008), 14, 121–62.

8. More recent works have followed in Goldberg's polemical footsteps: Ennio Caretto, *Quando l'America si innamorò di Mussolini* (Rome: Editori Internazionali Riuniti, 2014); Dinesh D'Souza, *The Big Lie: Exposing the Nazi Roots of the American Left* (Washington, DC: Regnery, 2017).

9. George H. Mead, "The Nature of Aesthetic Experience," *International Journal of Ethics* 36, no. 4 (1926): 382–93.

10. Richard's father, Horace Walter Child, owed his brother-in-law, the industrialist and politician Charles Sumner Bird, more than $10,000 in the 1920s. See Promissory Note, November 1, 1921, Folder "Bills and Receipts"; and Letter, Charles Sumner Bird to Horace Walter Child, June 24, 1924, Folder "General Correspondence, 1909–24." Both in Reel 1, Richard Washburn Child Papers, 1870–1927, Library of Congress, Washington, District of Columbia (hereafter cited as RWCP).

11. Richard Washburn Child, "My Classmate Sheffield," *Saturday Evening Post*, December 24, 1904.

12. "An Intimate Study of Richard Washburn Child, New Italian Ambassador," *Boston Sunday Post*, May 29, 1921.

13. Letter, Richard Washburn Child to Horace Walter Child, September 2, 1906. Letter, Richard Washburn Child to Horace Water Child, December 16, 1906. Both in Folder "General Correspondence, 1909–24," Reel 1, RWCP.

14. "Intimate Study of Richard Washburn Child," *Boston Sunday Post*.

15. Richard Sherman, "Charles Sumner Bird and the Progressive Party in Massachusetts," *New England Quarterly* 33, no. 3 (September 1960): 325–34.

16. Letter, Richard Washburn Child to Theodore Roosevelt, August 24, 1912, Folder "1881–1919," Reel 2, RWCP.

17. Letter, Richard Washburn Child to Horace Walter Child, September 2, 1906, Folder "General Correspondence, 1909–24," Reel 1, RWCP. Child, "Foreword," in *My Autobiography*, xvii–xix.

18. Richard Washburn Child, "Making the World Safe for Truth," *Frank Leslie's Weekly*, September 14, 1918.

19. John A. Morello, *Selling the President, 1920: Albert D. Lasker, Advertising, and the Election of Warren G. Harding* (Westport, CT: Praeger, 2001), 53, 67, 73.

20. "Intimate Study of Richard Washburn Child," *Boston Sunday Post*.

21. "Child and Schurman Named Ambassadors," *New York Times*, May 18, 1921.

22. *Embassy Weekly*, June 30, 1923, 865/1239, Record Group 59, Microcopy 527, National Archives and Records Administration, College Park, Maryland (hereafter cited as RG#, M#, NARA). Child, *Diplomat Looks at Europe*, 154; also published as Richard Washburn Child, "The Making of Mussolini," *Saturday Evening Post*, June 28, 1924.

23. "R. W. Child Opens Roosevelt Drive," *New York Times*, September 26, 1932.

24. Letter, Richard Washburn Child to Theodore Roosevelt, August 24, 1912, Folder "1881–1919," Reel 2, RWCP.

25. Child, *Diplomat Looks at Europe*, 14; also published as Richard Washburn Child, "Our American Diplomat," *Saturday Evening Post*, November 1, 1924.

26. David F. Schmitz, *The United States and Fascist Italy, 1922–1940* (Chapel Hill: University of North Carolina Press, 1988), 51–53, 56–57.

27. Letter, Richard Washburn Child to Horace Walter Child, February 13, 1924; Letter, Maude Parker to Mr. and Mrs. Horace Walter Child, October 24, 1923; both in Folder "1923–24," Reel 2, RWCP. "Coolidge Will Be a Candidate, Says R. W. Child," *Chicago Daily Tribune*, July 30, 1926. Memorandum, Franklin D. Roosevelt to William Phillips, February 21, 1934, Folder: Jan–March 1934, Official File 20 Dept. of State; Letter, Richard Washburn Child to Franklin D. Roosevelt, March 11, 1934, Folder: Endorsements for Minister, 1933–1946, Official File 218b. Both at Franklin D. Roosevelt Library, Hyde Park, New York (hereafter cited as FDRL).

28. For examples of Child's consumption of women and alcohol, see Letter, Richard Washburn Child to Horace Walter Child, November 14, 1925; and Letter, Richard Washburn Child to Horace Walter Child, March 17, 1926; both in Folder "General Correspondence, 1925–7," Reel 1, RWCP.

29. Folder "Genealogy," Reel 2, RWCP. Letter, Richard Washburn Child to Horace Walter Child, August 1916, Folder "General Correspondence, 1909–24," Reel 1, RWCP.

30. Letter, Richard Washburn Child to Horace Walter Child, Folder "Undated," Reel 1, RWCP.

31. Letter, Richard Washburn Child to Horace Walter Child, November 14, 1925, Folder "General Correspondence, 1925–7," Reel 1, RWCP.

32. Letter, Richard Washburn Child to Horace Walter Child, November 1925, Folder "General Correspondence, 1925–7," Reel 1, RWCP.

33. Jan Cohn, *Creating America: George Horace Lorimer and the Saturday Evening Post* (Pittsburgh: University of Pittsburgh Press, 1989), 3, 8, 10, 12, 141, 165.

34. "Intimate Study of Richard Washburn Child," *Boston Sunday Post*.

35. Marco Mariano and Federica Pinelli, *Europa e Stati Uniti secondo il New York Times: La corrispondenza estera di Anne O'Hare McCormick, 1920–1954* (Turin: Otto, 2000), 11–14.

36. J. Douglas Tarpley, "Anne O'Hare McCormick," in *American Newspaper Journalists, 1926–1950*, ed. Perry J. Ashley, *Dictionary of Literary Biography*, vol. 29 (Detroit: Gale, 1984), 194.

37. Teresa Beatrice O'Hare, "Love," *Songs at Twilight* (Columbus, OH: Columbus Printing Co., 1898), 40.

38. Carol Poh Miller and Robert A. Wheeler, "Cleveland: The Making and Remaking of an American City, 1796–1993," in *Cleveland: A Metropolitan Reader*, ed. W. Dennis Keating, Norman Krumholz, and David C. Perry (Kent, OH: Kent State University Press, 1995), 38–40.

39. The O'Hares were congregants at Saint Agnes, a new Catholic Church in a middle-class neighborhood of Cleveland. Anne's affection for, and perhaps gratitude to, Saint Agnes's, ran deep. She would later write a history of the church, describing how its beauty revealed itself slowly, like the "facets in the mind" of a good friend. Anne O'Hare McCormick, *St. Agnes Church, Cleveland, Ohio* (Cleveland: The Martin Printing Company, 1920), 33.

40. Mariano and Pinelli, *Europa e Stati Uniti secondo il New York Times*, 18–28.

41. Ibid., 29–30.

42. Anne McCormick, "Pompeii," *Bookman*, January 1918.

43. Mariano and Pinelli, *Europa e Stati Uniti secondo il New York Times*, 38–41.

44. Anne O'Hare McCormick, "New Italy of the Italians," *New York Times*, December 19, 1920.

45. Anne O'Hare McCormick, "Italy Rebels against Rebellion," *New York Times*, April 24, 1921; Anne O'Hare McCormick, "Il Duce Pictures the New State," *New York Times*, October 24, 1926.

46. Ministry of Popular Culture to Alberto Calza Bini, October 17, 1926, fascicolo "Giornalisti stranieri" (part 1), busta 256, Ministero della Cultura Popolare; Archivio Storico Diplomatico del Ministero degli Affari Esteri, Rome (hereafter cited as ASD).

47. For a typical article on Roosevelt's domestic policy, see Anne O'Hare McCormick, "As He Sees Himself," *New York Times*, October 16, 1938.

48. Marion Turner Sheehan, "Foreword," in *The World at Home: Selections from the Writings of Anne O'Hare McCormick*, ed. Marion Turner Sheehan (New York: Alfred Knopf, 1956), xi.

49. McCormick interviewed Hitler in his first year as chancellor. Anne O'Hare McCormick, "Hitler Seeks Jobs for All Germans," *New York Times*, July 10, 1933.

50. For examples, see Anne O'Hare McCormick, "Now We All Debate the Issues," *New York Times*, October 7, 1928; Anne O'Hare McCormick, "This America: A Re-Discovery," *New York Times*, September 9, 1934.

51. Mariano and Pinelli, *Europa e Stati Uniti secondo il New York Times*, 107–9.

52. "Abroad: A Tribute to Anne O'Hare McCormick," *New York Times*, May 31, 1954.

53. Paul David Pope, *The Deeds of My Fathers: How My Grandfather and Father Built New York and Created the Tabloid World of Today* (New York: Rowman & Littlefield, 2010), 38.

54. Pope, *Deeds of My Fathers*, 41–94; Philip V. Cannistraro, "Generoso Pope and the Rise of Italian American Politics, 1925–1936," in *Italian Americans: New Perspectives in Italian Immigration and Ethnicity*, ed. Lydio Tomasi (Staten Island, NY: Center for Migration Studies of New York, 1985), 264–73. Philip V. Cannistraro, "Pope, Generoso (1891–1950)," in *The Italian American Experience: An Encyclopedia*, ed. Salvatore J. LaGumina, Frank J. Cavaioli, Salvatore Primeggia, and Joseph A. Varacalli (New York: Garland, 2000), 487–88.

55. Pope, *Deeds of My Fathers*, 90.

56. Cannistraro, "Pope, Generoso," 487–88. "Il Progresso, Oldest Italian Daily Here, Sold," *New York Times*, September 30, 1928.

57. Cannistraro, "Generoso Pope and the Rise of Italian American Politics," 275–76.

58. "Il Progresso, Oldest Italian Daily Here, Sold," *New York Times*.

59. Cannistraro, "Pope, Generoso," 488. "To Buy *Corriere d'America*," *New York Times*, September 5, 1931.

60. "Il Gr. Uff. Generoso Pope a colloquio con Roosevelt," *Il Progresso Italo-Americano*, January 31, 1936; "Un'intervista del Gr. Uff. G. Pope col Segretario degli Esteri On. Hull," *Il Progresso Italo-Americano*, February 1, 1936.

61. "Honored by King of Italy," *New York Times*, May 11, 1926.

62. Fasciolo H407, "Raccomandato Pope Generoso New York Oggetto: 1928 onorificenza," busta 18, Segreteria particolare del Duce, carteggio ordinario, Archivio Centrale dello Stato, Rome (hereafter cited as ACS).

63. For examples, see "Remember Next Tuesday," *Il Progresso Italo-Americano*, November 2, 1930; Generoso Pope, "Gl'italoamericani e i pubblici uffici," *Il Progresso Italo-Americano*, January 5, 1933.

64. For an example of Pope's ties with Senator Wagner, see Letter, Robert Wagner to George Akerson, April 2, 1930, Folder Pope, Presidential Secretary's File, Herbert Hoover Papers, Herbert Hoover Library, West Branch, IA. For an example of his ties with Governor Roosevelt, see "Contro la disoccupazione," *Il Progresso Italo-Americano*, March 9, 1930.

65. Memorandum, Franklin Roosevelt to Edwin Watson, September 28, 1944, Folder: Pope, Generoso, President's Personal File 4617, FDRL. "Generoso Pope Sees Roosevelt," *New York Times*, October 18, 1944.

66. *Reminiscences of Herbert Wallace Schneider*, interviewed by Constance Myers, with John P. Diggins, 1976, Columbia Center for Oral History, Columbia University, New York.

67. *Reminiscences of Herbert Wallace Schneider*.

68. Ibid.

69. Herbert Wallace Schneider, "Instrumental Instrumentalism," *Journal of Philosophy* 18, no. 5 (March 1921): 113–17.

70. Herbert Wallace Schneider, "Science and Social Progress: A Philosophical Introduction to Moral Science" (PhD dissertation, Columbia University, 1920), 61, 37, 49.

71. Charles Merriam to Herbert Schneider, April 14, 1926, Folder, Correspondence, 1924–1929, 107/1/3, Selected Papers of Herbert W. Schneider, 1924–1976, Special Collections Research Center, University of Southern Illinois, Carbondale, IL (hereafter cited as SPHWS).

72. Herbert Wallace Schneider, *Making the Fascist State* (New York: H. Fertig, 1928); Herbert Wallace Schneider, "Italy's New Syndicalist Constitution," *Political Science Quarterly* 42, no. 2 (June 1927): 161–202; Herbert Wallace Schneider, "Giovinezza," *Century Magazine*,

December 1927; Herbert Wallace Schneider, "Phases of Fascism," *Historical Outlook* 19, no. 1 (January 1928): 7–13.

73. Charles Ellwood, review of *Making the Fascist State, American Journal of Sociology* 35, no. 2 (September 1929): 323–24. See also Leonard Manyon, review of *Making the Fascist State, American Historical Review* 34, no. 3 (April 1929): 597–99; Roscoe C. Martin, review of *Making the Fascist State, Southwestern Political and Social Science Quarterly* 11, no. 2 (September 1930): 202–3.

74. Edward A. Purcell, *The Crisis of Democratic Theory: Scientific Naturalism and the Problem of Value* (Lexington: University of Kentucky Press, 1973), 95–114.

75. William Yandell Elliott, review of *Making the Fascist State, American Political Science Review* 23, no. 2 (May 1929): 477–81.

76. Herbert Wallace Schneider and Shepard Bancroft Clough, *Making Fascists* (Chicago: University of Chicago Press, 1929).

77. Charles E. Merriam, *The Making of Citizens: A Comparative Study of Methods of Civic Training* (Chicago: University of Chicago Press, 1931), ix–xi, 223–32, 299–301. Merriam's comparative research drew on country studies of Austria-Hungary, France, Germany, Great Britain, Italy, Russia, Switzerland, and the United States.

78. Letter, Henry Haskell to Herbert Schneider, November 16, 1934, Folder, Correspondence, 1930–1935, 107/1/4, SPHWS.

79. Herbert Wallace Schneider, "Faith," *Journal of Philosophy* 21, no. 2 (January 1924): 36–40; Horace Leland Friess and Herbert Wallace Schneider, *Religion in Various Cultures* (New York: H. Holt, 1932).

80. Anne O'Hare McCormick, "The Drama of Pope and Premier," *New York Times*, June 14, 1931; Anne O'Hare McCormick, "Italy Puts the Yoke on Capital and Labor," *New York Times*, November 28, 1926.

81. Child, *Diplomat Looks at Europe*, 218–19; also published as Richard Washburn Child, "What Does Mussolini Mean?" *Saturday Evening Post*, July 26, 1924.

82. "Gli italiani nel mondo," *Il Progresso Italo-Americano*, August 4, 1929.

83. Herbert Schneider, *The Fascist Government of Italy* (New York: Van Nostrand, 1936), viii–x, 62.

84. Diggins, *Mussolini and Fascism*; D'Agostino, *Rome in America*, 158–257; Cannistraro, *Blackshirts in Little Italy*. Research into the support of many Italian Americans for fascism owes a debt to those historians who have described the effects of nativism and discrimination on ethnic communities. John Higham, *Strangers in the Land: Patterns of American Nativism, 1860–1925* (New Brunswick, NJ: Rutgers University Press, 2002); Matthew Frye Jacobson, *Whiteness of a Different Color: European Immigrants and the Alchemy of Race* (Cambridge, MA: Harvard University Press, 1998); Thomas A. Guglielmo, *White on Arrival: Italians, Race, Color, and Power in Chicago, 1890–1945* (New York: Oxford University Press, 2004); Peter G. Vellon, *A Great Conspiracy against Our Race: Italian Immigrant Newspapers and the Construction of Whiteness in the Early 20th Century* (New York: New York University Press, 2014).

85. Emilio Gentile, "Impending Modernity: Fascism and the Ambivalent Image of the United States," *Journal of Contemporary History* 28, no. 1 (January 1993): 7–29. Ruth Ben-Ghiat, *Fascist Modernities: Italy, 1922–1945* (Los Angeles: University of California Press, 2001). Roger Griffin, *Modernism and Fascism: The Sense of a Beginning under Mussolini and Hitler* (New York: Palgrave Macmillan, 2007).

86. Adrian Lyttelton, *The Seizure of Power: Fascism in Italy, 1919–1929* (Princeton, NJ: Princeton University Press, 1987). Robert O. Paxton, *The Anatomy of Fascism* (New York: Alfred Knopf, 2004), 121, 151–53.

Chapter 1. The Good Adventure: Fascist Squads in a War-Weary World

1. Anne O'Hare McCormick, "The Revolt of Youth," *New York Times*, June 5, 1921. McCormick, "New Italy of the Italians."
2. McCormick, "Revolt of Youth."
3. McCormick, "New Italy of the Italians."
4. McCormick, "Revolt of Youth."
5. Ibid.
6. Diggins, *Mussolini and Fascism*, 29–31.
7. John Dos Passos Notebook, August 26, 1917, cited by Peter G. Filene, *Him/her/self: Sex Roles in Modern America* (Baltimore: Johns Hopkins University Press, 1986), 101.
8. Christopher Capozzola, *Uncle Sam Wants You: World War I and the Making of the Modern American Citizen* (New York: Oxford University Press, 2008), 11; David M. Kennedy, *Over Here: The First World War and American Society* (New York: Oxford University Press, 2004), 105–6.
9. Child, "Making the World Safe for Truth."
10. United States Department of Treasury National War-Savings Committee, *United States Government War-Savings Stamps: What They Are and Why You Should Buy Them* (Washington, DC: U.S. Government Printing Office, 1917).
11. Kennedy, *Over Here*, 44.
12. Walter Lippmann, "The World Conflict in Relation to American Democracy," *Annals of the American Academy of Political and Social Science* 72 (July 1917): 7–8.
13. Letter, Richard Washburn Child to Horace Walter Child, August 19, 1917, Folder "1881–1919," Reel 2, RWCP.
14. John Dos Passos, *One Man's Initiation: 1917* (London: George Allen & Unwin, 1920); John Dos Passos, *Three Soldiers* (New York: George H. Doran, 1921).
15. George Creel, *How We Advertised America: The First Telling of the Amazing Story of the Committee on Public Information That Carried the Gospel of Americanism to Every Corner of the Globe* (New York: Harper Row, 1920), 4.
16. Barry Alan Marks, "The Idea of Propaganda in America" (PhD dissertation, University of Minnesota, 1957), 28–52. Brett Gary, *The Nervous Liberals: Propaganda Anxieties from World War I to the Cold War* (New York: Columbia University Press, 1999), 23–26.
17. Ronald Steel, *Walter Lippmann and the American Century* (New York: Vintage Books, 1981), 114–15.
18. On the pervasive disillusionment, see Kennedy, *Over Here*, 88–92, 292–95. On the distance between political idealism and political reality, see Thorstein Veblen, "Dementia Praecox," in *The Culture of the Twenties*, ed. Loren Baritz (Indianapolis: Bobbs-Merrill, 1970), 28–40. On the reality of death in France, see John Dos Passos, "The Body of an American," in *Culture of the Twenties*, 5–11.

19. Harold E. Stearns, "Preface," in *Civilization in the United States*, ed. Harold E. Stearns (London: Jonathan Cape, 1922), vii.

20. F. Scott Fitzgerald, *This Side of Paradise* (New York: Scribner's, 1920), 304.

21. Baritz, "Introduction," in *Culture of the Twenties*, xix.

22. McCormick, "New Italy of the Italians."

23. Schneider, "Giovinezza."

24. Child, *Diplomat Looks at Europe*, 158; also published as Child, "Making of Mussolini."

25. Child, *Diplomat Looks at Europe*, 162–63; also published as Child, "Making of Mussolini."

26. Letter, Richard Washburn Child to Horace Walter Child, October 14, [1919?], Folder "1881–1919," Reel 2, RWCP.

27. Cohn, *Creating America*, 135–53.

28. Schneider, *Making the Fascist State*, 93, 74, 153.

29. McCormick, "Italy Rebels against Rebellion."

30. Anne O'Hare McCormick, "The Old Woman in the New Italy," *New York Times*, July 15, 1923. Schneider, *Making the Fascist State*, 63.

31. McCormick, "Italy Rebels against Rebellion."

32. Anne O'Hare McCormick, "Politics à l'Italienne," *New York Times*, September 10, 1922.

33. Schneider and Clough, *Making Fascists*, 44.

34. Schneider, *Making the Fascist State*, 83.

35. Child, *Diplomat Looks at Europe*, 165–66, 157; also published as Child, "Making of Mussolini."

36. Schneider, *Making the Fascist State*, 83.

37. Anne O'Hare McCormick, "Italy and Popes and Parliaments," *New York Times*, July 24, 1921.

38. Child, *Diplomat Looks at Europe*, 166; also published as Child, "Making of Mussolini."

39. Child, *Diplomat Looks at Europe*, 255; also published as Richard Washburn Child, "What Europe Thinks," *Saturday Evening Post*, April 4, 1925.

40. Child, *Diplomat Looks at Europe*, 58, 102; published in part as Richard Washburn Child, "International Show Windows," *Saturday Evening Post*, December 20, 1924.

41. Child, *Diplomat Looks at Europe*, 233; also published as Richard Washburn Child, "The Day of the Money Lenders," *Saturday Evening Post*, February 28, 1925.

42. Anne O'Hare McCormick, "Europe under the Arc Light," *New York Times*, March 20, 1921.

43. Anne O'Hare McCormick, "Bored Americans Abroad," *New York Times*, September 11, 1921.

44. "I Am Bored Stiff with This Life," illustration, in McCormick, "Bored Americans Abroad."

45. Anne O'Hare McCormick, "Wild West's Own New York," *New York Times*, March 5, 1922.

46. Anne O'Hare McCormick, "Zenith Discusses 'Babbitt,' Epic of Pullmania," *New York Times*, October 22, 1922.

47. Harold E. Stearns, "Paris Artists Come to Primitive Barter," *Baltimore Sun*, April 29, 1922.

48. Sinclair Lewis, *Babbitt* (New York: Harcourt Brace, 1922), 4, 68, 74.

49. Anne O'Hare McCormick, "Trifles Light as Air in a Tottering World," *New York Times*, June 19, 1921.

50. McCormick, "Zenith Discusses 'Babbitt.'" Lewis, *Babbitt*, 50.

51. Anne O'Hare McCormick, "Keeping the 'K' Out of Our Culture," *New York Times*, May 28, 1922.

52. Schneider, *Making the Fascist State*, 40.

53. Mark Thompson, *The White War: Life and Death on the Italian Front, 1915–1919* (New York: Basic Books, 2010), 324; H. James Burgwyn, *The Legend of the Mutilated Victory: Italy, the Great War, and the Paris Peace Conference, 1915–1919* (Westport, CT: Greenwood Press, 1993). Schneider, *Making the Fascist State*, 17–18, 44.

54. Schneider, *Making the Fascist State*, 40.

55. Paolo Spriano, *L'occupazione delle fabbriche, settembre 1929* (Turin: Einaudi, 1964). Spriano emphasized the limitations of the labor movement. Lyttelton, *Seizure of Power*, 44–51; Michael Ebner, *Ordinary Violence in Mussolini's Italy* (New York: Cambridge University Press, 2011), 23–47. Lyttelton and Ebner stressed the importance of fascist violence for suppressing socialism in provincial towns, such as Ferrara and Bologna, and the surrounding countryside.

56. Schneider, *Making the Fascist State*, 63.

57. "Intimate Study of Richard Washburn Child," *Boston Sunday Post*.

58. According to the embassy, labor groups in Rome and Naples organized strikes in protest against fascist violence, rather than the other way round. This analysis suggested that squadrism was not necessary to suppress communism—rather, it exacerbated the rumblings of the far left. *Embassy Weekly*, November 15, 1921, 865.00/1008; *Embassy Weekly*, November 22, 1921, 865.00/1012; both in RG59, M527, NARA.

59. Anne O'Hare McCormick, "Italy and Bolshevism," *New York Times*, July 20, 1928; Anne O'Hare McCormick, "Italian Crisis in 1920," *New York Times*, July 28, 1928.

60. McCormick, "Italy Rebels against Rebellion"; McCormick, "Old Woman in the New Italy."

61. McCormick, "Italy Rebels against Rebellion."

62. McCormick, "Revolt of Youth." Schneider, *Making the Fascist State*, 234, 250. Although Schneider recognized the mixed makeup of the squads, he referred frequently to the students among them, and fascism's "characteristics of a student movement."

63. Salvatore Lupo, *Il fascismo: La politica in un regime totalitario* (Rome: Donzelli, 2005), 93. Lupo cites the statistics gathered by the squadrists themselves up to 1921, recognizing that these were likely to be inexact. Roberta Suzzi Valli, "The Myth of Squadrismo in the Fascist Regime," *Journal of Contemporary History* 35, no. 2 (April 2000): 137. Not surprisingly, Valli cites much higher student membership in Bologna and Florence, where between forty and fifty percent of squadrists were students. By contrast, in Reggio Emilia only two percent of squadrists came from student backgrounds.

64. Stephen H. Norwood, *Strikebreaking and Intimidation: Mercenaries and Masculinity in Twentieth-Century America* (Chapel Hill: University of North Carolina Press, 2002), 17, 31; Colin J. Davis, *Power at Odds: The 1922 National Railroad Shopmen's Strike* (Urbana: University of Illinois Press, 1997), 119–22.

65. Schneider, *Making the Fascist State*, 234.

66. Ibid., 250.

67. Matteo Millan, "Origins," in *The Politics of Everyday Life in Fascist Italy: Outside the State?*, ed. Joshua Arthurs, Michael Ebner, and Kate Ferris (New York: Palgrave Macmillan, 2017), 29.

68. See also McCormick, "Revolt of Youth," for the responses of the "starry-eyed little Italian woman"; and McCormick, "Trifles Light as Air in a Tottering World," for fascists' defense of the honor of a female post office worker.

69. McCormick, "Politics à l'Italienne."

70. Child, *Diplomat Looks at Europe*, 170, 177, 170; also published as Child, "Making of Mussolini," and Richard Washburn Child, "Open the Gates," *Saturday Evening Post*, July 12, 1924.

71. Paula S. Fass, *The Damned and the Beautiful: American Youth in the 1920's* (New York: Oxford University Press, 1977), 21–23; Frederick Lewis Allen, *Only Yesterday: An Informal History of the Nineteen-Twenties* (New York: Blue Ribbon Books, 1931), 88–112.

72. "The Socialists Themselves Have Created the Reaction," illustration, in Anne O'Hare McCormick, "Italy's Parliamentary Paradoxes," *New York Times*, May 8, 1921.

73. Anne O'Hare McCormick, "Old Woman in the New Italy."

74. McCormick, "Italy Rebels against Rebellion."

75. McCormick, "Italy and Popes and Parliaments." Christopher Duggan, *Fascist Voices: An Intimate History of Mussolini's Italy* (New York: Oxford University Press, 2013), 45. The fascists shouted at Misiano: "Out! Out with deserters! Here we do not offend the glorious dead of the war and revolution." They shaved and painted his head, tied a placard around his neck, and forced him to walk down the Corso to jeering crowds.

76. *Embassy Weekly*, December 19, 1921, 865.00/1040; *Embassy Weekly*, December 26, 1921, 865.00/1047; both RG59, M527, NARA.

77. McCormick, "Italy and Popes and Parliaments."

78. McCormick, "Revolt of Youth."

79. McCormick, "Italy Rebels against Rebellion."

80. Capozzola, *Uncle Sam Wants You*, 210–12; Christopher Nehls, "The American Legion and Striking Workers during the Interwar Period," in *The Right and Labor in America: Politics, Ideology, and Imagination*, ed. Nelson Lichtenstein and Elizabeth Tandy Shermer (Philadelphia: University of Pennsylvania Press, 2012), 27–41; "Demands Action at Once Against Reds," *Los Angeles Times*, November 13, 1919; "American Legion Chief Warns All Members against Taking Law into Their Own Hands," *New York Times*, December 23, 1919.

81. "Centralia Riots Live in Memory," *New York Times*, November 11, 1962; Nell Irvin Painter, *Standing at Armageddon: The United States, 1877–1919* (New York: Norton, 2008), 376–77.

82. Valli, "Myth of Squadrismo in the Fascist Regime," 135–36.

83. Child, *Diplomat Looks at Europe*, 171, 177; also published as Child, "Making of Mussolini," and Child, "Open the Gates."

84. Schneider, "Giovinezza."

85. Ibid.; Schneider, *Making the Fascist State*, 18, 40.

86. Child, *Diplomat Looks at Europe*, 171; also published as Child, "Making of Mussolini."

87. Child, *Diplomat Looks at Europe*, 171; also published as Child, "Making of Mussolini." McCormick, "Italy's Parliamentary Paradoxes."

88. McCormick, "Italy's Parliamentary Paradoxes."

89. McCormick, "Italy Rebels against Rebellion."

90. McCormick, "Revolt of Youth."

91. Child, *Diplomat Looks at Europe*, 161–62; also published as Child, "Making of Mussolini."

92. Letter, Richard Washburn Child to Horace Walter Child, November 5, 1921, Folder "1920–21," Reel 2, RWCP.

93. Letter, Maude Parker to Mr. and Mrs. Horace Walter Child, November 14, [1921?], Folder "1920–21," Reel 2, RWCP.

94. McCormick, "Italy Rebels against Rebellion."

95. McCormick, "Politics à l'Italienne."

96. McCormick, "Italy and Popes and Parliaments."

97. Telegram, Richard Washburn Child to Charles Evans Hughes, October 26, 1922, 865.00/1164; Telegram, Richard Washburn Child to Charles Hughes, October 28, 1922, 865.00/1165; both RG59, M527, NARA.

98. Letter, Richard Washburn Child to Horace Walter Child, October 13, 1922, Folder "1922," Reel 2, RWCP.

99. Letter, Maude Parker to Mr. and Mrs. Horace Walter Child, October 24, 1922, Folder "1922," Reel 2, RWCP. Child, *Diplomat Looks at Europe*, 178–79; also published as Child, "Open the Gates."

100. Child, *Diplomat Looks at Europe*, 191; also published as Child, "Open the Gates."

101. Child, *Diplomat Looks at Europe*, 194, 196; also published as Child, "Open the Gates."

102. Child, *Diplomat Looks at Europe*, 195; also published as Child, "Open the Gates."

103. "Bring Them Back Victorious! Buy Liberty Bonds," 1918, POS-WWI-US, no. 286; "Our Boys in the Trenches—Is There Anything They Need That You Would Not Give Them?" 1917, POS-WWI-US, no. 276; W. A. Rogers, "His Liberty Bond, Paid in Full," 1917, POS-US.R635, no. 1; all in Prints and Photographs Division, Library of Congress.

104. McCormick, "Bored Americans Abroad."

105. Child, *Diplomat Looks at Europe*, 196; also published as Child, "Open the Gates."

106. Anne O'Hare McCormick, "The Swashbuckling Mussolini," *New York Times*, July 22, 1923. McCormick inadvertently revealed her lack of direct knowledge of the March on Rome by describing the marchers as "dusty and dry." Anyone who was actually there, and who experienced the torrential downpours, would have attested to the opposite.

107. Child, *Diplomat Looks at Europe*, 195; also published as Child, "Open the Gates."

108. Child, *Diplomat Looks at Europe*, 197–98; also published as Child, "Open the Gates."

109. "Nation Rejoices at War's End; City Is Jubilant," *New York Times*, November 12, 1918. "City Already Astir with Parade Spirit," *New York Times*, March 23, 1919.

110. "Pay Silent Tribute to the Dead in War," *New York Times*, November 12, 1922.

111. "Walker Is Acclaimed," *New York Times*, November 5, 1922; "Harvard Team Has Last Hard Workout," *New York Times*, November 24, 1922; "Rome's Colosseum Outdone by Our Football Bowls," *New York Times*, November 5, 1922.

112. Child, *Diplomat Looks at Europe*, 196.

113. Schneider, *Making the Fascist State*, 82; McCormick, "Italy and Bolshevism."

114. Martin Blinkhorn, *Mussolini and Fascist Italy* (New York: Routledge, 1994), 22.

115. Lyttelton, *Seizure of Power*, 85–86.

116. Schneider, *Making the Fascist State*, 83.

117. McCormick, "Italy and Popes and Parliaments." Before this article was published in the *Times*, the newspaper's main section had carried only six articles referring to Mussolini (mainly in passing). *Embassy Weekly*, August 30, 1921, 865.00/944, RG59, M527, NARA.

118. Schneider, *Making the Fascist State*, 9–13; Child, *Diplomat Looks at Europe*, 172–73; *Embassy Weekly*, November 4, 1922, 865.00/1180, RG59, M527, NARA. See also *Reminiscences of Herbert Wallace Schneider*. Schneider claimed that *Il Popolo d'Italia* had received American funding during the war, channeled to Mussolini via Charles Merriam, who then worked for the Committee on Public Information in Rome. Merriam supported Schneider's 1927 research grant because he wanted Schneider to investigate whether American financial support had impacted Mussolini's editorial position during the war. Schneider's memory was sustained by subsequent scholarship. See Patrick D. Reagan, *Designing a New America: The Origins of New Deal Planning, 1890–1943* (Amherst: University of Massachusetts Press, 1999), 65.

119. Schneider, *Making the Fascist State*, 11.

120. *Embassy Weekly*, November 4, 1922, 865.00/1180, RG59, M527, NARA.

121. Child, *Diplomat Looks at Europe*, 173; also published as Child, "Making of Mussolini."

122. R.J.B. Bosworth, *Mussolini* (London: Arnold, 2004), 114.

123. *Embassy Weekly*, November 4, 1922, 865.00/1180, RG59, M527, NARA.

124. Schneider, *Making the Fascist State*, 8, 12.

125. Child, *Diplomat Looks at Europe*, 158; also published as Child, "Making of Mussolini."

126. Schneider, *Making the Fascist State*, 20.

127. McCormick, "Italy and Popes and Parliaments." *Mussolini as Revealed in His Political Speeches, November 1914–August 1923*, ed. and trans. Bernardo Barone Quaranta di San Severino (London: Dent, 1923), 196–200.

128. McCormick, "Italy Rebels against Rebellion."

129. Child, *Diplomat Looks at Europe*, 173. Telegram, Richard Washburn Child to Charles Evans Hughes, October 26, 1922, 865.00/1164, RG59, M527, NARA. In Child's official account of this meeting, Mussolini seemed less relaxed and more calculating.

130. Child, *Diplomat Looks at Europe*, 173–74; also published as Child, "Making of Mussolini."

131. Child, *Diplomat Looks at Europe*, 172; also published as Child, "Making of Mussolini." Schneider, "Giovinezza."

132. *Embassy Weekly*, May 20, 1922, 865.00/1114, RG59, M527, NARA. Mussolini, according to this report, had refused to retract an article, in which he criticized Missiroli.

133. McCormick, "The Swashbuckling Mussolini."

134. Schneider, *Making the Fascist State*, 81–82.

135. Ibid., 82; McCormick, "Swashbuckling Mussolini."

136. Letter, Richard Washburn Child to Horace Walter Child, August 19, 1917, Folder "1881–1919," Reel 2, RWCP.

137. McCormick, "Politics à l'Italienne."

138. McCormick, "Revolt of Youth."

Chapter 2. Mystic in a Morning Coat: Americans' Mussolini in the 1920s

1. Child, *Diplomat Looks at Europe*, 204–6; also published as Child, "What Does Mussolini Mean?"

2. Child, *Diplomat Looks at Europe*, 206; also published as Child, "What Does Mussolini Mean?"

3. Anne O'Hare McCormick, "The Age-Old Issue Stirs Rome," *New York Times*, October 10, 1926. See also Schneider, *Making the Fascist State*, 86.

4. Diggins, *Mussolini and Fascism*, 71–72. Diggins wrote that Mussolini "seemed to give expression to certain ideals rendered precarious by the sudden changes of the twenties." For similar observations, see Frank Costigliola, *Awkward Dominion: American Political, Economic, and Cultural Relations with Europe, 1919–1933* (Ithaca, NY: Cornell University Press, 1984), 96.

5. Warren Susman, "Culture Heroes: Ford, Barton, Ruth," in *Culture as History: The Transformation of American Society in the Twentieth Century* (New York: Pantheon, 1984), 141–49; Warren Susman, "'Personality' and the Making of Twentieth Century Culture," in *Culture as History*, 271–85. Steven Watts, *The People's Tycoon: Henry Ford and the American Century* (New York: Alfred Knopf, 2005), xii–xiii. Watts presents a similar explanation for Ford's popularity. David Riesman, with Nathan Glazer and Reuel Denny, *The Lonely Crowd: A Study of the Changing American Character* (New Haven, CT: Yale University Press, 1953), 13–26. Susman's distinction between "character" and "personality" bears many similarities to Riesman's distinction between "inner-direction" and "outer-direction."

6. Gian Giacomo Migone, *The United States and Fascist Italy: The Rise of American Finance in Europe*, trans. Molly Tambor (New York: Cambridge University Press, 2015). For a less scholarly rendition of a similar argument, see Caretto, *Quando l'America si innamorò di Mussolini*.

7. Schmitz, *United States and Fascist Italy*, 56; Costigliola, *Awkward Dominion*, 94; Anne O'Hare McCormick, "When Greek Greets Greek," *New York Times*, July 13, 1924; Anne O'Hare McCormick, "Climax Passed, League Faces Knotty Issues," *New York Times*, October 3, 1926; "Italy's Fiscal House in Order," *Il Progresso Italo-Americano*, February 3, 1929. Schneider, *Making the Fascist State*, 71. Schneider attributed much of this economic stability to Mussolini's choice of the liberal economist Alberto De Stefani as finance minister.

8. Child, *Diplomat Looks at Europe*, 222–23; also published as Child, "What Does Mussolini Mean?" Neglecting to mention the role of De Stefani, Child implied that Mussolini was directly responsible for the program's creation, and its apparent successes. Letter, Richard Washburn Child to Charles Evans Hughes, May 1, 1923, 865/1227, RG59, M527, NARA. More skeptical in his official missives, Ambassador Child suggested that the proposed budget cuts would be undermined by military expenditures.

9. Child, "The President."

10. Richard Washburn Child, "Mussolini Now," *Saturday Evening Post*, March 24, 1928.

11. Child, *Diplomat Looks at Europe*, 215; also published as Child "What Does Mussolini Mean?"

12. Diggins, *Mussolini and Fascism*, 160.

13. Alexander De Grand, *Italian Fascism: Its Origins and Development* (Lincoln: University of Nebraska Press, 2000), 66, 69–71.

14. McCormick, "Il Duce Pictures the New State."

15. Letter, Anne O'Hare McCormick to Benito Mussolini, July 15, 1926; "Intervista Mc Kormick [sic]"; Letter, McCormick to Giacomo Paulucci, July 26, 1926; Letter, McCormick to Paulucci, August 4, 1926. All in sotto-fascicolo "1926 Anna O'Hare Mc. Cormick," fascicolo "Interviste," busta 752, Ministero della Cultura Popolare, ASD. Mussolini was probably referring to an Associated Press interview with Robert H. Davis. See "Mussolini's Faith in Star," *Los Angeles Times*, September 14, 1926.

16. Anne O'Hare McCormick, "Main Street, Too, Winters in Florida," *New York Times*, February 22, 1925; Anne O'Hare McCormick, "Miracle Men on Florida's Gold Coast," *New York Times*, March 8, 1925; Anne O'Hare McCormick, "Making a Speedway of De Soto's Trail," *New York Times*, May 17, 1925.

17. McCormick, "Making a Speedway of De Soto's Trail."

18. Generoso Pope, "Ai lettori del Progresso," *Il Progresso Italo-Americano*, November 2, 1928.

19. Generoso Pope, "To Our Readers," *Il Progresso Italo-Americano*, November 4, 1928.

20. Italianità can be translated, simply, as Italian identity. But, as some historians have shown, in the context of a hostile environment in the United States in the late nineteenth and early twentieth centuries, it was sometimes underpinned by claims to the superiority of Italian civilization, and chauvinism toward people with darker skins than Italians' own. See Vellon, *Great Conspiracy against Our Race*.

21. "S. E. Mussolini mentre pronuncia . . . ," photograph, *Il Progresso Italo-Americano*, January 6, 1929.

22. "An Italian Genius, He Knows His Business," *Il Progresso Italo-Americano*, January 11, 1929. This article was a reprint of a piece published in William Randolph Hearst's *New York Evening Journal*.

23. "Presieduta da S.E. Benito Mussolini . . . ," photograph, *Il Progresso Italo-Americano*, March 24, 1929.

24. "'Come Mussolini prepara l'Italia futura'—Federzoni," *Il Progresso Italo-Americano*, December 2, 1929.

25. For the launch of the English-feature section, see Generoso Pope, "To the Readers of 'Il Progresso,'" *Il Progresso Italo-Americano*, November 18, 1928.

26. "Italo-Americans of Whom We Are Proud: Ferdinand Pecora," *Il Progresso Italo-Americano*, December 30, 1928. "Italo Palermo, in Four Years, Trebled Capital of Bank of Sicily Trust Co.," *Il Progresso Italo-Americano*, January 26, 1930.

27. I. C. Falbo, "Ai lettori del 'Progresso,'" *Il Progresso Italo-Americano*, November 2, 1928.

28. For these mafia connections, see Jack Vitek, *The Godfather of Tabloid: Generoso Pope Jr. and the National Enquirer* (Lexington: University Press of Kentucky, 2008), 16–18, 23–24.

29. For "maelstrom," see Marshall Berman, *All That Is Solid Melts into Air: The Experience of Modernity* (London: Verso, 1983), 15–16.

30. "He Is Big Enough to Scrap Caesar and Napoleon in Favor of Mussolini," illustration, in McCormick, "Il Duce Pictures the New State."

31. "S. E. Mussolini mentre pronuncia . . . ," photograph, *Il Progresso Italo-Americano*; "Presieduta da S.E. Benito Mussolini . . . ," photograph, *Il Progresso Italo-Americano*.

32. "Il gigante e il pigmeo della boxe," *Il Progresso Italo-Americano*, October 20, 1929; "Il Generale Italo Balbo . . . ," photograph, *Il Progresso Italo-Americano*, January 6, 1929.

33. See also "A Glimpse of Il Duce," photograph, *Il Progresso Italo-Americano*, March 31, 1929; "On. Benito Mussolini," photograph, *Il Progresso Italo-Americano*, April 21, 1929; "Benito Mussolini," photograph, *Il Progresso Italo-Americano*, April 21, 1929; "S. E. Benito Mussolini, Primo Ministro d'Italia," photograph, *Il Progresso Italo-Americano*, February 17, 1929.

34. Susman, "'Personality' and the Making of Twentieth Century Culture," 271–85.

35. Richard Weiss, *The American Myth of Success: From Horatio Alger to Norman Vincent Peale* (New York: Basic Books, 1969), 48–63.

36. For "therapeutic," see T. J. Jackson Lears, *No Place of Grace: Antimodernism and the Transformation of American Culture, 1880–1920* (Chicago: University of Chicago Press, 1981), 101–4, 194.

37. Luisa Passerini, *Mussolini immaginario: Storia di una biografia, 1915–1939* (Bari: Editori Laterza, 1991), 123. As Schneider recognized, Mussolini insisted that his opponents speak less than he. Schneider, *Making the Fascist State*, 86.

38. Sofia Serrenelli, "A Town for the Cult of the Duce: Predappio as a Site of Pilgrimage," in *The Cult of the Duce: Mussolini and the Italians*, ed. Stephen Gundle, Christopher Duggan, and Giuliana Pieri (Manchester, UK: Manchester University Press, 2013), 93–109. Passerini, *Mussolini immaginario*, 89.

39. McCormick, "Il Duce Pictures the New State."

40. Benito Mussolini, *My Autobiography*, 1–19; also published as Benito Mussolini, "Youth," *Saturday Evening Post*, May 5, 1928.

41. Child, "Mussolini Now." See also McCormick, "Il Duce Pictures the New State." "He Drinks Not at All" read the subheading of one section.

42. McCormick, "Il Duce Pictures the New State."

43. Child, "Mussolini Now."

44. "Un lavoratore formidabile," *Il Progresso Italo-Americano*, May 20, 1929. See also Antonio Cottafavi, "The New Italy," *Il Progresso Italo-Americano*, January 13, 1929.

45. Child, *Diplomat Looks at Europe*, 222; also published as Child, "What Does Mussolini Mean?"

46. Child, *Diplomat Looks at Europe*, 185; also published as Child, "Open the Gates." Mussolini, wrote Child, ordered the March on Rome because the movement was like a bubbling bottle of champagne. He needed to pop the cork "lest effervescence burst the bottle and waste the contents." Child, "Foreword," in *My Autobiography*, xiii; also published as Child, "Mussolini Now." Mussolini spoke, wrote Child, in sentences, "suddenly ejaculated."

47. Metaphors of ejaculation were in line with late-Victorian ideas of "passionate" manhood, which praised male sexuality as authentic and invigorating. See E. Anthony Rotundo, *American Manhood: Transformations in Masculinity from the Revolution to the Modern Era* (New York: Basic Books, 1993), 71–74, 231–32.

48. Child, "Foreword," in *My Autobiography*, xi–xiii; also published as Child, "Mussolini Now." Anne O'Hare McCormick, "Behind Fascism Stands a Philosopher," *New York Times*, September 26, 1926.

49. McCormick, "The Swashbuckling Mussolini"; Anne O'Hare McCormick, "There Were Giants in Those Days," *New York Times*, August 3, 1924. McCormick described the various phases of Mussolini's career as consistent with his commitment to Italy.

50. Passerini, *Mussolini immaginario*, 39. Schneider, *Making the Fascist State*, 125. In contrast to Child, McCormick, and Pope, Schneider adopted an ironic tone when discussing aspects of Mussolini's image. This comported with Schneider's belief that Mussolini's actual character mattered less than his ability to project aspects of character—including self-abnegation and responsibility—that enabled effective leadership.

51. Child, *Diplomat Looks at Europe*, 215; also published as Child, "What Does Mussolini Mean?"

52. Anne O'Hare McCormick, "The People's Own Dictators," *New York Times*, April 13, 1924.

53. Mussolini, *My Autobiography*, 6; also published as Mussolini, "Youth." See also Serrenelli, "A Town for the Cult of the Duce," 95.

54. "La famiglia del Duce per i bambini di Roma," *Il Progresso Italo-Americano*, January 2, 1929.

55. Child, "Mussolini Now."

56. "An Italian Genius, He Knows His Business," *Il Progresso Italo-Americano*. See also McCormick, "Behind Fascism Stands a Philosopher."

57. *Embassy Weekly*, June 30, 1923, 865/1239, RG59, M527, NARA, contains the text of Child's speech at the banquet of the Italo-American Society in Rome, June 28, 1923.

58. Child, "Foreword," in *My Autobiography*, xv; also published as Child, "Mussolini Now."

59. R.J.B. Bosworth, *Mussolini's Italy: Life under the Dictatorship, 1915–1945* (New York: Penguin Books, 2006), 241–43.

60. Fass, *Damned and the Beautiful*, 7, 13. For anxieties about young men in other periods of history, see Judy Hilkey, *Character Is Capital: Success Manuals and Manhood in Gilded Age America* (Chapel Hill: University of North Carolina Press, 1997); James Gilbert, *A Cycle of Outrage: America's Reaction to the Juvenile Delinquent in the 1950s* (New York: Oxford University Press, 1986).

61. McCormick, "When Greek Greets Greek."

62. McCormick, "Miracle Men on Florida's Gold Coast."

63. Richard Washburn Child, *Battling the Criminal* (Garden City, NY: Doubleday, 1925). Child's series on crime ran in the *Saturday Evening Post* under the title "The Great American Scandal," between August 1 and November 14, 1925. "Crime Commission Members Selected," *Washington Post*, November 16, 1925; "Commission Unable to Find Universal Panacea for Crime," *Baltimore Sun*, April 30, 1926. The Crime Commission ran its five-month course, impacting policy little, if at all.

64. Child, *Battling the Criminal*, 43–47, 66–67, 76; also published as Richard Washburn Child, "The Great American Scandal—Why We Have Crime," *Saturday Evening Post*, August 15, 1925; Richard Washburn Child, "The Great American Scandal—Youth and Felony," *Saturday Evening Post*, August 29, 1925.

65. Child, *Battling the Criminal*, 46; also published as Child, "The Great American Scandal—Why We Have Crime."

66. Child, "The President."

67. Child, *Battling the Criminal*, 46; also published as Child, "The Great American Scandal—Why We Have Crime."

68. Child, *Diplomat Looks at Europe*. 273–75; also published as "What Europe Thinks."

69. Child, *Battling the Criminal*, 121; also published as Richard Washburn Child, "The Great American Scandal—Take This Case," *Saturday Evening Post*, September 26, 1925.

70. Child, "The President."

71. McCormick, "Making a Speedway of De Soto's Trail."

72. Richard Washburn Child, "Scout Training Guides Youths through Shoals of Temptations," *New York Herald Tribune*, April 24, 1927.

73. Child, *Diplomat Looks at Europe*, 253; also published as Child, "What Europe Thinks."

74. Anne O'Hare McCormick, "The Mass Offensive of Women," *New York Times*, April 14, 1929.

75. Ibid.

76. For the decline of the culture of service and obligation, see *Embassy Weekly*, June 30, 1923, 865/1239, RG59, M527, NARA. For New Women, and their effects on youth, see Child, *Diplomat Looks at Europe*, 256–57; also published as Child, "What Europe Thinks." For juvenile delinquency, see Child, *Battling the Criminal*, 33, 68–69; also published as Child, "The Great American Crime Scandal—Why We Have Crime"; and Child, "The Great American Scandal—Youth and Felony." For modern art, see Child, *Diplomat Looks at Europe*, 256; also published as Child, "What Europe Thinks."

77. Child, *Diplomat Looks at Europe*, 256; also published as Child, "What Europe Thinks."

78. Child, *Diplomat Looks at Europe*, 24–25; also published as Child, "Our American Diplomat."

79. The following represents a small sample of Child's obsessive discussions about money: Letter, Richard Washburn Child to Horace Walter Child, October 15, 1923; Letter, Richard Washburn Child to Horace Walter Child, October 29, 1923; Letter, Richard Washburn Child to Horace Walter Child, October 10, 1924; all in Folder "1923–24," Reel 2, RWCP. Diggins, *Mussolini and Fascism*, 49. Diggins recognized that Child's personal papers revealed his constant interest in money.

80. Letter, Richard Washburn Child to Horace Walter Child, October 11, 1922, Folder "1922," Reel 2, RWCP.

81. Child, *Diplomat Looks at Europe*, 23; also published as Child, "Our American Diplomat." For his readers, Child ascribed these excesses to other expatriates in Rome. He wrote that, unlike these socialites, he resisted the "shirt front" and "soda mints." Child, "The President."

82. Letter, Richard Washburn Child to Horace Walter Child, March 17, [1926?]; Letter, Richard Washburn Child to Horace Walter Child, November 14, 1925; both in Folder "General Correspondence, 1925–27," Reel 1, RWCP.

83. Child, *Diplomat Looks at Europe*, 256; also published as Child, "What Europe Thinks."

84. Letter, Richard Washburn Child to Horace Walter Child, [No day given] November 1925, Folder "General Correspondence, 1925–27," Reel 1, RWCP.

85. "R. W. Child Files Divorce Action; Won't Tell Why," *Chicago Daily Tribune*, August 6, 1926; "Richard W. Child, Envoy and Author, Sues for Divorce," *Washington Post*, August 6, 1926.

86. Letter, Richard Washburn Child to Mr. and Mrs. Horace Walter Child, March 18 [1923?]; Letter, Richard Washburn Child to Horace Walter Child, August 5, 1923; both in Folder "1923–24," Reel 2, RWCP.

87. "Ambassador Child Is Merely on Leave," *New York Times*, October 9, 1923.

88. Letter, Richard Washburn Child to Horace Walter Child, February 13, 1924, Folder "1923–24"; Letter, Richard Washburn Child to Mr. and Mrs. Horace Walter Child, [Late July 1926?], Folder "1925–30"; both in Reel 2, RWCP. "Coolidge Will Be a Candidate, Says R. W. Child," *Chicago Daily Tribune*.

89. Letter, Richard Washburn Child to Horace Walter Child, September 27, 1926, Folder "General Correspondence, 1925–27," Reel 1, RWCP.

90. Letter, S. S. McClure to Giovanni Capasso Torre, August 12, 1926, fascicolo "Mac Clure [sic] e Rivetta," busta 256, Ministero Cultura Popolare, ASD. Initially, S. S. McClure pitched the idea of the autobiography to the regime. "I want to supervise the editing of a book telling the story of Italy.... In order to secure wide reading in all countries, the book should ultimately

bear the name of Mussolini." Kenneth Roberts, *I Wanted to Write* (Garden City, NY: Doubleday, 1949), 176–79. McClure then approached Lorimer for a ghost writer. Roberts, a regular contributor to the *Post*, was Lorimer's first choice for the job, but Roberts pulled out of the deal due to the conditions imposed by Margherita Sarfatti. Philip V. Cannistraro and Brian R. Sullivan, *Il Duce's Other Woman* (New York: Morrow, 1993), 358. Child sailed to Rome in the fall of 1927. By February of the following year, he had "cut McClure out of the deal."

91. Schneider, "Giovinezza."

92. Schneider and Clough, *Making Fascists*, 83–109, 178–82.

93. Merriam, *Making of Citizens*, 117–18, 226–32. Merriam did not deny that at least one of these "special patriotic organizations"—the Blackshirts—was the paramilitary arm of an uncompromising dictatorship.

94. Charles E. Merriam, "Editor's Preface," in Schneider and Clough, *Making Fascists*, vii.

95. Child, *Battling the Criminal*, 263–90; also published as Richard Washburn Child, "The Great American Scandal: Turning Back the Crime Tide," *Saturday Evening Post*, November 14, 1925; esp. Child, "Scout Training Guides Youths through Shoals of Temptations."

96. I. C. Falbo, "Ai lettori del 'Progresso.'" The historiography regarding Casa Italiana brims with vituperation. Diggins, *Mussolini and Fascism*, 255. Diggins wrote that "Fascism found a veritable home in America" through the Casa, and its head, the pragmatist philosopher, Giuseppe Prezzolini. Giuseppe Prezzolini, *The Case of the Casa Italiana* (New York: American Institute of Italian Studies, 1976). Prezzolini authored a slim but vicious volume, in which he denied each of Diggins's charges, accused Diggins of sloppy research, and claimed that there was no archival evidence to support the allegations of regime support for Casa Italiana. Elena Bacchin, "Prezzolini in America e il fascismo. Un memoriale," *Contemporanea* 11, no. 2 (April 2008): 243–56. More recent scholarship has found that Prezzolini viewed fascism favorably and that he became a card-carrying member of the Fascist Party in 1935.

97. Italo Falbo to Alessandro Chiavolini, December 11, 1928, fascicolo H407, "Raccomandato Pope, Generoso New York Oggetto:1928 onorificenza," busta 18, Segreteria particolare del Duce, carteggio ordinario, ACS.

98. "Generoso Pope Decorated," *New York Times*, February 6, 1929.

99. "La grande manifestazione in onore del Comm. Generoso Pope all'Hotel Biltmore," *Il Progresso Italo-Americano*.

100. "Il Comm. Pope arriva oggi a Napoli," *Il Progresso Italo-Americano*, June 24, 1929.

101. "Il S. Padre ha ricevuto nella sala del trono il Comm. Pope," *Il Progresso Italo-Americano*, July 5, 1929; "Un pranzo ufficiale in onore del Comm. G. Pope a Roma," *Il Progresso Italo-Americano*, July 2, 1929.

102. "L'entusiastico tributo de Arpaise al Comm. Pope alla signora ed ai figli," *Il Progresso Italo-Americano*, July 14, 1929.

103. "Il Primo Ministro On. Mussolini riceve il comm. Pope e l'On. Falbo," *Il Progresso Italo-Americano*, July 6, 1929.

104. Cannistraro, "Generoso Pope and the Rise of Italian American Politics," 276.

105. "Il Primo Ministro On. Mussolini riceve il Comm. Pope e l'On. Falbo," *Il Progresso Italo-Americano*.

106. "Il Duce posa col Comm. Pope," photograph, *Il Progresso Italo-Americano*, July 20, 1929.

107. "La grande manifestazione in onore del Comm. Generoso Pope all'Hotel Biltmore."

108. "Grande banchetto di onore al Comm. Pope e al Dr. Falbo," *Il Progresso Italo-Americano*, July 11, 1929.

109. "Justice Cotillo Lifelong Friend of Immigrant," *Il Progresso Italo-Americano*, March 24, 1929.

110. Pope, "To the Readers of 'Il Progresso.'"

111. "In Defense of the Family," *Il Progresso Italo-Americano*, March 2, 1929.

112. Waldo Frank, *The Re-Discovery of America: An Introduction to a Philosophy of American Life* (New York: Scribner's, 1929), 105; also published as Waldo Frank, "The Re-Discovery of America. IX: Gods and Cults of Power," *New Republic*, March 28, 1928.

113. Walter Lippmann, "The Problem of Unbelief," in *A Preface to Morals* (New York: Macmillan, 1929), 7.

114. Child, *Diplomat Looks at Europe*, 273; also published as Child, "What Europe Thinks."

115. Edward Corsi, "The Soul of America," *Il Progresso Italo-Americano*, June 9, 1929; Edward Corsi, "What Price Prosperity?" *Il Progresso Italo-Americano*, July 21, 1929.

116. Corsi, "What Price Prosperity?"

117. Anne O'Hare McCormick, "Nobody's Home Town: Washington," *New York Times*, July 14, 1929.

118. Ibid. Anne O'Hare McCormick, "America at Last Airs Its Mind," *New York Times*, November 4, 1928. Anne O'Hare McCormick, "C. W. Bryan—Who May Become President," *New York Times*, October 19, 1924. "Una dimostrazione," *Il Progresso Italo-Americano*, November 3, 1928.

119. Al Smith lost the 1928 presidential contest against Herbert Hoover. He was also unsuccessful in his bid for the Democratic nomination for president in 1924. Charles Wayland Bryan was the Democrats' vice-presidential candidate in the 1924 election, which the Democrats lost in a landslide to Calvin Coolidge and Charles Dawes.

120. Child, "The President."

121. Ibid.

122. McCormick, "America at Last Airs Its Mind."

123. Anne O'Hare McCormick, "Uncertain, the Farmer Waits," *New York Times*, March 31, 1929.

124. Anne O'Hare McCormick, "Bringing Politics Up to Date," *New York Times*, November 25, 1928.

125. Child, *Diplomat Looks at Europe*, 221; also published as Child, "What Does Mussolini Mean?"

126. Schneider, *Making the Fascist State*, 224–27; Anne O'Hare McCormick, "Fascism Takes Francis as Patron Saint," *New York Times*, September 12, 1926.

127. Amanda Minervini, "Face to Face: Iconic Representations and Juxtapositions of St. Francis of Assisi and Mussolini during Italian Fascism," in *TOTalitarian ARTs: The Visual Arts, Fascisms and Mass-Society*, ed. Mark Epstein, Fulvio Orsitto, and Andrea Righi (Newcastle, UK: Cambridge Scholars, 2017), 40–61.

128. Emilio Gentile, *Il culto del Littorio: La sacralizzazione della politica nell'Italia fascista* (Rome: Laterza, 1993).

129. For speech in the Chamber of Deputies, see Schneider, *Making the Fascist State*, 86; McCormick, "Age Old Issue Stirs Rome"; Mussolini, *My Autobiography*, 199; also published as Benito Mussolini, "The Death Struggle of a Worn-Out Democracy," *Saturday Evening Post*,

June 23, 1928. For appearance with prelates, see Schneider, *Making the Fascist State*, 230; Schneider and Clough, *Making Fascists*, 67. Prefiguring Emilio Gentile's argument, Schneider recognized the rapprochement for what it was: a power grab. He was no less admiring of Mussolini a result. See Schneider and Clough, *Making Fascists*, 74, 80; Schneider, *Making the Fascist State*, 222; Gentile, *Il culto del Littorio*.

130. McCormick, "Drama of Pope and Premier."

131. "Prossimo incontro del Papa col Duce," *Il Progresso Italo-Americano*, February 9, 1929.

132. "Dopo la conciliazione fra la Chiesa e lo Stato in Italia," *Il Progresso Italo-Americano*, February 17, 1929; Rastignac, "Significato e portata della conciliazione," *Il Progresso Italo-Americano*, February 9, 1929; Rastignac, "La pace tra la Chiesa e lo Stato," *Il Progresso Italo-Americano*, February 12, 1929.

133. "Dopo la conciliazione fra la Chiesa e lo Stato in Italia," *Il Progresso Italo-Americano*.

134. "La conciliazione tra Chiesa e Stato," photographs, *Il Progresso Italo-Americano*, February 8, 1929; "La firma dello storico atto," *Il Progresso Italo-Americano*, February 15, 1929.

135. Rastignac, "Rinnovamento spirituale in Italia," *Il Progresso Italo-Americano*, March 18, 1929.

136. Child, "Mussolini Now"; published in part in Child, "Foreword," in *My Autobiography*, xi.

137. Child, "Foreword," in *My Autobiography*, xviii–xix; also published as Child, "Mussolini Now."

138. Child, "Foreword," in *My Autobiography*, xix; also published as Child, "Mussolini Now."

139. Child, "Mussolini Now."

Chapter 3. The Dream Machine: The Fascist State in an Era of Democratic Disillusionment

1. Schneider, *Making the Fascist State*, 103, 158–59.

2. Elliott, review of *Making the Fascist State*.

3. For Dewey, see Robert B. Westbrook, *John Dewey and American Democracy* (Ithaca, NY: Cornell University Press, 1993).

4. Peter Vogt, "Herbert Schneider and the Ideal of an Intelligent Society," *Transactions of the Charles S. Peirce Society* 38, no. 3 (July 2002): 395.

5. Purcell, *Crisis of Democratic Theory*, 98. Stephen Jay Gould, *The Mismeasure of Man* (New York: Norton, 1996), 222–63.

6. *Reminiscences of Herbert Wallace Schneider*.

7. Purcell, *Crisis of Democratic Theory*, 98–104.

8. Paul V. Murphy, *The New Era: American Thought and Culture in the 1920s* (Lanham, UK: Rowman & Littlefield, 2011), 149–79.

9. Walter Lippmann, *Public Opinion* (New York: Harcourt Brace, 1922).

10. Benjamin F. Wright, "The Tendency Away from Political Democracy in the United States," *Southwestern Political and Social Science Quarterly* 7, no. 1 (June 1926): 25.

11. David M. Ricci, *The Tragedy of Political Science: Politics, Scholarship, and Democracy* (New Haven, CT: Yale University Press, 1984), 83.

12. Kent expressed some sympathies with fascism. See Frank R. Kent, "Mussolini Explains Aims of Fascism and Predicts its World-Wide Acceptance," *Baltimore Sun*, October 1, 1930.

13. Schneider, *Making the Fascist State*, 79–80.

14. McCormick, "Italy and Bolshevism."

15. Schneider, *Making the Fascist State*, 80.

16. McCormick, "Italy and Bolshevism." Mussolini, *My Autobiography*, 115–116, 163; also published as Mussolini, "Death Struggle of a Worn-Out Democracy"; and Benito Mussolini, "Toward Conquest of Power," *Saturday Evening Post*, July 21, 1928.

17. McCormick, "Italy and Bolshevism"; Richard Washburn Child, *The Writing on the Wall: Who Shall Govern Us Next?* (New York: Sears, 1929).

18. Schneider, *Making the Fascist State*, 80.

19. Mussolini, *My Autobiography*, 69; also published as Benito Mussolini, "Ashes and Embers," *Saturday Evening Post*, June 2, 1928. See also Schneider, *Making the Fascist State*, 88–98; Mussolini, *My Autobiography*, 214–26; also published as Benito Mussolini, "Five Years of Government," *Saturday Evening Post*, August 25, 1928. Both Schneider and Mussolini paid significant attention to the 1923 Acerbo law (which doctored elections in the fascists' favor), as well as the subsequent elections, and the murder in June 1924 of the socialist deputy Giacomo Matteotti, who had criticized these elections as a charade. Both argued that fascism's opponents had blocked the government, leaving Mussolini with no choice but to scrap multiparty politics. For more accurate analysis of these years, see Adrian Lyttelton, "Fascism in Italy: The Second Wave," *Journal of Contemporary History* 1, no. 1 (January 1966): 75–100; Mauro Canali, "The Matteotti Murder and the Origins of Mussolini's Totalitarian Fascist Regime in Italy," *Journal of Modern Italian Studies* 14, no. 2 (May 2009): 143–67.

20. Mussolini, "Death Struggle of a Worn-Out Democracy."

21. Letter, Richard Washburn Child to Horace Walter Child, October 10, 1924, Folder "1923–24," Reel 2, RWCP. "Lorimer of the Post is putting up five thousand for expenses and a fat price on each of ten articles—in fact a record price. In addition Maude has an order for articles which will make her prosperous," Child told his father. Child's articles were published in the *Post* between December 1924 and April 1925.

22. Child, *Writing on the Wall*, 1–4, 56–57, 72–74, 77–80, 85–87.

23. Ibid., 58–59, 62–63 70–71, 174, 183.

24. Ibid., 60, 146; Lippmann, *Public Opinion*, 72.

25. Anne O'Hare McCormick, "The Corn Belt Looks at Governor Smith," *New York Times*, September 23, 1928; Anne O'Hare McCormick, "Trailing the Elusive Farm Vote," *New York Times*, October 14, 1928; Anne O'Hare McCormick, "Enter Woman, the New Boss of Politics," *New York Times*, October 21, 1928.

26. "Senate Show to Open for Three-Month Run," *Il Progresso Italo-Americano*, December 2, 1928.

27. "Problems That Confront the New Congress," *New York Times*, April 7, 1929.

28. Anne O'Hare McCormick, "Senate and House in a Test of Strength," *New York Times*, May 19, 1929; "The Revolt in the Republican Party," *New York Times*, November 17, 1929; Anne O'Hare McCormick, "Over the Senate Insurgent Whips Snap," *New York Times*, November 17, 1929.

29. Anne O'Hare McCormick, "Congress: Mirror of the Nation," *New York Times*, May 5, 1929.

30. Child, *Writing on the Wall*, 229–30. E. Pendleton Herring, *Group Representation Before Congress* (Baltimore: Johns Hopkins University Press, 1929), 277–83. Herring, a political scientist, made the same estimation.

31. Child, *Writing on the Wall*, 54, 229, 234–36. Although Child bemoaned the influence of money power over political processes, the pressure groups that he identified as destructive were not the repositories of business and financial interests, but representative of more marginalized members of society.

32. Anne O'Hare McCormick, "Light on the Elusive Lobbyist," *New York Times*, November 3, 1929. Herring, *Group Representation before Congress*, 53. Like McCormick, Herring suggested that lobbyists' influence was derived primarily from their sectoral skills, and "general uptodateness."

33. McCormick, "Light on the Elusive Lobbyist"; "Sets Lobby Inquiry to Begin Tuesday," *New York Times*, October 11, 1929. McCormick's article on lobbying coincided with a senate hearing on lobbies, which investigated, among other cases, the influence of lobbyists on the tariff.

34. Child, *Writing on the Wall*, 224.

35. Ricci, *Tragedy of Political Science*, 82–83. Ricci refers to Arthur Holcombe's 1924 *The Political Parties of Today*, which argued that third parties arose when existing parties did not adequately address pressing issues.

36. Child, *Writing on the Wall*, 72, 223.

37. Ibid., 144. Charles E. Merriam and Harold F. Gosnell, *Non-Voting, Causes and Methods of Control* (Chicago: University of Chicago Press, 1924). Merriam and Gosnell produced the decade's most complete analysis of nonvoting, based on political behavior in Chicago's 1923 municipal elections. Although they warned against extrapolating too much from a discrete survey, Merriam's and Gosnell's contemporaries, including Walter Lippmann, frequently cited the report. Walter Lippmann, *The Phantom Public* (New York: Harcourt Brace, 1925), 17–18; Walter Lippmann, "The Causes of Political Indifference Today," *Atlantic Monthly*, February 1927.

38. Child, *Writing on the Wall*, 194, 153.

39. At almost fifty-seven percent, voter turnout in 1928 was about eight percent higher than it had been in the previous two presidential elections.

40. McCormick, "Now We All Debate the Issues."

41. Ibid.; Merriam, *Making of Citizens*, 298. Merriam also mused that that "adjustment" was the "watchword of modern life": the most successful programs of civic education (among which he implicitly ranked Italy's) were those that moved with the "changed and changing new world." The concept of institutional lag was derived from Ogburn's proposition that nonmaterial changes—for instance, in systems of government—lagged behind material ones. See William F. Ogburn, *Social Change with Respect to Culture and Original Nature* (New York: B. W. Huebsch, 1922), 249–52.

42. Westbrook, *John Dewey and American Democracy*, 307–8.

43. McCormick, "Bringing Politics Up to Date."

44. McCormick, "Italy Puts the Yoke on Capital and Labor."

45. Child, "Foreword," in *My Autobiography*, xv; also published as Child "Mussolini Now."

46. Schneider, *Making the Fascist State*, 94.

47. McCormick, "Behind Fascism Stands a Philosopher."

48. Schneider, *Making the Fascist State*, 202–3; "Elections in Italy," *Il Progresso Italo-Americano*, January 3, 1929; Child, *Writing on the Wall*, 212–13. As Child noted, the Grand

Council also had power to appoint men from outside the confederations' list entirely. He argued that this discretionary power bolstered expertise within parliament: if council members perceived that the national interest demanded the further elucidation of particular issues, they could select the best men to represent these concerns, he wrote.

49. "Presieduta da S.E. Benito Mussolini . . . ," photograph, *Il Progresso Italo-Americano*, March 24, 1929.

50. Lippmann, *Public Opinion*, 251–81. Purcell, *Crisis of Democratic Theory*, 102–4. Lippmann was by no means alone in calling for a greater role for experts in policymaking in the United States. Other proponents of elite rule included Harold Lasswell and Elton Mayo.

51. Child, *Writing on the Wall*, 212–13.

52. "Il Duce Explains New Chamber," *Il Progresso Italo-Americano*, April 14, 1929.

53. "La camera unanime approva gli accordi tra Italia e Vaticano," *Il Progresso Italo-Americano*, May 15, 1929. Arnaldo Cortesi, "Chamber Approves Vatican Accord," *New York Times*, May 15, 1929. *Il Progresso*'s report of a unanimous vote was false. Cortesi noted that two deputies actually voted against the accords. Their vote, he wrote, was "likely" a "mistake," which he supposed was due to unfamiliarity with the "machinery of voting."

54. "I lavori del nuovo parlamento," *Il Progresso Italo-Americano*, April 12, 1929. "Discorso della Corona," *Il Progresso Italo-Americano*, April 21, 1929.

55. Simonetta Falasca-Zamponi, *Fascist Spectacle: The Aesthetics of Power in Mussolini's Italy* (Berkeley: University of California Press, 2000), 132.

56. McCormick and Schneider occasionally conveyed some hesitancy about Italian corporatism. McCormick, "Light on the Elusive Lobbyist." McCormick conceded at the end of 1929 that the parliament was "so dominated by Mussolini that it has as yet no value as an experiment in government." As was usual, her more critical comments about the fascist state tended to appear in her reporting from outside Italy, almost hidden away, as a subclause of a sentence. Schneider, *Fascist Government of Italy*, 52–53. It was not until 1936 that Schneider acknowledged that, under the corporate system, parliament was "more a survival than a power."

57. "Come si preparano le elezioni," *Il Progresso Italo-Americano*, January 21, 1929. "Elections in Italy," *Il Progresso Italo-Americano*. "Fascist Council Busy Preparing Final Ticket for Election of Italian Chamber in Italy," *Il Progresso Italo-Americano*, February 21, 1929.

58. Child, *Writing on the Wall*, 195.

59. "Le elezioni plebiscitarie svoltesi in Italia tra scene di intenso entusiasmo," *Il Progresso Italo-Americano*, March 25, 1929. See also Schneider and Clough, *Making Fascists*, 157.

60. "Le elezioni in Italia—voti a favore del regime: 8,506,576—contrari: 136,198," *Il Progresso Italo-Americano*, March 26, 1929. Rastignac, "Plebiscito che consacra il fascismo rinnovatore delle fortune d'Italia," *Il Progresso Italo-Americano*, March 27, 1929.

61. Child, *Writing on the Wall*, 44, 216.

62. Rastignac, "Plebiscito che consacra il fascismo rinnovatore delle fortune d'Italia."

63. "Il Duce Explains New Chamber," *Il Progresso Italo-Americano*.

64. A. James Gregor, *Giovanni Gentile: Philosopher of Fascism* (New Brunswick, NJ: Transaction, 2001), 30. Stanley Payne, *Fascism: Comparison and Definition* (Madison: University of Wisconsin Press, 1980), 73–75. Gentile's ideas contributed to the conceptualization of totalitarianism, although these formulations remained vague in the late 1920s.

65. Mussolini, *My Autobiography*, 277, 294; also published as Benito Mussolini, "En Route," *Saturday Evening Post*, October 27, 1928.

66. "Intervista Mc Kormick [sic]," July 15, 1926, sotto-fascicolo "1926 Anna O'Hare Mc. Cormick," fascicolo "interviste," busta 752, Ministero della Cultura Popolare, ASD. Following an audience with Mussolini in 1926, McCormick wrote to Mussolini. She asked him whether he would say that the corporate state was "more representative of all the people" than a democracy. The regime's opaque answer was as follows: "I answer by recalling a phrase of the proclamation issued by me on the day when the syndical regulations were approved: 'Only today a people laboring in the various activities and categories in the Fascist State rises up to be the active and conscious agent of its own destiny.'" McCormick, "Il Duce Pictures the New State." In the final article, published in the *Times*, McCormick's question stood out much more than Mussolini's response.

67. Anne O'Hare McCormick, "The Mussolini of the Year IX," *New York Times*, January 25, 1931.

68. McCormick, "Old Woman in the New Italy."

69. "Benito Mussolini com'è visto dalle donne americane," *Il Progresso Italo-Americano*, February 10, 1929. "'Come Mussolini prepara l'Italia futura'—Federzoni," *Il Progresso Italo-Americano*.

70. Schneider, *Making the Fascist State*, 219, 223–24.

71. "'La volata' un nuovo sport italiano ideato da A. Turati," *Il Progresso Italo-Americano*, December 26, 1928. Augusto Turati was the secretary of the Fascist Party.

72. "La prima partita della 'volata,'" *Il Progresso Italo-Americano*, January 7, 1929.

73. Schneider and Clough, *Making Fascists*, 201.

74. "S.E. Mussolini insedia il nuovo presidente del Consiglio di Stato, S.E. il Prof. Santi Romano," photograph, and "Il Senato italiano chiude labori della XXVII legislatura . . . ," photograph. Both in *Il Progresso Italo-Americano*, January 13, 1929; "Presieduta da S.E. Benito Mussolini . . . ," photograph, *Il Progresso Italo-Americano*; "La seduta reale del 20 aprile scorso alla Camera dei Deputati," photograph, *Il Progresso Italo-Americano*, May 1, 1929.

75. "Al Colosseo—mentre parla Mussolini . . . ," photograph, *Il Progresso Italo-Americano*, April 28, 1929. "Il Duce assiste dal gigantesco podio . . . ," photograph, *Il Progresso Italo-Americano*, May 19, 1929.

76. "By an Exiled Anti-Fascist, 'Italians Were Asked to Vote Unanimously,'" *Baltimore Sun*, April 3, 1929; "Foe to Fascism Airs His Views," *Los Angeles Times*, April 11, 1929.

77. "Raccolta ufficiale delle leggi e dei decreti del Regno d'Italia," Article 57 and Article 72, 6090, 6098. This law stipulated the different appearances of the "yes" and "no" ballots. The voter ostensibly voted in secret, but had to leave his discarded ballot in an urn in the booth. He then had to bring his chosen ballot to a fascist official, who would "scrutinize" the ballot to "ensure" that it had been sealed.

78. Luisa Passerini, *Fascism in Popular Memory: The Cultural Experience of the Turin Working Class* (New York: Cambridge University Press, 1987). Passerini cites birth control, humor, graffiti, and *silence* as forms of opposition to fascism.

79. Johnathan Dunnage, *Twentieth Century Italy: A Social History* (Harlow, UK: Pearson, 2002), 72–84.

80. Schneider, *Making the Fascist State*, 212.

81. McCormick, "Italy Puts the Yoke on Capital and Labor."

82. Anne O'Hare McCormick, "Citadels of Resounding Ideas," *New York Times*, January 15, 1928. Fascism, argued McCormick, was not "intended for exportation."

83. Marcus Duffield, "Mussolini's American Empire," *Harper's*, November 1929. In late 1929, *Harper's* published an investigative report on Mussolini's support for grassroots fascist organizations in the United States. Alan Cassels, "Fascism for Export: Italy and the United States in the Twenties," *American Historical Review* 69, no. 3 (April 1964): 707–12; Diggins, *Mussolini and Fascism*, 89–94. Although a number of Duffield's claims were exaggerated, his basic observation that the fascist regime provided active support to Italian-American sympathizers through the Fascist League of North America was correct.

84. McCormick, "Light on the Elusive Lobbyist"; Child, *Writing on the Wall*, 215. For how these institutions worked in practice, see Charles S. Maier, "Between Taylorism and Technocracy: European Ideologies and the Vision of Industrial Productivity in the 1920s," *Journal of Contemporary History* 5, no. 2 (April 1970): 27–61; and Karl Lowenstein, "Occupational Representation and the Idea of an Economic Parliament," *Social Science* 12, no. 4 (October 1937): 424–25. In Germany's case, a council on economic affairs—the *Reichswirtschaftsrat*—"rarely progressed beyond stalemate and paralysis," according to Maier. In Czechoslovakia, an advisory board consulted the government on economic policy and legislation. According to Lowenstein, this body was an arm of the central government, which in no way complied with the "theoretical premises of the idea of functional representation." In Hungary and Romania, representatives of the professions were incorporated into the upper houses of the existing parliament. Making up only a small proportion of their chambers, they were "hardly in a position to influence parliament."

85. Child, *Writing on the Wall*, 174, 183. Samuel George Hobson, *National Guilds: An Inquiry into the Wage System and the Way Out* (London: G. Bell and Sons, 1914), 256–57, 263; Winston S. Churchill, *Parliamentary Government and the Economic Problem* (Oxford: Clarendon Press, 1930), 16; Geoffrey Foote, *The Labour Party's Political Thought: A History* (Basingstoke, UK: Palgrave MacMillan, 1997), 108–9, 117, 170. In Britain, corporate ideas were first associated with guild socialists. For instance, Hobson envisaged a "Guild Congress," which would deal with "industrial problems," while parliament would manage "affairs of State." Although the guild socialists' heyday was the immediate postwar period, their calls for "functional" assemblies persisted through the 1920s and gained renewed energy during the depression. Churchill was among those who called for an "economic sub-parliament" to confront industrial and financial problems. By this time, Oswald Mosly too suggested corporate arrangements as a solution to Britain's problems, but in contrast to other Britons' conceptions, Mosly's ideas were modeled directly on the Italian corporate state.

86. Oliver McKee Jr., "Lobbying for Good or Evil," *North American Review*, March 1929. McCormick, "Light on the Elusive Lobbyist"; Herring, *Group Representation before Congress*, 9–10; E. Pendleton Herring, "Legalized Lobbying in Europe," *Current History* 31, no. 5 (February 1930): 947. Like McCormick, Herring compared American lobbies to European economic parliaments.

87. McCormick, "Light on the Elusive Lobbyist." McCormick's piece ended with a note of pessimism. She doubted that Americans would be willing to innovate an entirely new institution of government in the foreseeable future. "[A]s a people we are slower to change our institutions than our habits," she wrote.

88. Child, *Writing on the Wall*, 151, 154, 195, 264, 268, 271. For the War Industries Board, see Kennedy, *Over Here*, 126–36.

89. Edward Corsi, "Mergers," *Il Progresso Italo-Americano*, June 30, 1929. Herbert Hoover, *American Individualism* (Garden City, NY: Doubleday, 1922), 28–31, 39–45. Incorporating cooperation and "community responsibility" into the concept of individualism, Hoover's ideas actually represented a departure from *laissez-faire* liberalism.

90. McCormick, "America at Last Airs Its Mind"; McCormick, "Uncertain, the Farmer Waits."

91. Ferdinand Schevill, review of *Making the Fascist State*, *International Journal of Ethics* 40, no. 1 (October 1929): 129–32.

92. McCormick, "Light on the Elusive Lobbyist."

93. Lippmann, *Public Opinion*, 268.

94. Ibid., 202–13. Lippmann discarded the possibility of corporate representation (in the form of guild socialism) as a solution to democracy's problems, mainly because he recognized that it would be impossible to reconcile the interests of various groups to arrive at the "common interest."

95. Child, *Writing on the Wall*, 215, 268.

Chapter 4. Man as the Measure of All Things: Sympathizing with Fascism in the Early Depression Years

1. Thomas B. Morgan, "Mussolini Becomes Champion of Poor Who Confide Their Troubles to Him," *Il Progresso Italo-Americano*, October 22, 1933. Morgan was head of the United Press office in Rome.

2. This story stood in stark—and perhaps intentional—contrast to the story told by the American Major General Smedley Butler in January 1931. Butler claimed that Mussolini's car had hit a child when motoring at seventy miles per hour. Mussolini had ordered his chauffer to drive on, shouting "What is one life in the affairs of a State," according to Butler. Butler's claims caused a scandal, and prompted the Department of State to issue a formal apology. See "Envoy Protests Gen. Butler's Talk," *New York Times*, January 27, 1931. Diggins, *Mussolini and Fascism*, 34–36.

3. For fascist economics, see Ralph Grimaldi, "New Deal Must Follow Fascist Evolution if It Is to Survive, Dr. Grimaldi Asserts," *Il Progresso Italo-Americano*, May 11, 1934.

4. "Mussolini's Wise Words," *Il Progresso Italo-Americano*, December 21, 1930.

5. I. C. Falbo, "Problemi del lavoro," *Il Progresso Italo-Americano*, October 9, 1930.

6. Generoso Pope, "Perché tutti possono lavorare," *Il Progresso Italo-Americano*, September 18, 1932. "5-Day Week Demand Is Put Up to Hoover," *New York Times*, July 21, 1932. Pope's editorial echoed an American Federation of Labor executive council statement made two months earlier.

7. Anne O'Hare McCormick, "A Year of the Hoover Method," *New York Times*, March 2, 1930. For a similar expression, see Matthew Josephson, *Portrait of the Artist as American* (New York: Harcourt, Brace and Company, 1930), x. "The suspicion grows that the child, beyond control, now menaces the parent," Josephson wrote of the relationship between man-made machines and men.

8. Anne O'Hare McCormick, "The Great Dam of Controversy," *New York Times*, April 20, 1930; Anne O'Hare McCormick, "Hunting the Elusive Paramount Issues," *New York Times*,

March 22, 1931; Anne O'Hare McCormick, "'East' and 'West': The Basic Issue," *New York Times*, October 23, 1932.

9. Anne O'Hare McCormick, "A New Americanism Is Emerging," *New York Times*, September 4, 1932.

10. Anne O'Hare McCormick, "The Average Italian Is Still Himself," *New York Times*, February 8, 1931. See also Anne O'Hare McCormick, "As Wall Street Sees a Changing World," *New York Times*, October 9, 1932: "My own impression is . . . that title without responsibility, the decline of individual business, paper gains and losses, tend to create apathy."

11. McCormick, "New Americanism Is Emerging."

12. Anne O'Hare McCormick, "The Mind behind the Radio Broadcast," *New York Times*, April 10, 1932; Anne O'Hare McCormick, "Hollywood: Weird Factory of Mob Art," *New York Times*, December 6, 1931. See also Anne O'Hare McCormick, "The Great Empire of Celluloid," *New York Times*, November 29, 1931; Anne O'Hare McCormick, "The Vastest Audience Ever Assembled," *New York Times*, December 20, 1931; Anne O'Hare McCormick, "The Radio: A Great Unknown Force," *New York Times*, March 27, 1932; Anne O'Hare McCormick, "Radio's Audience: Huge, Unprecedented," *New York Times*, April 3, 1932.

13. Franco Ciarlantini, "La vertiginosa New York," *Il Progresso Italo-Americano*, December 28, 1930. Gentile, "Impending Modernity." Gentile analyzes Ciarlantini's contribution to the fascist critique of American modernity.

14. Mary Todaro, "Our Immigrants and Their Problems," *Il Progresso Italo-Americano*, October 22, 1933. Mary Iacovella, "New York City—Modern Mecca of Art and Letters," *Il Progresso Italo-Americano*, September 11, 1932.

15. "Il triste dramma della disoccupazione fra le ricchezze e gli sperperi di N. Y.," *Il Progresso Italo-Americano*, November 16, 1930.

16. President's Research Committee on Social Trends, *Recent Social Trends in the United States; Report of the President's Research Committee on Social Trends* (New York: McGraw-Hill, 1933), xiii, also 144–51, 271, 283, 310. See also David M. Kennedy, *Freedom from Fear: The American People in Depression and War, 1929–1945* (New York: Oxford University Press, 1999), 21–24.

17. Anna Siomopoulos, "Entertaining Ethics: Technology, Mass Culture and American Intellectuals of the 1930s," *Film History* 11, no. 1 (1999): 45–54. Lewis Mumford, *Technics and Civilization* (New York: Harcourt Brace, 1934), 315–16.

18. David Welky, *Everything Was Better in America: Print Culture in the Great Depression* (Champaign: University of Illinois Press, 2007), 72, 136.

19. Typical of the boastful press was: "Il conto del tesoro alla fine d'ottobre," *Il Progresso Italo-Americano*, November 24, 1928; "Public Confidence Aids Italy's Rise in Industry," *Il Progresso Italo-Americano*, January 21, 1929.

20. "Dr. Badia Reports Italy Improving under Mussolini," *Il Progresso Italo-Americano*, February 15, 1931; "In Italia si vive meglio che in ogni altro paese d'Europa, dice il 'Post,'" *Il Progresso Italo-Americano*, September 25, 1932.

21. Schneider, *Fascist Government of Italy*, 86.

22. Ibid., 6, 15–16.

23. McCormick, "Average Italian Is Still Himself."

24. Ibid.

25. Anne O'Hare McCormick, "The Average American Emerges," *New York Times*, January 3, 1932; McCormick, "New Americanism Is Emerging."

26. Herbert Johnson, "The Silver Lining—Families Are Getting Acquainted Again," illustration, in Richard Washburn Child, "Unmasking Events," *Saturday Evening Post*, July 16, 1932.

27. "H. E. Ambassador De Martino Urges Italo-Americans Here to Heed United States Ideals," *Il Progresso Italo-Americano*, November 9, 1930.

28. "Our Fiftieth Anniversary," *Il Progresso Italo-Americano*, November 9, 1930.

29. Anne O'Hare McCormick, "Foggy Days under the Big Dome," *New York Times*, February 15, 1931.

30. Anne O'Hare McCormick, "The Two Conventions: Chicago Contrasts," *New York Times*, July 3, 1932.

31. McCormick, "Vastest Audience Ever Assembled."

32. McCormick, "Year of the Hoover Method."

33. Richard Washburn Child, "Low Tide in Politics," *Saturday Evening Post*, April 24, 1926.

34. "R. W. Child Opens Roosevelt Drive," *New York Times*.

35. "President Hoover's Message," *Il Progresso Italo-Americano*, December 13, 1931.

36. Louis W. Liebovich, *Bylines in Despair: Herbert Hoover, the Great Depression, and the U.S. News Media* (Westport, CT: Praeger, 1994); and Joan Hoff-Wilson, "Herbert Hoover: The Popular Image of an Unpopular President," in *Understanding Herbert Hoover: Ten Perspectives*, ed. Lee Nash (Stanford, CA: Hoover Institution Press, 1987), 1–23.

37. Passerini, *Mussolini immaginario*, 87–93; Duggan, *Fascist Voices*, 221–24.

38. "Il Duce nella dolce e serena intimità della famiglia," photograph, *Il Progresso Italo-Americano*, July 17, 1932.

39. "Mussolini's Birthplace Now Scene of Pilgrimage," *Il Progresso Italo-Americano*, February 20, 1929; "Mussolini' [sic] Native Village Rebuilt; His Home a National Monument," *Il Progresso Italo-Americano*, September 10, 1933.

40. "Una visita del Duce a Predappio," *Il Progresso Italo-Americano*, August 21, 1929.

41. "La recente visita del Duce alla bonifica di Maccarese, nella campagna romana," photograph, *Il Progresso Italo-Americano*, April 13, 1930; "Premier Mussolini Visiting Workers' Homes in Rome," photograph, *Il Progresso Italo-Americano*, October 19, 1930; "The Duce Addressing a Group of Old Countrywomen in Ostia," photograph, *Il Progresso Italo-Americano*, May 17, 1931; "Premier Mussolini Chatting with Laborers," photograph, *Il Progresso Italo-Americano*, May 1, 1932.

42. See fascicolo, "Invia materiale di propaganda negli Stati Uniti," busta 218, Stati Uniti 1934, Ministero della Cultura Popolare, direzione generale servizi della propaganda, archivio generale (1930–1943), ACS.

43. McCormick, "Average Italian Is Still Himself." Mussolini, wrote McCormick, was the only leader of a modern state who had prioritized the development of agriculture over industrial production. For observations linking fascist maternity care to Mussolini's veneration of his mother, see "Benito Mussolini com'è visto dalle donne americane," *Il Progresso Italo-Americano*.

44. Ministry of Popular Culture to Alberto Calza Bini, October 17, 1926, fascicolo, "Giornalisti stranieri" (part 1), busta 256, Ministero della Cultura Popolare, ASD.

45. McCormick, "Mussolini of the Year IX."

46. Richard Washburn Child, "Their Little Too Much," *Saturday Evening Post*, April 9, 1932.

47. Anne O'Hare McCormick, "A New Hoover Is Now Emerging," *New York Times*, February 7, 1932. Even when Hoover did take action, these observers argued that it was too little too

late, and that he continued to intervene in favor of corporations (as evidenced by the Reconstruction Finance Corporation) rather than the common man. This was a common critique. See Kennedy, *Freedom from Fear*, 85, 91.

48. Anne O'Hare McCormick, "Preparing for 'the New Deal,'" *New York Times*, January 15, 1933.

49. "R. W. Child Opens Roosevelt Drive," *New York Times*. For Lorimer's opposition to Roosevelt, see Cohn, *Creating America*, 234–37.

50. "Text of Governor Roosevelt's Appeal at Metropolitan Opera House," *New York Times*, November 4, 1932.

51. McCormick, "Year of the Hoover Method."

52. "Pensiamo ai poveri," *Il Progresso Italo-Americano*, October 23, 1932.

53. Richard Washburn Child, "Turning of Roosevelt to Sales Tax Proves His Bigness, Says R. W. Child," *New York American*, May 22, 1933. Child, "Foreword," in *My Autobiography*, xii; also published as Child, "Mussolini Now."

54. McCormick, "Mussolini of the Year IX"; Anne O'Hare McCormick, "'Let's Try It!' Says Roosevelt," *New York Times*, March 26, 1933.

55. McCormick, "Preparing for 'the New Deal.'" See also Anne O'Hare McCormick, "Roosevelt's View of the Big Job," *New York Times*, September 11, 1932.

56. Anne O'Hare McCormick, "The Nation Renews Its Faith," *New York Times*, March 19, 1933.

57. Generoso Pope, "Bilancio di due settimane," *Il Progresso Italo-Americano*, March 19, 1933; McCormick, "'Let's Try It!' Says Roosevelt."

58. For examples of these accusations, see Ira Katznelson, *Fear Itself: The New Deal and the Origins of Our Time* (New York: Liveright Norton, 2014), 161, 235–36.

59. Pope, "Bilancio di due settimane."

60. McCormick, "Drama of Pope and Premier"; Anne O'Hare McCormick, "The Man the World Watches," *New York Times*, September 1, 1935.

61. McCormick, "Nation Renews Its Faith."

62. "Veterans' City Named 'Littoria,'" *Il Progresso Italo-Americano*, May 15, 1932.

63. "Italy Uses Motor Caravans in Back-to-Farm Movement," *Il Progresso Italo-Americano*, April 20, 1930.

64. "Plan to Reclaim 200,000 Acres of Pontine Marshes," *Il Progresso Italo-Americano*, December 20, 1931. See also Schneider, *Fascist Government of Italy*, 111.

65. "Reclamation of Campagna Lands Nets Big Results," *Il Progresso Italo-Americano*, May 17, 1931. For a further example of precise accounting of individuals, see "Italy's Social Insurance Aid Shows Progress," *Il Progresso Italo-Americano*, August 16, 1931.

66. "Reclamation of Campagna Lands Nets Big Results."

67. "La guerra che preferiamo," *Il Progresso Italo-Americano*, August 16, 1933.

68. Memorandum, Ministry of Foreign Affairs, Press Office, for the attention of Mussolini, June 1, 1933. Memorandum, Ministry of Foreign Affairs, Press Office, for the attention of Mussolini, May 25, 1933. Both in fascicolo "Ministero per la Stampa e Propaganda Mac Cormick [*sic*] O'Hare Anna," busta 597, Ministero della Cultura Popolare, ASD.

69. Diggins, *Mussolini and Fascism*, 24, 38, 39, 44.

70. Galleazo Ciano to Valentino Orsolini Cencelli, November 23, 1933, fascicolo "Ministero per la Stampa e Propaganda Mac Cormick [*sic*] O'Hare Anna," busta 597, Ministero della Cultura Popolare, ASD.

71. Anne O'Hare McCormick, "Italy in the Year XII E. F.," *Ladies' Home Journal*, March 1934. "Veterans' City Named 'Littoria,'" *Il Progresso Italo-Americano*. By contrast, *Il Progresso* reported that the average plot size was twelve to fifteen acres.

72. McCormick, "Italy in the Year XII E. F."

73. Undated document, fascicolo "Ministero per la Stampa e Propaganda Mac Cormick [*sic*] O'Hare Anna," busta 597, Ministero della Cultura Popolare, ASD. McCormick asked the government for the average wages of skilled and unskilled labor. The government responded with a table, which demonstrated average incomes by economic sector, from the years 1929 to 1933. These statistics demonstrated that nominal wages in agriculture had declined by twenty percent over these years.

74. McCormick, "Italy in the Year XII E. F." McCormick, "Mussolini of the Year IX." In the *Times*, in 1931, McCormick had acknowledged more challenges in Italian public finances: increasing unemployment, a large budget deficit, and the threat of falling real wages.

75. Schneider, *Fascist Government of Italy*, 86–87, 112. Schneider presented the regime's 1935 *Annual Statistics*, which showed a decline in real wages in the early depression years followed by a more recent improvement, and ten percent higher per capita calories from food (as opposed to alcohol) in 1929–33 relative to 1910–14.

76. Jon S. Cohen, "Fascism and Agriculture in Italy: Policies and Consequences," *Economic History Review* 32, no. 1 (February 1979): 70–87.

77. Diane Ghirardo, *Building New Communities: New Deal America and Fascist Italy* (Princeton, NJ: Princeton University Press, 1989), 51–53.

78. Bosworth, *Mussolini's Italy*, 438.

79. Cohen, "Fascism and Agriculture in Italy." Cohen discusses the limitations of the data.

80. For examples of this balancing act, see McCormick, "Mussolini of the Year IX"; Schneider, *Fascist Government of Italy*, 85.

81. Anne O'Hare McCormick, "Ford Seeks a New Balance for Industry," *New York Times*, May 29, 1932.

82. Anne O'Hare McCormick, "The Future of the Ford Idea," *New York Times*, May 22, 1932.

83. "What Outlook for City Dwellers in Farming?" *Il Progresso Italo-Americano*, April 9, 1933.

84. "Agriculture—The Use of the Land Is the Best Form of Unemployment Insurance," photograph, in McCormick, "Ford Seeks a New Balance for Industry."

85. "Workers on Henry Ford's Experimental Farm," photograph, *Il Progresso Italo-Americano*, April 9, 1933.

86. "Contro la disoccupazione," *Il Progresso Italo-Americano*.

87. I. C. Falbo, "Ritorno alla terra," *Il Progresso Italo-Americano*, May 29, 1932. Other ethnic communities organized back-to-the-land movements of urban workers. For the efforts of the Jewish community to resettle New York City garment workers, which resulted in the Jersey Homestead, see Paul K. Conkin, *Tomorrow a New World: The New Deal Community Program* (Ithaca, NY: Cornell University Press, 1959), 260–76; Dona Brown, *Back to the Land: The Enduring Dream of Self-Sufficiency in Modern America* (Madison: University of Wisconsin Press, 2011), 157–62, 164–65.

88. Giovanni Macerata, "Come gli italiani in America possono contribuire alla soluzione della crisi," *Il Progresso Italo-Americano*, December 11, 1932. Macerata noted that his suggestions were in line with both fascist state policy and FDR's ideas.

89. Franklin D. Roosevelt, "Back to the Land," *Review of Reviews*, October 1931.

90. McCormick, "Roosevelt's View of the Big Job."

91. Lecture notes, Herbert W. Schneider, "The Discipline of American Agriculture," part of lecture series, "Lineamenti storici e ideali del conflitto economico-politico intorno di Roosevelt," Folder, "Manuscripts, L," 107/3/5, SPHWS.

92. For "evils," see the remarks of Secretary of the Interior Harold Ickes, in Memorandum for the Press, for release in the afternoon papers of October 12, 1933, Folder, Secretary to the President 1933–36, Subsistence Housing, 1933, Louis McHenry Howe Papers, FDRL. For "outcasts," see quote from M. L. Wilson, the chief of the Subsistence Homestead Division, in William E. Leuchtenburg, *Franklin D. Roosevelt and the New Deal, 1932–1940* (New York: Harper Torchbooks, 1963), 136.

93. Conkin, *Tomorrow a New World*, 43–58. Conkin points to the influence of the ideas of Elwood Mead on the Subsistence Homestead Program. Decades before, Mead had supervised reclamation and settlement projects in Australia. Pamphlet, "General Information Concerning the Purposes and Policies of the Division of Subsistence Homesteads," November 15, 1933, Division of Subsistence Homesteads, United States Department of the Interior, Folder, "Department of the Interior, Research on Subsistence Homestead," Accretion to John Ihlder Papers, Washington Housing and Development Matters, FDRL. Planning documents of the Subsistence Homesteads Division referenced the experiences of Denmark.

94. Translation of Memo, Italo Balbo to Mussolini; Source: Bollettino del Ministero degli Affari Esteri (Bulletin of the Ministry of Foreign Affairs), July 1933, Document created in November 1933, Folder: Long, Breckinridge, President's Personal File 434, FDRL.

95. "The De-Urbanization Movement," *Il Progresso Italo-Americano*, August 6, 1933.

96. Letter, James Farley to Franklin D. Roosevelt, December 8, 1933, Folder: Farley, James A., 1932–1939, President's Personal File 309, FDRL. The only evidence for a high-level New Dealer who expressed admiration, in broad terms, for Mussolini's agricultural program, comes from James Farley's 1933 trip to Europe. Farley wrote: "I was quite impressed with Mussolini's great drainage development where he converted marshes into fine farm lands." Farley was chair of both the New York State Democratic Committee and the DNC, as well as the post master general. He was not an economic policymaker. Ghirardo, *Building New Communities*, 129–30. Ghirardo finds little evidence that Italy was a source of inspiration for the Subsistence Homestead project. She notes that "low-level administrators" of resettlement projects perused "consular reports about subsistence projects in Germany, Italy, the Netherlands, and Norway."

97. Rexford Tugwell, Diary entries for October 20 and 22, 1934, Folder, Diary: March–Dec. 1934, Rexford Tugwell Papers, FDRL. Tugwell's diary revealed admiration for aspects of Italy's response to the depression: the regime's "systematic" construction projects and its "effectiveness of administration." But Tugwell expressed grave reservations about the suppression of freedom in Italy. Goldberg, *Liberal Fascism*, 11, 156. Goldberg neglects to mention these criticisms when he quotes the same diary entries, to create the impression that Tugwell was an unqualified fan of fascism.

98. For this merger, see Conkin, *Tomorrow a New World*, 113; Brown, *Back to the Land*, 150.

99. Lecture notes, Herbert W. Schneider, "The Discipline of American Agriculture," part of lecture series, "Lineamenti storici e ideali del conflitto economico-politico intorno di Roosevelt," Folder, "Manuscripts, L," 107/3/5, SPHWS.

100. Ghirardo, *Building New Communities*, 118; Anthony J. Badger, *The New Deal: The Depression Years, 1933–1940* (New York: Hill and Wang, 1989), 240.

101. Conkin, *Tomorrow a New World*, 237–304.

102. Michael A. Bernstein, "Why the Great Depression Was Great: Toward a New Understanding of the Interwar Economic Crisis in the United States," in *The Rise and Fall of the New Deal Order, 1930–1980*, ed. Gary Gerstle and Steve Fraser (Princeton, NJ: Princeton University Press, 1989), 32–54.

103. Schneider, *Making the Fascist State*, 164, 211–12; Mussolini, *My Autobiography*, 203–4; also published as Mussolini, "Five Years of Government."

104. Schneider, *Fascist Government of Italy*, 114, 118–19.

105. Anne O'Hare McCormick, "Mussolini Eager to Maintain Peace," *New York Times*, June 5, 1933.

106. Schneider, *Fascist Government of Italy*, 114, 118. According to Schneider, the six billion lire peak of the budget deficit in 1933 produced a reduction in unemployment from over 1.1 million men in 1933 to below nine hundred thousand in 1934. By 1935, according to these official statistics, Italy's unemployed numbered just six hundred thousand.

107. "Lavoro per 40 mila operai in Italia," *Il Progresso Italo-Americano*, August 10, 1930; "Lavori pubblici," *Il Progresso Italo-Americano*, November 10, 1932.

108. "Mussolini's Achievements in Italy Extolled by New Hampshire Judge," *Il Progresso Italo-Americano*, December 4, 1932.

109. McCormick, "Italy in the Year XII E. F."

110. "Italy and the 5-Day Week," *Il Progresso Italo-Americano*, September 11, 1932.

111. Schneider, *Fascist Government of Italy*, 83.

112. "La disoccupazione e l'Italia," *Il Progresso Italo-Americano*, June 24, 1933.

113. "Share the Work," *Il Progresso Italo-Americano*, October 9, 1932.

114. "La disoccupazione e l'Italia," *Il Progresso Italo-Americano*.

115. Gaetano Salvemini, "Italian Unemployment Statistics," *Social Research* 1, no. 3 (August 1934): 349.

116. Gianni Toniolo and Francesco Piva, "Unemployment in the 1930s: The Case of Italy," in *Interwar Unemployment in International Perspective*, ed. Barry Eichengreen and T. J. Hatton (Dordrecht, Netherlands: Kluwer, 1988), 237. The variation between 3 and 8.8 percent is due to the unreliability of any official estimates for unemployment (in the industrial sector alone). The authors derive the lower bound estimates of unemployment from official unemployment statistics and the upper bound from the industrial census. The authors note that, due to pervasive informality and underemployment in agriculture in this era, there is no way to calculate actual (un)employment rates in this sector. Victoria De Grazia, *The Culture of Consent: Mass Organization of Leisure in Fascist Italy* (New York: Cambridge University Press, 1981), 52. Less critical examination of the regime's statistics has prompted other historians to claim that, by 1935, public works employed around 500,000 of "several million" unemployed Italians.

117. Toniolo and Piva, "Unemployment in the 1930s," 224, 226; Anna Treves, *Le migrazioni interne nell'Italia fascista: Politica e realtà demografica* (Turin: Einaudi, 1976).

118. McCormick, "Italy in the Year XII E. F.," Undated document, fascicolo "Ministero per la Stampa e Propaganda Mac Cormick [sic] O'Hare Anna," busta 597, Ministero della Cultura Popolare, ASD. McCormick probably used data provided to her by the government to describe the Borgheses' economic conditions.

119. Bosworth, *Mussolini's Italy*, 270, citing "Review of the Political and Economic Situation in the Provinces," February 8, 1933.

120. "Hoover Suggests Aid by Federal Workers," *New York Times*, November 11, 1931; "700 Leaders Pledge Aid in Finding Jobs," *New York Times*, November 22, 1932. Hoover rejected any compulsory limits on working hours but supported voluntary efforts.

121. "L'iniziativa del 'Progresso' in favore dei disoccupati," *Il Progresso Italo-Americano*, March 23, 1930.

122. "Il Progresso Italo Americano pei disoccupati," *Il Progresso Italo-Americano*, April 6, 1930.

123. "The Share-the-Work Plan: Teagle Answers Its Critics," *New York Times*, January 15, 1933; "Job Drive Is Backed by Manufacturers," *New York Times*, October 3, 1932. Teagle, the president of Standard Oil, was the leader of the voluntary movement.

124. Generoso Pope, "Perché tutti possono lavorare," *Il Progresso Italo-Americano*, September 18, 1932.

125. McCormick, "Mussolini of the Year IX."

126. "L'Italia può far questo—noi, no," *Il Progresso Italo-Americano*, August 30, 1931.

127. "A Mussolini Might Help Solve Crisis," *Il Progresso Italo-Americano*, February 5, 1933; "L'Italia può far questo." These pieces were based on excerpts from the Hearst Press—the *Chicago American* and the *Evening Journal*. Hearst was both sympathetic toward Mussolini and vociferously critical of the Hoover administration. See Diggins, *Mussolini and Fascism*, 48–49; Welky, *Everything Was Better in America*, 20, 34.

128. Anthony J. Badger, *FDR: The First Hundred Days* (New York: Hill and Wang, 2008), 86.

129. Generoso Pope, "Dare lavoro ai disoccupati," *Il Progresso Italo-Americano*, July 24, 1932.

130. Generoso Pope, "Gl'insegnamenti della crisi," *Il Progresso Italo-Americano*, September 11, 1932.

131. The historiography of Hoover's response to the depression is contentious, but historians broadly agree that the president's fiscal conservatism and ideas of individualism constrained public works programs. Glen Jeansonne, *The Life of Herbert Hoover: Fighting Quaker, 1928–1933* (New York: Palgrave MacMillan, 2012), 201–2; William E. Leuchtenburg, *Herbert Hoover* (New York: Times Books, 2009), 109–12. In 1930, Hoover slashed his own Emergency Committee for Employment's recommended appropriation by eighty percent.

132. Pope, "Gl'insegnamenti della crisi."

133. Generoso Pope, "The Greatest Need," *Il Progresso Italo-Americano*, February 26, 1933. Pope also criticized Hoover's weak implementation of work-sharing schemes, which he believed had been used only to freeze out foreign-born workers from factories in the United States.

134. "Text of Governor Roosevelt's Appeal at Metropolitan Opera House," *New York Times*. Jonathan Alter, *The Defining Moment: FDR's Hundred Days and the Triumph of Hope* (New York: Simon & Schuster, 2006), 91. Alter argues that Governor Roosevelt's response to unemployment in New York was tardy and inadequate but that it nonetheless helped to shift notions of the positive role of government in protecting people from poverty and hunger.

135. For the intentional vagueness of Roosevelt's program during the campaign, see Alter, *Defining Moment*, 129, 132.

136. McCormick, "'Let's Try It!' Says Roosevelt."

137. "Prof Tugwell Denies He Spoke for Roosevelt," *Baltimore Sun*, January 27, 1933.

138. Generoso Pope, "Un programma coraggioso," *Il Progresso Italo-Americano*, January 29, 1933.

139. Richard Washburn Child, "R. W. Child Sees Trend to Sales Tax to Finance Federal Public Works," *New York American*, May 13, 1933. Richard Washburn Child, "R. W. Child Says Only Public Works Can Cure Worst Ill—Unemployment," Undated newspaper article, published by William Randolph Hearst's Universal Service Inc., with dateline, May 9, 1933. Attached as a clipping in Memo, Marvin McIntyre to Franklin D. Roosevelt, May 15, 1933, Folder: Child, Richard Washburn, President's Personal File 1760, FDRL.

140. Badger, *FDR: The First Hundred Days*, 98–101. These $3.3 billion were administered through the Federal Emergency Administration of Public Works, renamed the Public Works Administration in 1935.

141. Generoso Pope, "Si ritorna al lavoro," *Il Progresso Italo-Americano*, June 18, 1933.

142. Generoso Pope, "Problemi di oggi e di domani," *Il Progresso Italo-Americano*, September 4, 1933.

143. Glaucus, "Il 'Labor Day' trova gli Stati Uniti in piena lotta contro la crisi," *Il Progresso Italo-Americano*, September 3, 1933. Just as it did for Italy, *Il Progresso* used precise accounting to suggest that public works in the United States had the most human of effects. The precision of this figure obfuscated the fuzziness of the language. You can *begin* the process of distributing any amount of money, without spending much at all. As historians have shown, little money was actually spent on public works in 1933. See Kennedy, *Freedom from Fear*, 178–79.

144. Richard Washburn Child, "Our New Crisis," *New York American*, November 13, 1934.

145. Letter, Richard Washburn Child to Franklin D. Roosevelt, August 30, 1934, Folder: Child, Richard Washburn, President's Personal File 1760, FDRL.

146. Richard Washburn Child, "Public Debt and Bureaucratic Dictatorship Raising Grave New Issues—R. W. Child," *New York American*, July 19, 1934; Child, "Our New Crisis."

147. Letter, Richard Washburn Child to Franklin D. Roosevelt, May 11, 1933, Folder: Security Exchange Act, 1933 May 1–15, Official File 242, FDRL; Letter, Richard Washburn Child to Franklin D. Roosevelt, February 6, 1934, Folder: Bonds and Securities, 1934, Official File 242a, FDRL.

148. Letter, E. Paul Yaselli to Marvin McIntyre, May 10, 1933, Folder, Richard Washburn Child, President's Personal File 1760, FDRL.

149. Richard Washburn Child, "Preservation of Constitution to Be Vital Congress Issue," *New York American*, January 2, 1934; Richard Washburn Child, "Congress Must Not Become Mere Rubber Stamp for President, R. W. Child Warns," *New York American*, February 2, 1934.

150. Letter, Richard Washburn Child to Franklin D. Roosevelt, March 11, 1934, Folder: Endorsements for Minister, 1933–1946, Official File 218b, FDRL.

151. "De Valera Greets Our New Minister," *New York Times*, June 28, 1935. Diggins, *Mussolini and Fascism*, 205–6.

152. Memorandum, Franklin D. Roosevelt to William Phillips, February 21, 1934, Folder: Jan–March 1934, Official File 20 Dept. of State, FDRL. Letter, Stephen Duggan to Franklin D. Roosevelt, March 9, 1934; Letter, Franklin D. Roosevelt to Stephen Duggan, March 26, 1934; both in Folder, Duggan, Stephen, President's Personal File 1404, FDRL. The political scientist Stephen Duggan wrote to FDR expressing concern about this appointment, noting that Child was not a true friend of the New Deal. FDR replied: "Don't worry about the gentleman in question!"

153. Letter, Breckinridge Long to Franklin D. Roosevelt, May 23, 1934, Folder: Diplomatic Correspondence Italy, Long Breckinridge: 1933–1936, President's Secretary's File 41, FDRL.

154. Letter, Richard Washburn Child to Franklin D. Roosevelt, August 30, 1934, Folder: Child, Richard Washburn, President's Personal File 1760, FDRL.

155. Richard Washburn Child to Franklin Roosevelt, January 12, 1935, Folder: Child, Richard Washburn, President's Personal File 1760, FDRL.

156. Badger, *New Deal*, 199–200; Kennedy, *Freedom from Fear*, 175–76. Historians suggest that this kind of analysis underestimated FDR's *own* fiscal conservatism.

157. Generoso Pope, "La politica del lavoro," *Il Progresso Italo-Americano*, February 25, 1934.

158. "17 Billion Lire Spent on Public Works, Says Minister di Crollalanza," *Il Progresso Italo-Americano*, February 25, 1934.

159. Generoso Pope, "Un grande esperimento," *Il Progresso Italo-Americano*, August 13, 1933. Pope argued that Americans should seek solace in the "excellent results" under an Italian corporative system of "state control" and "class collaboration," suggesting that with the National Industrial Recovery Act, the United States, too, was on the right path.

160. Glaucus, "Per rimettere in azione il gigantesco ingranaggio industriale degli S. U.," *Il Progresso Italo-Americano*, August 20, 1933.

161. I. C. Falbo, "NRA e fascismo," *Il Progresso Italo-Americano*, September 17, 1933. "We regard strife as a luxury for the rich," wrote Mussolini in his English-language autobiography. Mussolini, *My Autobiography*, 281; also published as Mussolini, "En Route."

162. I. C. Falbo, "NRA e fascismo."

163. Translation of Memo, Italo Balbo to Mussolini, Source: Bollettino del Ministero degli Affari Esteri (Bulletin of the Ministry of Foreign Affairs), July 1933, Document created in November 1933, Folder: Italy, Government of 1933–1936, Official File 233, FDRL. Roosevelt never expressed more than a vague admiration for the corporate state. For instance, Balbo wrote to Mussolini, claiming that the president "spoke words of appreciation for the labor organization of our country" during their meeting in July 1933. Maurizio Vaudagna, "The New Deal and Corporativism in Italy," *Radical History Review* 4, nos. 2–3 (1977): 6–7. Of perhaps more significance are the NRA planning documents, cited by Vaudagna, which included a favorable assessment of the corporate state as enabling economic stability and class cooperation. Reports such as these were examples of New Dealers' willingness to reference models from all over the world, if aspects of them might be of use to the United States. Katznelson, *Fear Itself*, 93. In addition to keeping a portrait of Mussolini in his office, Johnson handed out a fascist pamphlet on the corporate state to cabinet members. But it seems that most members of the cabinet viewed Johnson, who was erratic and alcoholic, as a liability.

164. Kennedy, *Freedom from Fear*, 185–88; "Johnson Outlines 5 Chief Problems," *New York Times*, March 3, 1934.

165. Generoso Pope, "4 marzo 1933—4 marzo 1934," *Il Progresso Italo-Americano*, March 4, 1934.

166. Anne O'Hare McCormick, "The Mood of America on Election Eve," *New York Times*, November 4, 1934.

167. McCormick, "This America: A Re-Discovery"; McCormick, "Mood of America on Election Eve."

168. McCormick, "Mood of America on Election Eve."

169. McCormick, "This America: A Re-Discovery"; McCormick, "Mood of America on Election Eve."

170. Walter Lippmann, "The Acids of Modernity," in *Preface to Morals*, 51–67.

Chapter 5. The Garden of Fascism: Beauty, Transcendence, and Peace in an Era of Uncertainty

1. "Twelve Flights Have Been Tried over General Balbo's Route from Europe to America, but Only Five Succeeded," *Il Progresso Italo-Americano*, July 9, 1933. Robert Whol, *The Spectacle of Flight: Aviation and the Western Imagination, 1920–1950* (New Haven, CT: Yale University Press, 2005), 93. It was more difficult to fly across the Atlantic in an east to west direction than in the opposite direction; requiring close coordination, formation flights were much more difficult than solo flights.

2. Claudio G. Segre, *Italo Balbo: A Fascist Life* (Berkeley: University of California Press, 1987), 236–40; Whol, *Spectacle of Flight*, 92–93. "S. E. Balbo esalta il valore e la disciplina dei piloti," *Il Progresso Italo-Americano*, July 7, 1933; "La squadra di Balbo e pronta a spiccare il volo transatlantico," *Il Progresso Italo-Americano*, July 7, 1933.

3. "Italian Flyers Plan to Resume Trip Today," *Baltimore Sun*, July 8, 1933; "Rain and Fog Again Hold Up Italian Flyers," *Chicago Daily Tribune*, July 9, 1933.

4. "Mrs. Roosevelt Departs for Long Journey . . ." *Washington Post*, July 7, 1933. The *Post* reported that Child was chairman of the committee. But other newspapers named Major Reed Landis the chairman. See, for example, "Chicago to Mark Italo Balbo Day," *New York Times*, July 15, 1933.

5. Telegram, Richard Washburn Child to Marvin McIntyre, July 11, 1933, Folder: Child, Richard Washburn, President's Personal File 1760, FDRL.

6. "From Rome to Chicago," *Il Progresso Italo-Americano*, July 16, 1933; "Cheat Perils," *Washington Post*, July 18, 1933; Whol, *Spectacle of Flight*, 93; Segre, *Italo Balbo*, 241–42.

7. James O'Donnell Bennett, "Chicago Fetes Balbo Heroes in Heroic Style," *Chicago Daily Tribune*, July 17, 1933.

8. "5,000 Acclaim Balbo Flyers at Italian Dinner," *Chicago Daily Tribune*, July 17, 1933; "Southern Route Safer, Says Balbo," *New York Times*, July 17, 1933.

9. Italo Balbo, *La centuria alata* (Milan: Mondadori, 1934), 259.

10. See "Italian-Americans of Chicago Honor . . . ," photograph, in Bennett, "Chicago Fetes Balbo Heroes in Heroic Style"; "5,000 Acclaim Balbo Flyers at Italian Dinner," *Chicago Daily Tribune*.

11. "5,000 Acclaim Balbo Flyers at Italian Dinner," *Chicago Daily Tribune*. On the fascist salute as a transnational performance, see Joseph Fronczak, "The Fascist Game: Transnational Political Transmission and the Genesis of the U.S. Modern Right," *Journal of American History* 105, no. 3 (December 2018): 568–71.

12. "100,000 at Chicago Greet Balbo Fleet," *New York Times*, July 16, 1933; "5,000 Acclaim Balbo Flyers at Italian Dinner," *Chicago Daily Tribune*; "Aeronautics: Viva Balbo," *Time*, July 24, 1933. *Time* claimed that Child, not Balbo, called the roll. This does not seem likely. The *Tribune*'s next-day report that Balbo had called the roll is far more credible.

13. "5,000 Acclaim Balbo Flyers at Italian Dinner," *Chicago Daily Tribune*.

14. Telegram, William Phillips to Richard Washburn Child, July 12, 1933, Folder, Italy, Government of 1933–1936, Official File 233, FDRL; "5,000 Acclaim Balbo Flyers at Italian Dinner," *Chicago Daily Tribune*.

15. "Sul pontile del Floyd Bennett Field," photograph, *Il Progresso Italo-Americano*, July 20, 1933; "Moors in Jamaica Bay," *New York Times*, July 20, 1933.

16. "La partenza di S. E. Balbo per Washington," photograph, *Il Progresso Italo-Americano*, July 21, 1933.

17. "Italian Flyers Win New Acclaim Here; Honored by Mayor," *New York Times*, July 22, 1933; "Il ricevimento alla City Hall," *Il Progresso Italo-Americano*, July 21, 1933; "La trionfale giornata italiana di New York," *Il Progresso Italo-Americano*, July 22, 1933.

18. Generoso Pope, "Sulla via del ritorno," *Il Progresso Italo-Americano*, July 11, 1933. Pope summed up the sentiments of many Italian Americans when he stated that Balbo's flight meant that they could be prouder than ever of their *"italianità"*: the airmen's achievement signaled the "rebirth of Italy, thanks to the genius of Mussolini."

19. Bennett, "Chicago Fetes Balbo Heroes in Heroic Style." Bennett called him "D'Artagnan of the air."

20. "Balbo and His Men Honored in Capital," *Baltimore Sun*, July 21, 1933. The article noted the crowd's astonishment and delight with Balbo's public costume change at Anacostia airfield.

21. Segre, *Italo Balbo*, 52–53, 178–79.

22. Whol, *Spectacle of Flight*, 92; "Moors in Jamaica Bay," *New York Times*.

23. Pope, "Sulla via del ritorno."

24. "Balbo and His Men Honored in Capital."

25. Anne O'Hare McCormick, "1903—the Conquest of the Air—1928," *New York Times*, December 16, 1928. McCormick described flight as "triumph of independence and exactitude over vagarious wind." Whol, *Spectacle of Flight*, 93.

26. "5,000 Acclaim Balbo Flyers at Italian Dinner," *Chicago Daily Tribune*; "100,000 at Chicago Greet Balbo Fleet," *New York Times*; Bennett, "Chicago Fetes Balbo Heroes in Heroic Style"; "1,000,000 in Chicago Bid Balbo Good-Bye," *New York Times*, July 19, 1933.

27. "Italian Flyers Win New Acclaim Here; Honored by Mayor," *New York Times*. Balbo liked to reflect how Italian aviation itself was a story of breaking free of the limits imposed by nature. At the dinner at the Commodore Hotel, he noted that Italy's relative poverty, forced on it by its lack of natural resources, had not stood in the way of the development of a world-class aeronautical program.

28. "La crociera non ha alcuno scopo di natura militare," *Il Progresso Italo-Americano*, July 21, 1933.

29. Pope, "Sulla via del ritorno"; "Il saluto di Pope e le parole di Balbo," *Il Progresso Italo-Americano*, July 20, 1933.

30. "Un messaggio del Presidente al Re," *Il Progresso Italo-Americano*, July 22, 1933; Letter, William Phillips to Franklin Roosevelt, July 21, 1933, Folder: Italy, Government of 1933–1936, Official File 233, FDRL.

31. Letter, Franklin Roosevelt to Breckinridge Long, June 16, 1933, Folder: Long, Breckinridge, President's Personal File 434, FDRL.

32. "100,000 at Chicago Greet Balbo Fleet," *New York Times*. The *Times* parenthesized the protests of Italian antifascists in Chicago on July 15 as a "jarring note" in an otherwise joyful day.

And only the *Times* reported that the "first message that the General delivered to Chicago was a rebuke": he was angry because two American boats had cut across his path as he descended. Henrietta Nesbitt, *White House Diary* (New York: Doubleday, 1948), 92–93. A White House staffer noted that Balbo "looked unhappy and weary" prior to his meeting with Roosevelt.

33. Stefano Luconi, "Ethnic Allegiance and Class Consciousness among Italian-American Workers, 1900–1941," *Socialism and Democracy* 22, no. 3 (September 2008): 138.

34. David Eldridge, *American Culture in the 1930s* (Edinburgh: Edinburgh University Press, 2008), 52–54; Morris Dickstein, *Dancing in the Dark: A Cultural History of the Great Depression* (New York: Norton, 2009), 219, 426, 433, 436, 360, 524.

35. Zygmunt Bauman, *Modernity and Ambivalence* (Cambridge: Polity Press, 1991), 20; Zygmunt Bauman, *Modernity and the Holocaust* (Cambridge: Polity Press, 1989).

36. Kennedy, *Freedom from Fear*, 218.

37. Lucius Jones, "Society-Slants: 'How Can They Be Hungry Full as I Am,'" *Atlanta Daily World*, December 16 1934.

38. Kennedy, *Freedom from Fear*, 219–42.

39. Charles Magee Adams, "Who Bred These Utopias?" *North American Review*, June 1935.

40. Kennedy, *Freedom from Fear*, 292–96.

41. Arthur M. Schlesinger Jr., *The Age of Roosevelt: The Politics of Upheaval: 1935–1936* (New York: Mariner, 2003), 292; Badger, *New Deal*, 136.

42. Lecture notes, Herbert W. Schneider, "Industry and Labor under the Roosevelt Regime," part of lecture series, "Lineamenti storici e ideali del conflitto economico-politico intorno di Roosevelt," Folder, Manuscripts L, 107/3/5, SPHWS.

43. Glaucus, "F. D. Roosevelt ed i gravi problemi nazionali," *Il Progresso Italo-Americano*, April 4, 1937. See also Generoso Pope, "Scioperi e prosperità," *Il Progresso Italo-Americano*, April 11, 1937.

44. George Gallup and Claude Robinson, "American Institute of Public Opinion—Surveys, 1935–38," *Public Opinion Quarterly* 2, no. 3 (July 1938): 382.

45. Lecture notes, Herbert W. Schneider, "Survey of Various Interests and Traditions in U.S.," part of lecture series, "Lineamenti storici e ideali del conflitto economico-politico intorno di Roosevelt," Folder, Manuscripts L, 107/3/5, SPHWS.

46. Gallup and Robinson, "American Institute of Public Opinion," 388.

47. Schmitz, *United States and Fascist Italy*, 135–205.

48. Letter, Henry Haskell to Herbert Schneider, November 16, 1935, Folder, Correspondence, 1930–1935, 107/1/4, SPHWS. For Butler and fascism, see Diggins, *Mussolini and Fascism*, 255–57. By the mid-1930s, Butler had become critical of fascism, identifying similarities between, and alarming tendencies within, totalitarian regimes.

49. Report, Carlo Boidi to Benito Mussolini, November 29, 1935, sotto-fascicolo 36, "On Boidi—crociera del GUF in America," busta 8, Ministero della Cultura Popolare, gabinetto 1926–1944, ACS.

50. Letter, Angelo Flavio Guidi to Ottavio de Peppo, April 14, 1936, fascicolo "Propaganda nel nord America," busta 220, Stati Uniti 1935–1936, Ministero della Cultura Popolare, direzione generale servizi della propaganda, archivio generale (1930–1943), ACS. Letter, Pietro Gorgolini to Dino Alfieri, September 29, 1936, fascicolo 450, "Centro Italiano di Studi Americani, Gorgolini prof. Pietro," busta 74, Ministero della Cultura Popolare, gabinetto 1926–1944, ACS. By 1936, Guidi was a member of the directorship of the Fasci all'Estero (the fascist party abroad).

51. Letter, Fulvio Suvich to Ministry of Foreign Affairs and Ministry of Press and Propaganda, February 4, 1937, fascicolo "Propaganda straniera negli Stati Uniti," busta 222, Stati Uniti 1937, Ministero della Cultura Popolare, direzione generale servizi della propaganda, archivio generale (1930–1943), ACS.

52. *Reminiscences of Herbert Wallace Schneider*. Schneider claimed that his "chief" objective in writing *The Fascist Government of Italy* in 1936 had been to demonstrate that fascism had "no relation to Nazism."

53. "What Price Naziism?" *Il Progresso Italo-Americano*, July 15, 1934.

54. "Il Duce Leaving Littoria after the Harvest," photograph, *Il Progresso Italo-Americano*, August 12, 1934.

55. See Mariano Pierro to Giuseppe Sapuppo, March 17, 1934; and Anne O'Hare McCormick to Galeazzo Ciano, April 9, 1934. Both in fascicolo "Ministero per la Stampa e Propaganda Mac Cormick [sic] O'Hare Anna," busta 597, Ministero della Cultura Popolare, ASD.

56. Anne O'Hare McCormick, "New Italy: Fact or Phrase," *New York Times*, May 17, 1936.

57. Angelo Flavio Guidi, "La Roma verdeggiante; la città delle piante e dei fiori," *Il Progresso Italo-Americano*, October 18, 1934.

58. "Extensive Improvements in All Towns Are Accomplished," *Il Progresso Italo-Americano*, August 11, 1935; Guidi, "La Roma verdeggiante."

59. Anne O'Hare McCormick, "Mussolini Willing to Guarantee Enforcement of an Arms Treaty," *New York Times*, April 14, 1934.

60. Guidi, "La Roma verdeggiante"; "Italy, the Country of Harmony, Is a Famous Land Everyone Admires," *Il Progresso Italo-Americano*, May 3, 1936.

61. "Extensive Improvements in All Towns Are Accomplished," *Il Progresso Italo-Americano*; Thomas B. Morgan, "Once the Noisiest City, Rome Is Now the Quietest Due to Ban on Auto Horns," *Il Progresso Italo-Americano*, January 27, 193; Guidi, "La Roma verdeggiante."

62. McCormick, "Mussolini Willing to Guarantee Enforcement of an Arms Treaty."

63. Generoso Pope, "Ritorno dall'Italia," *Il Progresso Italo-Americano*, June 25, 1937.

64. Anne O'Hare McCormick, "Dreams of Empire Kindle Rome," *New York Times*, August 25, 1935.

65. "L'inagurazione di importanti lavori a Roma," photograph, *Il Progresso Italo-Americano*, November 4, 1934; "Big Clearance Work Begun by Mussolini," *Il Progresso Italo-Americano*, November 18, 1934.

66. "Modern Apartment House in Ancient Rome," photograph, in McCormick, "Italy in the Year XII E. F."

67. "Rome Magnificent under Fascist Rule," *Il Progresso Italo-Americano*, June 14, 1936.

68. Ghirardo, *Building New Communities*.

69. McCormick, "This America: A Re-Discovery."

70. Anne O'Hare McCormick, "Fear Over Europe—Hope Here," *New York Times*, August 2, 1936.

71. Ibid.

72. Generoso Pope, "Risanamento edilizio," *Il Progresso Italo-Americano*, May 20, 1934.

73. Peter Marcuse, "The Beginnings of Public Housing in New York," *Journal of Urban History* 12, no. 4 (August 1986): 353–90; Gail Radford, *Modern Housing for America: Policy Struggles in the New Deal Era* (Chicago: University of Chicago Press, 1996), 146–98.

74. Glaucus, "Vasto programma edilizio americano e i problemi della sua attuazione," *Il Progresso Italo-Americano*, January 20, 1935. Glaucus's characterization of these various plans was quite accurate. "Work Relief Corporation, to Spend 8 to 9 Billions, Hopkins Plan to End Dole," *New York Times*, November 29, 1934. The *Times* described "cheap housing" as the principal aim of Hopkins's $9 billion spending plan, while Glaucus implied that all $9 billion would be devoted to housing.

75. Glaucus, "Vasto programma edilizio americano."

76. Glaucus, "Il 'Labor Day' trova gli Stati Uniti in piena lotta contro la crisi."

77. "Qual è la via che dovrà battere il nuovo Congresso per superare la crisi attuale?" *Il Progresso Italo-Americano*, January 13, 1935. "Aboliamo la disoccupazione," *Il Progresso Italo-Americano*, June 6, 1937.

78. Generoso Pope, "Ciò che il popolo attende," *Il Progresso Italo-Americano*, June 23, 1935; Generoso Pope, "Ritorno al lavoro," *Il Progresso Italo-Americano*, July 28, 1935; Generoso Pope, "Provvedere e in tempo utile," *Il Progresso Italo-Americano*, November 22, 1937; Generoso Pope, "Lavoro per tutti," *Il Progresso Italo-Americano*, December 12, 1937.

79. Generoso Pope, "Il discorso del Gov. Lehman," *Il Progresso Italo-Americano*, January 3, 1937.

80. "Job Relief Drive of Nine Billions Up to Roosevelt," *Washington Post*, January 12, 1934.

81. Badger, *New Deal*, 241–42; "Whittling Down the Housing Bill," *New York Times*, August 7, 1937; "Senate Passes Housing Bill with $4,000 a Family Limit," *New York Times*, August 7, 1937; *United States Housing Act of 1937, as Amended* (Washington, DC: Federal Works Agency, U.S. Housing Authority, 1939).

82. "Extensive Improvements in All Towns Are Accomplished," *Il Progresso Italo-Americano*.

83. See Guidi, "La Roma verdeggiante"; Morgan, "Once the Noisiest City"; and "Rome Magnificent Under Fascist Rule," *Il Progresso Italo-Americano*.

84. Guidi, "La Roma verdeggiante."

85. McCormick, "Dreams of Empire Kindle Rome." Mussolini wanted to free the "past from the overlay of centuries," according to McCormick.

86. Schneider, *Fascist Government of Italy*, 14. McCormick, "Dreams of Empire Kindle Rome." McCormick observed that Mussolini invoked Rome's imperial past to generate "national pride."

87. McCormick, "Italy in the Year XII E. F." Joshua Arthurs, *Excavating Modernity: The Roman Past in Fascist Italy* (Ithaca, NY: Cornell University Press, 2012), 50. Mussolini himself described his plans for ancient Rome as a large-scale gardening project, which would "liberate the trunk of the great oak from all that still constrains it."

88. McCormick, "Dreams of Empire Kindle Rome."

89. Schneider, *Fascist Government of Italy*, 7.

90. Schneider, *Making the Fascist State*, 228–29.

91. McCormick, "Italy in the Year XII E. F."

92. "Italy, the Country of Harmony, Is a Famous Land Everyone Admires," *Il Progresso Italo-Americano*.

93. Angelo Flavio Guidi, "Giovani italiani di tutto il mondo," *Il Progresso Italo-Americano*, September 11, 1935.

94. Telespresso, Under-Secretariat for Press and Propaganda to Luce Institute, June 22, 1935, fascicolo "Pellicole di propaganda per gli Stati Uniti," busta 219, Stati Uniti 1935, Ministero della Cultura Popolare, direzione generale servizi della propaganda, archivio generale (1930–1943), ACS.

95. "La Demolizione delle case intorno al Mausoleo di Augusto e i nuovi quartieri nella zona di Piazza Bologna," November 1934, B0576; "Lido di Roma. Giornate di sole dell'inverno romano," January 1934, B0404; "Italia Roma. Foro romano. Lavori di scavo," May 1934, B0469. All in *Giornale Luce*, accessed at archvioluce.com on June 12, 2020.

96. Anne O'Hare McCormick, "Hitler Seeks Jobs for All Germans," *New York Times*, July 10, 1933; Anne O'Hare McCormick, "The Three the World Watches," *New York Times*, August 12, 1934; Anne O'Hare McCormick, "Munich Becoming 'Capital' of Nazis," *New York Times*, February 11, 1934.

97. Arnaldo Cortesi, "Vatican Fearful of German Curbs," *New York Times*, July 3, 1934.

98. Anne O'Hare McCormick, "Frankfurt's Banks Still Run by Jews," *New York Times*, June 20, 1933.

99. McCormick, "Three the World Watches."

100. The *borgata* (suburban community) of Primavalle was notorious for its poor conditions. See Ghirardo, *Building New Communities*, 39–40, 192; and Borden W. Painter, *Mussolini's Rome: Rebuilding the Eternal City* (New York: Palgrave MacMillan, 2005), 94–95.

101. McCormick, "Dreams of Empire Kindle Rome." The observation that Italians feel Mussolini's renovation of Rome as they would "scars" on their body was made by Marta Marsili, a local historian and guide, who showed me the physical results of the fascist project for Rome on April 18, 2017.

102. Marilyn D. McShane and Frank P. Williams III, ed., *Encyclopedia of Juvenile Justice* (London: Sage, 2002), 365. These ideas were closely associated with the work of the University of Chicago sociologists Clifford Shaw and Henry McKay. See Clifford Shaw, Frederick Zorbaugh, Henry McKay, and Leonard Cottrell, *Delinquency Areas: A Study of the Geographic Distribution of School Truants, Juvenile Delinquents, and Adult Offenders in Chicago* (Chicago: University of Chicago Press, 1929).

103. Clifford Shaw and Henry McKay, "Social Factors in Juvenile Delinquency," in *Report on the Causes of Crime*, vol. 2 (Washington, DC: U.S. Government Printing Office, 1931).

104. Frederic Thrasher, "Gangsters: Why? A Resounding Question," *New York Times*, March 17, 1935.

105. McCormick, "Fear Over Europe—Hope Here"; "Let Laboratory Find Crime Cure, Scientist Says," *Chicago Daily Tribune*, April 7, 1930; Shaw and McKay, "Social Factors in Juvenile Delinquency," 34, 45, 55, 76, 128.

106. Generoso Pope, "Per il buon nome italiano," *Il Progresso Italo-Americano*, March 22, 1934.

107. McCormick, "Italy in the Year XII E. F."

108. Schneider and Clough, *Making Fascists*, 83–109, 178–82.

109. Schneider, *Fascist Government of Italy*, 46, 145–46.

110. Shaw and McKay, "Social Factors in Juvenile Delinquency," 3, 4, 327, 333.

111. "Italy Meets Crime Through 'Balilla,'" *Il Progresso Italo-Americano*, June 7, 1936.

112. McCormick, "Italy in the Year XII E. F."; McCormick, "Average Italian Is Still Himself"; Schneider, *Fascist Government of Italy*, 46.

113. "Le colonie marine e montane dei bimbi d'Italia e dei loro fratelli d'America," *Il Progresso Italo-Americano*, July 2, 1933.

114. Angelo Flavio Guidi, "Un accampamento che è un mondo," *Il Progresso Italo-Americano*, September 18, 1936.

115. "Italy's Great Youth Movement Harks Back to Caesar and Nero," *Il Progresso Italo-Americano*, March 7, 1937.

116. McCormick, "Italy in the Year XII E. F." "The 50,000 'Avanguardists' of Camp Dux, at the Holy Mass, Celebrated in the Open Air," photograph, *Il Progresso Italo-Americano*, October 1, 1933.

117. "Training Italy's Future Mothers," *Il Progresso Italo-Americano*, January 14, 1934. Tracy H. Koon, *Believe, Obey, Fight: Political Socialization of Youth in Fascist Italy, 1922–1943* (Chapel Hill: University of North Carolina Press, 1985), 96–98.

118. "Training Italy's Future Mothers," *Il Progresso Italo-Americano*.

119. McCormick, "Italy in the Year XII E. F."

120. "Maternity Centers in Italy Great Boon to Mothers and Children," *Il Progresso Italo-Americano*, September 30, 1934.

121. "The Italian Government Will Help Child Welfare," *Il Progresso Italo-Americano*, February 10, 1935.

122. "Il ciclismo italiano tuttora all'avanguardia," illustration, *Il Progresso Italo-Americano*, February 10, 1935. Generoso Pope, "Il primo campione italiano," *Il Progresso Italo-Americano*, July 1, 1933. Similarly, Generoso Pope wrote that Primo Carnera's victory as world heavyweight boxing champion in June 1933 was proof of the "magical Mussolinian impulse" at work on the youth of Italy.

123. "Italian Youth Movement Is Patterned on Roman Method," *Il Progresso Italo-Americano*, November 15, 1936.

124. Glaucus, "Nel XII annuale della marcia su Roma Marconi inaugura l'ora italiana," *Il Progresso Italo-Americano*, October 28, 1934.

125. "The Italian Government Will Help Child Welfare," *Il Progresso Italo-Americano*.

126. McCormick, "Italy in the Year XII E. F."

127. "La crociata del Gr. Uff. Generoso Pope per prevenire la delinquenza giovanile," *Il Progresso Italo-Americano*, July 11, 1937.

128. "La crociata del Gr. Uff. Generoso Pope per prevenire la delinquenza giovanile," *Il Progresso Italo-Americano*, April 4, 1937; "La crociata del Gr. Uff. Generoso Pope per prevenire la delinquenza giovanile," *Il Progresso Italo-Americano*, April 25, 1937.

129. "Campaign Opened to Assist Young People," *Il Progresso Italo-Americano*, October 25, 1936.

130. Ibid.; "Le colonie marine e montane dei bimbi d'Italia e dei loro fratelli d'America," *Il Progresso Italo-Americano*; "La crociata del Gr. Uff. Generoso Pope per prevenire la delinquenza giovanile," *Il Progresso Italo-Americano*, July 11, 1937.

131. "Un escursione a Villa Saint Joseph, oasi di amore e di pace, nido giocondo," *Il Progresso Italo-Americano*, August 19, 1934; Generoso Pope, "St. Joseph Villa: 1929–1934," *Il Progresso Italo-Americano*, March 10, 1935.

132. Generoso Pope, "Pel campeggio di villa St. Joseph," *Il Progresso Italo-Americano*, April 28, 1935.

133. "Crime Waves, Rackets Are Unknown in Italy under Fascist Regime," *Il Progresso Italo-Americano*, April 15, 1934. For a historical assessment of the fascist record in fighting the mafia, see Christopher Duggan, *Fascism and the Mafia* (New Haven, CT: Yale University Press, 1989).

134. "During One of Their Greatest Gatherings in Rome, the Balilla Presenting Il Duce with a Magnificent Vision of Youth and Discipline . . . ," photograph, *Il Progresso Italo-Americano*, August 11, 1935.

135. "The Contest Held at Piazza Siena, in Rome . . . ," photograph, *Il Progresso Italo-Americano*, August 2, 1936.

136. "Il Duce at the Child Welfare Show in Rome," photograph, *Il Progresso Italo-Americano*, July 18, 1937. According to the caption, this photo demonstrated, Mussolini's "love for the little ones."

137. Letter, Luigi Villari to the Director General of Propaganda, September 25, 1937, fascicolo "Propaganda negli Stati Uniti nuovo centro Italian Library of Information," busta 223, Stati Uniti 1938, Ministero della Cultura Popolare, direzione generale servizi della propaganda, archivio generale (1930–1943), ACS.

138. Schneider, *Fascist Government of Italy*, 20; "Maternity Centers in Italy," *Il Progresso Italo-Americano*.

139. McCormick, "Italy in the Year XII E. F."

140. "Italian-American Boys, Guests of the Fascist Government at Cortina," photograph, *Il Progresso Italo-Americano*, August 12, 1934.

141. Guidi, "Giovani italiani di tutto il mondo."

142. Matteo Pretelli, *La via fascista alla democrazia americana: Cultura e propaganda nella comunità italo-americane* (Viterbo: Sette Città, 2012), 97–98.

143. Anne O'Hare McCormick, "Confusion of Aims Is Seen in Germany," *New York Times*, June 14, 1933.

144. McCormick, "New Italy: Fact or Phrase."

145. McCormick, "Italy in the Year XII E. F."

146. See for instance, Telespresso, Augusto Rosso to the Undersecretary for Press and Propaganda, December 10, 1934, fascicolo "Materiale di propaganda per gli Stati Uniti," busta 219, Stati Uniti 1935, Ministero della Cultura Popolare, direzione generale servizi della propaganda, archivio generale (1930–1943), ACS. Ambassador Rosso included a clipping from the *Baltimore Sun* of a photograph of fascist youth carrying guns, inspected by the Austrian Chancellor von Schuschnigg on his visit to the Foro Mussolini. Rosso wrote that such images were "not useful for the effects of propaganda on this country."

147. Koon, *Believe, Obey, Fight*, 102.

148. Gentile, *Il culto del Littorio*.

149. Koon, *Believe, Obey, Fight*, 95–96. Balilla leaders were usually also children's schoolteachers; enrollment forms were sent home from school with children, and parents had to provide a "written explanation" if they opted not to enroll their child.

150. Victoria De Grazia, *How Fascism Ruled Women: Italy, 1922–1945* (Berkeley: University of California Press, 1993), 166–68.

151. Koon, *Believe, Obey, Fight*, 96.

152. Bosworth, *Mussolini's Italy*, 291.

153. "Two Hold Back in Geneva," *New York Times*, October 11, 1935.

154. "A Moral Embargo," *New York Times*, November 23, 1935; "President Gives Sharp Warning to War Shippers," *Chicago Daily Tribune*, October 31, 1935.

155. Roland N. Stromberg, "American Business and the Approach of War 1935–1941," *Journal of Economic History* 13, no. 1 (January 1953): 64–65; Brenda Gayle Plummer, *Rising Wind: Black*

Americans and U.S. Foreign Affairs, 1935–1960 (Chapel Hill: University of North Carolina Press, 1995), 51; "Hull Studies Neutrality," *New York Times*, December 5, 1935; "Neutrality Policy Pliant in New Bill," *New York Times*, January 1, 1936.

156. Anne O'Hare McCormick, "As Italy Faces the Test of Sanctions," *New York Times*, November 10, 1935.

157. "Natives Taught to Build Good Roads in Ethiopia," *Il Progresso Italo-Americano*, November 3, 1935; "Ethiopia's Virgin Territory Same as during Queen Sheba's Reign," *Il Progresso Italo-Americano*, March 21, 1937. For Ethiopian realities, see James McCann, *People of the Plow: An Agricultural History of Ethiopia, 1800–1990* (Madison: University of Wisconsin Press, 1995), 48, 58–60, 133–36, 157–68.

158. Sem Benelli, "Come amano e come odiano gli etiopi," *Il Progresso Italo-Americano*, April 5, 1936.

159. "Italian Advance in Ethiopia: Life in the Conquered Land," *Il Progresso Italo-Americano*, April 12, 1936; Generoso Pope, "4 Settembre: A Ginevra," *Il Progresso Italo-Americano*, September 4, 1935.

160. Generoso Pope, "La vertenza italo-abissina," *Il Progresso Italo-Americano*, March 3, 1935. Jean Allain, "Slavery and the League of Nations: Ethiopia as a Civilised Nation," *Journal of the History of International Law* 8, no. 2 (2006): 213–44. Slavery, it was true, did persist in Ethiopia. But the notion that Haile Selassie had failed to take any effective action to abolish it was false. The emperor had institutionalized a gradual approach to emancipation that, however imperfect from a human rights perspective, satisfied the standards of British abolitionists who monitored the country's progress.

161. "La regina etiope che, per serbarsi bella, prendeva il bagno nel sangue umano," *Il Progresso Italo-Americano*, August 18, 1935. "Ugandha Asura, Once the Favorite Slave Dancer of the King of Kings of Ethiopia, Who Has Escaped from Her Banishment from the Royal Court and Made Her Way to Italy," photograph, *Il Progresso Italo-Americano*, October 20, 1935.

162. "Ethiopian Soldiers Desert to Italians; Show Fealty, Dancing," *Il Progresso Italo-Americano*, April 5, 1936.

163. Benelli, "Come amano e come odiano gli etiopi."

164. Telegram, Dino Alfieri to Galeazzo Ciano [undated, but probably late October 1935], sotto-fascicolo 1, "Primo viaggio," fascicolo 283, busta 47, Corrispondenza Africa Orientale, S. E. Ciano, Ministero della Cultura Popolare, gabinetto 1926–1944, ACS.

165. "La quotidiana tragedia di un impero senza orgogli, senza glorie e senza fede," *Il Progresso Italo-Americano*, June 9, 1935, "Scene e paesaggi dell'Etiopia millenaria," *Il Progresso Italo-Americano*, December 29, 1935.

166. For a few examples of the literature on empire and wilderness, see Keith Pluymers, "Taming the Wilderness in Sixteenth- and Seventeenth-Century Ireland and Virginia," *Environmental History* 16, no. 4 (October 2011): 610–32; Patrick Brantlinger, *Taming Cannibals: Race and the Victorians* (Ithaca, NY: Cornell University Press, 2011); Denis Cosgrove, "Habitable Earth: Wilderness, Empire, and Race in America," in *Wild Ideas*, ed. David Rothenberg (Minneapolis: University of Minnesota Press, 1995), 27–41.

167. Guglielmo, *White on Arrival*, 120.

168. Anne O'Hare McCormick, "Africa Plan Final, Mussolini Insists," *New York Times*, May 24, 1935.

169. "La scoperta dell'America e la S.D.N," illustration, *Il Progresso Italo-Americano*, January 23, 1936.

170. Generoso Pope, "Il primo versamento," *Il Progresso Italo-Americano*, November 17, 1935.

171. Fascicolo "Invio di materiali varie negli Stati Uniti," busta 222, Stati Uniti 1937, Ministero della Cultura Popolare, direzione generale servizi della propaganda, archivio generale (1930–1943), ACS. This folder contains two undated photographs of road building in East Africa, to be distributed in the United States. Telegram, Dino Alfieri to Galeazzo Ciano [undated, but probably late October 1935], sotto-fascicolo 1, "Primo viaggio," fascicolo 283, busta 47, Corrispondenza Africa Orientale, S. E. Ciano, Ministero della Cultura Popolare, gabinetto 1926–1944, ACS. As part of the advice Alfieri offered to Ciano for an upcoming radio transmission to the United States, Alfieri wrote: "Insist on the character of peaceful systematization of the occupied territory—roads."

172. "Ethiopia's Virgin Territory Same as during Queen Sheba's Reign," *Il Progresso Italo-Americano*.

173. Anne O'Hare McCormick, "Italy Welcomes a 'Truce,'" *New York Times*, June 2, 1935. "Military Sanitation Curing the Natives . . . ," photograph, *Il Progresso Italo-Americano*, December 8, 1935. "La riorganizzazione della vita civile nei territori conquistati in Etiopia," *Il Progresso Italo-Americano*, January 5, 1936.

174. "Italy's Civilizing Mission in Ethiopia: Free Clinics Opened," *Il Progresso Italo-Americano*, April 19, 1936.

175. "Italy Transforms Addis Ababa from Native Hut Village into Roman City," *Il Progresso Italo-Americano*, October 11, 1936.

176. Telegram, Dino Alfieri to Galeazzo Ciano [undated, but probably late October 1935], sotto-fascicolo 1, "Primo viaggio," fascicolo 283, busta 47, Corrispondenza Africa Orientale, S. E. Ciano, Ministero della Cultura Popolare, gabinetto 1926–1944, ACS.

177. Schneider, *Fascist Government of Italy*, 12. McCormick, "Dreams of Empire Kindle Rome"; Generoso Pope, "Fine della prepotenza inglese," *Il Progresso Italo-Americano*, August 22, 1935.

178. Schneider, *Fascist Government of Italy*, 12, 139–41.

179. McCormick, "As Italy Faces the Test of Sanctions."

180. "La conquista etiopica e la bonifica integrale dell'uomo e dell'ambiente," *Il Progresso Italo-Americano*, January 12, 1936.

181. Glaucus, "Le ali d'Italia nel cielo d'Etiopia," *Il Progresso Italo-Americano*, October 20, 1935.

182. Letter, Anne O'Hare McCormick to Benito Mussolini, May 21, 1935, fascicolo "Ministero per la Stampa e Propaganda Mac Cormick [sic] O'Hare Anna," busta 597, Ministero della Cultura Popolare, ASD. McCormick, "Africa Plan Final, Mussolini Insists."

183. Anne O'Hare McCormick, "New Dreams of African Empire," *New York Times*, June 16, 1935.

184. Anne O'Hare McCormick, "Italians Prepare for Sanction War," *New York Times*, December 3, 1935.

185. Generoso Pope, "Per la neutralità americana," *Il Progresso Italo-Americano*, October 27, 1935; Generoso Pope, "Rispettare la neutralità," *Il Progresso Italo-Americano*, November 27, 1935; "Generoso Pope, "Ritorno alla legge," *Il Progresso Italo-Americano*, December 4, 1935; Generoso Pope, "Neutralità significa pace," *Il Progresso Italo-Americano*, December 26, 1935.

186. "Il Gr. Uff. Generoso Pope a colloquio con Roosevelt," *Il Progresso Italo-Americano*; "Un'intervista del Gr. Uff. G. Pope col Segretario degli Esteri On. Hull," *Il Progresso Italo-Americano*.

187. Robert A. Divine, *The Illusion of Neutrality* (Chicago: University of Chicago Press, 1962), 150–52; Cordell Hull and Andrew Henry Thomas Berding, *The Memoirs of Cordell Hull*, vol. 1 (New York: Macmillan, 1948), 464–65.

188. Letter, Herbert Schneider to Nicholas Murray Butler, January 25, 1936, Folder, Correspondence, 1936–1941, 107/1/5, SPHWS.

189. Anne O'Hare McCormick, "Italy Squeezed," *New York Times*, November 24, 1935.

190. McCormick, "Italians Prepare for Sanction War."

191. "Building Moral Resistance Source of Pride for Mothers," *Il Progresso Italo-Americano*, March 15, 1936.

192. "All'appello della patria tutti gl'italiani rispondono 'presente!,'" *Il Progresso Italo-Americano*, November 8, 1935. Alluding to the traditional squadrist roll call, a November 8 headline read "To the Call of the Country, All Italians Respond 'Present!'"

193. "I primi $100,000 della sottoscrizione versati da Pope al Console Gen. d'Italia," *Il Progresso Italo-Americano*, November 17, 1935.

194. "La nostra sottoscrizione: l'ultimo versamento," *Il Progresso Italo-Americano*, October 18, 1936.

195. "Ora per la patria," *Il Progresso Italo-Americano*, December 1, 1935.

196. Clipping from *Il Messagero*, June 12, 1937, in fascicolo H407, "Raccomandato Pope, Generoso New York Oggetto: 1928 onorificenza," busta 18, Segreteria particolare del Duce, carteggio ordinario, ACS.

197. Glaucus, "Le ali d'Italia nel cielo d'Etiopia."

198. "The Resurrection," image; "After the Victorious Battle of Lake Ascianghi...," photograph. Both in *Il Progresso Italo-Americano*, April 12, 1936.

199. For Ethiopian's adaptable, diverse, and environmentally sustainable system of agriculture, see McCann, *People of the Plow*. For the efficacy of both traditional and modern medicine in Ethiopia, see Makonnen Bishaw, "Promoting Traditional Medicine in Ethiopia: A Brief Historical Review of Government Policy," *Social Science and Medicine* 33, no. 2 (1991): 193–200.

200. Alberto Sbacchi, "Poison Gas and Atrocities in the Italo-Ethiopian War," in *Italian Colonialism*, ed. Ruth Ben-Ghiat and Mia Fuller (New York: Palgrave Macmillan, 2005), 47–56; Giorgio Rochat, "L'impiego dei gas nella guerra d'Etiopia, 1935–36," *Rivista di Storia Contemporanea* 17, no. 1 (January 1988): 74–109.

201. Charles Schaefer, "Serendipitous Resistance in Fascist-Occupied Ethiopia, 1936–1941," *Northeast African Studies* 3, no. 1 (1996): 87–115; Haile Larebo, "Empire Building and Its Limitations: Ethiopia (1935–1941)," in *Italian Colonialism*, 83–94.

202. "Ethiopia's Trade Hit by Occupation," *New York Times*, January 5, 1938; Larebo, "Empire Building and Its Limitations," 91.

203. Gianluca Podestà, "Emigrazione e colonizzazione in Libia e Africa orientale," *Altreitalia* 42 (2011): 40; Larebo, "Empire Building and Its Limitations," 90–91.

204. Mia Fuller, "Wherever You Go, There You Are: Fascist Plans for the Colonial City of Addis Ababa and the Colonizing Suburb of EUR," *Journal of Contemporary History* 31, no. 2 (April 1996): 403–4.

205. Schaefer, "Serendipitous Resistance in Fascist-Occupied Ethiopia"; Larebo, "Empire Building and Its Limitations."

206. For Italian Americans' support for the Ethiopian invasion, see Fiorello B. Ventresco, "Italian-Americans and the Ethiopian Crisis," *Italian Americana* 6, no. 1 (1980): 4–27. For active opposition of the minority of Italian Americans, see Neelam Srivastava, "Anti-Colonialism and the Italian Left: Resistances to the Fascist Invasion of Ethiopia," *Interventions* 8, no. 3 (2006): 413–29. For the response of African Americans, see Plummer, *Rising Wind*, 37–82.

207. Telespresso, Augusto Rosso to the Undersecretary for Press and Propaganda, December 10, 1934, fascicolo "Materiale di propaganda per gli Stati Uniti," busta 219, Stati Uniti 1935, Ministero della Cultura Popolare, dir. gen. servizi della propaganda, archivio generale (1930–1943), ACS. Letter, Fulvio Suvich to Ministry of Foreign Affairs and Ministry of Press and Propaganda, February 4, 1937, fascicolo "Propaganda straniera negli Stati Uniti," busta 222, Stati Uniti 1937, Ministero della Cultura Popolare, direzione generale servizi della propaganda, archivio generale (1930–1943), ACS.

208. "Nazi Link Is Denied at Camp's Opening," *New York Times*, July 19, 1937.

209. "12,000 at Nazi Fete Hear Boycott Plan," *New York Times*, September 6, 1937.

210. For the corporate state, see Schneider, *Fascist Government of Italy*, 66–100. For competent executives, see ibid., 47–51.

211. Ibid., ix.

212. For imperialism, see ibid., 133–41. For the single paragraph on the militia, see ibid., 47. On page 33, Schneider promised that he would "consider in turn . . . the army, navy and royal police." He did not.

213. Henry Spencer, review of *The Fascist Government of Italy*, *American Political Science Review* 30, no. 5 (October 1936): 991–92.

214. Herman Finer, review of *The Fascist Government of Italy*, *Public Opinion Quarterly* 1, no. 2 (April 1937): 148–50.

215. Letter, Anne O'Hare McCormick to Benito Mussolini, January 27, 1937, fascicolo "Ministero per la Stampa e Propaganda Mac Cormick [sic] O'Hare Anna," busta 597, Ministero della Cultura Popolare, ASD.

216. Anne O'Hare McCormick, "Mussolini Anxious over Spanish War," *New York Times*, February 2, 1937.

217. Letter, Anne O'Hare McCormick to Benito Mussolini, January 27, 1937, fascicolo "Ministero per la Stampa e Propaganda Mac Cormick [sic] O'Hare Anna," busta 597, Ministero della Cultura Popolare, ASD.

218. "What Is Moscow's Game?" *Il Progresso Italo-Americano*, October 25, 1936; I. C. Falbo, "Da una settimana all'altra," *Il Progresso Italo-Americano*, November 1, 1936; "Volunteers in Spain," *Il Progresso Italo-Americano*, February 7, 1937.

219. Glaucus, "Le cause della guerra civile in Ispagna," *Il Progresso Italo-Americano*, August 16, 1936.

220. Glaucus, "Franco e i suoi piani di ricostruzione," *Il Progresso Italo-Americano*, November 15, 1936.

221. Generoso Pope, "L'Italia e la libertà religiosa," *Il Progresso Italo-Americano*, May 23, 1937. See also Generoso Pope, "Respect Commands Respect," *Il Progresso Italo-Americano*, May 2, 1937.

Conclusion. Searching for Soul under the Sign of the Machine

1. Josephson, *Portrait of the Artist as American*, ix–x.

2. Joseph Wood Krutch, *The Modern Temper: A Study and a Confession* (New York: Harcourt Brace, 1929).

3. Gutzon Borglum, "Our Ugly Cities," *North American Review*, November 1929.

4. McCormick, "Trifles Light as Air in a Tottering World."

5. For expatriates' individualism, see Warren Susman, "Pilgrimage to Paris: The Backgrounds of American Expatriation" (PhD dissertation, University of Wisconsin, 1957), 297–99.

6. McCormick, "Politics à l'Italienne."

7. For the complex relationship between futurism and fascism, see Adrian Lyttelton, "Futurism, Politics, and Society," in *Italian Futurism 1909–1944: Reconstructing the Universe*, ed. Vivien Greene (New York: Solomon R. Guggenheim Museum, 2014), 58–76.

8. Berman, *All That Is Solid Melts into Air*, 15–16.

9. Matteo Millan, "The Institutionalisation of Squadrismo: Disciplining Paramilitary Violence in the Italian Fascist Dictatorship," *Contemporary European History* 22, no. 4 (November 2013): 551–73.

10. Paul Corner, *The Fascist Party and Popular Opinion in Mussolini's Italy* (Oxford: Oxford University Press, 2012), 182.

11. "Child Gets Final Call," *Los Angeles Times*, February 1, 1935.

12. "R. W. Child Mass Today," *New York Times*, February 2, 1935.

13. "R. W. Child Funeral," *New York Times*, February 3, 1935.

14. Merriam, "Editor's Introduction," in Schneider and Clough, *Making Fascists*, vii–xii.

15. "Italy and Germany Ready to Aid Franco," *Los Angeles Times*, January 16, 1937; "Goering Predicts Showdown on Reds," *Baltimore Sun*, January 19, 1937; "Reich Holds Talks Cover Wide Field," *New York Times*, January 15, 1937.

16. Generoso Pope, "Il secondo quadriennio," *Il Progresso Italo-Americano*, January 17, 1937; Generoso Pope, "Per i residenti che non sono in regola con le leggi degli S.U.," *Il Progresso Italo-Americano*, January 24, 1937.

17. "Goering's Visit," *Il Progresso Italo-Americano*, January 17, 1937; I. C. Falbo, "Hitler e la situazione europea," *Il Progresso Italo-Americano*, January 31, 1937.

18. "Mussolini, with Sabre, Outsteps Gen. Goering," *Il Progresso Italo-Americano*, January 17, 1937.

19. Anne O'Hare McCormick, "In Europe: Contrast of Visits of Goering and Bishops to Rome," *New York Times*, February 1, 1937.

20. Anne O'Hare McCormick, "Italy Woos English Opinion by Outraging It," *New York Times*, May 10, 1937. This article was also critical of the fascist government's control of the press.

21. "Mussolini and Hitler to Meet Auspiciously," *New York Times*, September 19, 1937.

22. Anne O'Hare McCormick, "Mystic and Realist—a Fateful Meeting," *New York Times*, September 26, 1937.

23. Anne O'Hare McCormick, "Europe: Spanish War Is a Struggle between Italy and France," *New York Times*, April 12, 1937.

24. Telegram, Dino Alfieri to Fulvio Suvich, November 4, 1937, fascicolo "Ministero per la Stampa e Propaganda Mac Cormick [sic] O'Hare Anna," busta 597, Ministero della Cultura Popolare, ASD.

25. Letter, Anne O'Hare McCormick to Benito Mussolini, November 11, 1937, fascicolo "Ministero per la Stampa e Propaganda Mac Cormick [sic] O'Hare Anna," busta 597, Ministero della Cultura Popolare, ASD.

26. Telegram, Fulvio Suvich to Ministry of Press and Propaganda, November 5, 1937, fascicolo "Ministero per la Stampa e Propaganda Mac Cormick [sic] O'Hare Anna," busta 597, Ministero della Cultura Popolare, ASD.

27. Memorandum, Guido Rocco to Galeazzo Ciano, November 13, 1937, fascicolo "Ministero per la Stampa e Propaganda Mac Cormick [sic] O'Hare Anna," busta 597, Ministero della Cultura Popolare, ASD.

28. For "debatable points," see Letter, Anne O'Hare McCormick to Benito Mussolini, November 11, 1937, fascicolo "Ministero per la Stampa e Propaganda Mac Cormick [sic] O'Hare Anna," busta 597, Ministero della Cultura Popolare, ASD. Suvich had been undersecretary of foreign affairs, while Mussolini was the nominal minister of foreign affairs, between 1932 and 1936, immediately prior to his appointment as ambassador to Washington. Michael A. Ledeen, "Italian Jews and Fascism," *Judaism: A Quarterly of Jewish Life and Thought* 18, no. 3 (1969): 294–95, 297; Renzo De Felice, *Storia degli ebrei italiani sotto il fascismo* (Turin: Einaudi, 1988), 182–83. According to Ledeen and De Felice, Suvich represented an older way of thinking within the foreign service, which opposed closer Italian-German relations. These authors argue that Suvich's replacement as foreign minister, Ciano, advocated for stronger ties with the Nazis and paved the way for the adoption of racial laws.

29. Handwritten note, November 10, 1937, fascicolo "Ministero per la Stampa e Propaganda Mac Cormick [sic] O'Hare Anna," busta 597, Ministero della Cultura Popolare, ASD. This note, made by an official within the Ministry of Press and Propaganda, observed that an official from the Ministry of Foreign Affairs had "telephoned, informing that Mc Cormick will not be granted an audience with the Duce."

30. Generoso Pope, "Un viaggio trionfale," *Il Progresso Italo-Americano*, September 27, 1937; I. C. Falbo, "Il Duce in Germania," *Il Progresso Italo-Americano*, September 26, 1937.

31. "London and Rome Both Seeking an Agreement," *New York Times*, September 19, 1937; "Duce Off to Try to Get Aid for Anti-Red Axis," *Washington Post*, September 30, 1937; Schmitz, *United States and Fascist Italy*, 181–84.

32. "Text of Roosevelt's Speech at Chicago," *Baltimore Sun*, October 6, 1937; Schmitz, *United States and Fascist Italy*, 182–83.

33. Dorothy Borg, "Notes on Roosevelt's 'Quarantine' Speech," *Political Science Quarterly* 72, no. 3 (September 1957): 430–33; Travis Beal Jacobs, "Roosevelt's 'Quarantine Speech,'" *Historian* 24, no. 4 (August 1962): 485–88.

34. "Jews in Italy Told to Curb Anti-Naziism," *Baltimore Sun*, May 26, 1937; "Jews Must Back Duce or Leave, Paper Asserts," *Washington Post*, May 26, 1937; "Duce Orders Jews to Back Fascism or Leave Italy," *Atlanta Constitution*, May 26, 1937; "Italian Jews Told to Uphold Fascism or Leave Country," *New York Times*, May 26, 1937; "Join Fascists or Quit Italy, Duce to Jews," *Chicago Daily Tribune*, May 26, 1937; "Mussolini Warns Jews," *Los Angeles Times*, May 26, 1937. The story was on the front page of all these papers, save the *Los Angeles Times*.

35. Pope, "L'Italia e la libertà religiosa."

36. See for example, "Il Gr. Uff. Pope ricevuto dal ministro Pietro Parini e dall'ambasciatore degli SU," *Il Progresso Italo-Americano*, June 8, 1937; "Alta onorificenza conferita dal Re a Generoso Pope," *Il Progresso Italo-Americano*, June 10, 1937; "Il Comm. Pope ricevuto dal Re Imperatore," *Il Progresso Italo-Americano*, June 14, 1937.

37. Generoso Pope, "Gli ebrei in Italia," *Il Progresso Italo-Americano*, July 4, 1937; Generoso Pope, "The Jews in Italy," *Il Progresso Italo-Americano*, July 4, 1937. Pope's account of the meeting conveyed his own discomfort about the discussion; he told his readers that he first apologized to Mussolini for his "indiscreet" request.

38. "Generoso Pope Returns," *New York Times*, June 25, 1937.

39. Pope, "Gli ebrei in Italia"; Pope, "The Jews in Italy."

40. "Fascist Savants Decide Italians Are Aryan Race," *Chicago Daily Tribune*, July 15, 1938.

41. "Italy Plans Racial Terror à la Nazi," *Chicago Defender*, July 30, 1938. "L'Italia non altera la sua politica verso gli ebrei," *Il Progresso Italo-Americano*, July 16, 1938. See also, "L'Italia non intende iniziare un'era di persecuzione contro gli ebrei; i loro diritti civili sono rispettati," *Il Progresso Italo-Americano*, July 31, 1938. Based on a then-recent article in *Il Giornale d'Italia*, this article compared Italy's anti-Jewish policy to the United States' immigration restrictions of 1924. It argued that democracies, too, had "racial policies."

42. Generoso Pope, "Italiani ed ebrei d'America," *Il Progresso Italo-Americano*, August 28, 1938; Generoso Pope, "Italians and Jews in America," *Il Progresso Italo-Americano*, August 28, 1938.

43. "Italy Exiles Jews Entering since '19," *New York Times*, September 2, 1938. "Le nuove misure adottate ieri dal governo italiano," *Il Progresso Italo-Americano*, September 2, 1938.

44. "Schools of Italy to Keep Out Jews," *New York Times*, September 3, 1938; "Nuove misure del Consiglio dei Ministri," *Il Progresso Italo-Americano*, September 3, 1938.

45. Stefano Luconi, "The Response of Italian Americans to Fascist Antisemitism," *Patterns of Prejudice* 35, no. 3 (July 2001): 3–23.

46. Stefano Luconi, "*Il Grido della Stirpe* and Mussolini's 1938 Racial Legislation," *Shofar—An Interdisciplinary Journal of Jewish Studies* 22, no. 4 (2004): 67–79.

47. Ronald H. Bayor, "Italians, Jews and Ethnic Conflict," *International Migration Review* 6, no. 4 (1972): 385–86.

48. Generoso Pope, "Nervi a posto," *Il Progresso Italo-Americano*, September 11, 1938.

49. Luconi, "Response of Italian Americans to Fascist Antisemitism," 8. Luconi writes that Pope must also have been aware that his power within the Democratic Party could be damaged by tensions between the two ethnic communities.

50. "Suvich Will Head Insurance Firm," *New York Times*, September 13, 1938. Suvich was on annual leave, he never returned to the post of ambassador or another post in government. Suvich's departure represented the distancing of the old (and more moderate) guard of the foreign policy establishment from the regime.

51. Telespresso, Giuseppe Cosmelli to Ministry of Foreign Affairs, September 13, 1938, fascicolo "Ebraismo," busta 47, Serie affari politici 1931–45, Stati Uniti, ASD.

52. Stefano Luconi, "Fascist Antisemitism and Jewish-Italian Relations in the United States," *American Jewish Archives Journal* 56, no. 1 (2004): 152.

53. Telegram, Giuseppe Cosmelli to Ministry of Foreign Affairs, September 14, 1938, fascicolo "Ebraismo," busta 47, Serie affari politici 1931–45, Stati Uniti, ASD. The day after he transmitted

his analysis of Pope's "Nervi a posto" article, Cosmelli wrote again to the Ministry of Foreign Affairs. "I consider it my duty to report that the provisions regarding Italian Jews, considered as measures that will precede more comprehensive acts, have created a very delicate collective psychological attitude among Italian Americans." "Until now Italians and Jews have felt a lot of communality, as minorities vis-à-vis Anglo-Saxons," Cosmelli noted. Italian Americans, according to the chargé d'affaires, were anxiously awaiting the Grand Council's deliberations on the matter but the prevalent sentiments were "not only of momentary uncertainty and perplexity but . . . a deeper incomprehension."

54. Telegram, Giuseppe Cosmelli to Ministry of Foreign Affairs, September 15, 1938, fascicolo "Ebraismo," busta 47, Serie affari politici 1931–45, Stati Uniti, ASD.

55. Telegram, Galeazzo Ciano to Italian Embassy in Washington DC, September 19, 1939, fascicolo "Ebraismo," busta 47, Serie affari politici 1931–1945, Stati Uniti, ASD.

56. The Grand Council approved laws that banned marriage between Caucasian Italians and those of Jewish or African origins and limited Jewish property and business holdings. These laws went into effect on November 17, 1938. See Michele Sarfatti, *The Jews in Mussolini's Italy: From Equality to Persecution*, trans. John Tedeschi and Anne Tedeschi (Madison: University of Wisconsin Press, 2006), 129; De Felice, *Storia degli ebrei*, 302–7.

57. Telegram, Salvatore Cotillo to Benito Mussolini, October 7, 1938, fascicolo "Ebraismo," busta 47, Serie affari politici 1931–45, Stati Uniti, ASD.

58. Telegram, Galeazzo Ciano to Giuseppe Cosmelli, October 8, 1938, fascicolo "Ebraismo," busta 47, Serie affari politici 1931–45, Stati Uniti, ASD.

59. Diggins, *Mussolini and Fascism*, 342–43.

60. "L'Italia provvederà alla sistemazione degli ebrei," *Il Progresso Italo-Americano*, October 7, 1938; "20,000 ebrei italiani sono stati esclusi da tutte le misure restrittive," *Il Progresso Italo-Americano*, October 10, 1938; "Gli ebrei italiani ammontano a 49,160," *Il Progresso Italo-Americano*, October 13, 1938.

61. Diggins, *Mussolini and Fascism*, 343; Generoso Pope, "For a Better Understanding," *Il Progresso Italo-Americano*, December 25, 1938.

62. Sarfatti, *Jews in Mussolini's Italy*, 121–41; Giorgio Israel, *Il fascismo e la razza: La scienza italiana e le politiche razziali del regime* (Bologna: Mulino, 2010), 202–19.

63. For a contemporary, and accurate, critique of Pope's position on fascism's anti-Jewish policies, see "Is Mr. Pope a Fascist?" *Il Mondo*, July 15, 1941.

64. Anne O'Hare McCormick, "Europe: Why Is an Artificial Race Problem Raised in Italy?" *New York Times*, July 18, 1938.

65. Anne O'Hare McCormick, "In Europe: Anti-Jewish Decrees Displease and Puzzle Italian People," *New York Times*, January 30, 1939.

66. Translation of McCormick's article, "In Europe: Anti-Jewish Decrees Displease and Puzzle Italian People," January 29, 1939, fascicolo "Direzione generale per il servizio della stampa estera, McComrick [*sic*] O'Hare Anna," busta 554, Ministero della Cultura Popolare, ASD. The word "explusion" ("*espulsione*") was handwritten at the top of the translation.

67. "Times Man Killed," *New York Times*, July 27, 1956; "Cortesi Is Ordered to Give Up News Post," *New York Times*, December 13, 1938; "Arnaldo Cortesi Is Dead at 69," *New York Times*, November 27, 1966. An American citizen of Italian parentage, Cianfarra had stepped into Arnaldo Cortesi's shoes after the regime had ordered all Italian citizens who worked for foreign

news agencies either to quit their jobs or to leave the country. Cortesi chose to leave Italy so as to continue his work for the *Times*.

68. Officials first assumed that Cianfarra was responsible for the article and moved to expel him, before Cianfarra corrected them. Memorandum, Director General of Foreign Press, for the Attention of the Minister of Popular Culture, January 30, 1939; Memorandum, Ministry of Popular Culture, Dir. Gen. Stampa Estera, for the attention of the Minister, February 1, 1939. Both in fascicolo "Direzione generale per il servizio della stampa estera, Cianfarra, Camillo," busta 556, Ministero della Cultura Popolare, ASD.

69. Memorandum, Ministry of Popular Culture, Dir. Gen. Stampa Estera, for the attention of the Minister, February 1, 1939, fascicolo "Direzione generale per il servizio della stampa estera, McComrick [sic] O'Hare Anna," busta 554, Ministero della Cultura Popolare; ASD. This memorandum was stamped, "Seen by the Duce" (*"Visto dal Duce"*).

70. Anne O'Hare McCormick, "Europe: No Outside Power Cared to Save Austrian Freedom," *New York Times*, March 14, 1938. For similar analysis, see Anne O'Hare McCormick, "Europe: Rome and Berlin Still Doubt Durability of Their Axis," *New York Times*, February 21, 1938. Anne O'Hare McCormick, "Europe: Der Fuehrer to Meet Il Duce in a More Wary Rome," *New York Times*, May 2, 1938. This meeting did nothing to alter McCormick's estimation that Italian-German relations were poor.

71. Anne O'Hare McCormick, "Europe: The President's Timetable in the Munich Crisis," *New York Times*, October 31, 1938; Anne O'Hare McCormick, "Europe Weighs Strength of Berlin-Rome Axis," *New York Times*, April 30, 1939.

72. Anne O'Hare McCormick, "Europe: Mussolini Has the Chance to Aid Cause of Peace," *New York Times*, January 28, 1939; Anne O'Hare McCormick, "Europe: Relief Felt in Italy over Tone of Mussolini's Speech," *New York Times*, April 22, 1939.

73. McCormick, "Europe: Relief Felt in Italy over Tone of Mussolini's Speech."

74. Anne O'Hare McCormick, "In Europe: In the Final Test One Man Stands against the World," *New York Times*, August 28, 1939.

75. See Anne O'Hare McCormick, "In Europe: Italy the Pendulum—Where Will It Swing?" *New York Times*, September 11, 1939. See also Anne O'Hare McCormick, "Europe: Pressing of War Still Awaits Final Line-Up of Neutrals," *New York Times*, October 23, 1939; Anne O'Hare McCormick, "Europe: Rome Plays a Cautious Game but Leans toward Allies," *New York Times*, December 9, 1939.

76. Anne O'Hare McCormick, "Europe: Italy Now Turns toward Us, Seeing Some Like Aims," *New York Times*, January 8, 1940.

77. Anne O'Hare McCormick, "Italy Faces Decisive Hour, Beset by Clashing Desires," *New York Times*, April 20, 1940; Anne O'Hare McCormick, "Hitler by Threat and Suasion Presses Italy to Aid Him," *New York Times*, April 22, 1940.

78. Anne O'Hare McCormick, "Italians Not Surprised," *New York Times*, May 11, 1940.

79. Schmitz, *United States and Fascist Italy*, 193, 194, 201, 203.

80. Ibid., 205–206, citing William Phillips's diary.

81. Memorandum, Directorate General of Foreign Press, for the attention of the Minister of Popular Culture, January 12, 1940, fascicolo "Direzione generale per il servizio della stampa estera, McComrick [sic] O'Hare Anna," busta 554, Ministero della Cultura Popolare, ASD.

82. Anne O'Hare McCormick, "Europe: Tragic Paradox in Italy's Arguments for War," *New York Times*, June 3, 1940. In this article, she reflected back on a conversation she had had with "an important official" (perhaps Guido Rocco), in January 1940 regarding the likelihood of the United States' entry into the war. Upon his inquiry, she had told him that the United States' policy of nonbelligerence would likely change if Italy went in on Germany's side.

83. McCormick, "Europe: Italy Now Turns toward Us, Seeing Some Like Aims."

84. Letter, Anne O'Hare McCormick to Benito Mussolini, April 30, 1940, fascicolo "Direzione generale per il servizio della stampa estera, McComrick [sic] O'Hare Anna," busta 554, Ministero della Cultura Popolare, ASD.

85. Fono-Bollettino, n. 113, April 22, 1939. The Ministry of Popular Culture learned that McCormick was in Italy because the Italian Embassy in Washington forwarded a summary of an article that she had written from Rome. Someone in the ministry scribbled "She's in Rome?" (*"È a Roma?"*) under the embassy's press summary. Telegram, Ascanio Colonna to Alessandro Pavolini, November 16, 1939. Ambassador Colonna telegrammed the minister of popular culture, informing him that McCormick was traveling once more to Italy and had requested an audience with Mussolini and the minister. Colonna wrote that, taking account of ministerial orders, he had counseled McCormick against travel to Italy. McCormick had ignored his advice. Memorandum, Directorate General of Foreign Press, for the attention of the Minister of Popular Culture, April 23, 1940. On McCormick's last stay in Rome before Italy's entry into the war, an official in the foreign press section asked the minister of popular culture whether they should "invite her to distance herself" from Italy, or whether McCormick's assurances that she was in Rome only on a holiday, would not be filing any correspondence, and would be leaving in the first half of May were a sufficient check on her activities. McCormick remained in Rome and filed a news story just before she departed. All in fascicolo "Direzione generale per il servizio della stampa estera, McComrick [sic] O'Hare Anna," busta 554, Ministero della Cultura Popolare, ASD. For McCormick's story, see McCormick, "Italians Not Surprised."

86. Anne O'Hare McCormick, "Europe: Italy, Poised on Brink of War, Dreads German Victory," *New York Times*, May 25, 1940; McCormick, "Revolt of Youth."

87. McCormick, "Europe: Tragic Paradox in Italy's Arguments for War."

88. Similarly, in interview in 1976, Herbert Schneider denied that Italian fascism's flaws were "intrinsic" to its structure: he suggested that its failure was due to poor policies—namely, an attempt to resolve economic crisis through imperial expansion and the decision to ally Italy with Germany. *Reminiscences of Herbert Wallace Schneider*.

89. Diggins, *Mussolini and Fascism*, 334–35. Diggins cites an October 1938 Gallup poll that asked, "If you absolutely HAD to decide which dictator you liked best—Mussolini, Stalin, or Hitler—which would you choose?" Fifty-three percent of respondents chose Mussolini, compared to Stalin (thirty-four percent) and Hitler (thirteen percent).

90. Letter, Frank Mason to Generoso Pope, May 31, 1938, fascicolo 300, "Articoli offensivi contro l'Italia," busta 48, Ministero della Cultura Popolare, gabinetto, 1926–1944, ACS.

91. The fascist government had instructed Pope to counteract and try to suppress Westbrook Pegler's and Ernest Hemingway's critiques of fascist Italy. Letter, Fulvio Suvich to Dino Alfieri, June 16, 1938, fascicolo 300, "Articoli offensivi contro l'Italia," busta 48, Ministero della Cultura Popolare, gabinetto 1926–1944, ACS.

92. Foreign Agents Registration Act, Public Law 75-583, *U.S. Statutes at Large* 52 Stat. 631 (1938).

93. Letter, Fulvio Suvich to Dino Alfieri, June 16, 1938, fascicolo 300, "Articoli offensivi contro l'Italia," busta 48, Ministero della Cultura Popolare, gabinetto 1926–1944, ACS. Pellegrino Nazzaro, *Fascist and Anti-Fascist Propaganda in America: The Dispatches of Italian Ambassador Gelasio Caetani* (Youngstown, NY: Cambria Press, 2008), 165–66. In addition to the correspondence of May 1938, Pope wrote to the Ministry of Popular Culture twice in 1939, reminding the regime that his dailies were "at the service of the Fascist regime and Italy," and that Pope was "available personally and through his newspapers" to advance the fascist cause. Nazzaro cites letters from Pope and *Il Progresso*'s Rome correspondent, Vincent Giordano, to the Ministry of Popular Culture, of March 3, March 7, May 21, May 25, and June 2, 1939, from World War II captured enemy records.

94. Generoso Pope, "I diritti dell'Italia," *Il Progresso Italo-Americano*, December 4, 1938.

95. McCormick suggested frequently that no country was really morally, or even strategically, neutral, in the war. See McCormick, "Europe: Pressing of War Still Awaits Final Line-Up of Neutrals"; McCormick, "Italy Faces Decisive Hour"; Generoso Pope, "America ed Europa," *Il Progresso Italo-Americano*, March 19, 1939; Generoso Pope, "A ostilità iniziate," *Il Progresso Italo-Americano*, September 2, 1939.

96. Generoso Pope, "Mentre si combatte," *Il Progresso Italo-Americano*, September 3, 1939; also published as Generoso Pope, "Let Us Have Peace," *Il Progresso Italo-Americano*, September 3, 1939.

97. Generoso Pope, "United for Peace," *Il Progresso Italo-Americano*, September 10, 1939; also published as Generoso Pope, "Italia e Stati Uniti," *Il Progresso Italo-Americano*, September 8, 1939.

98. Generoso Pope, "L'Italia in guerra," *Il Progresso Italo-Americano*, June 11, 1940.

99. For Italian antifascists' long-standing opposition to Pope, see Marcella Bencivenni, *Italian Immigrant Radical Culture: The Idealism of the Sovversivi in the United States, 1890–1940* (New York: New York University Press, 2011), 77, 202.

100. Philip V. Cannistraro, "Introduction," in *Italian Fascist Activities in the United States*, ed. Philip V. Cannistraro (New York: Center for Migration Studies, 1977), xxv, xxvii; Rudolph J. Vecoli, "The Making and Un-Making of the Italian Working Class," in *The Lost World of Italian American Radicalism: Politics, Labor, and Culture*, ed. Philip V. Cannistraro and Gerald Meyer (Westport, CT: Praeger, 2003), 62–63.

101. "War of Nerves: Hitler's Helpers," *Fortune*, November 1940; "The Foreign Language Press," *Fortune*, November 1940; Diggins, *Mussolini and Fascism*, 345. See also, "Americanization of Mr. Pope," *Time*, September 22, 1941, for a discussion of the influence of *Il Mondo*.

102. "Says Consuls Aid Fascist Aims Here," *New York Times*, October 5, 1938.

103. "Closing of Consulates Bares Network of Fascist Agencies," *Baltimore Sun*, June 22, 1941.

104. Letter, J. Edgar Hoover to William Hassett, October 4, 1944, Folder: Pope, Generoso, President's Personal File 4617, FDRL.

105. Vecoli, "Making and Un-Making of the Italian Working Class," 62–63.

106. Diggins, *Mussolini and Fascism*, 349, citing captured records, July 25, 1941.

107. "Is Mr. Pope a Fascist?" *Il Mondo*. As *Il Mondo* observed, and Colonna implied, Pope tried to have it both ways, publishing editorials that were critical of Italy in English, and articles

that were far more forgiving in Italian. "Americanization of Mr. Pope," *Time*. According to *Time*, Pope avoided writing editorials that were critical of Mussolini in Italian until *Il Mondo* challenged him to do so, in mid-September 1941.

108. *Il Progresso Italo-Americano*, September 12, 1941. Cited by John Norman, "Repudiation of Fascism by the Italian-American Press," *Journalism Quarterly* 21, no. 1 (March 1944): 3.

109. "Americanization of Mr. Pope," *Time*.

110. Telegram, Generoso Pope to Franklin D. Roosevelt, December 8, 1941, Folder: Pope, Generoso, President's Personal File 4617, FDRL.

111. Letter, Generoso Pope to Stephen T. Early, December 16, 1941, Folder: Pope, Generoso, President's Personal File 4617, FDRL.

112. Nazzaro, *Fascist and Anti-Fascist Propaganda in America*, 166.

113. Handwritten note, attached to letter, Generoso Pope to Franklin D. Roosevelt, December 27, 1941, Folder: Pope, Generoso, President's Personal File 4617, FDRL.

114. Memorandum, William D. Hassett, March 15, 1943, Folder: Pope, Generoso, President's Personal File 4617, FDRL.

115. Memorandum, Franklin Roosevelt to Edwin Watson, July 31, 1940, Folder: Pope, Generoso, President's Personal File 4617, FDRL.

116. For Pope's new role within the DNC, see "Democrats to Join Labor on Electors," *New York Times*, September 23, 1940. Stefano Luconi, "The Impact of World War II on the Political Behavior of the Italian-American Electorate in New York City," *New York History* 83, no. 4 (2002): 406–9, 413. The Italian-American vote for the Democratic Party nonetheless fell off dramatically in 1940. For instance, in New York, only forty-two percent of Italian Americans voted for FDR in 1940, down from seventy-nine percent in 1936.

117. Memorandum, Oscar Ewing to Franklin Roosevelt, September 23, 1944, Folder: Pope, Generoso, President's Personal File 4617, FDRL.

118. Memorandum, Franklin D. Roosevelt to Edwin Watson, September 28, 1944, Folder: Pope, Generoso, President's Personal File 4617, FDRL. Luconi, "Impact of World War II on the Political Behavior of the Italian-American Electorate," 413. In 1944, the Republican candidate and governor of New York, Thomas E. Dewey, won a plurality of the Italian-American votes in New York.

119. Transcription of Edward Flynn's telephone calls, Edwin Watson to Franklin Roosevelt, October 9, 1944, Folder: Pope, Generoso, President's Personal File 4617, FDRL. For the relationship between Flynn and Pope, according to antifascists, see "Is Mr. Pope a Fascist?" *Il Mondo*. *Il Mondo* claimed that while Flynn needed Pope to get out the Italian-American vote, Pope had relied on Flynn and other "Tammany connections" to increase the price of sand and gravel in the Bronx and Manhattan, to Pope's great benefit.

120. "Generoso Pope Sees Roosevelt," *New York Times*.

121. Letter, J. Edgar Hoover to William Hassett, October 4, 1944, Folder: Pope, Generoso, President's Personal File 4617, FDRL.

122. Franklin Roosevelt to James M. Barnes, Eugene Casey, Jonathan W. Daniels, and David K. Niles, April 4, 1944, Folder: Pope, Generoso, President's Personal File 4617, FDRL.

123. *Reminiscences of Herbert Wallace Schneider*.

124. "The Death of Fascism," *Il Progresso Italo-Americano*, July 26, 1943.

125. Letter, Anne O'Hare McCormick to Franklin Roosevelt, May 21, 1941, Folder, New York Times (Anne O'Hare McCormick), 1936–1937, President's Personal File 675 FDRL. Underlining in the original.

REFERENCES

Primary Sources

Archival Materials

ARCHIVIO CENTRALE DELLO STATO, ROME

Segreteria particolore del Duce, carteggio ordinario
Ministero della Cultura Popolare, direzione generale servizi della propaganda
Ministero della Cultura Popolare, gabinetto

ARCHIVIO STORICO DIPLOMATICO DEL MINISTERO DEGLI AFFARI ESTERI, ROME

Ministero della Cultura Popolare
Serie affari politici, 1931–45, Stati Uniti

COLUMBIA CENTER FOR ORAL HISTORY, COLUMBIA UNIVERSITY, NEW YORK

Reminiscences of Herbert Wallace Schneider, interviewed by Constance Myers, with John P. Diggins, 1976

LIBRARY OF CONGRESS, WASHINGTON, DISTRICT OF COLUMBIA

Prints and Photographs Division
Richard Washburn Child Papers, 1870–1927

NATIONAL ARCHIVES AND RECORD ADMINISTRATION, COLLEGE PARK, MARYLAND

RG 59, Department of State

NATIONAL ARCHIVES AND RECORD ADMINISTRATION, FRANKLIN D. ROOSEVELT LIBRARY, HYDE PARK, NEW YORK

Accretion to John Ihlder Papers, Washington Housing and Development Matters
Louis McHenry Howe Papers
President's Official File
President's Personal File
Rexford Tugwell Papers

NATIONAL ARCHIVES AND RECORD ADMINISTRATION, HERBERT HOOVER LIBRARY, WEST BRANCH, IOWA

Presidential Secretary's File

SPECIAL COLLECTIONS RESEARCH CENTER, UNIVERSITY OF SOUTHERN ILLINOIS, CARBONDALE, ILLINOIS

Selected Papers of Herbert W. Schneider, 1924–1976

Newspapers, Magazines, and Journals

American Journal of Sociology
American Historical Review
American Political Science Review
Annals of the American Academy of Political and Social Science
Atlanta Constitution
Atlanta Daily World
Atlantic Monthly
Baltimore Sun
Bookman
Boston Sunday Post
Century Magazine
Chicago Daily Tribune
Chicago Defender
Current History
Fortune
Frank Leslie's Weekly
Harper's
Historical Outlook
Il Mondo
Il Progresso Italo-Americano
International Journal of Ethics
Journal of Philosophy
Ladies' Home Journal

Los Angeles Times
New Republic
New York American
New York Herald Tribune
New York Times
North American Review
Political Science Quarterly
Public Opinion Quarterly
Review of Reviews
Saturday Evening Post
Social Research
Social Service Review
Southwestern Political and Social Science Quarterly
Time
Washington Post

Books

Allen, Frederick Lewis. *Only Yesterday: An Informal History of the Nineteen-Twenties*. New York: Blue Ribbon Books, 1931.

Balbo, Italo. *La centuria alata*. Milan: Mondadori, 1934.

Baritz, Loren, ed. *The Culture of the Twenties*. Indianapolis: Bobbs-Merrill, 1970.

Child, Richard Washburn. *Battling the Criminal*. Garden City, NY: Doubleday, 1925.

———. *A Diplomat Looks at Europe*. New York: Duffield and Company, 1925.

———. *The Writing on the Wall: Who Shall Govern Us Next?* New York: Sears, 1929.

Churchill, Winston S. *Parliamentary Government and the Economic Problem*. Oxford: Clarendon Press, 1930.

Creel, George. *How We Advertised America: The First Telling of the Amazing Story of the Committee on Public Information That Carried the Gospel of Americanism to Every Corner of the Globe*. New York: Harper Row, 1920.

Dos Passos, John. *One Man's Initiation: 1917*. London: George Allen & Unwin, 1920.

———. *Three Soldiers*. New York: George H. Doran, 1921.

Fitzgerald, F. Scott. *This Side of Paradise*. New York: Scribner's, 1920.

Frank, Waldo. *The Re-Discovery of America: An Introduction to a Philosophy of American Life*. New York: Scribner's, 1929.

Friess, Horace Leland, and Herbert Wallace Schneider. *Religion in Various Cultures*. New York: H. Holt, 1932.

Herring, E. Pendleton. *Group Representation before Congress*. Baltimore: Johns Hopkins University Press, 1929.

Hobson, Samuel George. *National Guilds: An Inquiry into the Wage System and the Way Out*. London: G. Bell and Sons, 1914.

Hoover, Herbert. *American Individualism*. Garden City, NY: Doubleday, 1922.

Hull, Cordell, and Andrew Henry Thomas Berding. *The Memoirs of Cordell Hull*. Vol. 1. New York: MacMillan, 1948.

Josephson, Matthew. *Portrait of the Artist as American*. New York: Harcourt Brace, 1930.
Krutch, Joseph Wood. *The Modern Temper: A Study and a Confession*. New York: Harcourt Brace, 1929.
Lewis, Sinclair. *Babbitt*. New York: Harcourt Brace, 1922.
Lippmann, Walter. *The Phantom Public*. New York: Harcourt Brace, 1925.
———. *A Preface to Morals*. New York: Macmillan, 1929.
———. *Public Opinion*. New York: Harcourt Brace, 1922.
McCormick, Anne O'Hare. *The World at Home: Selections from the Writings of Anne O'Hare McCormick*. Edited by Marion Turner Sheehan. New York: Alfred Knopf, 1956.
Merriam, Charles E. *The Making of Citizens: A Comparative Study of Methods of Civic Training*. Chicago: University of Chicago Press, 1931.
Merriam, Charles E., and Harold F. Gosnell. *Non-Voting, Causes and Methods of Control*. Chicago: University of Chicago Press, 1924.
Mumford, Lewis. *Technics and Civilization*. New York: Harcourt Brace, 1934.
Mussolini, Benito. *Mussolini as Revealed in His Political Speeches, November 1914–August 1923*. Edited and translated by Bernado Barone Quaranta di San Severino. London: Dent, 1923.
———. *My Autobiography*. Edited by Richard Washburn Child. New York: Scribner's, 1928.
Nesbitt, Henrietta. *White House Diary*. New York: Doubleday, 1948.
Ogburn, William F. *Social Change with Respect to Culture and Original Nature*. New York: B. W. Huebsch, 1922.
O'Hare, Teresa Beatrice. *Songs at Twilight*. Columbus, OH: Columbus Printing Co., 1898.
Roberts, Kenneth. *I Wanted to Write*. Garden City, NY: Doubleday, 1949.
Schneider, Herbert Wallace. *The Fascist Government of Italy*. New York: Van Nostrand, 1936.
———. *Making the Fascist State*. New York: H. Fertig, 1928.
Schneider, Herbert Wallace, and Shepard Bancroft Clough. *Making Fascists*. Chicago: University of Chicago Press, 1929.
Shaw, Clifford, Frederick Zorbaugh, Henry McKay, and Leonard Cottrell. *Delinquency Areas*. Chicago: University of Chicago Press, 1929.
Stearns, Harold E., ed. *Civilization in the United States*. London: Jonathan Cape, 1922.

Miscellaneous

Foreign Agents Registration Act, Public Law 75-583. *U.S. Statutes at Large* 52 Stat. 631 (1938).
President's Research Committee on Social Trends. *Recent Social Trends in the United States; Report of the President's Research Committee on Social Trends*. New York: McGraw-Hill, 1933.
"Raccolta ufficiale delle Leggi e dei decreti del regno d'Italia." Vol. 6. Rome: Provveditorato Generale dello Stato, 1928.
Schneider, Herbert Wallace. "Science and Social Progress: A Philosophical Introduction to Moral Science." PhD dissertation, Columbia University, 1920.
Shaw, Clifford, and Henry McKay. "Social Factors in Juvenile Delinquency." In *Report on the Causes of Crime*, Vol. 2. Washington, DC: U.S. Government Printing Office, 1931.
United States Department of Treasury National War-Savings Committee. *United States Government War-Savings Stamps: What They Are and Why You Should Buy Them*. Washington DC: U.S. Government Printing Office, 1917.

"United States Housing Act of 1937, as Amended." Washington, DC: Federal Works Agency, United States Housing Authority, 1939.

Selected Secondary Sources

Arthurs, Joshua. *Excavating Modernity: The Roman Past in Fascist Italy*. Ithaca, NY: Cornell University Press, 2012.
Badger, Anthony J. *The New Deal: The Depression Years, 1933–1940*. New York: Hill and Wang, 1989.
Bauman, Zymunt. *Modernity and Ambivalence*. Cambridge: Polity Press, 1991.
Ben-Ghiat, Ruth. *Fascist Modernities: Italy, 1922–1945*. Berkeley: University of California Press, 2001.
Berman, Marshall. *All That Is Solid Melts into Air: The Experience of Modernity*. New York: Penguin Books, 1988.
Bernstein, Michael A. "Why the Great Depression Was Great: Toward a New Understanding of the Interwar Economic Crisis in the United States." In *The Rise and Fall of the New Deal Order, 1930–1980*, edited by Gary Gerstle and Steve Fraser, 32–54. Princeton, NJ: Princeton University Press, 1989.
Bosworth, R.J.B. *Mussolini*. London: Arnold, 2004.
———. *Mussolini's Italy: Life under the Dictatorship, 1915–1945*. New York: Penguin Books, 2006.
Brown, Dona. *Back to the Land: The Enduring Dream of Self-Sufficiency in Modern America*. Madison: University of Wisconsin Press, 2011.
Cannistraro, Philip V. "Generoso Pope and the Rise of Italian American Politics, 1925–1936." In *Italian Americans: New Perspectives in Italian Immigration and Ethnicity*, edited by Lydio Tomasi, 264–88. Staten Island: Center for Migration Studies of New York, 1985.
Capozzola, Christopher. *Uncle Sam Wants You: World War I and the Making of the Modern American Citizen*. New York: Oxford University Press, 2008.
Caretto, Ennio. *Quando l'America si innamorò di Mussolini*. Rome: Editori Internazionali Riuniti, 2014.
Cohn, Jan. *Creating America: George Horace Lorimer and the Saturday Evening Post*. Pittsburgh: University of Pittsburgh Press, 1989.
Conkin, Paul K. *Tomorrow a New World: The New Deal Community Program*. Ithaca, NY: Cornell University Press, 1959.
De Grand, Alexander. *Italian Fascism: Its Origins and Development*. Lincoln: University of Nebraska Press, 2000.
De Grazia, Victoria. *How Fascism Ruled Women: Italy, 1922–1945*. Berkeley: University of California Press, 1993.
Dickstein, Morris. *Dancing in the Dark: A Cultural History of the Great Depression*. New York: Norton, 2009.
Diggins, John P. *Mussolini and Fascism: The View from America*. Princeton, NJ: Princeton University Press, 1972.
Duggan, Christopher. *Fascist Voices: An Intimate History of Mussolini's Italy*. New York: Oxford University Press, 2013.
Ebner, Michael. *Ordinary Violence in Mussolini's Italy*. New York: Cambridge University Press, 2011.

Eldridge, David. *American Culture in the 1930s.* Edinburgh: Edinburgh University Press, 2008.

Falasca-Zamponi, Simonetta. *Fascist Spectacle: The Aesthetics of Power in Mussolini's Italy.* Berkeley: University of California Press, 2000.

Fuller, Mia. "Wherever You Go, There You Are: Fascist Plans for the Colonial City of Addis Ababa and the Colonizing Suburb of EUR '42." *Journal of Contemporary History* 31, no. 2 (April 1996): 397–418.

Gentile, Emilio. *Il culto del Littorio: La sacralizzazione della politica nell'Italia fascista.* Rome: Laterza, 1993.

———. "Impending Modernity: Fascism and the Ambivalent Image of the United States." *Journal of Contemporary History* 28, no. 1 (January 1993): 7–29.

Ghirardo, Diane. *Building New Communities: New Deal America and Fascist Italy.* Princeton, NJ: Princeton University Press, 1989.

Goldberg, Jonah. *Liberal Fascism: The Secret History of the American Left from Mussolini to the Politics of Meaning.* New York: Doubleday, 2008.

Griffin, Roger. *Modernism and Fascism: The Sense of a Beginning under Mussolini and Hitler.* Basingstoke, UK: Palgrave Macmillan, 2007.

Israel, Giorgio. *Il fascismo e la razza: La scienza italiana e le politiche razziali del regime.* Bologna: Mulino, 2010.

Katznelson, Ira. *Fear Itself: The New Deal and the Origins of Our Time.* New York: Liveright Norton, 2014.

Kennedy, David M. *Freedom from Fear: The American People in Depression and War, 1929–1945.* New York: Oxford University Press, 1999.

———. *Over Here: The First World War and American Society.* New York: Oxford University Press, 2004.

Koon, Tracy H. *Believe, Obey, Fight: Political Socialization of Youth in Fascist Italy.* Chapel Hill: University of North Carolina Press, 1985.

Lears, T. J. Jackson. *No Place of Grace: Antimodernism and the Transformation of American Culture, 1880–1920.* Chicago: University of Chicago Press, 1981.

Luconi, Stefano. "The Response of Italian Americans to Fascist Antisemitism." *Patterns of Prejudice* 35, no. 3 (July 2001): 3–23.

Lyttelton, Adrian. *The Seizure of Power: Fascism in Italy, 1919–1929.* Princeton, NJ: Princeton University Press, 1987.

Mariano, Marco, and Federica Pinelli. *Europa e Stati Uniti secondo il New York Times: La corrispondenza estera di Anne O'Hare McCormick, 1920–1954.* Turin: Otto, 2000.

Marks, Barry Alan. "The Idea of Propaganda in America." PhD dissertation, University of Minnesota, 1957.

Mead, George H. "The Nature of Aesthetic Experience." *International Journal of Ethics* 36, no. 4 (1926): 382–93.

Migone, Gian Giacomo. *The United States and Fascist Italy: The Rise of American Finance in Europe.* Translated by Molly Tambor. New York: Cambridge University Press, 2015.

Millan, Matteo. "The Institutionalisation of Squadrismo: Disciplining Paramilitary Violence in the Italian Fascist Dictatorship." *Contemporary European History* 22, no. 4 (2013): 551–73.

Passerini, Luisa. *Mussolini immaginario: Storia di una biografia, 1915–1939.* Bari: Editori Laterza, 1991.

Pope, Paul David. *The Deeds of My Fathers: How My Grandfather and Father Built New York and Created the Tabloid World of Today*. New York: Rowman & Littlefield, 2010.

Pretelli, Matteo. *La via fascista alla democrazia americana: Cultura e propaganda nella comunità italo-americane*. Viterbo: Sette Città, 2012.

Purcell, Edward A. *The Crisis of Democratic Theory: Scientific Naturalism and the Problem of Value*. Lexington: University Press of Kentucky, 1973.

Sarfatti, Michele. *The Jews in Mussolini's Italy: From Equality to Persecution*. Translated by John Tedeschi and Anne Tedeschi. Madison: University of Wisconsin Press, 2006.

Schmitz, David F. *The United States and Fascist Italy, 1922–1940*. Chapel Hill: University of North Carolina Press, 1988.

Segre, Claudio G. *Italo Balbo: A Fascist Life*. Berkeley: University of California Press, 1987.

Susman, Warren I. *Culture as History: The Transformation of American Society in the Twentieth Century*. New York: Pantheon, 1984

Vaudagna, Maurizio. "The New Deal and Corporativism in Italy." *Radical History Review* 4, nos. 2–3 (1977): 3–35.

Welky, David. *Everything Was Better in America: Print Culture in the Great Depression*. Champaign: University of Illinois Press, 2007.

Westbrook, Robert B. *John Dewey and American Democracy*. Ithaca, NY: Cornell University Press, 1993.

Whol, Robert. *The Spectacle of Flight: Aviation and the Western Imagination, 1920–1950*. New Haven, CT: Yale University Press, 2005.

INDEX

Acerbo, Giacomo, 17
agriculture: back-to-the-land movement and, 96, 100–102, 203n87; Battle for Grain and, 96, 98; democracy and, 70–73; depression years and, 96–101, 112, 201n42; Ethiopia and, 138, 219n199; farmers and, 3, 32, 70, 82, 90, 94, 98–101, 113, 144; gardens and, 100–101; labor-saving machines and, 140; land reclamation and, 96–103, 153; Mussolini's public persona and, 124; sharecroppers and, 97; squads and, 32; subsistence, 100–102, 204n92; U.S. crisis in, 70
Alfieri, Dino, 139–40, 168, 226n91
Alger, Horatio, 49, 53, 59, 92
American Chamber of Commerce, 47
American Legion, 33, 110
American Political Science Review, 146–47
Amos 'n' Andy (radio show), 88
anarchism, 18, 26–27, 33
antifascism, 17, 79, 82, 104, 120, 149, 167, 169–70
antisemitism, 157–62, 166
Armistice Day, 38
Ascoli, Max, 170
Associated Press, 46
Atlanta Daily World (newspaper), 122
austerity, 42–43, 50, 60–61, 63
Avanti (newspaper), 39

Balbo, Italo; aviation and, 48–49, 101–2, 116–21, 131, 145, 209n12; Child and, 116–17, 209n11; garden metaphor and, 120; on Italy's poverty, 210n27; Pope and, 117–19, 210n18; Roosevelt and, 101–2, 117, 119
balilla (fascist boy scouts), 57, 132–33, 137
Baltimore Sun, 119
Battle for Grain, 96, 98
Battling the Criminal (Child), 53
Bauman, Zygmunt, 120–21
Ben-Ghiat, Ruth, 20
Berlin, 69, 135, 147, 162, 167
Berman, Marshall, 152
Bible, 17, 150
Blackshirts, 146
Boidi, Carlo, 123–24
Bolshevism, 6, 24, 26, 31, 41, 51, 147, 152
Borah, William, 60
Borglum, Gutzon, 151
boycotts, 146, 159
Brownshirts, 136, 146
Bryan, Charles Wayland, 60
Bryan, William Jennings, 60
Butler, Nicholas Murray, 123
Butler, Smedley, 199n2

Cabinet of Foreign Affairs, 46
Caesar, 129
Camp Nordland, 146
Cannistraro, Philip, 4
capitalism, 11, 18, 76, 85, 96, 122
Cappa, Benedetta, 142
Carnegie Endowment for International Peace, 17, 123, 132, 154
Carnera, Primo, 48–49
Catholic Action, 130

237

238 INDEX

Catholics, 177n39; Cannistraro on, 4; Child and, 154; cult of St. Francis and, 61; D'Agostino on, 4; democracy and, 70, 78; Diggins on, 4, 18; farmers and, 70; fascism and, 4, 17–18, 61, 78, 129, 133, 137, 149, 155; Hitler and, 130; Klausener and, 130; Lateran Accords and, 61–62, 75, 78; McCormick and, 11, 18, 61, 70, 78, 129–30, 133, 137, 155; Mussolini and, 4, 18, 61, 129, 155; Nazis and, 130, 149, 155; Polish, 15; youth organizations and, 133

Catholic Universe (newspaper), 11

Catholic World magazine, 11

Central State Archives, 6

Century magazine, 34, 57

Century of Progress exhibition, 119

Chamberlain, Neville, 158, 162

Chamber of Deputies, 28, 33, 39, 42–43, 61

charity, 51–52, 55, 105, 135

Chicago Defender (newspaper), 158

Child, Anne, 154

Child, Constance, 154

Child, Horace Walter, 175n10

Child, Richard Washburn: alcohol and, 37, 176n28; as ambassador to Italy, 1, 8, 26, 31, 35, 37, 42, 44, 51–53, 110; background of, 1, 6–9, 16–18; Balbo and, 116–17, 209n11; *Battling the Criminal* and, 53; Catholics and, 154; communism and, 26–27, 34–35; conservatism and, 18, 109–11; conservatives and, 8, 18; Coolidge and, 8, 56, 60; cultural issues and, 9, 19, 24, 53, 55, 151, 153; death of, 154; democracy and, 3, 16, 67–69, 72, 77, 81–82; depression and, 90–91, 94–96, 107–11; education and, 18; fascism and, 1, 3, 6–9, 18–20, 24, 31–44, 51–52, 57, 72, 74, 78–82, 91, 95–96, 117, 132–37, 150–54, 161, 173; foreign policy and, 6, 142; Hoover and, 8; influence of, 6, 8–9, 17–18, 25, 83, 109, 150; *Italia disprezzata* (despised Italy) and, 26–27; labor and, 18, 26, 31, 45, 52, 100; liberalism and, 52, 67–69, 77; Lorimer and, 9, 26, 57, 69, 94, 109; millenarianism and, 25; modernity and, 3, 19–21, 42–57, 60–63, 67–74, 77–83, 95–96, 135, 150–51, 153; morals of, 56; National Crime Commission and, 53; neutrality and, 39; on American affluence, 54–56; peace and, 116–17; postwar years and, 24–28, 31–41; propaganda and, 19, 24, 50, 151–52; as prophet, 69; public image of Mussolini by, 1, 42–45, 48–57, 60–63; Republicans and, 16, 91; *Ridgway's* and, 6–7; Rome and, 1, 9, 31, 34–40, 56, 69, 72, 110, 152; Roosevelt and, 53, 94–95, 107, 109–11, 117; *Saturday Evening Post* and, 1, 6–7, 9, 26–27, 36, 44, 50, 62, 68, 90, 94, 109; searching for soul and, 150–54, 173; socialism and, 26, 31, 34; source material on, 6; squads and, 24, 31–32, 34, 36, 38, 40–42, 117, 152–53; State Department and, 56, 110; War Industries Board (WIB) and, 81; *The Writing on the Wall* and, 69

Christian Basilica of Santa Maria, 129

Christian Front, 159

Cianfarra, Camille, 161, 225n68

Ciano, Galeazzo, 143, 155, 156, 218n171

Ciarlantini, Franco, 88

Circus Maximus, 129

city planning, 121, 124–31, 145, 153

Civilian Conservation Corps, 126

Civil Works Administration (CWA), 110

Collier's magazine, 7–8

Colonial Sand & Stone Company, 13

Colonna, Ascanio, 170, 227n107

Columbia University, 3, 15, 58

Columbus, Christopher, 139

Committee on Public Information (CPI), 24–25

communism: apathy toward, 41; Child and, 26–27, 34–35; fascism and, 24, 31–35, 39, 41, 155; Goering on, 155; McCormick and, 31–34, 39, 41; Misiano and, 28, 33; Schneider and, 34, 41; squads and, 24

complexities, 43–46, 63, 127

conservatism: Child and, 8, 18, 109–11; depression years and, 94, 107, 109–11; Glaucus and, 128; Goldberg and, 4–5;

McCormick and, 18; peace and, 126, 128; *Saturday Evening Post* and, 94
consumerism, 53–54, 85, 88, 122, 127
Coolidge, Calvin, 8, 56, 60
Cornelia, 142
corporate state: democracy and, 19, 74–83, 196n56; exporting of, 80–82; *Il Progresso* and, 81; Italy and, 19, 45–47, 67, 74–83, 111, 146, 152–53; lobbyists and, 80–81; Mussolini and, 45–47, 67, 74, 77, 80, 111, 153; Roosevelt and, 208n163; War Industries Board (WIB) and, 81
Corsi, Edward, 60, 81
Cortesi, Arnaldo, 97, 224–25n67
Cosmelli, Giuseppe, 158–60, 223–24n53
Costello, Frank, 13
Cotillo, Salvatore, 160
Coughlin, Charles, 122, 159
Creel, George, 25
crime, 48, 53–54, 60, 131–35, 190n76, 215n133
cultural issues: Child and, 9, 19, 24, 53, 55, 151, 153; depression years and, 88, 96–101, 112; disillusionment and, 40, 70–73; heroes and, 42–44; Italy and, 3, 5, 9, 11, 18–20, 28, 40, 58, 72–73, 96, 101, 129, 131, 138, 151, 159, 164, 168, 170; McCormick and, 11, 19, 29, 32, 46, 53, 55, 70, 112, 138, 151, 164; mass production and, 29; materialism and, 20, 39, 53, 88–89, 97; Ministry of Popular Culture and, 129, 158–59, 164, 226n85, 227n93; modernity and, 43–44, 46, 53, 55, 58, 63–64; peace and, 120, 129, 131, 138; Pope and, 19, 58, 151, 159, 168, 170; Schneider and, 19, 151; United States and, 5, 9, 11, 18–20, 24, 29, 32, 40, 43–44, 46, 53, 58, 63–64, 70, 72–73, 88, 96, 99, 101, 112, 120, 129, 131, 138, 151, 159, 164, 168, 170
Czechoslovakia, 80, 163, 168

D'Agostino, Peter, 4
Daladier, Édouard, 162
Davis Island, 46
debt, 13, 26, 68, 76, 103
decentralization, 73

De Martino, Giacomo, 90
democracy: agriculture and, 70–73; Catholics and, 70, 78; Child and, 3, 16, 67–69, 72, 77, 81–82; corporate state and, 19, 74–83, 196n56; decentralization and, 73; decline of, 68–74; Dewey and, 65–66; dictatorship and, 16, 67, 69, 82; disillusionment with, 65–83; dynamic society and, 19; efficiency and, 67–68, 74, 76, 81, 83; elections and, 68, 70, 72–73, 76–79, 81; Germany and, 69, 80; Hoover and, 70, 72–73, 81; *Il Progresso* and, 69–70, 74–82; immigrants and, 70; industry and, 69, 72–73, 81; intelligence tests and, 66; labor and, 74, 76, 78, 80; liberalism and, 67–69, 77–78, 128, 155; lobbies and, 71–72, 80–81; McCormick and, 3, 16, 21, 67–74, 78–83, 128, 197n66; modernity and, 67, 72, 75, 80, 83; moral issues and, 66; multiparty system and, 67, 69, 72; neutrality and, 75; peace and, 128; pluralism and, 123; Pope and, 3, 16, 67–68, 79, 82; propaganda and, 75; *Saturday Evening Post* and, 67–68, 82; Schneider and, 16, 65–68, 74, 78–80, 82, 123, 128, 155; searching for soul and, 155, 173–74; spirituality and, 67, 76, 79, 83; tradition and, 68, 75, 78, 81; voting and, 14, 65, 72, 76–79, 83; weakened state of, 68–74
Democratic Council for Americans of Italian Origin, 172
Democratic National Committee (DNC), 172
Democrats, 14–16, 21, 142, 171, 228n116
depression years: agriculture and, 96–101, 112, 201n42; Child and, 90–91, 94–96, 107–11; conservatism and, 94, 107, 109–11; cultural issues and, 88, 96–101, 112; efficiency and, 91; governance issues and, 91–94; Hoover and, 87, 88, 91–92, 94, 105–7, 206n131; *Il Progresso* and, 84–112; immigrants and, 89–90, 96; industry and, 86, 89, 100–103, 108, 111; interwar years and, 23, 29; Italy and, 84–85, 89–90, 93–106, 108, 110–12, 115; labor and, 86, 88–90, 96, 98, 100–101, 108, 111–15; liberalism and, 91;

depression years (*continued*)
McCormick and, 86–87, 112–14; machine-made crisis and, 85–89; materialism and, 88–89, 97; mechanical production and, 88; modernity and, 85, 88, 95–96, 115; moral issues and, 100, 108; New Deal and, 120, 122, 126–28, 131, 145; Pope and, 86, 90, 94–96, 99–100, 105–12; poverty and, 85, 89, 92, 99, 108; production and, 85–86, 88, 90, 96, 98, 100, 111, 115; propaganda and, 19, 88, 92–94, 96, 98, 115; public works and, 102–8, 110, 112, 126–27; recovering from, 169; Roosevelt and, 8, 94–96, 100–102, 107–14; Schneider and, 89, 96, 98–104, 110; socialism and, 109; spirituality and, 96, 100; technology and, 84–85, 91, 95–96, 99–100, 106, 115, 173; tradition and, 92–93, 96, 98, 109, 113; United States and, 85, 89–102, 106, 108–9, 111–13, 115

De Stefani, Alberto, 103, 186n8

Dewey, John, 15, 65–66, 73, 88

Dickstein, Samuel, 169

dictatorship: American perceptions and, 145; Child on, 69; democracy and, 16, 67, 69, 82; Hitler and, 121, 156–57; journalists and, 161; Mussolini and, 50–52, 67, 128, 156–57, 166; Nazi-Soviet pact and, 163; Pope on, 170; propaganda and, 50, 92

Dies, Martin, 169

Diggins, John, 4–5, 18, 23–24, 43–44, 160, 179n84, 191n96

Diocletian's baths, 129

Directorate General of Foreign Press, 156

education: Child and, 18; civic, 155; fascism and, 65; McCormick and, 11, 97; Schneider and, 15, 17, 132; youth training and, 63, 121, 132, 134–35, 138, 145, 153, 155

efficiency: democracy and, 67–68, 74, 76, 81, 83; depression years and, 91; land reclamation and, 96–103, 153; modernity and, 60–61; Mussolini and, 1, 68, 128, 151–52; peace and, 128

elections: democracy and, 68, 70, 72–73, 76–79, 81; fascism and, 33, 76–77, 141; Hoover and, 107; *Il Progresso* and, 15, 77, 79, 81; Italy and, 67–68, 76–77, 79; plebiscites and, 76–79, 151, 162; Roosevelt and, 15, 94, 107, 172; United States and, 15, 60–61, 70, 72–73, 81, 94, 107, 141, 172

elitism, 5, 18, 32, 47, 68, 75–76, 81

Elliott, William Yandell, 17

embargoes, 138, 141–42, 159

Eritrea, 139

ethics, 16, 50, 52, 54, 77–81, 132

Ethiopia: Abyssinia and, 138–39, 144, 153; agriculture and, 138, 219n199; garden metaphor and, 19, 138–44, 145; *Il Progresso* on, 138–43; Italian invasion of, 121, 123, 138–46, 153–54, 220n206; Jews in, 160; labor and, 141; League of Nations and, 138–39, 142–43; Pope and, 158; production and, 140; slavery and, 139, 217n160

Everson, Dorothy, 154

Ewing, Oscar, 172

exercise, 63, 125

factories, 27, 104, 108, 113, 125

Falbo, Italo Carlo, 47–48, 58, 86, 100, 111, 157

fascism: antifascism and, 17, 79, 82, 104, 120, 149, 167, 169–70; antisemitism and, 157–62, 166; architecture and, 130; *balilla* (boy scouts) and, 57, 132–33, 137; Catholics and, 4, 17–18, 61, 78, 129, 133, 137, 149, 155; Child and, 1, 3, 6–9, 18–20, 24, 31–44, 51–52, 57, 72, 74, 78–82, 91, 95–96, 117, 132–37, 150–54, 161, 173; communism and, 24, 31–35, 39, 41, 155; corporate state and, 19, 45–47, 67, 74–83, 111, 146, 152–53; democratic disillusionment and, 65–83; depression years and, 84 (*see also* depression years); difficulty in defending, 155–57; Diggins on, 4–5, 18, 23–24, 43–44, 160; elections and, 33, 76–77, 141; explaining sympathies for, 18–21; futurism and, 142, 152, 221n7; garden metaphor of, 19,

120–26, 128, 130, 133, 135, 137–49, 153; Goering on, 55; liberalism and, 4–5, 18, 33, 52, 77–78, 128, 155, 170; McCormick and, 6, 9, 18–24, 31–41, 45, 68, 74, 78–83, 88, 91, 93, 95–96, 98, 104, 121, 124–42, 146–47, 150–56, 161–69, 173–74; as machine with a soul, 1, 3, 20, 76, 83, 150–54; March on Rome and, 23–24, 35–38, 40, 68, 72, 82, 152–53, 184n106, 188n46; moral issues and, 6, 17, 23–24, 33, 37, 39, 57, 123, 133–34, 160, 173; neutrality and, 17, 143, 163, 169; New Deal and, 41, 85, 101, 120, 122, 126, 131, 145; plebiscites and, 76–79, 152, 161; Pope and, 6, 14, 18–20, 58–59, 61, 79, 82, 95–96, 106, 110, 121, 125, 131, 135–36, 138, 140, 142, 146–55, 158–62, 167–74; promise of new world and, 25, 28, 30, 40–41, 43; propaganda and, 17, 19, 24, 33, 51, 61, 64, 75, 92–94, 96, 98, 115, 124, 136, 140, 145, 151–52, 161, 169; renewing war and, 30–35; as replacing God, 150; road to war and, 162–67; Schneider and, 6, 16–20, 24, 30–34, 38, 40–41, 57, 65–68, 78–80, 82, 96, 98, 121–23, 128, 132, 136, 146–47, 150–55, 173–74, 212n52; searching for soul and, 150–74; squads and, 19 (*see also* squads); youth and, 63, 78–79, 121, 131–38, 145, 152–53, 155

Fascist Government of Italy, The (Schneider), 146–47, 212n52

Federal Bureau of Investigation (FBI), 170–72

Federal Emergency Relief Agency, 127

Federal Housing Administration, 127

Finer, Herman, 146–47

Fitzgerald, F. Scott, 25

Florence, 31–35, 89, 103–5

Florida real-estate boom, 6, 46, 53

Flynn, Ed, 172, 228n119

Ford, Henry, 43, 99–101, 115

Foreign Agents Registration Act, 168

foreign policy, 6, 121, 123, 142, 144, 147, 155, 162

Foro Mussolini, 135

Fortune magazine, 169

Franco, Francisco, 147, 155

Frank, Waldo, 60

Franklin Roosevelt Library, 6

Freud, Sigmund, 54, 150

futurism, 142, 152, 221n7

gardens: agriculture and, 100–101; Balbo and, 120; Bauman on, 120–21; Ethiopia and, 19, 138–45; factories and, 113; farming and, 100; as fascist metaphor, 19, 120–26, 128, 130, 133, 135, 137–49, 153; Italy and, 19, 123; urban planning and, 124–28, 130, 145; youth and, 133, 135, 137, 145

Gentile, Emilio, 20, 192n129

Gentile, Giovanni, 74, 77, 196n64

German American Bund, 146

Germany: Catholics and, 149; democracy and, 69, 80; Ethiopia and, 138; Hitler and, 12, 121, 123–24, 130, 147, 156–58, 162–63, 165, 167, 170; Nazis and, 12, 19, 121–24, 130, 136–38, 145–47, 149, 154–67, 170; Sudetenland and, 168; youth movements and, 137

"Giovinezza" (Youth), 34, 37, 78

Glaucus, 108, 111, 122, 126–28, 141, 143, 145, 147, 207n143, 213n74

Goering, Herman, 155

Goldberg, Jonah, 4–5, 204n97

Gosnell, Harold, 72, 195n37

governance issues, 27, 152, 173

Gracchi, 142

Grand Council, 47, 74–77, 160–61, 195n48, 224n56

Great War, 23–24, 28, 36, 41, 65, 151, 169

Griffin, Roger, 20

Guidi, Angelo Flavio, 124–25, 132, 136

Gumps, The (comic strip), 88

Harding, Warren, 8, 56

Harvard University, 6, 17, 32, 38

Hawley-Smoot tariff bill, 71–72

healthcare, 78, 97, 137

Hearst, William Randolph, 109, 207n127

Hemingway, Ernest, 226n91

heritage, 25, 112

Hitler, Adolf: Catholics and, 130; dictatorship of, 121, 156–57; "Heil Hitler!" and, 146; *Il Progresso* and, 124, 157, 170; McCormick and, 121, 123–24, 130, 147, 156–58, 162–63, 165, 167, 170; modernity and, 130; Mussolini and, 12, 121, 123–24, 147, 156–58, 162–67, 170; Nazis and, 12, 121, 123–24, 130, 147, 156–58, 162–63, 165, 167, 170; Night of the Long Knives and, 130; road to war and, 162–67
Hollywood, 86, 88
homelessness, 86
Hoover, Herbert: Child and, 8; democracy and, 70, 72–73, 81; depression years and, 87, 88, 91–92, 94, 105–7, 206n131; individualism and, 199n89; McCormick and, 60–61, 70, 72–73, 81, 87, 91, 94; modernity and, 60–61
Hoover, J. Edgar, 170
Hopkins, Harry, 127
Horner, Henry, 116–17
House Committee on Un-American Activities (HUAC), 169
House of Motherhood and Infancy, 133
housing, 103, 126–31, 134
Housing Act, 128
Hughes, Charles Evans, 53
Hull, Cordell, 109, 138, 141
Hungary, 80, 138, 161
hymns, 15, 34, 37, 59

Ickes, Harold, 127, 204n92
identity, 37, 86, 105, 129, 149, 159, 162, 169, 173, 187n20
"If Italy Can Do This, Why Can't We?" (*Il Progresso*), 106
Il Corriere d'America (newspaper), 158
Il Duce. See Mussolini, Benito
Il Grido della Stirpe (*The Cry of the Bloodline*) (newspaper), 150
Il Mondo (newspaper), 169, 171
Il Popolo d'Italia (newspaper), 39, 157
Il Progresso (newspaper): antisemitism and, 158–60; corporate state and, 81; crusade against juvenile delinquency and, 134–35; democracy and, 69–70, 74–82; Democrats and, 14–15; depression years and, 84–112; elections and, 15, 77, 79, 81; Ethiopia and, 138–43; Falbo and, 47–48, 58, 86, 100, 111, 157; Glaucus and, 108, 111, 122, 126–28, 141, 143, 145, 147; goal of, 46–47; Goering and, 155; Hitler and, 124, 157, 170; "Italo-Americans of Whom We Are Proud" series and, 47; land reclamation and, 96–103; modernity and, 46–52, 58–62, 75, 88, 95, 133, 135, 152, 155; National Recovery Administration (NRA) and, 110–12, 122; peace and, 122, 124–29, 132–43, 148, 152, 155, 157–60, 168, 170; Pope and, 14, 46–47, 58–60, 90, 95, 105, 110–12, 127–28, 134, 140, 142, 152, 155, 157–60, 168, 170; portrayal of Mussolini by, 48–52, 58–62; public works and, 102–8, 110, 112; Red Cross and, 143; Roosevelt and, 14, 95, 122, 125; women and, 133–35
immigrants: democracy and, 70; depression years and, 89–90, 96; McCormick and, 9; modernity and, 47–48, 58, 60; Pope and, 12, 18
imperialism, 139, 146
Industrial Workers of the World, 33
industry: construction, 48; democracy and, 69, 72–73, 81; depression years and, 86, 89, 100–103, 108, 111; factories and, 27, 104, 108, 113, 125; interwar years and, 33, 46, 48; Labour Party and, 69; McCormick and, 11, 21; modernity and, 21; National Industrial Recovery Act (NIRA) and, 108; National Recovery Administration (NRA) and, 122; Pope and, 167; production and, 3, 21, 23, 29, 85–86, 88, 90, 96, 98, 100, 111, 115, 144, 150, 153; suffering under, 11; tourist, 46; War Industries Board (WIB) and, 81
inflation, 68, 75, 144
instrumentalism, 15, 18, 65–66
interventionism, 39, 51, 145, 153
Istanbul, 69
Italia disprezzata (despised Italy), 25–28

Italian Consul General, 14, 58, 93, 154
"Italo-Americans of Whom We Are Proud" series (*Il Progresso*), 47
Italy: antisemitism and, 157–62, 166; Caporetto defeat and, 30, 39; Child as U.S. ambassador to, 1, 8, 26, 31, 35, 37, 42, 44, 51–53, 110; city planning and, 121, 124–31, 145, 153; corporate state and, 19, 45–47, 67, 74–83, 111, 146, 152–53; cultural issues and, 3, 5, 9, 11, 18–20, 28, 40, 58, 72–73, 96, 101, 129, 131, 138, 151, 159, 164, 168, 170; debt and, 26, 68, 76, 103; depression years and, 84–85, 89–90, 93–106, 108, 110–12, 115; elections and, 67–68, 76–77, 79; Ethiopia and, 19, 121, 123, 138–46, 153–54, 158, 160; inflation and, 68, 75, 144; invasion of Ethiopia by, 121, 123, 138–46, 153–54, 220n206; invasion of France by, 171–72; March on Rome and, 23–24, 35–38, 40, 68, 72, 82, 152–53, 184n106, 188n46; modernity and, 18–21, 48, 72, 96, 115, 147, 150–53; multiparty system in, 67; postwar malaise of, 25–28; promise of new world for, 25, 28, 30, 40–41, 43; public works and, 102–5; renewing war and, 30–35; Rome and, 1 (*see also* Rome); study methodology on, 5–6; unification of, 22; war weariness of, 22–41

Jacobs, Judge, 103
Jews, 19, 130, 146, 149, 155, 157–62, 166, 203n87, 224n53
Johnson, Hugh, 111–12
Josephson, Matthew, 150
juvenile delinquency, 54–55, 131, 134–35

Kelly, Edward, 116–17
Kent, Frank, 66
Klausener, Erich, 130
Knox, Frank, 110
Krutch, Joseph, 150

labor: administrative superlabor and, 45; agriculture and, 3, 32, 70–73, 82, 90, 94, 96–101, 112–13, 138, 144, 153, 201n42;
back-to-the-land movement and, 96, 100–102, 203n87; capital and, 11, 18, 76, 96, 122; child, 78; Child and, 18, 26, 31, 45, 52, 100; consumerism and, 53–54, 85, 88, 122, 127; democracy and, 74, 76, 78, 80; depression years and, 86, 88–90, 96, 98, 100–101, 108, 111–15; Ethiopia and, 140–41; factories and, 27, 104, 108, 113, 125; forty-hour work week and, 103–4; Industrial Workers of the World and, 33; interwar years and, 26, 28, 31–33, 45, 52, 63; land reclamation and, 96–103, 153; McCormick and, 11, 28; machines and, 11, 86, 96, 101, 108, 140; mass production and, 21, 88, 90, 100–101, 150; mechanical production and, 88; modernity and, 11, 45, 62, 63, 80; movements for, 26, 31–33, 100–101; National Industrial Recovery Act (NIRA) and, 108; National Labor Relations Act and, 122; peace and, 122–23, 140–41; Pope and, 13, 18, 108, 112, 140; production and, 3, 21, 23, 29, 85–86, 88, 90, 96, 98, 100, 111, 115, 144, 150, 153; public works and, 102–8, 110, 112, 126–27; radical movement for, 26; Schneider and, 18, 31, 101, 122, 141; skilled/unskilled wages and, 203n73; slave, 3, 139, 217n160; spirituality and, 27; strikes and, 26–28, 32, 68, 122, 182n58; Subsistence Homestead and, 102, 204n93; unemployment and, 44, 86, 88, 91, 100–108, 119, 121–22, 205n116; women and, 78, 105, 137; work ethic and, 50, 54

Labor Day, 108
Labour Party, 26, 69
Ladies' Home Journal, 97–98, 105, 125, 129, 131, 133, 136
Lateran Accords, 61–62, 75, 78
Lausanne, 28
League of Nations, 138–39, 142–43
League of Republicans for Roosevelt, 107, 109
leftists, 26, 31, 34, 41
Legionnaires, 33–34
Lewis, Sinclair, 29–30
Liberal Fascism (Goldberg), 5

liberalism: Child and, 52, 67–69, 77; democracy and, 67–69, 77–78, 128, 155; depression years and, 91; fascism and, 4–5, 18, 33, 52, 77–78, 128, 155, 170; Goldberg and, 4–5; leftists and, 26, 31, 34, 41; McCormick and, 18, 27, 33, 38, 41, 67, 78, 128; Misiano and, 28; modernity and, 52; peace and, 128; Schneider and, 18, 27, 67–68, 78, 128, 155
liberty bonds, 36
Lions Club, 55
Lippmann, Walter, 24–25, 66, 88
Littoria, 96–97, 124, 133
loans, 70, 106–7, 128
lobbyists, 71–72, 75, 80–81, 83
London, 69, 116, 146
Long, Huey, 122
Lorimer, George Horace, 9, 26, 57, 69, 94, 109
Luce Institute, 129
Lupis, Giuseppe, 169
lynching, 19, 32–34

McClure, S. S., 190n90
McClure's (magazine), 7
McCormick, Anne O'Hare: access of, 93–94; American affluence and, 54–56; antisemitism and, 161–62; background of, 3, 6, 9–12, 17–18; Catholics and, 11, 18, 61, 70, 78, 129–30, 133, 137, 155; communism and, 31–34, 39, 41; conservatives and, 18; cultural issues and, 11, 19, 29, 32, 46, 53, 55, 70, 112, 138, 151, 164; cutting ties with Italy by, 173–74; democracy and, 3, 16, 21, 67–74, 78–83, 128, 197n66; Democrats and, 16; denied interview of Mussolini, 156–57; depression years and, 86–87, 112–14; education and, 11; fascism and, 6, 9, 18–24, 31–41, 45, 68, 74, 78–83, 88, 91, 93, 95–96, 98, 104, 121, 124–42, 146–47, 150–56, 161–69, 173–74; foreign policy and, 6, 142; Goering and, 155; Hitler and, 121, 123–24, 130, 147, 156–58, 162–63, 165, 167, 170; Hoover and, 60–61, 70, 72–73, 81, 87, 91, 94; immigrants and, 9; industry and, 11, 21; influence of, 6, 11–12, 17–18, 80, 83, 97, 112, 131, 156, 166, 168; interwar years and, 22–55, 60–62; invasion of Ethiopia and, 138–42; *Italia disprezzata* and, 25–28; journalistic license of, 46, 97–98; labor and, 11, 28; *Ladies' Home Journal* and, 97–98, 125, 129, 131, 133, 136; liberalism and, 18, 27, 33, 38, 41, 67, 78, 128; modernity and, 11, 19–21, 29, 42–55, 60–62, 88, 95–96, 125, 150–51, 153; neutrality and, 141–42, 164–65, 168–69; *New York Times* and, 3, 6, 9, 11–12, 18, 28, 33, 40, 46–47, 54, 82, 97–98, 113, 125, 129–31, 133, 136, 156, 162, 164, 168; peace and, 121, 124–42, 146–47; portrayal of Mussolini by, 43–55, 60–62; postwar weariness and, 28–30; propaganda and, 19, 50, 93, 98, 136, 151–52, 156, 161, 164; Pulitzer Prize of, 12; road to war and, 162–67; Rome and, 11, 22, 24, 32, 37–38, 40, 97–98, 138, 142, 147, 152, 155–56, 161–66, 226n85; Roosevelt and, 12, 95, 107, 113–14, 147, 157, 164–65, 174; searching for soul and, 150–57, 161–69, 172–74; socialism and, 27, 31, 33–34, 39; squads and, 24, 31–35, 38, 40–41, 152–53; tradition and, 33
McCormick, Francis, 11
Madison Square Garden, 117, 148
Madrid, 69
mafia, 48, 215n133
Making the Fascist State (Schneider), 65–66
March on Rome, 23–24, 35–38, 40, 68, 72, 82, 152–53, 184n106, 188n46
Marsili, Marta, 214n101
martial code, 32–33
masculine ideals, 48, 53–60, 63
Mason, Frank E., 167–68
mass production, 21, 29, 85, 88, 90, 100–101, 150
materialism, 20, 39, 53, 88–89, 97
Mazzini Society, 170–71
Mead, Elwood, 204n93
Mead, George 6
Merriam, Charles, 16–17, 57, 72, 132, 179n77, 185n118, 195n37, 195n41
middle class, 30, 55

millenarianism, 25
Ministry of Foreign Affairs, 6, 158–59
Ministry of Popular Culture, 129, 158–59, 164, 226n85, 227n93
Ministry of Press and Propaganda, 93, 136, 156, 161, 216n146
Misiano, Francesco, 28, 33, 183n75
modernity: Berman and, 152; Child and, 3, 19–21, 42–57, 60–63, 67–74, 77–83, 95–96, 135, 150–51, 153; complexities of, 43–46, 63, 127; cultural issues and, 43–44, 46, 53, 55, 58, 63–64; democracy and, 67, 72, 75, 80, 83; depression years and, 85, 88, 95–96, 115; efficiency and, 60–61; Hitler and, 130; Hollywood and, 86, 88; Hoover and, 60–61; *Il Progresso* and, 46–52, 58–62, 75, 88, 95, 133, 135, 152, 155; immigrants and, 47–48, 58, 60; industry and, 21; interwar years and, 25, 29, 42–50, 56, 60, 63–64; Italy and, 18–21, 48, 72, 96, 115, 147, 150–53; labor and, 11, 45, 62–63, 80; liberalism and, 52; McCormick and, 11, 19–21, 29, 42–55, 60–62, 88, 95–96, 125, 150–51, 153; moral issues and, 55, 57; peace and, 125, 133, 135, 147; Pope and, 19–21, 44–49, 58–63, 95–96, 125, 147, 150–53; propaganda and, 50–51, 61, 64; radio and, 86, 88; Schneider and, 19–21, 44, 51, 57, 63, 96, 150–51, 153; socialism and, 51–52, 61; spirituality and, 43, 61–63; squads and, 42; technology and, 20; tradition and, 3, 11, 20–21, 54, 63–64, 147; United States and, 3, 18–19, 21, 42, 48, 53–57, 67, 72, 96, 115, 150–52
Moffett, James, 127
moral issues: Child and, 56; democracy and, 66; depression years and, 100, 108; Dewey and, 15; ethics and, 16, 50, 52, 54, 77–81, 132; fascism and, 6, 17, 23–24, 33, 37, 39, 57, 123, 133–34, 160, 173; fighting communism and, 24, 33; Great War values and, 28; interwar years and, 23–24, 28, 30, 32–33, 37, 39, 54–55, 57; manners and, 32; martial codes and, 32; materialism and, 20, 39, 53, 88–89, 97; modernity and, 55, 57; neutrality and, 39; new world and, 30; objectivity and, 17; peace and, 123, 133–35, 138; Schneider and, 6, 17; squads and, 24, 32–33; youth and, 32–33
Mosley, Oswald, 198n85
multiparty system, 67, 69, 72, 194n19
Mumford, Lewis, 88
Mussolini, Benito: ability to handle complexity, 43–46, 63, 127; antisemitism and, 157–62, 166; autobiography of, 1, 9, 50–52, 57, 62–63, 68, 77, 194n19; *Avanti* and, 39; aviation and, 52, 119, 155; car of hits child, 199n2; Catholics and, 4, 18, 61, 129, 155; Chamber of Deputies speech of, 42–43; childhood home of, 50–52, 92; Child's portrayal of, 42–45, 48–57, 60–63; city planning and, 124–25, 128–31; corporate state and, 19, 45–47, 67, 74, 77, 80, 111, 153, 196n56; democratic disillusionment and, 67–68, 73–80; depression years and, 84–85, 89, 92–103, 106, 110–11, 115; dictatorship of, 50–52, 67, 128, 156–57, 166; efficiency and, 1, 68, 128, 151–52; explaining sympathies for, 18–21; fabricated austerity of, 42–43, 50, 60–61, 63; fascism and, 3 (*see also* fascism); as genius, 45, 47, 62–63; Goering and, 155; Hitler and, 12, 121, 123–24, 147, 156–58, 162–67, 170; as *Il Duce*, 1, 4, 14, 45–53, 58, 61–62, 74, 84–85, 93, 124–25, 135, 141, 147, 160, 162, 164, 168; *Il Popolo d'Italia* and, 39, 157; *Il Progresso*'s portrayal of, 48–52, 58–62; intolerance of, 39; as Italy's Alger, 48–53; land reclamation and, 96–103, 153; Lateran Accords and, 61–62; McCormick's portrayal of, 43–55, 60–62; masculine ideals and, 48, 53–60, 63; modernity and, 42 (*see also* modernity); mysticism and, 43, 54, 62; peace and, 117–25, 128–35, 139, 141, 143, 146–48; Piedmontese drive of, 84–85, 96; Pope's portrayal of, 44–49, 58–63; as prime minister, 24, 42–45; public persona of, 42–64, 92–94, 124, 147; public works and, 103, 106, 110; rise of, 38–40; road to war

Mussolini, Benito (*continued*)
and, 163–67; Schneider's portrayal of, 44, 51, 57, 63; as shadowy figure, 38–39; spirituality and, 1, 43, 61–63, 152; study methodology on, 5–6; technology and, 20, 84–85, 95, 115; timed publishing of, 46; "Viva Mussolini!" and, 146
Mussolini, Bruno, 143
Mussolini, Vittorio, 92, 143
Mussolini and Fascism: The View from America (Diggins), 4
mysticism, 43, 54, 62

National Archives and Records Administration, 6
National Broadcasting Company, 167
National Crime Commission, 53
National Industrial Recovery Act (NIRA), 108
nationalism, 28, 33, 37, 167
National Labor Relations Act (NLRA), 122
National Recovery Administration (NRA), 110–12, 122
National Socialists (Nazis): Catholics and, 130, 149, 155; Czechoslovakia and, 163; Germany and, 12, 19, 121–24, 130, 136–38, 145–47, 149, 154–67, 170; Goering and, 155; Hitler and, 12, 121, 123–24, 130, 147, 156–58, 162–63, 165, 167, 170; Poland and, 163; Soviet Pact and, 163; spirituality and, 130, 136; youth and, 136–37
Native Americans, 139
neutrality: Child and, 39; democracy and, 75; Ethiopian invasion and, 138, 141–43; fascism and, 17, 143, 163, 169; interwar years and, 39; Italy and, 163–65; McCormick and, 141–42, 164–65, 168–69; peace and, 138, 141–43; Pope and, 141–42, 168–69; Schneider and, 17, 39, 142; searching for soul and, 163–66, 168–69; United States and, 138, 141–42, 163, 165, 168–69
New Deal: depression years and, 85, 95, 101, 108–13, 114, 120, 122, 126–28, 131, 145; fascism and, 41, 85, 101, 120, 122, 126, 131, 145; public works and, 108, 110, 112, 126–27; Roosevelt and, 21, 85, 95, 101, 108–13, 114, 120, 122, 126–28, 131, 145; urban planning and, 126–28
new world, 25, 28, 30, 40–41, 43
New York American, 109
New York Post, 170
New York Supreme Court, 160
New York Times: antisemitism and, 159, 162; Cortesi and, 97; delayed publishing of, 46; depression years and, 86, 97, 100, 113; McCormick and, 3, 6, 9, 11–12, 18, 28, 33, 40, 46–47, 54, 82, 97–98, 113, 125, 129–31, 133, 136, 156, 162, 164, 168; Van Anda and, 11
New York World Telegram, 107
Night of the Long Knives, 130
North American Review, 80, 122
nurseries, 78, 133–35, 137

Office of War Information (OWI), 171
O'Hare, Teresa, 9–11
O'Hare, Thomas, 9–10
Organization for Maternity and Childhood, 78
Owsley, Alvin, 110

parades, 22, 37–38, 40, 117, 166
Paris Peace Conference, 30
Parker, Maude, 9, 35–36, 40, 56, 154
Passos, John Dos, 24–25
patriotism, 7, 23, 28, 31, 33–34, 51, 57, 59, 152, 166, 173
Paulucci, Giacomo, 46
Pavolini, Alessandro, 164
peace: appeasement and, 142, 144, 168; Carnegie Endowment for International Peace and, 123; Child and, 116–17; city planning and, 124–31; conservatism and, 126, 128; cultural issues and, 120, 129, 131, 138; democracy and, 128; *Il Progresso* and, 122, 124–29, 132–43, 148, 152, 155, 157–60, 168, 170; invasion of Ethiopia and, 121, 123, 138–46, 153–54; labor and, 122–23, 140–41; liberalism and, 128; McCormick and, 121,

124–42, 146–47; modernity and, 125, 133, 135, 147; moral issues and, 123, 133–35, 138; Mussolini and, 117–25, 128–35, 139, 141, 143, 146–48; neutrality and, 138, 141–43; Pope and, 117–21, 125–28, 131, 134–43, 146–49; propaganda and, 123–24, 136, 139–40, 145; Roosevelt and, 117, 119, 122–23, 138, 142, 147, 157, 162, 164; Schneider and, 121–23, 127–29, 132, 136, 140–42, 146–47; socialism and, 137–38, 145; squads and, 117; tradition and, 117, 133, 147

Pecora, Ferdinand, 47
Pegler, Westbrook, 226n91
Philippines, 91
Phillips, William, 157, 163
Piazza della Repubblica, 129
Piazza Venezia, 37
Pirandello, Luigi, 60
Pius XI, 58, 61–62
plebiscites, 76–79, 152, 161
police, 32–33, 57, 96, 117, 122
"Pompeii" (McCormick), 11
Pope, Anthony, 58
Pope, Catherine, 58
Pope, Fortune, 58
Pope, Generoso: antisemitism and, 158–62; background of, 3, 6, 12–18, 58; Balbo and, 117–19, 210n18; as *Camerata Casagrande*, 168; Colonial Sand & Stone Company and, 13; cultivated image of, 57–59; cultural issues and, 19, 58, 151, 159, 168, 170; cutting ties with Italy by, 173–74; democracy and, 3, 16, 67–68, 79, 82; Democrats and, 16, 172; depression years and, 86, 90, 94–96, 99–100, 105–12; Ethiopia and, 138–43, 158; Falbo and, 58; fascism and, 6, 14, 18–20, 58–59, 61, 79, 82, 95–96, 106, 110, 121, 125, 131, 135–36, 138, 140, 142, 146–55, 158–62, 167–74; FBI and, 170–72; foreign policy and, 6, 142; Goering and, 155; growing opposition to, 169–70; Hemingway and, 226n91; *Il Progresso* and, 14, 46–47, 58–60, 90, 95, 105, 110–12, 127–28, 134, 140, 142, 152, 155, 157–60, 168, 170; immigrants and, 12, 18; industry and, 167; influence of, 6, 13–14, 17–18, 58, 100, 131, 139, 150, 157, 168–69, 171–72; labor and, 13, 18, 108, 112, 140; Mason and, 167–68; Ministry of Popular Culture and, 227n93; modernity and, 19–21, 44–49, 58–63, 95–96, 125, 147, 150–53; neutrality and, 141–42, 168–69; Order of the Chevalier of the Crown of Italy and, 14; peace and, 117–21, 125–28, 131, 134–43, 146–49; Pegler and, 226n91; portrayal of Mussolini by, 44–49, 58–63; propaganda and, 19, 136, 140, 151–52; Rome and, 14, 59, 138, 143, 159–61, 167, 170–71; Roosevelt and, 14–15, 94–96, 100, 108, 110, 142, 157, 170–72, 174; searching for soul and, 150–62, 167–74; squads and, 153; Villa St. Joseph and, 135

populism, 122
poverty, 49–50, 52, 59, 85, 89, 92, 99, 108, 119, 210n27
pragmatism, 4, 15, 18, 51, 62, 95, 102, 115, 137, 156
Predappio, Romagna, 50–52, 92
production: back-to-the-land movement and, 96, 100–102, 203n87; Battle for Grain and, 96, 98; depression years and, 85–86, 88, 90, 96, 98, 100, 111, 115; Ethiopia and, 140; Ford and, 101; labor and, 3, 21, 23, 29, 85–86, 88, 90, 96, 98, 100, 111, 115, 144, 150, 153; land reclamation and, 96–103, 153; mass, 21, 29, 85, 88, 90, 100–101, 150; public works and, 102–5; Subsistence Homestead and, 102, 204n93

progressivism, 4–5, 7, 11, 18, 21, 25, 78, 109, 111
propaganda: Battle for Grain and, 96; Child and, 19, 24, 151–52; democracy and, 75; depression years and, 19, 88, 92–94, 96, 98, 115; dictatorship and, 50, 92; effects of war and, 24–25; fascist and, 17, 19, 24, 33, 51, 61, 64, 75, 92–94, 96, 98, 115, 124, 136, 140, 145, 151–52, 161, 169; HUAC and, 169; interwar years and, 24–25, 50–51, 61, 64; McCormick and, 19, 50, 93, 98, 136, 151–52, 156, 161, 164; Ministry of Press and Propaganda and, 93, 136, 156, 161, 216n146; modernity and,

propaganda (*continued*)
    50–51, 61, 64; Mussolini's public image and, 42–64, 92–94, 124, 147; peace and, 123–24, 136, 139–40, 145; Pope and, 19, 136, 140, 151–52; Schneider and, 17, 19, 136, 151–52; Villari and, 136
Protestants, 15
protests, 26–28, 82, 120, 142, 182n58
psychology, 54, 66–67, 167
Public and Its Problems, The (Dewey), 73
public opinion, 5, 74, 146, 157, 164, 166
Public Opinion Quarterly, 146
public works, 102–8, 110, 112, 126–27
Public Works Administration (PWA), 126–27
Pulitzer Prize, 12

Quintavalle, Ugo, 116–17
Quirinale, 37

radicals, 24, 26, 31–32
radio, 70, 72, 82, 86, 88, 95, 100, 169
raids, 33, 37
recession, 121
Reconstruction Finance Corporation (RFC), 106–7, 201n47
Red Cross, 143
Republicans, 8, 16, 44, 91, 94, 107, 109
Ridgway's magazine, 6–7
Rocco, Guido, 156–57
Romania, 80
Rome: Alfieri and, 168; birthday of, 22; Child and, 1, 9, 31, 34–38, 40, 56, 69, 72, 110, 152; Colonna and, 170; Cortesi and, 97; great parkways of, 130; Hitler/Mussolini meeting in, 167; as imperial city, 121, 128–29, 140; McCormick and, 11, 22, 24, 32, 37–38, 40, 97–98, 138, 142, 147, 152, 155–56, 161–66, 226n85; March on, 23–24, 35–38, 40, 68, 72, 82, 152–53, 184n106, 188n46; Marsili and, 214n101; Phillips and, 157; Pope and, 14, 59, 138, 143, 159–61, 167, 170–71; poverty of, 52; Rastignac and, 77; road to war and, 163; Schneider and, 17, 101–2, 122; spirituality and, 129; unemployment and, 104; urban planning and, 121, 124–31, 145, 153
Roosevelt, Franklin D.: back-to-the-land movement and, 100–102; Balbo and, 101–2, 117, 119; Child and, 8, 53, 94–95, 107, 109–11, 117; common touch of, 94–96; corporate state and, 208n163; depression years and, 8, 94–96, 100–102, 107–14; elections and, 15, 94, 107, 172; fascist sympathizers' support of, 95–96; FBI and, 170–72; as governor, 100; humanizing government and, 94; *Il Progresso* and, 14, 95, 122, 125; invasion of Ethiopia and, 140–42; League of Republicans for Roosevelt and, 107, 109; McCormick and, 12, 95–96, 107, 113–14, 147, 157, 162, 164–65, 174; National Crime Commission and, 53; New Deal and, 21, 85, 95, 101, 108–13, 114, 120, 122, 126–28, 131, 145; peace and, 117, 119, 122–23, 138, 142, 147, 157; Pope and, 14–15, 94–96, 100, 108, 110, 142, 157, 170–72, 174; progressives and, 5; public works and, 107–8, 110, 112, 126–27; quarantine speech of, 157; road to war and, 162–64; Schneider and, 122, 174; urban planning and, 126–28
Roosevelt, Theodore, 7–8, 62
Rotary Club, 55
Rough Riders, 33
Russia, 6, 26, 28

Sabaudia, 96–97
Sacco, Nicola, 26
St. Francis of Assisi, 61
Salvemini, Gaetano, 104
sanctions, 138–39, 142–43
Sanderson, Eva, 56
Saturday Evening Post: austerity propaganda of, 50; *Battling the Criminal* and, 53; beach picture of, 1, 2; Child and, 1, 6–7, 9, 26–27, 36, 44, 50, 62, 68, 90, 94, 109; conservatism and, 94; democracy and, 67–68, 82; depression years and, 90; *Italia disprezzata* (despised Italy) and, 26–28; Lorimer

and, 9, 26, 57, 69, 94, 109; Mussolini autobiography and, 1, 9, 50, 68–69; Roosevelt and, 94; socialism and, 26; spirituality and, 62; war-weary world and, 26–28, 36

savings, 24, 42, 44, 53

Schneider, Herbert Wallace: background of, 3, 6, 15–18; Carnegie Endowment and, 154; communism and, 34, 41; cutting ties with Italy by, 173–74; democracy and, 16, 65–68, 74, 78–80, 82, 123, 128, 155; depression years and, 89, 96, 98–104, 110; Dewey and, 65–66; education and, 15, 17, 132; fascism and, 6, 16–20, 24, 30–33, 34, 38, 40–41, 57, 65–68, 78–80, 82, 96, 98, 121–23, 128, 132, 136, 146–47, 150–55, 173–74; *The Fascist Government of Italy* and, 146–47, 212n52; Finer on, 146–47; foreign policy and, 6, 142; influence of, 6, 17–18, 150; instrumentalism of, 15, 18, 65–66; intelligence tests and, 66; interwar years and, 24, 26–27, 30–34, 38–41, 44, 51, 57, 63; *Italia disprezzata* (despised Italy) and, 26–27; labor and, 18, 31, 101, 122, 141; liberalism and, 18, 27, 67–68, 78, 128, 155; *Making the Fascist State* and, 65–66; Merriam and, 16–17, 57, 132; modernity and, 19–21, 44, 51, 57, 63, 96, 150–51, 153; moral issues and, 6, 17; neutrality and, 17, 39, 142; peace and, 121–23, 127–29, 132, 136, 140–42, 146–47; political affiliation of, 16; portrayal of Mussolini by, 44, 51, 57, 63; propaganda and, 17, 19, 136, 151–52; road to war and, 165; Rome and, 17, 101–2, 122; Roosevelt and, 122, 174; searching for soul and, 150–55, 173–74; Social Science Research Council and, 154; squads and, 10, 24, 31–32, 34, 38, 40–41, 152–53

sex, 27, 37, 40, 51, 60, 188n47

Sinclair, Upton, 122

slavery, 3, 139, 217n160

Smith, Adam, 103

Smith, Al, 60, 70, 72, 192n119

socialism: apathy toward, 41; *Avanti* and, 39; Child and, 26, 31, 34; depression years and, 109; interwar years and, 24, 26–27, 31, 33–34, 39–41, 51–52, 61; McCormick and, 27, 31, 33–34, 39; media imagery of, 33; modernity and, 51–52, 61; National Socialists and, 137–38, 145; peace and, 137–38, 145; *Saturday Evening Post* and, 26; squads and, 24

Social Science Research Council, 16, 154

Somalia, 138–39

Spain, 69, 147–49, 155

spirituality: democracy and, 67, 76, 79, 83; depression years and, 96, 100; despondency and, 33; fascist Rome and, 129; labor and, 27; mass hunger for, 153; modernity and, 43, 61–63; Mussolini and, 1, 43, 61–63, 152; Nazis and, 130, 136; sacrifice and, 143; technology and, 11; war effects and, 26; youth training and, 134, 137

squads: anger of, 39; Child and, 24, 31–32, 34, 36, 38, 40–42, 117, 152–53; communism and, 24, 31; Diggins and, 23–24; as forces for order, 24; intolerance of, 33; McCormick and, 24, 31–35, 38, 40–41, 152–53; March on Rome and, 23–24, 35–38, 40, 68, 72, 82, 152–53, 184n106, 188n46; martial code of, 32–33; modernity and, 42; moral issues and, 24, 32–33; peace and, 117; Pope and, 153; raids and, 33, 37; renewing war and, 30–35; rise of, 31, 34; Schneider and, 10, 24, 31–32, 34, 38, 40–41, 152–53; socialism and, 24; torture by, 32; tradition and, 32–33, 117, 152; violence of, 19, 31–36, 182n55, 182n58

State Department, 56, 110, 138

Stearns, Harold, 25, 29

strikes, 26–28, 32, 68, 122, 182n58

Subsistence Homestead program, 102, 204n93

Superman (comic strip), 88

Susman, Warren, 43–44, 49

Suvich, Fulvio, 145, 156–57, 222n28, 223n50, 226n91

Tagore, Rabindranath, 54
tariffs, 71–72
technology: depression years and, 84–85, 91, 95–96, 99–100, 106, 115, 173; human intelligence and, 173; mass production and, 21, 88, 90, 100–101, 150; modernity and, 20; Mussolini's relationship with, 20, 84–85, 95, 115; radio, 70, 72, 82, 86, 88, 95, 100, 169; spirituality and, 11
Tomb of the Unknown Soldier, 37
tourists, 29, 34–36, 46
Townsend, Francis, 122
tradition: declining values and, 9, 21, 54; democracy and, 68, 75, 78, 81; depression years and, 92–93, 96, 98, 109, 113; German Pietist, 15; heritage and, 25, 112; interwar years and, 25, 32–33, 54, 64; McCormick and, 33; modernity and, 3, 11, 20–21, 54, 63–64, 147; peace and, 117, 133, 147; squads and, 32–33, 117, 152
Trajan's market, 129
Treasury Department, 24
Tugwell, Rexford, 101–2, 107
Tunney, Gene, 72
Turkey, 69

Uncle Sam, 86, 87, 134
unemployment, 44, 86, 88, 91, 100–108, 119, 121–22, 205n116
United States: affluence of, 54–56; antisemitism and, 157–62, 166; city planning and, 124–31; Congress and, 7, 10, 49, 67, 70–72, 81, 91, 126, 128, 138, 141, 168–69; cultural issues and, 5, 9, 11, 18–20, 24, 29, 32, 40, 43–44, 46, 53, 58, 63–64, 70, 72–73, 88, 96, 99, 101, 112, 120, 129, 131, 138, 151, 159, 164, 168, 170; democracy and, 71–72 (*see also* democracy); Democrats and, 142, 171; depression years and, 85, 89–102, 106, 108–9, 111–13, 115; elections and, 15, 60–61, 70, 72–73, 81, 94, 107, 141, 172; Florida real estate boom and, 6, 46, 53; gods of, 60; governance issues and, 91–94; Italian invasion of Ethiopia and, 123, 139–42, 145–46, 154; modernity and, 3, 18–19, 21, 42, 48, 53–57, 67, 72, 96, 115, 150–52; neutrality of, 138, 141–42, 163, 165, 168–69; New Deal and, 21, 85, 95, 101, 108–13, 114, 120, 122, 126–28, 131, 145; public works and, 105–8, 110, 112, 126–27; Republicans and, 8, 16, 44, 91, 94, 107, 109; State Department and, 56, 110, 138; study methodology on, 5–6; Uncle Sam and, 86, 87, 134; voting behavior and, 14, 72; War Industries Board (WIB) and, 81
urbanization, 73, 100–101, 115, 124, 131
urban planning, 121, 124–31, 145, 153
U.S. Supreme Court, 122

Van Anda, Carr, 11
Vanzetti, Bartolomeo, 26
Via Aracoeli, 22–23, 35, 41, 166
Via del Mare, 125
Villari, Luigi, 136, 216n137
Villa St. Joseph, 135
Vittorio Emanuele III, 14, 37, 117, 119
volata sport, 78–79
voting, 14, 169; democracy and, 65, 72, 76–79, 83; elections and, 15 (*see also* elections); lack of secrecy in, 79; League of Nations and, 138; Philippines and, 91; plebiscites and, 76–79, 151, 162

Wagner, Charles, 54
Wagner, Robert, 14, 106, 128, 178n64
Wagner Act, 122
Walker, Jimmy, 13–14, 58–59
Walker, Mickey, 38
Wall Street, 1, 112
War Industries Board (WIB), 81
welfare, 51–52, 78, 93, 98, 135, 151
Welles, Sumner, 164
Westfield, Elizabeth, 8–9
Whalen, Grover, 111
Wilson, Woodrow, 7–8
women: American, 29, 90; apolitical, 23; Cornelia and, 142; House of Motherhood and Infancy and, 133; *Il Progresso*

and, 133–35; labor and, 78, 105, 137; *Ladies' Home Journal* and, 97–98, 105, 125, 129, 131, 133, 136; New, 55; nurseries and, 78, 133–35, 137; Organization for Maternity and Childhood and, 78; peasant, 84; squads' martial code and, 32; wedding ring donations and, 142–43

Works Progress Administration, 126

World War I, 23–24, 28, 36, 39–41, 65, 82, 111, 151, 169

World War II, 164, 174

Wright, Benjamin, 66

Writing on the Wall, The (Child), 69

youth, 189n60; *balilla* (boy scouts) and, 57, 132–33, 137; fascism and, 63, 78–79, 121, 131–38, 145, 152–53, 155; gangs and, 132; garden metaphor and, 133, 135, 137, 145; House of Motherhood and Infancy and, 133; juvenile delinquency and, 54–55, 131, 134–35; moral issues and, 32–33; Nazis and, 136–37; nurseries and, 78, 133–35, 137; spirituality and, 134, 137; squads and, 34 (*see also* squads); training programs for, 63, 121, 132, 134–35, 138, 145, 153, 155; Villa St. Joseph and, 135; *volata* and, 78–79

"Youth" (Mussolini), 1

A NOTE ON THE TYPE

This book has been composed in Arno, an Old-style serif typeface in the classic Venetian tradition, designed by Robert Slimbach at Adobe.

GPSR Authorized Representative: Easy Access System Europe - Mustamäe tee 50, 10621 Tallinn, Estonia, gpsr.requests@easproject.com